7

By Steve Randisi

Published in the USA by:
BearManor Media
P O Box 71426
Albany, Georgia 31708
www.bearmanormedia.com

ISBN: 978-1-62933-365-6
BearManor Media, Albany, Georgia
Printed in the United States of America
Book design by Robbie Adkins, www.adkinsconsult.com

Table of Contents

For Bob Shanks,
and in memory of MERV GRIFFIN

ACKNOWLEDGEMENTS

The following individuals and organizations provided invaluable assistance in the preparation of this book: Robbie Adkins, the late Jayne Meadows Allen, Gina Anzivino, Kaye Ballard, Peter Barsocchini, the Billy Rose Theater Division of the New York Public Library for the Performing Arts, William Childers, George Clark, Michael Daly, Brittany Jacobus Darpino, Michael B. Druxman, Anthony DiFlorio, III, the Free Library of Philadelphia Theatre Collection, Tony Garofalo, George Blood Audio, Patricia Giannascoli, Phil Gries, Jan Alan Henderson, Paul D. Inglesby, the late Cole Johnson, the late Don Kane, Dan Khoury, Max Klein, Scott MacGillivray, Steve Massa, Colin McCullough, Kliph Nesteroff, New Jersey Legal Copy, Ben Omart, Andy Patilla, Herbie J Pilato, Andrew Randisi, Monti Rock, III, Sean Robins, Jack Roth, Kevin Sasaki, Rick Saphire, Chris Sasse, Steve Stoliar, Jeffrey Vance, John Wells, the Team at Philadelphia Photographics, and Tom Wilson.

Special thanks go to Mark Fleischer, Esq., The Griffin Group, Inc., Bob Shanks, Julann Griffin, Tony Griffin, Albert Fisher, Rob Sinclair, David Peck and Tom Gulotta of Reelin' in the Years Productions.

An important note about some of the *Merv* shows reviewed herein, which exist only in audio format, with no corresponding videotapes or kinescopes. These include: the review of Merv's *Tonight Show* appearance with Sophia Loren (1962); Merv's New Year's Eve show (1962); Montgomery Clift's interview (1963); Joan Crawford's interview (1963); Bert Lahr's interview (1963); Merv's last NBC show (1963); Judy Garland subbing for Merv (1968); the Tiny Time Wedding Parody (1969); Merv's New Year's Eve show (1969); Abbie Hoffman/Virginia Graham/Tim Dolan debate (1970); Merv's First Anniversary on CBS (1970); Arthur Treacher's farewell (1970); Merv's Last New York show (1970); "The Year 2000" (1970). I am grateful to my research consultant, Rob Sinclair, and Phil Gries, for making available rare audio recordings of these programs that would have been lost but for their good sense to preserve them.

Any materials, including copyrights, trademarks, likeness rights owned or controlled by Merv Griffin and any related entity are used with permission.

Steve Randisi,
Philadelphia, PA

FOREWORD

The classic monthly magazine, *The Readers Digest*, used to have a column in every issue titled "The Most Fascinating Person I Ever Met." While I have been blessed with a long career in the entertainment industry that has put me in close proximity with many "fascinating" persons, certainly right up at the top of my list would be the name Mervyn Edward Griffin, Jr. I first met Merv in 1962 when I was head of TV and movies for the Seattle World's Fair. That one-day encounter would last a lifetime.

When Merv was selected to host his own talk show for Westinghouse Broadcasting in 1965, he brought me on board as head of promotion, publicity, and public relations. I also took on the added duty as show photographer, which neatly tied in with my other responsibilities. Consequently, I was actively involved in all the day-to-day functions of the series with the golden opportunity to interact closely with the entire production staff, musicians, and guests. More important, I was able to be with Merv, not only on a professional basis, but also on personal level with his family. It was a joy to become close friends. Many, many weekends were spent with the Griffins on their Califon, New Jersey farm where Merv taught me how to skeet shoot; and his wife, Julann, taught me how to make her famous Parmesan baked chicken. Over these casual weekend getaways from New York City, the Griffin clan became the close-knit family I never had.

It was back at our offices at The Little Theatre where *The Merv Griffin Show* originated that I was able to learn and grow the most. In the beginning, I simply knew Merv as the affable TV personality, host, and singer. But the real learning curve for me was witnessing, close up, Merv's immense talent as an entrepreneur and businessman with an intensive and unquenchable appetite for a mind-boggling array of interests.

One of Merv's most touching and admirable qualities was his profound compassion for virtually everyone he encountered, be they world famous or man-on-the street. An incident that has forever remained close to my heart involved one of our most important and memorable guests on the show, the Reverend Dr. Martin Luther King, Jr. Merv had long wanted to do a one-on-one sit down interview with Dr. King, and on July 6, 1967, Dr. King appeared at the Little Theatre with his friend Harry Belafonte. With Merv's keen talents to extract the most out of a guest, Dr. King's interview was open, heartwarming, candid, and enlightening. It was one of the most profound and unforgettable appearances on any episode of *The Merv Griffin Show* (as detailed later in this book).

Nine months later, on Thursday, April 4, 1968, we were about half way through videotaping another day's episode when tragedy struck. As we did for every show, producer Bob Shanks and I sat next to one another in the first row of the theatre, giving us quick access to the stage during commercial breaks. We would confer with Merv, chat with the guests, and I had moments to take candid close-up photos of everyone.

As the commercial break was about to begin, one of the pages came down to Bob and me. He knelt down and whispered into our ears: "Martin Luther King has been shot! He has been rushed to a hospital in Memphis and there is no word on his condition." We asked to be kept quietly informed during the breaks. Bob and I agreed that there was no sense in breaking this news to Merv in the middle of the show, since we had no definitive word on the situation. The show continued and over the course of the next few breaks, to the best of our knowledge, Dr. King was still alive. Merv could see the commotion going on around us, and asked what was up. Bob wisely told him it was nothing to be concerned about. Then, during the last break, with less than a minute to go in the show, Bob broke the news to Merv that Dr. King had been shot, but was still alive in the hospital, which was all anyone knew at that time.

When the show ended, Merv did something that still resonates deeply in my heart to this day. He walked to the edge of the stage to be as close to the audience as possible and motioned them to remain in their seats. He commented that perhaps some audience members had noticed the staff running back and forth to Bob and me. Merv then announced to the audience the stunning, tragic news out of Memphis. A loud gasp and cries of anguish erupted from the theatre. He recalled that just a few months earlier, Rev. King had sat on that very stage, discussing non-violence, peace and love for one another, and reflected emotionally on the enormous impact King's preaching and insights had had on him and, of course, the world.

Impulsively, Merv then asked the entire audience to stand and hold hands as he led them in prayer for Dr. King to survive this terrible attack. Merv quietly asked the audience to go home to their loved ones, as he was planning to do, and to keep Dr. King in their thoughts and prayers.

It would have been easier for Merv to say little or do nothing that day; just let the audience depart the theatre. But that was not how Merv Griffin lived his life—in public or private. He was unabashed to show his emotions, grief, compassion, and heartfelt empathy. In that one evening, Merv climbed higher in stature to this young broadcaster.

We all remember Merv's larger-than-life successes; his legendary career broke many milestones as an entertainer, producer, and real estate tycoon. I am blessed to have known him as a man of character, integrity and compassion. Hopefully, readers of this book will discover for themselves the exceptional and very special Merv Griffin.

Albert Fisher,
Los Angeles, CA

1. THE MAN BEHIND THE MICROPHONE

"Your wife will tell you she watches Merv Griffin
for his boyish charm. Don't count on it."—Trade ad,
1967

In March 1979, while honoring Merv Griffin at a testimonial dinner, Orson Welles extolled the talk show as the only legitimate art form to emerge from television. The legendary filmmaker acknowledged Griffin as a true master of the format, possessing all the attributes of the "classic talk-show host."

Welles wasn't merely dispensing empty praise. As countless hours of video can attest, Griffin displayed the same panache with superstars, ranging from John Wayne to Jane Fonda, as he did with the up-and-comers he enthusiastically nurtured. His interviews in the political category—and there were plenty of them—offered compelling insight into powerful leaders like Martin Luther King, Jr., Robert F. Kennedy, Adam Clayton Powell, Richard Nixon, Jimmy Carter and Ronald Reagan. These "heavyweights" usually shared the bill with other front-page luminaries. Day after day, year after year, an array of singers, comedians, writers, artists, athletes, raconteurs, and newsmakers could be seen chatting fluently with the always affable Merv.

This book is not a full-scale biography of Merv Griffin. Rather, it's the story of the television program bearing his name. *The Merv Griffin Show* journeyed through multiple lives—constantly growing and adapting as changing times and tastes dictated. Debuting on October 1, 1962, the first incarnation was a 55-minute entry on NBC's afternoon lineup. From the beginning, Griffin was a groundbreaker, bringing to daytime television an unprecedented blend of guests and topics as colorful as the network's famous peacock. The early reviews couldn't have been more flattering. *Look* magazine proclaimed the show as "one of the few bright lights on TV." The *New York Daily*

News praised the host as "a sophisticated wit." Even the *Christian Science Monitor* weighed in favorably, noting how Griffin "patiently aids his duller guests, and seldom misses an opportunity for humor." Rarely are such accolades expressed so boldly in a field where talent, intelligence, and charm are commonplace.

Success didn't materialize overnight for Griffin; his "dues" had been paid long before he began ad-libbing behind a desk. He'd been a piano-playing prodigy at age four, and a nationally known radio crooner by the time he was 19. Over the course of his career, Griffin would prosper as a big-band singer, recording artist, movie actor, composer, and game show impresario, before finding his niche as a literate purveyor of conversation. "Merv Griffin, in short, is an individual plurality," observed *TV Guide* in 1963.

Despite critical acclaim and a loyal following, the first *Merv Griffin Show* did not win its time slot and was canceled after a six-month run. The program would make a quiet return in May 1965, when the Westinghouse Broadcasting Company revived it in a 90-minute format for first-run syndication. Conceived as a late-night offering, but seen mostly in late-afternoon or earlyevening time slots, Griffin's Westinghouse series would evolve into one of the most influential talk shows of all time. It was during this second wave of popularity that Merv Griffin permanently re-established himself as a thought-provoking interviewer as well as a versatile entertainer.

In August 1969, CBS wooed Griffin out of his comfy syndication deal and thrust him into a three-way, late-night race against NBC's powerhouse, *The Tonight Show Starring Johnny Carson*, and ABC's *The Joey Bishop Show*. Though Griffin competed vigorously under the CBS banner, his efforts would prove futile owing to several inescapable factors. CBS owned fewer stations than NBC, making it impossible for *Merv* to win the ratings race. There was also a dwindling roster of illustrious guests on the New York scene, which necessitated changes in venue and format. One year after taking on the late-night shift, Griffin moved his show to Hollywood where he would master the format for which he's best remembered—the "theme show." While the ratings never increased, the pressures, tensions, and skirmishes between network and star did. Finally, after two-and-a-half acrimonious years, CBS and Griffin parted ways.

In March 1972, *The Merv Griffin Show* returned to the turf on which it had enjoyed its greatest success—syndication. This version of the show, which would eventually be cut back to an hour, would endure until Merv's final sign off on September 5, 1986.

How does a talk show evolve, and eventually thrive, in the fiercely competitive realm of television? It's accomplished through the dedication of producers, directors, writers, talent coordinators, musicians, and technicians, all of whom strive to make the show, and the star, look good. After the behind-the-scenes tasks are completed, it's up to the star to make the finished product come off as "spontaneous." Through this process, a talk-show host emerges as a consistent personality that the viewer gets to know as a friend. This is why people often refer to TV talkers by their first names. During the 1960s and '70s it was not uncommon to hear someone say: "Did you see who was on Merv last night?" or: "How about what Merv said to Zsa Zsa Gabor?" In recent years, we've heard things like: "*Oprah* has had some great shows lately!" and "Did you happen to catch *Ellen* yesterday?"

Several strengths distinguished Merv Griffin from his contemporaries. First, and obviously, Merv was a host without any sharp edges. Even so, he never lost sight of the fact that it was *his* show. He had no problem interrupting guests when they spoke too much (like Henny Youngman frequently did), or chiming in when a guest wouldn't speak at all (as Andy Warhol once did). When the situation demanded it, Merv could be uncharacteristically blunt, as record producer Phil Spector found out one night in 1965. Spector kept mentioning rival hosts Johnny Carson and Les Crane, despite negative reactions from Merv, who pointedly said, "cut it out." Spector kept it up. Then, in an unmistakable annoyed tone, Merv asked, "Did you come here tonight to plug other people's shows?" Spector cut it out.

Maintaining control of an interview requires acute listening. Merv knew when to talk and when not to. "I'm a good listener, a good reactor, and I'm terribly curious," he told *Look* magazine in 1968.

"You care about people," TV host and producer David Susskind told Griffin on the air. "You're not thinking of the next joke and you haven't got a prepared *shtick*. You listen with all your might and that's the secret of great interviewing." Lucille Ball was equally forthright in her appraisal of Griffin. "Sometimes I'm not paying attention to what the other person is saying," she told him during an interview. "I am watching *you* listen!"

Second, and equally important, was Griffin's meticulous attention to preparation, even in a format generally perceived as unscripted. Rather than relying on notes or summaries from staffers, Griffin would actually read the books his guests had written, screen their films, and review as much relevant material as his schedule would allow.

"Merv prepared," says Peter Barsocchini, Griffin's producer from 1979 to 1986. "It's a myth to say that he *didn't* prepare. Merv had an uncanny ability to sit down and read four or five sets of notes and retain them. He'd have the note cards on his desk, but he could do an interview without having to look at them. He would sit with the interviewers and talent coordinators before the show, read that set of notes, ask a few questions, and then it all sunk in."

Being a guest on a talk show can be an intimidating, if not terrifying, ordeal. It may look easy to walk out in front of a studio audience and chat with a congenial host, but it isn't. Uninhibited people, famous or not, make the best guests on these shows. Even performers with decades of experience on their resumés can become unnerved when that red light on the camera flashes on. Griffin had an amazing faculty for recognizing stagefright, and could quell someone's fears with the simplest of techniques. The trick was to make the guest feel comfortable in what is essentially an uncomfortable environment. To accomplish this, Griffin would express intense interest in even the dullest of subjects. It's practically impossible to watch the man and *not* notice his unbridled enthusiasm.

As a means of establishing intimacy between his guests and the studio audience, Griffin would often interview certain personalities (usually the lead star) at center stage, just a few feet away from the first row. Even more striking was his tendency to lean toward a guest with a heightened eagerness and murmur his questions softly.

"The guy's really at his best with a nervous guest," said talent coordinator Paul Solomon in 1970. "I've seen people go on shaking and stuttering and then come off saying, 'That man is terrific; it was a lot of fun and I'd love to do it again.'"

Actress/singer Kaye Ballard (*The Mothers-In-Law*) is a veteran of some150 talk show appearances. "Jack Paar, Merv Griffin, Johnny Carson, Mike Douglas, I worked with them all," says Ballard. "And what I remember most about Merv is that he was always so down to earth. With Johnny Carson, you were on tenterhooks all the time. Jack Paar was a brilliant conversationalist and easy to talk to. But I'd have to say that Merv was easier, and the atmosphere on his show was always completely relaxed."

Another notable trait of Griffin's was a penchant for exploring new ideas, thereby offering his audience food for thought. The turbulent '60s provided stimulating topics that were either addressed lightly, or avoided altogether, on other daytime variety/talk shows of the period. Merv was the first of the important daytime talkers to tackle controversial subjects potently, but tastefully. Civil unrest stemming from racial tensions, political assassinations, the burgeoning use of psychedelic drugs, the war in Vietnam, and the contempt for authority demonstrated by American youth, were all fodder for comprehensive discussion on Griffin's daily talker.

On the lighter side, Griffin's program was a much sought-after venue for fresh talent. Though Griffin's show wasn't the only game in town, it was the one that was the most feasible, in terms of landing a booking, for newcomers. Many of today's younger viewers are surprised to learn that several iconic performers (e.g., Richard Pryor, Tiny Tim, Lily Tomlin, Jerry Seinfeld, and Whitney Houston) got their first big break on the Griffin stage. Through the years, writers and historians have sometimes credited *The Ed Sullivan Show* or *The Tonight Show* for giving inventive comics like Pryor, and several others, their first national exposure. This genuinely irked Griffin. As early as 1969, he complained: "We got pretty tired of being an audition ground for the late-night shows—especially when they would introduce someone I discovered and add the announcement, 'making his first network appearance.'"

On the flip side of Griffin's list of first-timers is an equally impressive tally of final farewells. Judy Garland, Groucho Marx, Rosalind Russell, Totie Fields and Orson Welles are among the greats who basked in the limelight one last time via *The Merv Griffin Show*.

The roster of legends wasn't limited to those who'd earned fame onstage or in front of a camera. Many influential and groundbreaking directors sat on Griffin's sofa throughout the years. Alfred Hitchcock, Otto Preminger, William Wyler, Federico Fellini, Roman Polanski, Franco Zeffirelli, Martin Scorsese, and Francis Ford Coppola invariably found *Merv* to be a worthy platform on which to discuss their esteemed works.

Though Merv was not a comedian, he could toss one-liners alongside the best in the business. Rather than going for the big laugh, Merv frequently underplayed it, scoring just as heavily with a light retort. One night he was discussing the growing acceptance of cosmetic surgery with a prominent Beverly Hills plastic surgeon. Totie Fields, the lead guest, recalled a man who had offered to reshape her face. "Was he a doctor?" Merv quipped. The look on Totie's face was priceless. She chuckled; the audience roared.

Then there was the time Kenny Kingston, the self-proclaimed "psychic to the stars," told the audience that he constantly had three spirits around him—his grandfather, Chief Running Bull, and actor Clifton Webb. "You could be the Kingston Trio," cracked Merv. "You'll do very well around here," he added, as Kingston chuckled.

The "hip choir boy," as Griffin was frequently characterized, wasn't above the risqué *double-entendre* or a saucy "setup." In a late '70s segment, Sophia Loren and Charles Nelson Reilly were among several participants in an amusing poker-playing exhibition. "Do you have a pair, Sophia?" asked Merv, glancing impishly at the buxom actress. "She certainly *does!*" said Reilly enthusiastically.

Then there was the time Merv and Don Rickles subjected themselves to acupuncture. With large needles dangling from their faces, the two men sat there, staring at each other beseechingly. "I'll pull yours out if you'll pull mine out!" Merv offered, challenging the censor. "Let's not get *that* close," Rickles retorted.

Whether blatantly broad or extremely subtle, Griffin's quips never shattered anyone's dignity. In fact, the most pervasive criticism of Merv was the notion that he could be overly solicitous. By the early 1980s, Griffin's affable persona was so entrenched that it had become a springboard for parody and satire. Rick Moranis, on NBC's *SCTV Network*, lampooned Merv in a series of sketches, portraying him as a chubby, fawning host who prefaces or concludes every sentence with a resounding "*ooooooooh*" or "*aaaaaaaah.*" Such good-natured ribbing was to be expected, given Merv's tendency to speak in italics ("*Gee, what BEAUTIFUL girls they are*").

Griffin's rapture was patently genuine. Unfortunately, the same can't be said of all who sat next to him. Some celebrities make the rounds on talk shows solely to push whatever they're selling, be it a movie, book, concert tour, or whatever. Thus, extracting a cohesive interview from an uncommunicative guest often requires the skill of an experienced trial lawyer. In a 1981 segment, Ringo Starr dodged questions about the breakup of The Beatles, and his impending marriage to Barbara Bach, who occupied the seat next to him. Starr wanted to focus exclusively on his new film, *Caveman* (1981), and not much else. Awkward situations like this can sometimes work in a host's favor. Carson, for example, could perk up a stagnant interview with a double take or sardonic one-liner. Griffin would go the opposite route, playing the nice guy card to win the guest over. If he didn't, as in the case with Ringo, he'd simply move on to the next topic or the next guest.

On another occasion, actor Al Pacino expressed annoyance when he thought Merv had asked him a dumb question. Pacino hadn't yet achieved full-fledged stardom from his work in *The Godfather* (1972). He was an up-and-comer appearing as part of an ensemble in a Broadway show. "How did you make it from the Bronx to Broadway?" Merv asked. "By subway!" Pacino answered dryly. Merv cut to a commercial.

Aside from what viewers could see on the tube—an attractive host with a bouncy energy and innate curiosity about people—there was Merv Griffin, the producer, media mogul, and entrepreneur.

According to those who worked for Griffin, he was a "hands-on" exec. "He worked harder on that show than anyone else," says Don Kane, a Griffin talent booker who would ultimately rise to the rank of associate producer. "Virtually every aspect of the program was overseen by him."

The combined pressures of hosting a daily talk show, running multiple production companies, and overseeing a diverse range of ancillary enterprises can be daunting. Just as Merv knew when it was time to break for a commercial, he knew when it was time to break away from the endless cycle of showbiz stress.

"If we were taping two shows on a Thursday," recalls Barsocchini, "he'd be looking at his watch and I could tell he was already mentally on his airplane. He couldn't wait to get up to Carmel for the weekend. And after three days of Carmel, he needed the action and couldn't wait to get in the plane and come back to Los Angeles. Merv was somebody that was constantly hitting the refresh button. That's the way he liked it.

"Merv was not one to sit still for very long. He thrived on having the activity going on. He'd get up in the morning and often play tennis before going to work. But once he came into work, it was all non-stop and that's what he wanted. He kept in with the stuff that he liked, such as the game shows. He really didn't want to sit in on business negotiations, and meetings about crunching numbers and things like that, even though he did have a great sense of business."

Anyone who thinks hosting or producing a talk show is easy should talk to Peter Barsocchini. "It definitely *is* a pressure cooker," Barsocchini admits. "And with a talk show, we were turning out five 90-minute shows a week. We were doing six a lot of the time, trying to fill in for the times Merv would go on vacation. And that's a lot of pressure. It's a business for young people, because it's hard to have a family, or a normal life, because you're working around the clock."

What's the hardest part of the process? "Part of it is the realization that the show *must* go on," Barsocchini laughs. "But the hardest thing, actually, was keeping it fresh. You're talking about 30 guests a week, and you don't have a budget where you could fly people in from all over the world. And trying to get someone special would be even harder today because there are 80 billion outlets! Then, everybody was competing. Merv didn't want some big star, like Jane Fonda, right after she'd been on with somebody else; it was a big fight as to who was going to get her first. And it was also a matter of getting it on the air first. It was a lot like a newspaper because you were constantly churning out new material. You're in the middle of production complications during the day, while trying to put something together for tomorrow. Then you're thinking of something you'll be shooting in New York!"

While Griffin knew instinctively which celebrities would generate respectable ratings, he didn't rely solely on the name value of his guests. "Much of *The Merv Griffin Show* focused on conversation," observes Kevin Sasaki, a Los Angeles-based public relations executive who worked for Griffin from 1991 to 2007. "It wasn't just movie stars, music stars, or comedians on his show. He'd have people on who were running companies, politicians, astronauts, artists, and scientists. You name it, he had it," says Sasaki. "And some of the people who were guests on his show were not necessarily there to plug a book, a movie, or a product. They would all *stay* for the duration of the show. It was like a party. Today, it's one chair and one guest at a time. The guest is on for three minutes, and then it's on to the next guest.

"Merv would have people on that weren't the top music artists of the day. He would have them on, of course, but he'd also have people like Zsa Zsa Gabor, who had nothing to promote other than being Zsa Zsa. He had people who made great conversation, like Totie Fields, and others that weren't A-list stars, but were entertaining and loved to sit and talk. Merv liked to *dish*. He loved little bits of gossip, and loved to hear about people. When we'd get together to discuss business, he would take the time to talk personal. 'What did you hear about this one? What did you hear about that one?' He never lost his curiosity about the world and it kept him *up* about things. He was very into what young people were looking at. And with me being quite a bit younger, he looked to me for a perspective on places to go. So I took him to a few places where the younger stars would hang out, and he wanted to see them. A lot of that was because he was formulating the club at his hotel, and I think he wanted to get a sense of what the kids were jamming to."

As an employer, Griffin was known to hire young people for entry-level jobs. If they wanted to keep those jobs, they had to carry their weight. "He'd offer you an opportunity," says Barsocchini. "But Merv was not one to suffer fools gladly. When I was offered the job to produce his show around the end of 1979, I was 27-years-old. Not a lot of the shows back then would have made that offer. Now I had been working there and had shown what I could do. But if things had gone south, I would have been given a handshake and a 'see-you-later!' That's the nature of show business, generally speaking. Show business is not a get-rich-quick scheme. You can elevate quickly and you can also descend quickly."

"Merv had certain rules and guidelines that his employees had to abide by," offers Sasaki. "Some of that probably wasn't easy for his assistants, because Merv was a 24/7 kind of man. He was very dynamic. He didn't like people who went against his rules, or people he felt he couldn't trust, which was understandable. If by chance, an employee's performance was not up to par, you would very quietly hear that that person was no longer there."

With Griffin, the task at hand was far more important than personal reactions. "I once overheard people who were working for Merv talk about him behind his back," recalls Julann Griffin, who was married to the star from 1958 to 1976. Julann immediately brought the matter to her husband's attention. "I told him about it, and he said, 'Don't bother me with that. I don't care what they say. I just want them to do their jobs.' He didn't believe in getting mixed up with 'small stuff.' To him, the big stuff was getting the job done."

Unlike many other powerful showbiz moguls, Griffin remained accessible to his employees. "He *wanted* to talk to you," Sasaki recalls. "It wasn't as though you had to go through five people, even though he was on the phone all the time."

Off-camera, Griffin was pretty much like his on-screen persona. "The bottom line with Merv was—and I say this after having worked for him many years—what you saw was what you got," says Barsocchini. "He wasn't a phony. Being a celebrity is more complicated than most people think, and it gets old fast. When you're dealing with the public, some people are rude and you can spot them. Merv knew how to handle them *all*, ranging from the curious onlooker to the intrusive fan.

"Many times in Vegas, there'd be someone who'd say, 'Merv, may I shake your hand?' And Merv would say, 'Hi, how are you?' He'd put his arm around them to take the picture, sign whatever it was, and say, 'Nice to meet you.' And he would start to move on. Then you'd hear, 'Oh, wait, Merv, would you do this, or do that?' They wouldn't let it go. But Merv knew how to handle the public."

"He knew how to get through a crowd easily," recalls Julann Griffin. "He always smiled and looked in everyone's eyes as he rushed by them. It was as though he had made contact with everybody. And whenever he looked at people, he could kind of empathize what they were going through. He saw everybody as interesting."

One thing Merv never lost, from his days as a radio singer to his years as a media mogul, was a zest for performing. "Merv remained the consummate host," says Sasaki, referring to the period during which Griffin owned the Beverly Hilton Hotel. "He would participate in many things, and everybody wanted to stage their event as his hotel, especially because of that great ballroom, which could really support major TV productions such as award shows, and the like. Charities would always ask him to emcee, and they loved it if he would sing a song. I think Merv genuinely liked that; it was his joy."

Throughout his life in the public eye, Griffin personified the master showman. "With Merv, the bottom line was to produce the most satisfying show possible," says Don Kane. "He was willing to do whatever was necessary to keep his guests and audiences happy."

Making people happy was something that came naturally to Mervyn Edward Griffin, Jr. He was born on July 6, 1925 in San Mateo, California, a place he fondly recalled as: "A wonderful little community about 18 miles out of San Francisco."

He was the second child of Rita Robinson and Mervyn Edward Griffin, Sr. Merv, Jr. had one sibling, a sister, Barbara, born in 1923. "He was a Depression-era child," says Julann Griffin, "and he did not have an easy childhood. His father was never around. He had a weight problem. But he also had an active mind and a genuine interest in people."

The Griffins were among millions of American families affected by the Great Depression. When Mervyn, Sr., who worked at a sporting goods store, couldn't keep up the payments on his house, the family was forced to move in with Merv's grandmother.

If the men in the Griffin family had one thing in common, it was an unwavering passion for tennis. On a 1963 Griffin segment, screenwriter Adela Rogers St. Johns appreciatively recalled how Merv had come from a long line of tennis champs, on his father's side. Tennis for the Griffins was a way of life, something to be taken very seriously. "Your uncle Peck," St. Johns beamed, "was one of the great champions." Nodding in agreement, Merv added that while all the Griffins were pros, it was his Uncle *Elmer* who had been the family's undisputed champ.

"I've got a lot of uncles," Merv smiled. "You see, my name is really Mervyn," he explained, as though no one had been aware of that. "I'm Mervyn, Junior. My father's name was Mervyn. And his brother was Elmer. His other brother was Clarence. And there was another brother, Milton. And there was Frank. We never knew how a *Frank* got in there. And they were all great tennis players— the Irish Griffins with their lace curtain names."

To distinguish Mervyn, Jr. from Mervyn, Sr., the younger Griffin was nicknamed Buddy. Rita Griffin decided Buddy should take piano lessons and enlisted her sister Claudia to give him lessons. "He used to play beautifully when he was four," Claudia said of her nephew/prodigy in 1963. "He was so little, he had to play standing up. I loved him. He was just a doll."

Merv, Sr. knew nothing of his son's musical abilities until someone casually mentioned that they'd seen Buddy perform at a recital. When confronted by his dad, Buddy responded by simply offering a snappy performance of "Tea for Two." Long before he would enter his teens, Buddy's devotion to music was sealed forever.

"He was a slightly unusual child," recalled Rita Griffin. "He was always putting on shows. He took our clothes to costume his actors."

When he wasn't playing the piano or singing in the school choir, Buddy could be seen organizing backyard productions with his friends, the way Judy Garland and Mickey Rooney did in the old MGM musicals. An enterprising lad, Buddy also mowed lawns, sold magazines door-to-door, and published his own one-page newspaper detailing what his neighbors and classmates were up to. (Could this have been an early indication of Merv's proficiency for dishing gossip?)

Another favorite activity in the Griffin household was the word game "Hangman," which Buddy would play regularly with his sister and classmates. This simple pastime would one day provide the basis for one of television's most enduring game shows.

As a teenager, Merv ventured to Los Angeles to spend summer vacation with his Uncle Elmer, the family *bon vivant* who hobnobbed with the Hollywood elite. It was during this period that Merv got to meet his childhood idol, Errol Flynn, who happened to be Elmer's house-guest. Flynn, who starred in such unforgettable screen classics as *Captain Blood* (1935) and *The Adventures of Robin Hood* (1938), gave Merv his first autograph.

That summer, Merv would also encounter another of his Hollywood heroes, the renowned character actor Monty Woolley, nicknamed "The Beard" because of his distinctive white whiskers. Woolley had achieved a respectable degree of fame for starring in the stage and motion picture adaptations of *The Man Who Came to Dinner* (1942).

On screen, Woolley epitomized the feisty but grandfatherly curmudgeon. That wasn't the image Woolley presented when 14-year-old Merv encountered him at a posh country club. What he saw, to his utter disappointment, was a lecherous old man hitting on women at the bar. Nevertheless, Merv did what any teenage fan would do: he asked for an autograph. Woolley responded with two words: "Fuck off." It was then and there that Merv vowed that if he ever achieved any level of fame in show business, he'd never refuse to give autographs to fans or pose for pictures.

Following graduation from San Mateo High School, Merv worked at a number of nondescript jobs unrelated to the entertainment industry. He continued to offer his services as a pianist at church socials, weddings, and funerals. Following brief stints at San Mateo Junior College, and the University of San Francisco, he curtailed his education to pursue a full-time career in show business.

In 1944, at the insistence of a friend, Griffin applied for a staff musician's job at radio station KFRC in San Francisco. What the 19-year-old hopeful didn't realize, however, was that the station was seeking the talents of a singer, not a pianist. Merv auditioned for the job and was instantly hired to sing on a 15-minute oddity called *San Francisco Sketchbook*. One week later, the station manager not only raised his salary, he changed the title of the program to *The Merv Griffin Show*.

Soon, the Mutual network began broadcasting the program nationwide. Fan letters began to flood the station, requesting autographed pictures of Merv Griffin. All well and good, except for one potentially embarrassing problem. At five feet, ten inches tall, and weighing 240 pounds, Merv hardly fit the description of "America's Romantic Singing Star," as he'd come to be known. In addition to the excess weight, he had to deal with a chronic acne condition.

The enterprising station manager, Bill Pabst, came up with a shrewd plan. Henceforth, Merv Griffin would be billed as America's Romantic *Mystery* Voice. The autographs would be sent, but not on pictures. As Merv's voice continued to enthrall female fans coast to coast, his face would remain unseen. The only exceptions would occur during live performances, which Griffin did on weekends to earn extra money.

One day in 1946, an overzealous fan sneaked into the radio station hoping to meet her idol, Merv Griffin. In an effort to shoo the woman away, the receptionist said that Merv was rehearsing in the studio, an area "off limits" to the public. Equally disappointing was the fact that *The Merv Griffin Show* did not invite a studio audience. Because the visitor had never seen Merv, she didn't recognize him as he stood several feet away in the reception area. As luck would have it, a secretary called out to Merv, telling him he was wanted on the telephone. The woman stared at Merv for a few unforgiving seconds, then burst into spasms of cruel laughter. That laughter would echo in Merv's ears for the rest of his life, especially whenever he'd contemplate a sumptuous meal or high-calorie dessert.

America's Romantic Singing Star wasn't looking or feeling very romantic. Producer Bill Dozier (best remembered today for the 1960s *Batman* series) had heard Merv on the air and believed a romantic voice such as his would be perfect for movies. Then he got a good look at him in person and changed his mind. Likewise, singer Joan Edwards (of radio's *Your Hit Parade*) thought Merv's vocal talents could be exploited beyond the confines of radio. It was Edwards who told him, rather bluntly, to get rid of the "blubber." He did.

The Griffin diet menu was simple: nothing but steak and salad. The strict regimen lasted three months, resulting in a slender, 150-pound Merv Griffin who could meet and greet his adoring public without fear of embarrassment. A national fan club was soon established, with a west coast chapter headed by an enthusiastic teenager named Carol Burnett.

In 1948, bandleader Freddy Martin heard Griffin on the air, and offered him a job as the lead vocalist for his orchestra. Griffin accepted the job, albeit at a substantial cut in salary. He accepted the assignment with the expectation of greener pastures, and the exhilaration of cross-country travel.

Over the next several years, Griffin would become an increasingly popular personage at all the hot venues across the country, including the Cocoanut Grove in Hollywood. By 1951, Merv's name had become a household word, thanks to a novelty song called "I've Got a Lovely Bunch of Cocoanuts," which he sang with a delightfully convincing Cockney accent. More than a million copies of the record were sold, and the catchy ditty shot up to number one on the nation's "Hit Parade." Merv was signed as a solo artist by RCA Victor, and scored a second triumph with "Eternally," performed with Hugo Winterhalter and His Orchestra. Recorded in late 1951, the song ranked high on the *Billboard* charts by the third week of January 1952. Additional hits followed: "Wilhelmina," "Dream Street," "Never Been Kissed." Throughout this career, Griffin would hold recording contracts with several major labels, including Dot, Decca, Carlton, and MGM Records.

With the recent success of his recordings, Griffin took leave of the Martin orchestra and embarked on a solo tour. He once said that there probably wasn't a major hotel or nightclub that he hadn't played at least once, either as a band singer with the Martin orchestra or as a single.

It was during this period that Doris Day, a major star at Warner Bros., happened to catch Merv's nightclub act. Day, herself a former band singer, was on the lookout for a new male co-star. Impressed with Griffin's good looks and charismatic presence, she arranged a screen test for the boyish baritone.

In 1952, Griffin finally bid goodbye to Freddy Martin, joining the ranks of contract players at Warner Bros. Over the next two years, making movies would be the focal point of his existence. After a small role in the low-budget, black-and-white *Cattle Town* (1952), the crooner-turned-actor was cast in a Doris Day film. Unfortunately, anyone who blinks at the wrong moment is likely to miss his "performance" in Day's *By the Light of the Silvery Moon* (1953). In this Technicolor musical, Merv is afforded *one line* as a bullhorn-toting announcer. This cameo contrasts sharply with an expanded role in *So This Is Love* (1953), in which he's the romantic lead opposite the star, Kathryn Grayson. A lavish production based on the life of opera star Grace Moore, *Love* would provide Griffin an ample opportunity to exploit his appeal as a singer. Though Merv got to sing "I Kiss Your Hand, Madame," the kiss he would recall most fervently was the one he gave Kathryn Grayson.

On his show, and in various interviews, Merv would claim that his smooching scene with Grayson represented the first open-mouthed kiss in a mainstream movie. (Not to detract from Merv's ardor, but open-mouthed kisses were depicted in films that pre-date his birth!)

Griffin's other screen credits include *Three Girls and a Sailor* (1953), *The Boy From Oklahoma* (1954), and *Phantom of the Rue Morgue* (1954). In *Oklahoma*, Griffin played the unlikely role of a deputy sheriff. By his own admission, Griffin looked "ridiculous" in the role. In the scene in which his character is required to fire a gun, he does so, but with an expression that registers nothing less than sheer panic.

When Griffin wasn't working before the cameras, he was busy behind the microphones. Any *bona fide* Merv Griffin fan will definitely recognize his melodious tones in such diverse films as *The Beast from 20,000 Fathoms* (1953), and the Hitchcock thriller, *I Confess* (1953). His voice would also be heard on the radio, promoting major Warner Bros. releases such as John Wayne's *Hondo* (1953).

The early '50s would mark a tenuous time for young actors in Hollywood. The availability of desirable screen roles was on the wane, as was the studio contract system itself. "That's because the major studios were losing money left and right," said actor Jack Larson, best remembered as Jimmy Olsen on the 1950s TV series *Adventures of Superman*. "And one reason was a restructuring of the way films were distributed to theaters."

Larson became acquainted with Griffin at Warners. "We were both contract players there at the same time," the actor recalled. "There was a sense that Merv, this young Irish-Catholic fellow with a good voice, was being groomed as the next Bing Crosby." Although the two of them worked in *Three Sailors and a Girl* (1953), they did not have any scenes together. "Jack E. Leonard was also in the picture," recalled Larson, "and in later years, he would be a frequent guest on Merv's show."

Larson observed that up until the early '50s, the contract system had "keyed" the studios. "They had always kept their people under contract and turned out product like General Motors turned out cars. At Warner Bros., they'd turn out two Bette Davis pictures a year, two Errol Flynns, two Humphrey Bogarts. And they knew, in advance, where they were going to book these films. But during the fifties, there was a deregulation ruling concerning how the major studios distributed their films. That had to do with what was called block-booking, forcing exhibitors to buy the studio's films in groups, or blocks, which was considered unfair to the independent filmmakers who had become very aggressive."

Declining profits were attributable not only to the rise of the independents, but also the foreign market which, in the years following World War II, had begun to crank out more and more movies.

Another major blow to Hollywood was television, which had become more popular than movies. On Tuesday nights, when Milton Berle was on the air, many movie theaters closed early because people were at home watching Uncle Miltie on their newly purchased TV sets. The new medium was now more of a threat than radio had ever been. Along with that, the industry had to reassess how it would produce films for distribution. The studios had to either slow down or *close* down, and that situation contributed to the demise of the once lucrative contract system.

Merv hated the tedium associated with filmmaking. Sitting around all day waiting to be called to a set, and then delivering one or two lines in a miscast role, hardly seemed like a feasible path to stardom. The thing he enjoyed most was driving his white Buick convertible through the studio gate each morning, waiving to the guard who addressed him as "Mr. Griffin." That, more than anything else, made him feel like a star. Even so, he wanted out. After two years of walk-ons, voice-overs, and small roles, a discouraged Griffin bought out his contract. His status as a free agent came with a price tag: he would be precluded from working at any other movie studio for the next two years.

No one would cast more zingers at Griffin's failed film career than Griffin himself. Over the years, he would frequently joke that a "Merv Griffin Film Festival," comprising *all* his scenes spliced together, would run *four* minutes!

In 1954, with his movie contract effectively ended, Griffin decided that the best place to jump-start his career would be New York. Before heading east, however, he would enhance his resumé considerably by opening for the legendary Tallulah Bankhead at the Sands Hotel in Las Vegas. Years later, Bankhead would return the favor by making several memorable appearances on Merv's Westinghouse series.

Beginning life anew in the Big Apple, Griffin soaked up as much work in radio and television as he could find. He spent the summer of 1954 co-hosting a twice-a-week series with Betty Ann Grove, telecast under the tile *Song Snapshots on a Summer Holiday*. Premiering on the CBS television network on June 24, the first installment was set in Central Park and featured such popular tunes as "Three Coins in a Fountain," "Hooray for Love," and "My Friend."

Merv's next big break came the following winter, when he landed the role of Woody Mahoney, the young romantic hero, in the Broadway musical *Finian's Rainbow*. In his review for the *New York Journal-American*, John McClain wrote: "Merv Griffin, new to the stage and Broadway, is an assured and prepossessing performer with a good voice."

Despite positive reviews, Merv acknowledged his lack of discipline for Broadway, and came to terms with the fact that the stage held no more allure for him than movies did. Undaunted, the young star continued to reinvent himself in Manhattan, the epicenter of the television industry, with its vast resources and enticing opportunities. It was at this point that Merv decided he'd rather talk than sing for his supper. Over the next few years, he would zealously pursue the electronic medium, filling in for various stars or emcees, and by appearing regularly on such diverse offerings as CBS's *The Morning Show*, *The Robert Q. Lewis Show*, *The Arthur Murray Party*, and a religious program on ABC called *Look Up and Live*.

While Griffin was sharpening his emceeing skills for television, a phenomenon within the medium itself was unfolding late at night. It was a potent development that would alter the career of Merv Griffin, and scores of other entertainers for decades to come.

2. MAKE TALK, NOT LOVE

Programs like *The Merv Griffin Show*, which fall into the variety/talk category, have their roots in late-night television. In 1950, TV stations that didn't offer old movies or local programming in the post-11:00 p.m. period simply signed off until the next day.

The programming genius that paved the way for late-night talk shows was a broadcaster named Sylvester "Pat" Weaver (Sigourney's father). Weaver's background was in radio, where he had achieved considerable success as an advertising executive. He made the transition to television in 1949, having joined the NBC network as head of programming, and would ultimately serve as its president from 1953 to 1955.

Pat Weaver was a visionary in many respects, not the least of which was his conviction that television would have an ineffable impact on the world. He rightly predicted that the medium would ultimately make adults out of children (although some contemporary sociologists might argue that it's the other way around).

During his tenure at NBC, Weaver would be responsible for developing several of the network's earliest hits: *Howdy Doody*, *Your Show of Shows*, *The All Star Revue*, and *The Colgate Comedy Hour*, among many others. Many of his concepts and innovations are still widely used today. A notable example is the "live" magazine format that would materialize in the form of the *Today* show. Another is videotape, a revolutionary device that Weaver immediately employed when it became widely available in 1958.

In 1950, Weaver began pitching the idea that significant revenue could be earned in the post-11:00 p.m. hours. His colleagues were skeptical; they contended that most people, at that time of night, were either sleeping or making love. Nevertheless, Weaver's goal for live, late night entertainment would be realized in a vaudeville-style venture called *Broadway Open House*.

The man hired to host this after-hours experiment was a largely unknown comic named Don "Creesh" Hornsby. His nickname was earned by yelling "Creesh! Creesh!" as he frantically ran through the smoke-filled clubrooms in which he performed. Unfortunately, Creesh never went on the air. He died of polio two weeks before the premiere of the program.

Nevertheless, on May 29, 1950, *Broadway Open House* quietly made its debut with comedian Jerry Lester serving as host. Lester would alternate on the program with actor-comic Morey Amsterdam (remembered today as the acerbic comedy writer Buddy Sorrell on the 1960s hit, *The Dick Van Dyke Show*). Amsterdam's tenure on the show would be brief—four months. Lester, however, went on to make a name for himself and the program, essentially becoming television's first late-night star. The program peaked fairly quickly, particularly with the introduction of a bosomy, golden-haired bombshell nicknamed Dagmar (Jennie Lewis), who would serve as the show's foil. Also on hand was an assortment of zany comics, up-and-coming comedians (including Lenny Bruce), wild stunts with members of the studio audience, and a house band led by accordionist Milton DeLugg.

Broadway Open House was anything but a talk show. Its format was devoid of monologues, interviews, and serious discussion. What it *did* have was a party-like ambiance that kept viewers glued to the tube during hours traditionally spent sleeping, studying, partying, and making whoopee. More important, it paved the way for future programming in the post-11:00 p.m. "graveyard" shift.

The task of devising fresh comedy material five nights a week proved more demanding than anyone had anticipated. Additionally, Lester was said to have become disgruntled when Dagmar's popularity eclipsed his. After a mere nine months on the air, the show was beginning to wear thin. The ratings began to drop. Then, in May 1951, Lester quit the program. Dagmar remained, but without a strong comic presence, the series' days were numbered. A significant number of NBC affiliates, irate over lost revenue, began to drop the program in lieu of old movies. Finally, on August 24, 1951, *Broadway Open House* closed its doors for good.

Pat Weaver continued to develop fresh ideas for programs molded in the magazine-style format. Riding high on the success of *Today*, which debuted in January 1952, Weaver began to map out ideas for a similar series styled for the midnight hour. His attention would soon be focused on a local late-night personality who was essentially doing on local New York television what he had done on a Los Angeles radio station. The young host was a multi-faceted performer whose bag of tricks consisted of ad-libbed comedy, music, interviews, and lots of free-wheeling stunts and sight gags. His name was Steve Allen.

Jayne Meadows Allen, Steve's widow, recalled that: "*Broadway Open House* was gone and NBC was looking for something new. And there was Steve's local show seen only in New York on NBC's local station, WNBT-TV. This was in 1953. After Steve's show had been on the air for almost a year, Pat Weaver happened to tune in one night by accident. The next day, he called a meeting of all his executives and told them, 'Put that genius on the network *immediately.*' And they did. Going network was a big step up, because with a local show, you don't get the money you get when you're on a network. Pat told Steve he'd be on the network, with one proviso: 'your show is called The Steve Allen Show. I've brought Dave Garroway in from Chicago and I renamed his show *Today.* We awaken the country with *Today.* And since you'll be the last thing we have at night, I would like to change the title to *Tonight!*'"

Meadows recalled the pre-show jitters of comedian Louie Nye, one of Allen's regulars: "Louie said, 'Jayne, America will never understand us. We're too new, too experimental, and we're going to be a flop. You've got to be *hip* to understand Steve Allen.' I told him, 'Louie, darling, Monday will be your first Tonight Show. It's my birthday, and I predict that this show will someday be the longest running show in television. You're going to take America by storm because everybody in the country is going to love it. It's different. It's not a vaudeville show or a game show, and it's not like anything that was ever done in radio. This is a one-of-a-kind thing.'" Meadows didn't believe one word of what she had said. "I was just saying this to put Louie at ease," she said. "But it all came true."

On September 27, 1954 the program formerly known as *The Steve Allen Show* joined the NBC network under the title *Tonight!* The Hudson Theater, the venue for the Allen's local series, was retained as the home base for its network successor.

"Pat Weaver created the *title* of the program," Meadows recalled. "He was a brilliant advertising man and was good with slogans. But not one soul created anything on that show except Steve. And he did it without any writers!"

The Tonight Show, as the program came to be known, would endure longer than anyone could have anticipated, but not always with Steve Allen at the helm. Although the program was a critical and financial success, its frantic pace was a draining exercise for even the most energetic of hosts.

In October 1956, comedian Ernie Kovacs was hired to host the program on Monday and Tuesday nights. By January 1957, NBC decided that Steve Allen was far too valuable to be confined to the darkness of the late-night shift. The network moved him into its prime-time schedule, on Sunday nights, in an effort to challenge CBS's ratings winner, *The Ed Sullivan Show*. On January 25, 1957, viewers saw the last installment of Steve Allen's *Tonight!*

The NBC network sought to retain its status as the pioneer in late-night programming. The execs remained acutely aware of the moneymaking potential in those midnight hours. Indeed, the Allen show had proven itself to be eminently profitable in its relatively short run, and the network remained committed to what was fast becoming a national habit. Though enormously successful in terms of ratings and revenue, Allen's *Tonight!* was by no means devoid of criticism, even within the ranks of the NBC hierarchy. Several execs felt that the program, with its offbeat guests, wild stunts, and unrestrained zaniness, was too artless—even for midnight consumption. In an effort to broaden the range of audience appeal, the network would develop a format with more substance— one that consisted of news coverage, remote broadcasts, and diverse entertainment.

By this time, Pat Weaver had departed the halls of NBC after a heated disagreement with chairmen of the board, Robert Sarnoff, Jr. With Weaver gone, it was up to the other execs to come up with a magic formula to fill the void left by Allen. What they came up with was a radically different concept called *Tonight! America After Dark*. It was not a talk show. Instead, the program would focus on American nightlife as reported via studio segments and mobile cut-ins from various "hot spots." The host, Jack Lescoulie, was supported by a line-up of notable columnists who would report from various cities: Hy Gardner and Earl Wilson in New York; Irv Kupcinet in Chicago; and Vernon Scott in Los Angeles.

Though boldly innovative and technically sophisticated for its time, *After Dark* proved to be an unmitigated disaster. Audiences accustomed to Steverino's brand of buffoonery rejected the show instantly. Critical reaction was equally negative.

Jayne Meadows Allen recalled the level of desperation of the NBC brass: "They tried every gimmick imaginable, including cutting from city to city with various news and entertainment features. They even came up with the idea of adding a ski report, presumably to attract the nation's avid skiers. But nothing worked. It was pretty bad."

How bad? So bad that, according to one of its writers, Walter Kempley (a future Griffin writer/producer), viewers disliked the show so much they'd go next door and shut it off.

Unfortunately, Jack Lescoulie was no Steve Allen. He was fired less than a month after the show had been on the air. To replace Lescoulie, the producers hired the equally forgettable Al "Jazzbo" Collins who, like Steve, had been a successful disc jockey. Collins couldn't make a go of it either. As a result, *Tonight! America After Dark* actually *went* dark on June 26, 1957. The program did have an impact on the career of a 24-year-old man whose contributions to the medium of television would be incalculable. The young man was future *Merv Griffin Show* producer Robert H. Shanks.

The Illinois-born, Indiana-raised Shanks ("Bob" to everyone who knows him) recalls the dawn of the late-night variety/talk show. "Steve Allen is really the one who is responsible for the television variety/talk shows, although he didn't realize it at the time. But he was truly amazing. I loved the old Allen show and wanted to become a part of it. As it turned out, I'd gotten a coffee pour job on *Tonight! America After Dark* and got to meet a few people who would later go on to work for Jack Paar, who took over the *Tonight Show* in July of 1957. One of these people was John Carsey, who later became the husband of producer Marcy Carsey. He was the unit manager of the Paar show and I had lunch with him one day.

'Would you like to be a talent coordinator on the Paar show?' he asked. And I said, 'God, John, I'd kill for that.' And it happened that night. I was hired and went into the studio and met the producer. I saw the show that night and met Jack afterward."

Jack Paar had subbed successfully on Allen's *Tonight!* in mid-1956, and knew the mechanics of the format forward and backward by time he was hired to take over the show on a permanent basis. Paar, who would influence the video career of Merv Griffin more than anyone else, adhered to a basic philosophy to insure talk show success. "You want an electric undercurrent that keeps the audience from knowing what's going to happen next," he advised Griffin. "You be ready with your next question, but know when to let the show run itself."

Tonight Starring Jack Paar had its unceremonious debut on July 29, 1957. Whether it's a rerun of Merv, Johnny, or any of the current talkers, the modern viewer is actually watching the format refined by Jack Paar. It was Paar who popularized the now familiar desk-and-sofa combo that has become the hallmark of the American talk show, although some historians attribute that innovation to "Steverino."

"Paar was a very complex man," recalled Jayne Meadows. "But he was also a brilliant and talented man." Adjectives like "unpredictable" and "mercurial" were also frequently used to describe Paar's interviewing style. An overtly emotional man, he had no qualms about expressing his likes and dislikes on the air. Certain performers wouldn't be seen on his show (even if they were brilliant) simply because he didn't like them. He disliked shaking hands with people he didn't know, and avoided the elevators in the RCA Building (where his show relocated in 1959) because he didn't want to be spoken to by strangers.

In the absence of big name stars, Paar generated excitement from a blend of personalities who were colorful—and readily available. Some of his favorites included the renowned party-giver Elsa Maxwell, author-humorist Alexander King, Zsa Zsa Gabor, comedienne Dody Goodman; actor-comedian Cliff Arquette (in character as the lovable "Charley Weaver"); British star Hermione Gingold, the French-born actress Genevieve, and the delightfully neurotic actor-pianist Oscar Levant. In the mid-to-late sixties, many of these stalwarts would turn up regularly on the syndicated *Merv Griffin Show*.

While millions of people adored Paar, many disliked him. Yet almost everybody watching television late at night was watching *The Jack Paar Show*, as the program had been renamed in 1959.

Described by one observer as "a bull in his own china shop," Paar regularly sparred with important columnists, including Walter Winchell and Dorothy Kilgallen, whenever he felt they had treated him unfairly. The host also took on politicians, sponsors, his head writer Jack Douglas, TV host Ed Sullivan, and even his own guests. In fact, Paar once threw Mickey Rooney off the show because he thought the actor was drunk.

Despite such rancor, Bob Shanks maintains that Jack Paar was not a difficult man to work for. "The only problem was that he was always a nervous wreck," Shanks recalls. "His nervousness radiated and you picked up all that energy and anxiety. He was actually a sweet guy, but he could also be sarcastic and quick. When you had a bad booking, almost everybody would run. And the situation would fester. Carsey told me, 'Bob, when you have a rotten booking—and you will because every talent coordinator does—make sure you're the first face Jack sees when he comes off the stage. Don't say anything. Just be right there in his face.'"

Shanks decided to try doing just that when he'd had a bad booking one night. "Jack said, 'What the hell was that all about, kid?' And he went right by me, then forgot about it. That was one of many good pieces of advice I got from John Carsey."

Paar's best-remembered battle was the one he waged against his own network. One night in February 1960, he told a joke on the air involving a "W.C.," the British term for water closet, or, more succinctly, *toilet*. Paar saw the bit as nothing more than a cute story full of *double entendres*. The NBC censor thought otherwise and excised it from the tape without informing the star. The following night, still highly infuriated that he hadn't been consulted, Paar reacted with the same fury he'd demonstrated in the past. This time, however, he quit the show while on the air. The announcer, Hugh Downs, finished the program that night. Out of respect for his boss, Downs conducted the interviews from his seat on the panel rather than the host's chair.

Bob Shanks wasn't present for the famous walk-off because he was on his honeymoon. "I thought, here I am, just married, and out of a job," recalls Shanks.

Everyone connected with the show was nervous. Paar's viewers were nervous. The *network* was nervous. Over the next several days, the Paar-NBC feud would remain front-page worthy news. Paar wasn't around to read any of it. He had fled to Hong Kong.

After weeks of frantic head scratching at NBC, the wayward host returned to the NBC studios on March 11, 1960. "When I walked off, I said there must be a better way of making a living," said Paar, after the applause died down. "Well, I've looked, and there isn't. Be it ever so humble, there is no place like Radio City."

If a lesson had been learned from the Paar *Tonight Show* years, it's that the talk show is at its best when there's a spark of raw energy or a moment of unexpected drama. Paar had a term for such occurrences: "planned chaos."

3. GAME SHOWS AND SUB-HOST GIGS

If the name Merv Griffin is associated with anything other than daytime chitchat, it's that enduring phenomenon known as the game show. From the earliest days of television, game shows have been a career-boosting device for the budding star as well as the established genius. Jack Paar, Johnny Carson, Carl Reiner, and others all hosted game shows before their names became household words. Long *after* their names had become household words, Groucho Marx, Fred Allen, Ernie Kovacs, and even Jackie Gleason quizzed, puzzled, and challenged a procession of willing participants.

Merv's connection to the genre stretches back to the late 1950s, an era during which contestants competed on enormously popular "quiz" shows like *The $64,000 Question, Dotto,* and *Twenty One.* With nail-biting tenseness, viewers would tune in to witness the players sweat out answers to difficult questions on national television. The winnings were astronomical and so were the ratings. But when ratings began to decline (partially due to the fact that the shows were competing against each other) the producers resorted to rigging. Certain contestants were given the correct answers in advance to pump up the sagging ratings and enhance the competitive nature of the games.

In 1958, a series of scandals exposed several of the most popular shows (including the ones aforementioned) as having been "fixed." The impact of the scandals would be intense and far-reaching. Quiz shows began to vanish from the airwaves. Public reaction was decidedly negative, with most Americans convinced that the deception on the part of the producers, sponsors, and networks, had violated the trust of the nation. In 1960, after a myriad of investigations, lawsuits, and hearings, Congress amended the Communications Act of 1934, making it illegal to "fix" the outcome of any contest or game.

In his book *Making the Good Life Last*, Griffin draws a distinction between a "quiz show" and a "game show." According to the book, a quiz show tests a person's knowledge for money; a game show, on the other hand, involves a certain skill or activity for which the winning contestant is awarded a prize. Today, the consensus among many aficionados is that "quiz shows" became known as "game shows" in order to distance the newer programs from the ones tainted by scandal, and to suggest a more leisurely undertone.

The producers *least* affected by the scandals were Mark Goodson and Bill Todman. In the early fifties, the Goodson-Todman organization popularized a format in which a contestant would be pitted against three or four celebrities on a panel. The panelists functioned much like a repertoire company, lending an air of class and sophistication to the game itself, which often seemed secondary.

All of the half-hour Goodson-Todman programs originated from small studios in New York City. The company's first megahit was *What's My Line?*, which debuted on CBS on February 2, 1950. Its premise was simple; the panelists merely had to guess the occupation of the contestant. The best part of each telecast was the last segment during which the blindfolded panelists had to identify a celebrity "mystery guest."

Premiering on June 2, 1952, *I've Got a Secret* proved more challenging. The panelists had to uncover the contestant's "secret," which was usually a humorous or heartwarming life experience.

Most intriguing of all was *To Tell the Truth*, a winner from its first airing in December 1956, largely because it underscored an important human instinct: the ability to determine if someone was telling the truth.

A few Goodson-Todman offerings did not feature celebrity panelists. On those programs, it was incumbent upon the contestants to demonstrate skills that might involve physical dexterity (*Beat the Clock*) or knowledge of a particular subject (*The Price Is Right*). These half-hour formats would be updated and revived for the syndicated market over the course of several decades.

In 1957, Goodson-Todman was in the process of developing a new quizzer called *Play Your Hunch*. The producers began to audition emcees for the new show to be broadcast "live" each weekday.

Play Your Hunch was designed to gauge the intuition of its contestants. After being presented with a problem, players would have to choose one of three solutions labeled X, Y, and Z. It would essentially be a game of observation and deduction, much like *To Tell the Truth*, but with more action and panache. A contestant might have to deduce which of three square-dancing couples was a husband and wife team. He might have to figure out which of three men, all wearing kilts, could actually play the bagpipes. Though *Hunch* would not feature a celebrity panel, the producers intended to offer as many showbiz personalities as possible, especially for the show's more elaborate (and often slapstick) stunts.

Merv Griffin was unemployed during the first few weeks of 1957. He would soon be hosting a Florida-based travel program on ABC called *Going Places*, which, ironically, went nowhere. The show barely lasted eight months. By the fall, he was still employed by ABC, this time as host of a live radio program. The network spared no expense in promoting the new series, taking out full-page ads in the trade papers. The centerfold ad in the October 16, 1957 issue of *Variety* boasted that: "The new *Merv Griffin Show* puts a peppy portion of showmanship, salesmanship on American Radio every weekday night, 7:15 to 7:55 p.m." The show focused on music and songs performed by guest artists, as well as a cast of regulars that included a grown-up Darla Hood (the dark-haired sweetheart of the *Our Gang* comedies) and The Spellbinders. Doug Browning served as announcer, while Jerry Bresler and Lyn Duddy handled the musical production aspects.

After his contract with ABC expired, Griffin learned from his agent, Marty Kummer, that Goodson-Todman was auditioning emcees for its newest project. The prospective host had to be able to sing, dance, and perform admirably in skits. Knowing that Griffin excelled in all these areas, Kummer thought the new program would be a perfect vehicle for his client. Griffin thought otherwise. Hosting a game show wasn't exactly what the ambitious 32-year-old star had in mind.

Up until now, each phase of the young entertainer's career had been exceedingly ill-timed. His first success was achieved in radio not long before that medium would be overshadowed by television.

Next, he joined the Freddy Martin Orchestra as its lead singer just as the big bands were winding down. Then, he signed on with Warner Bros. at a time when the studio contract system was rapidly fizzling out. Now he was about to plunge into a television game show at a time when such programs were under intense legal scrutiny.

With considerable ambivalence, Merv auditioned for producer Mark Goodson in late 1957. He was hired almost instantly. The next hoop the star had to jump through was the taping of the requisite "pilot" episode that would be pitched to, and ultimately purchased by, CBS in the winter of 1958.

Hunch would serve as a significant springboard in Griffin's business career. In addition to a steady paycheck, the half-hour series would also provide a rudimentary education in the nuts-and-bolts of game shows. The tasks Merv would master with this new venture would serve him immeasurably in years to come.

Things were beginning to look up for Griffin, whose life and career until then had been somewhat peripatetic. On May 18, 1958 he married Julann Elizabeth Wright, the vivacious actress/comedienne he'd met two years earlier on *The Robert Q. Lewis Show.*

Julann caught a glimpse of her future husband during his brief stint on the Broadway stage in *Finian's Rainbow.* "That's where I first saw him," recalls Julann. "I just couldn't believe that voice! And a week later, while I was on *The Robert Q. Lewis Show,* guess who showed up? I couldn't believe it. I felt as thought I'd known him all along. He was like a family member right from the beginning."

Merv was instantly attracted to Julann's wholesomeness and fun-loving sense of humor. They made each other laugh. "When I first met him," says Julann, "my impression was that he was warm and funny. He was just so open and full of life. I thought he was funny, and he thought I was funny, so that worked out well."

Julann's first meeting with Bob Shanks occurred at *The Tonight Show.* "Julann Griffin had a great sense of humor," recalls Shanks. "She had walked by a jewelry store one day and saw something that said, 'If you're royalty, come in and try on this tiara.' The thing was worth millions, and she walked in and said, 'I'm a fairy princess!' And an enterprising public relations guy thought that was great.

She tried it on, they photographed her, and it got a lot of press. So we booked her on the Paar show."

"That actually wasn't a great thing for me," says Julann, "because I was an ad-lib comedienne and I never chewed my cabbage twice. Paul Keyes was the one who interviewed me for the Paar show, and they all laughed when I told them that story. I didn't think much of it. But, lo and behold, Jack Paar asked me about it that night. I couldn't believe it because I thought it was old stuff. I was so naïve!"

Play Your Hunch, which debuted over the CBS airwaves on June 30, 1958, was fast-paced and well received by critics. Though praised by the *New York Post* as "the best of the new arrivals," the program wasn't strong enough to compete against NBC's blockbuster game show *Treasure Hunt*. Consequently, CBS canceled *Hunch* after a six-month run. ABC, the third-ranked network at the time, picked up the show on January 5, 1959—and canceled it seven months later.

Griffin didn't lose any video exposure or career momentum as a result of the cancellations. In fact, he was ubiquitous on television during the second half of 1959. "He seemed to be all over the dials," as Julann fondly remembers. Merv's post-*Hunch* assignments were extensive and varied. Goodson-Todman put him before the cameras as substitute host for the vacationing Bill Cullen on *The Price is Right*, for two weeks, beginning on August 3.

That same week, Griffin was signed for multiple appearances on *The Arthur Murray Party*, a weekly variety series hosted by dance instructors Arthur and Kathryn Murray. Debuting on ABC in July of 1950, the program was staged like an actual party, with guest stars dressed to the nines, performing various dance steps. The program was actually a thinly veiled promotional vehicle for the famous Arthur Murray Dance Studios.

Griffin teamed up with singer Jane Harvey for the August 17 telecast, which also featured songwriter Johnny Burke. Griffin and Harvey offered a delightful medley of Burke's songs, including "Imagination," "Swinging on a Star," and "Pennies from Heaven." On another memorable telecast in the series, Griffin and Harvey offered a medley of songs by Bob Merrill, who was also showcased.

As if his schedule wasn't hectic enough, Griffin took over hosting chores from Carl Reiner on the prime time game show, *Keep*

Talking. Produced by Wolf Productions for ABC, this exercise in ad-libbing separated its celebrity players into two teams. One member on each team, after being given a word, would have to relate a story without using that particular word. The other team members then had to continue the story, hence the show's title. It was a simple premise that tested the quick-wittedness of comedy mavens like Morey Amsterdam, Orson Bean, Jayne Meadows, Joey Bishop, and numerous others.

Griffin was also Goodson-Todman's first choice to fill in for the vacationing Bud Collyer on *To Tell the Truth*. When Griffin subbed on one edition of the program in 1961, the panel happened to include a spirited, dark-haired young man named Johnny Carson. A few years later, after Griffin had begun his daily talk show, the company offered him the host's chair on *I've Got a Secret*. Owing to the demands of his syndicated series, Griffin declined. Steve Allen took the job.

Goodson-Todman respected Griffin not only as a stellar host, but also as a competent program consultant and strategist. The company would benefit from several of his recommendations, which called for more entertainment and audience participation to the tried-and-true *Play Your Hunch* formula. Griffin's ideas proved successful. As a result, a "new and improved" version of the show was sold to NBC. The half-hour programs, now recorded on videotape in the RCA Building, would air in color each weekday morning. The NBC premiere of *Hunch* would coincide with a major event in the lives of the Griffins—the birth of their only child, Anthony Patrick, on December 8, 1959.

In the early months of 1960, Griffin was still contractually obligated to three network series: *Play Your Hunch, Keep Talking,* and *The Arthur Murray Party*. "The only trouble I have keeping up with the shows," Griffin told writer Jack Leahy, "is that they're all so different. *Play Your Hunch* is an informal daytime quiz show. *Keep Talking* is another ad-lib affair but in a more formal and professional style. *The Arthur Murray Party* has an entirely different format and unlike the other two, demands rehearsals."

By the fall of 1960, Griffin would be adding yet another credit to his rapidly expanding resumé. NBC tapped him to preside over

Saturday Prom, a blatant attempt to inherit the young viewers of ABC's recently canceled *Dick Clark Saturday Night Beech-Nut Show*.

According to network press releases, *Saturday Prom* promised to be a "new and exciting shindig" that would showcase various teen-age recording favorites in a New York studio each Saturday evening. The show would feature a live orchestra, led by Bobby Vinton, and hundreds of kids dancing to the latest steps.

With this latest undertaking, Griffin became one of the most traveled TV personalities in show business. There would be obligatory sojourns to various cities each weekend, where Merv would meet the deejays promoting all the popular tunes performed on the Saturday night telecast.

Griffin knew as much about the recording industry as anyone in the business, having sold millions of copies of "I've Got a Lovely Bunch of Cocoanuts." After the release of his last major hit, "I Keep Running Away from You" (written by Irving Berlin), Griffin was convinced his recording days were over. Joe Carlton, of Carlton Records, believed otherwise.

Carlton was convinced that the time was ripe for another Griffin hit. "If you have six television shows a week," he told the young host, "you have a large audience that knows you. You should have a record out which would appeal to your audiences." The result was "Banned in Boston," an ancient ditty brought up to date with a decidedly rock-and-roll beat. The lyrics tell of a girl whose "wiggle" was apparently bawdy enough to get her banned in Boston— among other cities. Music publicist and biographer Peter Levinson described the song thusly: "Behind Merv Griffin's voice in the hit record is a happy-go-lucky chorus of 'yeh yeh's,' and a twangy combination of guitars, Fender basses, and tenor saxophone providing the musical accompaniment."

Released as a single, the novelty tune proved so popular that it was also included on *Merv Griffin's Dance Party*, an LP distributed under the Carlton label. "Merv sings and swings 'The Charanga' plus eleven exciting twists/cha-chas/ponies/slops/& bops," boasted the album's trendy cover.

Despite the advantage of "live" (as opposed to "lip synched") performances from major artists, *Saturday Prom* didn't generate much in the way of publicity or ratings. NBC dropped the show in January 1961, after a mere three-month run. In no way did the cancellation curtail Griffin's demanding schedule. Aside from his daily hosting chores on *Play Your Hunch*, he had a record to promote. His weekend jaunts to places like Baltimore, Washington D.C., Pittsburgh, Allentown, and Cincinnati, included visits to hops, deejay shows, and assorted promotional events.

Not since his days with the Freddy Martin Orchestra had Merv experienced so many appreciable on-the-road encounters. "I got to see what people thought of me and of both our shows," he told a reporter. "In New York, people don't even blink an eye when they see a television personality on the street. As I walked down the streets of the various cities I visited, I would get questioning looks and could overhear whispers from passers-by who recognized me from TV."

Much of that recognition was attributable to the mounting popularity of his morning game show. Thanks to the "magic" of videotape, Griffin was able to stockpile episodes of *Play Your Hunch* in advance, thereby allowing more time for travel and hobnobbing. One amusing encounter with the record librarian of a Boston radio station stuck in his memory. "He was watching *Play Your Hunch* on his TV set in his office," Merv recalled. "When he turned around and saw me watching myself on TV, he couldn't believe his eyes and remarked excitedly, 'But you can't be here—you're on the air *now!*' Actually, that sort of thing happened to me more than once."

With *Play Your Hunch* now established as a bona fide hit on NBC's morning schedule, the network moved the program into prime time, first on a trial basis in 1960, then as a summer replacement for *The Bob Newhart Show* in 1962. Interestingly, one of Newhart's writers on that award-winning comedy/variety series, which ran from October 1961 to June 1962, was future Griffin executive producer Ernest Chambers.

Primetime success notwithstanding, Merv knew that *Hunch* had finally come into its own when the producers finally authorized the marketing of the *Play Your Hunch Home Game*. Manufactured by Transogram, the boxed game was sold in stores and presented on the air—to the losers—as a consolation prize.

Another perk was to be derived from *Hunch*: an opportunity for Merv to form his own orchestra. The result was the long-awaited, but short-lived, Merv Griffin and His Play Your Hunch Band. "We're the only new young band around," Griffin told *TV Guide* in 1960. "First we play an old song as it was originally written and recorded. Then we do a second chorus as it might be played today, then combine the two styles in the third chorus. For example, if we were to do a Count Basie number, the third chorus might be a combination of Basie and cha-cha-cha."

Unfortunately, only a handful of episodes of *Play Your Hunch* are known to have survived. Existing only in black-and-white kinescope form, the films have been replayed from time to time on game show networks. Loss of the complete library of episodes is truly unfortunate, especially since a bevy of comedy greats ranging from The Three Stooges to Carol Burnett, periodically indulged themselves in several of the show's more outlandish stunts.

The move to the "peacock network" provided a few unequivocal perks. First, Griffin's video visibility was significantly greater, since NBC had far more affiliates than CBS and ABC. Second, the young host would be working under the same roof with a personage he genuinely admired—Jack Paar. Like millions of Americans, Merv was an ardent viewer of *The Tonight Show*. He watched Paar each evening with absolute fascination, contemplating a fervent desire to sub-host for him. This wasn't far fetched, since Paar would take every Monday night off, with no qualms about leaving the show in the hands of a competent substitute host. Merv was well acquainted with the Paar regime, having appeared on Jack's show as a singer on August 27, 1957 and January 23, 1959. He would eventually get to sit behind the host's desk, but not before making a third appearance on the late-night series, this time with his wife, on July 17, 1961.

Merv and Julann Griffin epitomized the youthful optimism that defined the early sixties. An attractive pair, the Griffins were also intelligent and energetic conversationalists, qualities that every talent coordinator yearns for in a prospective talk-show guest. With Merv now a rising star in the NBC ranks, he and Julann were invited to appear together, along with comedian Jack E. Leonard and

Cliff Arquette. The booking would mark Merv's first meeting with Bob Shanks. Griffin took a liking to the young producer and was especially appreciative of the attentive manner in which he prepped him and his wife for the show. The Griffins' segment was so well received that it was repeated as a "Best of Paar" telecast on September 29, 1961.

With several successful *Tonight* appearances under his belt, Griffin now felt confident enough to bandy words with the skittish Paar whenever he ran into him in the halls at NBC. More significantly, the two hosts would soon appear on television together again, but not in a way that either of them could have ever envisioned.

4. THE NERVE OF MERV

There's usually a hush in the studio when a game-show host tells contestants to "think it over" before giving an answer. That wasn't the case on *Play Your Hunch* one day in mid-January 1962. As Merv instructed the players to weigh their answers carefully, he was startled by a sudden burst of applause. He turned around and saw, to his utter astonishment, Jack Paar. One of Paar's well-known quirks was an avoidance of elevators. He didn't like being gawked at or spoken to by strangers, so he would frequently take a short cut from Studio 6-B on the sixth floor (where his show was taped), up to the seventh floor where his offices were located. On this particular day, however, Paar had arrived at work earlier than usual. "Jack wandered into the studio while Merv was taping his game show," recalls Shanks. "He didn't know that anyone else used his studio during the day." Paar was stunned to see a flurry of activity on *his* stage. The applause that greeted the late-night star was nearly deafening, such was his popularity at the time.

Griffin looked Paar in the eye and delivered what he would later describe as his first ad-lib on television. "What do you want?" he asked nonchalantly. Since no tapes, kinescopes, or audio recordings of this fortuitous moment are known to exist, it's not possible to assess if Merv's opening line was an expression of self-assuredness or simply a nervous reaction to being caught off guard. Whatever the case, the extemporaneous banter that followed scored a big hit with the studio audience and home viewers. Virtually everything the two of them said generated gales of laughter. In fact, they were so funny that some people thought the bit had been prearranged.

Paar left the studio that morning with a very favorable opinion of Griffin. He liked the way the young emcee had handled the unexpected encounter. "Jack told us about it that night," recalls Shanks. "He said, 'You know, that kid is very good.' Paar used to take Monday nights off, the way Johnny Carson would do years later. And, eventually, Merv was asked to fill in for Jack on one of those Monday nights."

Subbing for the Paar was the momentous gig that Merv and his agent, Marty Kummer, had been clamoring for. On Monday, January 29, 1962, the long-awaited opportunity had finally materialized—along with several overwhelming obstacles.

First, the producer, Paul Orr, could not (or *would* not) be present for the early-evening taping. "Nobody wanted to be saddled with producing for the sub-host," Shanks confides. That's because if the sub-host bombed, all those associated with him would also bear the blemish of failure. "But I held my hand up and they let me produce," recalls Shanks. "That's how Merv and I got to be close."

Second, there was a problem with guest procurement. No major star wanted to go on the nation's hottest talk show with a substitute host, particularly one that was known primarily for a quirky novelty song and a daytime game show. By airtime, however, Shanks had enlisted actor Wally Cox (*Mr. Peepers*), Dagmar (*Broadway Open House*), Howard Morris (best remembered for his recurring role on *The Andy Griffith Show*), Dr. Cleo Dawson, and "double-talk" comic Al Kelly. Also on the bill was a vivacious young singer who would be making her national television debut. Her name was Aretha Franklin.

With the guest list finalized, only one problem remained—Merv. The usually calm and collected host was overcome by a bundle of unrelenting nerves. Nevertheless, he pulled himself together and managed to get through the opening monologue, clearly the most demanding portion of the program for *any* host.

"The show was going superbly," Shanks recalls. "Merv had come up with the idea for a funny bit with Al Kelly, who excelled at double-talk, and they worked well together. Merv then introduced Aretha, and went to a commercial. I was backstage at that point, something that would lead to a life-long habit. And Merv came off and walked right by me. I said, 'Merv, where are you going?' He told me, 'I can't do this!' And I said, 'What do you mean? You're off to a great start.' He was terrified because there were six million people watching. I told him, 'No. Just one—*me*. What if I stood by the camera . . . would that help you? Could you deliver the show just to me?' I talked him down a little and he went back out there while I stood by the camera. And for most of the next six years, that's where I stood, by the first camera."

Griffin channeled his nervousness into a brisk performance that resonated well with viewers. The big break he had longed for had finally come his way. The evening had also provided a life altering opportunity for Shanks, who proved his proficiency as a producer by taking control of the entire program and making it run smoothly. As the credits rolled, Merv wiped the sweat off his forehead. He thanked his "producer" for the enormous support he'd demonstrated throughout the taping. "That night changed his life—and mine," says Shanks. "And it was the beginning of a long-term professional relationship."

Merv's *Tonight Show* reviews were excellent. Not one critic had found fault with his performance behind the desk. Merv knew he had finally found his niche, a conviction abetted by Paar's insistence that he continue to guest-host the program on a regular basis. "Merv loved it," recalls Julann Griffin. "The format fit him like a glove."

Griffin's second fill-in for Paar, on February 12, 1962, featured comedienne Pat Carroll, Jack E. Leonard, Larry Storch (several years before *F Troop* would catapult him to major stardom), and baseball legend Jimmy Piersall. It was on this edition of the program that Merv featured his wife Julann in a comedy skit by supposedly "discovering" her sitting in the studio audience. "He had me on," says Julann, "to help him feel more comfortable."

By now, there was no doubt in anyone's mind that Griffin was a consistently witty and erudite host. Suddenly, Paul Orr and his production staff couldn't do enough for him whenever he was scheduled to fill in for Paar. Griffin, whose confidence now rested solely in Bob Shanks, insisted that the young talent coordinator assume all responsibilities of production whenever he subbed.

Merv's final night of subbing for Paar was March 1, 1962, when he welcomed comedian Milt Kamen, actor Wally Cox, and singers Kaye Ballard and Judy Johnson. Now that Griffin had hit his stride, he was hit with something else—the starling news that Jack Paar was leaving *The Tonight Show*.

Rare audio recordings reveal that Paar had hinted at his impending departure from the late-night program as early as November

23, 1961. On that date, he speculated that his successor *might* be Johnny Carson. Paar gave NBC a deadline, March 30, 1962, to make a decision as to who would replace him.

One thing was certain. Paar's departure wouldn't be a repeat of his highly publicized walk-off in 1960. This time he would *not* be coming back. When word reached the vigilant showbiz columnists, there was wide speculation that Griffin might soon be sitting behind the famous desk on a permanent basis. What the press didn't know was that NBC had already selected and signed a new host, but was keeping mum as to who had been given the coveted job. Like Griffin, the successor happened to be a daytime game show host who had subbed successfully on *Tonight*. Eventually, it was revealed that the heir apparent was indeed Johnny Carson.

Like Steve Allen, Carson had achieved success in local radio. By 1951, he'd moved to Los Angeles where he landed a staff announcer's job at KNXT-TV, the CBS affiliate, where he would soon host a live hodgepodge called *Carson's Cellar*. One of Carson's admirers was Red Skelton, who eventually hired the young comedian as a writer. One day in 1954, Skelton injured himself during a rehearsal and was unable to perform. He wisely requested that Carson take his place on the program that night. This fortunate happenstance ultimately resulted in *The Johnny Carson Show*, a prime time variety offering that ran a mere 39 weeks on CBS in 1955. A daytime version would remain on the network through 1956. The following year, Carson moved to New York and began hosting the daytime game show *Who Do You Trust?*, a job he would hold until *The Tonight Show* beckoned him.

The last edition of the *The Jack Paar Show* (as the program had been officially renamed) aired on March 29, 1962. Unfortunately for NBC, when Paar said goodbye, so did the audience and the advertisers. Though all of the sub-hosts were captivating, many viewers had tuned out simply because Paar was gone. Many of the long-time sponsors were gone too, although a multitude of new ones were lined up for the October premiere of Carson. As the weeks wore on, the caliber of guest stars had sharply diminished, along with the network's ratings and profits.

During this interregnum, only two men racked up ratings that were comparable to Paar's. One was Merv Griffin; the other was Jerry Lewis.

"Merv and Jerry were good friends," says Rick Saphire, who had a long association with Jerry Lewis. Saphire, who once managed the comedian's career, hailed from a show business family. Saphire's uncle, Ernest Gluckman, who had produced *The Colgate Comedy Hour*, also served as associate producer of the *Tonight Show* episodes hosted by Lewis.

Saphire recalls that, "*The Tonight Show* took quite a dip after Jack Paar left, and not all of the guest hosts were headline-makers. They were all terrific in their own way; they *had* to be, because the *Tonight Show* was an institution by that time. Soupy Sales, for instance, was on there hosting, but he was out of his element. Not being the Soupy that we remember as taking a pie in the face, he proved to be charming and entertaining. As other guest hosts, Soupy succeeded in showing the nation another side of his personality.

"Then Jerry came on and immediately began kidding the sponsors' products. If the sponsor happened to be a cigarette company, he'd take a cigarette and break it into a million pieces, or stick it in his nose. You didn't do that kind of thing to sponsors. But he could get away with it."

In the wake of Lewis's incredible *Tonight Show* success, ABC would give him a weekly talk show of his own in the fall of 1963. The result was *The Jerry Lewis Show*, a frantic variety/talk offering seen on Saturday nights from 9:00 to 11 p.m.

"Jerry took over the El Capitan Theater on Vine Street in Hollywood," says Saphire. "He renamed it The Jerry Lewis Theater. But after the cancellation of Jerry's show, just 13 weeks after its debut, ABC bought the theater from Jerry and renamed it The Hollywood Palace."

Less than a decade later, the Hollywood Palace would become the permanent home base of *The Merv Griffin Show*.

The period between Paar's departure and Carson's arrival would see a diverse array of celebrities keeping the *Tonight Show* franchise afloat. During the spring and summer months, the parade of talent included Art Linkletter, Arlene Francis, Soupy Sales, Jan Murray,

Peter Lind Hayes and Hugh Downs. During the two weeks Merv hosted in April, his reviews couldn't have been better if he'd hired a publicist to write them.

"Merv Griffin is by far the best replacement for Paar to date," observed Jack O'Brian in the *The New York Journal American* (May 1, 1962). "The 'Tonight' job is TV's toughest and Merv Griffin is settling into it neatly, better each night."

The *Cincinnati Post and Times Star* declared that, "Merv Griffin stands out among Paar replacements" (May 4, 1962). The publication noted that the current *Tonight Show* booked twice as many guests, "but Merv sees to it that nobody is ignored and all are made to feel welcome and important."

The most persuasive observation of all appeared in the *Detroit Free Press*: "Griffin's two weeks have been the high spot. Personable Griffin must have made NBC wonder if they should have gone to the bother of getting Johnny Carson to take over in October" (May 25, 1962).

During his stint as guest host, Merv exuded the same sparkling repartee that had earned him critical acclaim on his first late-night outing. Acutely aware of the good job Griffin was doing, the network execs and show producers put him behind the desk several more times during April, and scheduled him for more appearances later that summer.

Most people today are unaware that *The Tonight Show*, in its early years, had a running time of one hour and 45 minutes. That meant that during the weeks Griffin hosted the late-night program, he was responsible for more than 11 hours of programming, factoring in the half hour spent on *Play Your Hunch*.

One of Merv's favorite guests was comedy writer/comic Woody Allen, who had made his talk show debut a year earlier with Paar. At first, the chemistry between Allen and Paar was nonexistent. Not only did Paar disapprove of the young comic's material, which he deemed too risqué, he found him unfunny and physically unappealing. (Typical Allen humor: "The difference between sex and death is, death you can do alone and nobody will laugh at you.") Merv thought Allen was brilliant and got him booked for multiple appearances on the show, the first of which occurred occurred in mid-July.

One evening, Griffin chatted with an English character actor he'd worked with several years earlier on *Play Your Hunch*.

Arthur Treacher had earned a considerable degree of fame by masterfully portraying stuffy servants and acerbic dignitaries in dozens of movies. His extensive stage work made him a sought-after talent for many "live" TV anthologies like *The All Star Revue*, *Goodyear Playhouse*, *Armstrong Circle Theatre*, *Kraft Theatre*, and *Climax*. He occasionally turned up on oddities such as *You're in the Picture*, a game show so astoundingly bad that its host, Jackie Gleason, apologized to viewers on its second, and final, airing.

Treacher, in contrast with his dour screen persona, possessed a razor-sharp wit, and cracked wise with Merv on *The Tonight Show*. There was an unmistakable affinity between the young host and the veteran character actor. By this time, Griffin knew how to extract the best retorts from *any* guest, and his banter with this famous "gentleman's gentleman" proved highly amusing. Even Merv's guests (which included the Smothers Brothers) were duly impressed. At one point during the program, Merv leaned over and told Treacher that if he ever got a talk show of his own, he'd hire him as his "second banana." The aging actor took the compliment to heart and pressed it in his memory book. The two men went their separate ways and wouldn't see each other again, on a professional basis, for three years.

With the increased exposure from *Tonight*, Griffin began to attract more and more attention from the press. In fact, viewer and critical response was so overwhelmingly enthusiastic that the network tapped Griffin to host the show for two consecutive weeks in late July. Although no kinescopes or videotapes of the interim *Tonight Show* with Griffin are known to exist, rare audio recordings provide a tantalizing sample of the program's flavor.

On July 30, 1962, announcer Hugh Downs announced Merv's *Tonight Show* line up in this order: Zsa Zsa Gabor, Dan Dailey, Felicia Sanders, Lou Holtz, Ginny Tiu, Sophia Loren (on film), and Skitch Henderson and the NBC Orchestra.

"Thank you so much," said Merv after the applause subsided. "I can't tell you how nice it is to be back. And first of all, I want to thank all the emcees that filled in for *me* during my vacation!

I must tell you I got a chance in the last three or four months to look in at the Tonight Show and see all of the emcees. And it's been very good and interesting, because everybody brought a little bit of their own personality to the show. So it's been very diverse programming with comics, singers, and talkers. Jerry Lewis's two weeks were wild, marvelous. It was like watching a two-week telethon for the benefit of nervous collapse!"

The most notable aspect of the evening would be Merv's first "remote" segment, an interview filmed on location for inclusion in the program, as Paar had frequently done. It was at a party given by producer Joseph E. Levine that Merv's crew was permitted to set up a 16mm sound camera to showcase Sophia Loren. Merv was about to regale viewers with a rare insight into the international star. More important, the fast-paced little film would demonstrate just how smoothly Merv could handle a star of Loren's magnitude.

Without any prepared questions, Merv charmed Loren to such an extent that she persuaded her husband, director Carlo Ponti, to join the conversation. Before you knew it, Merv had scored an exclusive scoop from Ponti about his impending film projects. Although some critics assessed Merv's style as a bit obsequious, others marveled at the successful connection he'd made with the celebrated couple. It was clearly one of Merv's finest nights on the late-night series.

By mid-summer, the NBC had become keenly aware that Merv Griffin was a draw, and thus destined for big things in television. Not wanting to lose a hot property to another network, the network entered into negotiations with Griffin's agent, and ultimately signed the 37-year-old entertainer to a two-year contract. The result would be *The Merv Griffin Show*, a 55-minute "strip," meaning it would air on multiple consecutive days, in this case, Monday through Friday. The job Griffin really wanted, but would never get, was *The Tonight Show*—on a permanent basis. Nevertheless, he was happy to settle for his niche in the afternoon, along with the perennial soap operas and game shows.

5. BRINGING "TONIGHT" TO DAYTIME

The chairman of Federal Communications Commission, Newton B. Minow, in his controversial (and now legendary) speech before the National Association of Broadcasters in May 1961, referred to television as "a vast wasteland." Minow blatantly contended that commercial television did not serve the best interests of the American public.

A cursory review of program listings for the 1962–63 TV season painfully corroborates Minow's conviction. The daytime schedules, in particular, were flagrantly banal. From Monday through Friday, the daytime "wasteland" served up a stream of soap operas, game shows, and reruns of canceled sitcoms and dramatic anthologies.

As a midday entry, *The Merv Griffin Show* would offer a refreshing alternative to the humdrum fare that saturated all three networks. In its publicity campaign, the NBC press department promised a "wide variety of entertainment features, ranging from Griffin's versatile talents as host and performer to guest stars, conversations with interesting and amusing personalities, music, and a measure of the unusual and unexpected."

Each installment of the Griffin show would open with that well-remembered intro: "The following program is brought to you in living color on NBC." The NBC network had been a trailblazer in the development of color television. As far back as 1946, NBC and rival CBS were experimenting with the transmission of color images, and both networks had petitioned the FCC for acceptance of their respective systems. By 1949, the Commission was holding hearings on matters pertaining to color television. Although the commission approved CBS's proposed system in 1950, the go-ahead ultimately went to NBC and its National Television Standard Committee ("NTSC") on December 17, 1953. The following year, RCA—NBC's parent company at the time—began to manufacture and market color sets. Soon thereafter, several of NBC's daytime programs, such as the live anthology series *Matinee Theatre*, were airing in color solely for the purpose of promoting the new sets. The emergence of the peacock logo would exemplify the network's leadership in the technological breakthrough. Soon, NBC would be heralded as "the full color network."

The NBC programming execs placed Griffin in the 2:00 p.m. time slot as a replacement for *The Jan Murray Show.* Opposite Griffin on CBS were two immensely popular programs. The first half-hour was occupied by the Goodson-Todman game show *Password,* hosted by the ultra-congenial Allen Ludden. The second half-hour belonged to *Art Linkletter's House Party.*

Linkletter had been an enormously popular personality in broadcasting since the 1940s. In fact, *House Party* had actually begun its long run on CBS (and later, ABC) radio in 1945. The program, produced by John Guedel (*You Bet Your Life*) moved to CBS television in 1952. Linkletter was extremely successful with his predominantly female audience. His lighthearted fare included interviews with celebrities and interesting people from all walks of life, as well as entertainment acts, and lots of audience-participation buffoonery.

Across the dials, ABC was offering *Day in Court,* followed by a moderately successful game show called *Seven Keys,* hosted by Jack Narz. The Griffin show would not have the advantage of a strong lead-in, since the network had turned the 1 to 2 p.m. time slot over to its affiliates for local programming. There wasn't anything particularly enticing about what followed Griffin. At 2:55 p.m., NBC presented the live, five-minute *NBC News Mid-Afternoon Report,* followed by reruns of *The Loretta Young Theater.*

The NBC executives told Griffin that they essentially wanted a program in the same vein as *The Tonight Show.* This was more of a safety net rather than a plan to restructure the network's daytime strategy. "We were in the bullpen for Carson," explains Bob Shanks, "because NBC had no idea at that point if Johnny would work out. They wanted us to do a nighttime show to see if Merv could handle it on an ongoing basis. And if Carson failed, they'd have Merv ready to go in."

The show was expected to offer the sophistication and spontaneity of late-night television, with its unwavering allure, to the daytime audience. That is not to say that Griffin was expected to

emulate Jack Paar. After nine months of intermittent subbing on
The Tonight Show, Merv had firmly established his own on-air persona. There would be no outbreaks of emotion, feuds, or walk-
offs (at least from the host) on Merv's show. Nevertheless, certain
elements of the Paar formula would *have* to be infused into the
afternoon program, particularly that all important "undercurrent of
excitement." The only problem was that no one, including Griffin
and the network executives, was certain if the format that proved
successful at midnight would also work in midday. Because it was
a midday program, it had to appeal to the largest demographic that
made up the afternoon audience at that time—women.

"It's a tremendous women's audience," Griffin said in a 1962
interview. "And after all, women pretty well control the dials, day
and night." Griffin said he wanted the program to represent a
departure from the games and soaps. "We're going to give them
politics and books and interesting people—all set in a framework of
music and entertainment and comedy, the kind of atmosphere that
automatically relaxes your guest stars."

This was a bold and ambitious goal. It was also an unprecedented
gamble on the part of NBC and the sponsors. No network had
ever attempted to broadcast a Paar-like program, replete with literate conversation, at two in the afternoon.

Meticulous care was taken in hiring the best available talent to put
the show together. By this time, Merv had cultivated a professional
relationship with Bob Shanks. The talent coordinator-turned-pro-
ducer had guided him painlessly through a rapid progression: from
guest, to guest host, and now, host. Griffin told the NBC execs he
wanted Shanks to produce the show. The network agreed.

In an interview with *The New York Herald-Tribune*, Griffin
explained why he had remained loyal to Shanks. "When my agent
persuaded Jack Paar to let me replace him one Monday, the whole
staff of the Tonight Show took the night off in my honor," Griffin
recalled. "Only the associate producer, Bob Shanks, stayed. They let
him produce the show that night. It was a good show. They let us
try again. The production staff took that night off, too, muttering
'that bum again.' It was another good show. When NBC bought
this show, I hired Bob Shanks to produce it." Griffin also told the

publication that his new gig would be a *Tonight Show* for all the housewives who can't stay up late at night. (Imagine a TV host making such a comment in today's world!)

Bob Shanks believes that television is a producer's medium, just as film is said to be a director's medium. He took special care to select the finest talent available. When it came time to hire staff writers, a proficient trio was chosen: Dick Cavett, Pat McCormick, and David Lloyd. All three would go on to great success as television writers and/or personalities.

Griffin would also have the luxury of two associate producers, Monty Morgan and George Vosburgh, rather than the traditional one. Interestingly, women would hold key jobs on Griffin's staff. Mary Ann Minster would assist the producer, while Jean Meegan would team up with Larry Holofcener as talent coordinator. Meegan and Holofcener would remain with Griffin well into his tenure at Westinghouse.

Art director Tom Trimble, who had designed the famous *Tonight Show* desk-and-sofa configuration, was brought in to construct a similar set for Griffin.

In 1962, Tony Garofalo was a recent college grad with high aspirations. He got his foot in the door at 30 Rock with a coveted job on the NBC Page staff. "We all had dreams of becoming another James Dean or a director or producer. Mine was to write comedy and songs," says Garofalo. He sent a note to Griffin, who was still presiding over *Play Your Hunch*. Garofalo was amazed when the star answered his note and agreed to hear one of his songs titled "Pretty Girl." After the young man sang and strummed his way through the song, Griffin asked him to perform it on a segment of *Hunch*. Garofalo recalls: "There I was, an NBC page, on live TV, listening to Merv Griffin tell America that "Pretty Girl" would be his next single. It was undeniably the highlight of my young life."

Garofalo was ultimately hired as a production assistant on Merv's talk show. Like numerous other staffers, Garofalo would remain in Griffin's employ into the 1980s.

With its key positions now filled, *The Merv Griffin Show* was touted as an exhilarating new entry on the NBC's mid-afternoon lineup. The program would be "packaged" by Milbarn Enterprises, the corporate forerunner of Merv Griffin Productions, in association with the NBC network.

6. AND NOW, HERE'S MERV!

Although October 1, 1962 is not an important date in world history, it is a significant marker in the annals of television. Anyone who is a student of television history (or showbiz trivia) is likely to know that Johnny Carson became the new custodian of *The Tonight Show* on that date. Few, however, are aware that *The Merv Griffin Show* premiered on the same day, or that Griffin and Carson taped their respective programs in the same studio: NBC's Studio 6-B. Merv would tape at 12:15 p.m., and as soon as his team wrapped for the day, an NBC crew would dismantle the Griffin set and replace it with the famous *Tonight Show* desk-and-sofa setup.

Griffin boasted that his show was "completely sold out" to sponsors even before it went on the air. With advertisers waiting in line, things were looking rosy for the rookie who once earned his living subbing for the vacationing, retiring, or under-the-weather TV hosts.

One of the more interesting, yet little known, aspects of Merv's NBC program was its musical performances, not necessarily those who sang them, but those who *played* them. "After we signed Frank Simms as our announcer, there was a problem when it came time to select a competent musical director," Bob Shanks recalls. "Merv, of course, wanted an in-house orchestra and we were able to hire 11 players. And we had a wonderful solution to the problem of hiring a musical director because we couldn't find anyone that we liked. It was Merv who had come up with the solution. He said to me, 'There are all these great bandleaders hanging around doing nothing. Why don't you call Duke Ellington, Count Basie, and some of the others, and see if they'd like to guest-conduct for a week.' So I called them and that's what we did. They'd come to the studio with their classic charts and do one week at a time. Basie, Ellington, Tito Puente, Xavier Cugat, and several others led the orchestra. It turned out to be a wonderful solution."

Each week a different bandleader would bring in his own arrangements for the members of the NBC orchestra to play. Even Hugh Downs (Paar's former announcer/sidekick) offered to take a crack at conducting the band, and did so with his own composition called "Sandwriting."

For the series opener, Griffin welcomed comedian Shelley Berman, singer Patrice Munsel, journalist/screenwriter Adela Rogers St. Johns, and 28-year-old-pianist Peter Nero. The irascible Berman was in top form with a succession of hilarious ad-libs, several of which involved the touchy subject of religion, something not generally joked about on daytime television in 1962. He got away with it, but wisely covered himself, and the network, by telling viewers in a half-joking, half-serious manner *not* to write complaint letters. Minutes later, a commercial for a laxative product spawned a few more ad-libs about another delicate topic—constipation.

The conversation took on a more docile tone with St. Johns. She spoke of the halcyon days of the motion picture industry, the illustrious stars she'd known and worked with, and her latest book, *Final Verdict*. Munsel sang, and Nero, who had recently won a Grammy for "Best New Artist," offered a selection on the piano.

The following day, *Variety* observed a trait of Griffin's that would stick with him for the duration of his talk-show career. "Griffin showed a disposition once more to be slightly over solicitous and traditionally 'show biz' in his approach to interviews." Aside from this one "idiosyncrasy," the reviewer said: "Griffin comes close to being as pleasant as any TV host around. There's something about his ease and self-effacement that smacks of Garry Moore, and that's pretty good."

The show had gotten off to a good start, but it suffered a mild setback during its second week. Coverage of the baseball playoffs, beginning on October 8, necessitated the pre-emption of two Griffin shows. Loss of momentum can be detrimental to any new series that's still finding its audience. Fortunately, the Griffin show had no difficulty getting back into the groove in its third week and continued to garner positive reviews.

The Griffin crew made good use of the "down time." Merv and Bob Shanks flew to England to film several "remote" interviews, like the one they'd done with Sophia Loren. One of the actors on their radar was Peter O'Toole.

Though O'Toole was relatively unknown at the time, an interview with him was considered something of a triumph because the film he'd just completed, *Lawrence of Arabia* (1962), was expected to be an international blockbuster.

Bob Shanks recalls how the interview with the Irish actor almost didn't happen.

"Things were more casual in those days, and you didn't have to go through eight press agents. We had agreed to meet in a tavern up in Hampstead Heath. So we arrived, looked around, and didn't see anyone there who looked like Peter O'Toole. And after a half hour or so we left, and got a hold of the publicist who told us, 'He was there!' And I said, 'Well, why didn't we see him? You'd think a good-looking blond guy like that would. . . .'" And the publicist said, 'He's *not* a blond.' They dyed his hair blond for the title role in *Lawrence of Arabia*. I asked if he still would do the interview and he said, 'Sure he will.' I said, 'Let me get a crew, and confirm that we have it. Let's try to set it up at the Ritz Hotel. And that's what happened. He came to the hotel and we did a terrific interview, with one director of photography shooting 16mm film, an assistant, and a sound man.'"

The interview with the brown-haired O'Toole was played on the air in October. Shortly after *Lawrence of Arabia* had gone into general release, O'Toole showed up as expected at NBC, all set for another wonderful interview with "that delightful Griffin chap." What no one at the network knew was that Columbia Pictures, in keeping with its publicity campaign, had O'Toole dye his hair blond to match his appearance in the film.

In order to maintain a balance of energy and spontaneity, talk show hosts generally do not meet with guests prior to taping unless, of course, they are close friends. Consequently, Merv had no idea that a golden-haired O'Toole was about to walk onto the stage. It seems unfathomable that Merv wouldn't recognize the man simply because his hair was a now a different color. Yet that's exactly what happened. When O'Toole walked through the curtain, Merv thought his staff had pulled a prank on him. "You are *not* Peter

O'Toole!" he said resolutely. That assertion marked the beginning of a painfully awkward exchange during which the annoyed actor answered every question with a one-syllable answer. Teetering on the brink of disaster, the interview lasted a mere nine minutes. When it was over, O'Toole exited the set on a sour note. He called Merv a son of a bitch, loud enough for the studio audience to hear, as he retreated to his dressing room. In the years to come, O'Toole would make additional appearances on talk shows. *The Merv Griffin Show* was not among them.

By early November 1962, the program was in full gear, thanks to the steady stream of high-caliber guests Griffin was attracting. Cognizant of the fact that NBC wanted a daytime replica of *Tonight*, Griffin's producer and talent coordinators sought to book an illustrious mix of talent in order to comply with the network's expectations. Thus, the luminaries who sat next to Merv on the early broadcasts were certainly befitting of any major variety show, daytime or otherwise. The list included Bob Hope, Greer Garson, Gloria Swanson, Ann Sothern, Anthony Perkins, Anthony Quinn, Victor Borge, Basil Rathbone, Elsa Lanchester, Jack Haley, Peter Lorre, Walter Slezak, Eli Wallach, and a young future Oscar winner by the name of Liza Minnelli.

Danny Kaye caused a minor uproar one day in November 1962. After a cigarette commercial played on the air, Kaye began talking about the joys of smoking. He started to cough more and more, until, finally, he couldn't talk at all. Everyone, including Merv, thought it was an exceedingly funny bit. NBC didn't see it that way, and deleted the entire routine from the tape to avoid offending the sponsor.

The next day, in his opening monologue, Merv announced that his show was "in the news." He began to explain why a two-minute section of the previous edition had been cut, and replaced by an "insert" of Labor Leader George Meany. Suddenly, a voice interrupted him. "Are you Mr. Griffin?" yelled a tall man in a trench coat and derby hat, clutching an attaché case in one hand and an umbrella in the other. It was Danny Kaye. He gave a phony name, claiming to represent the "Sponsor's Protective Association." In the course of chastising Merv for the events of the previous day, he began to puff vigorously on a long cigar. Everyone knew what was coming next. Sure enough, Kaye pretended to choke, but only mildly and momentarily. He was so wildly uninhibited that Merv allowed him to take over the show, which was made all the more erratic by a laryngitis-stricken Shelley Berman, actor Peter Cook, singer Dolores Wilson, and Dr. Cleo Dawson.

Along with the major Hollywood stars, the show also booked an impressive succession of literary figures, including William Saroyan, Adela Rogers St. Johns (who was so captivating on the first telecast that Merv invited her back regularly), entertainment critic Cleveland Amory, and the provocative Norman Mailer.

Griffin also managed to secure appearance commitments from writers who generally didn't do talk shows. Among them were British journalist and media personality Malcolm Muggeridge, and the English poet W.H. Auden, whose works blended politics, pop culture, and religion. "We had Auden on our Christmas show with Santa Claus in 1962," recalls Bob Shanks, "along with all the staff's kids." Auden read his poems while the not-too-attentive kids opened their gifts from Santa!

Rounding out every show was at least one comic well known on the talk-show circuit. The short list includes Jonathan Winters, Henry Morgan (dubbed "The Rebel Without a *Pause*"), Henny Youngman, Woody Allen (who made 11 appearances in 26 weeks), Buddy Hackett, Carl Reiner, Jack E. Leonard, and Milt Kamen. A good singer was also essential to each show, preferably one who could converse engagingly on the panel.

Griffin learned an important lesson at NBC with regard to the booking of certain guests. Networks are corporations, and corporations have "blacklists." That is, a list of people who, for one reason or another, are not in the good graces of the company. Merv went to bat for several performers who had been blacklisted (e.g., Judy Holliday, Jack Gilford, et al.) and booked them anyway.

When it came to guest procurement, the Griffin show held a distinct advantage over its competitors. As a contract player at a major movie studio, Merv had rubbed elbows with the Hollywood elite on a daily basis. He didn't realize it at the time, of course, but he was building up an impressive list of contacts that would prove invaluable in his future career as a television talk-show host. The actors, directors, screenwriters, and moguls knew him—and trusted him. Consequently, he could snag commitments from certain stars that other hosts couldn't. As Adela Rogers St. Johns had pointed out on her first appearance, it was Merv who had squired young Elizabeth Taylor around town during her first extended tour of New York in the fifties. To the glitterati of Hollywood, Merv was more than just a talker on the fluorescent tube; he was a trusted friend.

Shortly after the debut of *The Merv Griffin Show*, the world stood by as the United States and the Soviet Union would come dangerously close to nuclear war. A 13-day confrontation, stemming from Soviet missiles stationed in Cuba, had commenced on October 16, 1962. As everyone remained transfixed on the standoff between the two superpowers, the showbiz columnists focused on a cold war that was being waged at NBC.

It was apparent to many within the television industry that a rivalry existed between the Griffin and Carson camps, despite a shared network affiliation. Booking the big names, more than anything else, was the root of the problem. Merv was getting the iconic stars. Johnny wasn't.

Tony Garofalo confides that while Carson and Griffin weren't friendly at that time, they weren't exactly enemies. "In years to come, they would eventually appear on each other's programs," says Garofalo. "And it's funny when you stop and think of how uptight they both were back then. You have hosts competing with each other today, but I don't think they're anywhere near as uptight. During the first year of Carson's residency, the competition was so fierce that when an actor [Mickey Shaughnessy] mentioned 'Merv Griffin' on *The Tonight Show*, the name was conspicuously bleeped."

Griffin regarded the bleeping as something more than a mild annoyance, especially since it had occurred on *his* network. The situation wasn't helped when Merv, on his own program, suggested that the *Tonight Show* producer should have bleeped the entire soundtrack!

As one would expect, the press took delight in noting how the act of censorship had triggered a skirmish between the two shows. It was Dave Tebet, one of NBC's many execs, who quickly and quietly effectuated a truce. Part of Tebet's job was to make certain that the talent was kept happy. He not only took care of on-the-air personalities, but the behind-the-scenes honchos as well. Tebet was known to pamper stars and VIPs with various amenities to keep them smiling. One can only imagine how many gifts he had to dole out in order for peace to reign supreme between the network's budding talk-show stars.

On December 31, 1962, the mercury in every thermometer in New York City plummeted drastically. Amazingly, neither the freezing cold nor the gridlock holiday traffic could deter the 500 fans lined up at Studio 6-B to attend the last Merv Griffin show of the year. "We don't believe what's happening to us here," said Merv in his opening monologue. "The temperature is zero—or close to it. And winds, they say, are up to 80 miles an hour. It's a terrible day." Nevertheless, he succeeded in warming up his audience with a barrage of New Year's Eve jokes, topped by a lively rendition of "You Make Me Feel So Young." The big musical attraction, however, was that week's guest conductor, Guy Lombardo. The legendary bandleader was the perfect choice for the occasion. Lombardo's name had become synonymous with New Year's Eve, thanks to his annual telecasts from New York's Waldorf Astoria, which included a live "remote" from Times Square at midnight. Lombardo closed out the show with "Auld Lang Syne," a heartwarming selection for the festive season. Unfortunately, the coming year wouldn't be heartwarming or festive for *The Merv Griffin Show*.

As anyone even vaguely familiar with the television business surely knows, ratings are, and always have been, the bottom line. NBC was far from impressed with Griffin's latest numbers. The show continued to generate rave reviews from critics, but the ratings told another story.

Password, a game show produced by Goodson-Todman, Merv's former employers, and Art Linkletter's *House Party*, were winning the 2:00 p.m. slot by a substantial margin. In fact, both back-to-back programs were steadily pulling in 50 percent shares for CBS.

On a snowy day in January 1963, Griffin and Shanks learned that their show would soon be getting the ax. This was galling, particularly in light of the rave reviews Griffin was getting. One observer went so far as to say that *The Tonight Show* never looked as good as it does in the daytime with Merv. That same month, *Look* magazine ran a feature about Griffin's amazing rise in the macrocosm of television talk shows. "Griffin lifts the whole show above the sudsy soporifics of daytime TV," the magazine noted.

It was strictly a matter of numbers. Griffin made a valiant effort, even in the face of cancellation, to pump up the sagging ratings. In reaching out to some of his old Hollywood chums, Merv scored a commitment from someone he'd known for over a decade—actor Montgomery Clift.

Words like "sensitive" and "moody" are often used to describe Montgomery Clift, one of Hollywood's iconic leading men of the 1950s. Monty, as his friends and colleagues knew him, had skillfully embraced his roles in major films like *A Place in the Sun* (1951), Hitchcock's *I Confess* (1953), *From Here to Eternity* (1953), *Judgment at Nuremberg* (1961), and others, which solidified his place in cinema history.

Though Clift never won an Academy Award, he had been nominated several times during the course of a screen career that spanned two decades. In his prime, he was one of Hollywood's hottest properties and was in constant demand. Then, in 1956, Clift was injured in a near-fatal auto accident that destroyed his matinee-idol looks. After a long and painful recovery, which necessitated multiple surgeries and a wired jaw, the 35-year-old actor stoically resumed his career. Considering the magnitude of his injuries, Clift's face didn't look bad, but it looked significantly different. His facial features in *Raintree County* (1957) vary discernably, owing to the fact that some scenes had been filmed pre-accident, while others were shot post-accident. Nevertheless, Clift's reputation for brilliance in front of the cameras remained unscathed. Despite a slide into alcoholism, prescription drug addiction, and erratic behavior, Clift was still a hot talent sought by television producers and casting directors. Fans were clamoring to see him—in any venue. His appearance with Merv would not only be a "first" for the Griffin show, but for the NBC network as well.

"From New York, it's the Merv Griffin show," blared Frank Simms. "Merv's guests today are Montgomery Clift, Don Adams, Nancy Andrews, Val Pringle, and Sasha Ramaroul, with Al Finelli conducting the NBC Orchestra, and I'm Frank Simms. *And now here's Merv!*"

Merv assured the audience that "Monty" would be the first guest. Everyone, from the top members of the production team down to the pages, was excited at the notion of seeing this beloved star—in person.

Tony Garofalo was assigned the task of getting the actor to the studio on that brutally cold day—February 4, 1963. "It was snowing and I could barely get him into the limo," Garofalo recalls. "He was inebriated and that was sad. I don't remember anything he said. It was toward the end of his life. I'm not exactly sure how Merv knew him, but I assume they had been friendly from their Hollywood movie days. To my knowledge, I don't think he ever did any other talk show."

Except for his movies, Montgomery Clift had rarely been seen on television. A short time before he agreed to appear on Merv's show, Clift had submitted to a one-on-one chat on New York columnist Hy Gardner's program. As Garofalo notes, the actor had never appeared on a talk show with a studio audience.

When Clift finally arrived at the studio, Merv was already on the air. When the time came for Clift's segment, it was obvious that he was in no condition to go on. In fact, the drama backstage was more jarring than *anything* that would be seen on television that day. As the staff poured as much black coffee into Clift as he could stand, the producer alerted Merv as to what was transpiring behind the set. There wasn't much else to do except bring out Don Adams, then appearing regularly on *The Perry Como Show.* Adams, who was two years away from achieving sitcom immortality with *Get Smart*, kept the studio audience moderately amused with his tried-and-true stand-up routines. Meanwhile, Bob Shanks was backstage, frantically deciding what to do about the "special" guest.

"We had dealt with alcoholics before, and unless it was going to be an embarrassment, I'd put them on," the producer recalls. "If they were really bad, I'd say, 'Look, you're really not in shape to do the show. Why don't we rebook you?' But Monty wanted to do it. He wanted to go on, and he went out there and got through it."

When Adams's segment finally ended, *the* moment had arrived. Although Merv had been made aware of Clift's condition, he had no idea what to expect when the actor stepped through the curtain. He nervously began the intro: "One of our most distinguished actors is with us today," he said proudly. "I guess I've seen just about every picture this man has made. Speaking personally, he's never done a show like this before and I'm delighted that he's doing this as a favor. I am proud to welcome Montgomery Clift."

The actor strode through the curtain with a remarkable air of confidence. He sat behind the desk, on Merv's left. "I've got to tell you about this new thing called television," said Merv lightheartedly. "Wha' *hoppens* here?" said Monty, trying to mask his nervousness. "Just relax and talk," said Merv reassuringly.

They began with a discussion of Clift's work in *Freud* (1962). "Shall I predict it now—Academy Award?" said Merv beseechingly. The audience roared its approval. "Every year, you make the best picture of the year. It must be very exciting." Clift was obviously taken aback by the compliment. "Thank you, Merv," he said softly.

Monty said the nature of pulling off a complicated role like Freud was nearly impossible. "There's nothing working for you," he complained. "It's like doing a mental western; it's all happening up here," he said, pointing to his head. "He [Freud] has to be *almost* as sick as the people he's talking to. He was the first man to psychoanalyze himself. Now you *have* to be pretty upset to get to that point."

Merv asked if playing such an intense role had affected his private life. "You don't have a private life when you're in pictures," Clift responded. "It's like being in prison. You get up at 5:30 a.m. and go to the studio. You get done studying at two; and you're lucky if you get four hours sleep."

Merv continued to praise the actor, noting that he hadn't done enough films. "Like most actors, you'll do whatever good part comes along. I'll take that one, I'll take this one. Then you seem to lay back and wait a long time before you decide to take a role." "No, no, no!" Monty disagreed. "Once I was out of work for two years because I didn't find anything I liked. Then, unfortunately, I found three that I liked and only had time to have bronchitis in between them. So I did all three."

Merv changed the subject to the one that was ripe for intense discussion: Marilyn Monroe. Only six months had passed since the actress had been found dead in her Brentwood home. Her name was still a hot topic in 1963.

Merv recalled Monty's work with Monroe in her final film, *The Misfits* (1961). "I have read that you were also a friend of hers," said Merv. "Not as a woman, but as an actress. What *kind* of actress was she?"

A solemn expression crossed the actor's face. "It's very easy to talk nicely about people who are dead," he reasoned. "And I don't mean what I say lightly because I meant it when she was living. She was really the most marvelous person I had ever encountered. You played a scene with her and you met her eyes. And what came back, you met again. And everything was up a ladder; it raised every scene to a new height. I have nothing but the most lovely words for her." These comments drew applause from the audience as well as everyone on the panel.

Was Monroe was a "raw talent" or a "study"? Clift thought for a moment. "It's hard to say, because as an actor, you have to be just as studied in keeping yourself *un*-studied. To be *spontaneous*, you have to work hours, and yet nobody knows that. Not that that's necessary," he said.

Clift recalled how Monroe had labored mightily during the filming of *The Misfits*. "My God, how she worked," he said emphatically. "And it was marvelous how she'd give you such reassurance."

The program was nearly over. "Where does the world take you now?" Merv asked the actor. "Another motion picture? I wish you would do television, but you won't, will you?" Clift thought for a moment. "I'm here, aren't I?" he answered, incredulously. "I'm not signed to a studio, so I'm not committed to three pictures or four pictures." The actor said he had no idea where or when his next film assignment would take place. "It's always that way," he said solemnly. "I do something and I hope I don't die as a result. And then I accept it as something that I like. It seems to me if you're not really interested in a part, you can't very well expect the audience to be interested. So to do it for the so-called *gelt* [money] that comes in is silly, because you don't get to keep much of it anyway. So maybe you can hang on to a little integrity while you're doing it."

With Clift running out of steam, Merv did his best to keep the conversation fluent. "Are you going to travel now?" Merv asked. Monty's deadpan reaction would have rivaled Jack Benny's. "Am I going to travel *now?*" he repeated, as though he hadn't heard right. The audience snickered. "Ya see," Merv chimed in. "He's one of these guys who pins you down to *everything* you're saying!"

The 55-minute episode, which had been a nerve-wrecking ordeal, was coming to a close. "Monty, I can't tell you how much we appreciate your being here today," Merv smiled. "It's been a first for us, and a first for you, in this format. You've been a great guest and I wish you continued success." Clift got up to leave, but Merv beckoned him to remain seated. "I don't want you to leave on that trip just yet," he told him. What Merv was really concerned about was whether or not the actor would be able to make it back to the Green Room without passing out.

As Merv announced the next day's guests (Henry Morgan, Ronnie Schell, Francis Bittle, and Sue Bennett), the band struck up the theme and the lights came down—with Clift still on the set. Years later, Merv would claim that Clift managed to reach the backstage area where he collapsed—while the audience was still applauding vigorously.

Montgomery Clift's final performance would be realized in a French/German thriller titled *The Defector* (1966). He died of a heart attack on July 23, 1966, several months before the film was released.

On March 7, 1963, Griffin scored another hit with a Hollywood superstar: Joan Crawford. Also featured were journalist Adela Rogers St. Johns and Pulitzer Prize-winning novelist Allen Drury (*Advise and Consent*, 1962).

"In the halls at NBC, you can always tell when a star is about to appear on a show," said Merv in his monologue. "There's lots of milling around, things are being said like, 'Is she here yet?' 'What room is she in?' There's an electricity about a star, and I'm not talking about these lamps here."

Crawford agreed to do the show, with one proviso—Merv had to sing a song. "And so, today in her honor," said the flattered host, "I have selected the entire third act of Madame Butterfly!" He didn't sing *that*, of course. He offered instead a pleasant rendition of "All I Do Is Dream of You."

The orchestra greeted Crawford with "Makin' Whoopee." She seemed genuinely touched by the standing ovation she received. "Those are your people, Miss Crawford," said Merv, "your whole fan club is here today." In an effort to make his guest as "comfortable as possible," Griffin opened a few bottles of Pepsi. [As anyone familiar with Crawford's career knows, the actress had long been associated with the soft drink company as a board member and spokesperson.]

Griffin wasted no time in getting down to business. He called attention to Crawford's recently published (and ghostwritten) memoir, *A Portrait of Joan*, which had weathered considerable criticism. Some reviewers, no doubt expecting a scornful expose, felt that the actress had "softened" the facts, particularly with regard to Bette Davis, who had recently co-starred with Crawford in *What Ever Happened to Baby Jane?* (1962). "Did you tell the whole truth in here, and nothing but?" asked Merv, holding up the slender volume. "So help me God!" said Crawford, smiling. "It doesn't mean that I *didn't* soften it," she added. "I was criticized, Merv, because a lot of people thought I should have been more vicious. And I think you can sell a book without being vicious." Crawford said she didn't *feel* vicious towards anyone. She was grateful, she admitted, for those who had come into her life, or had crossed her path, for better or worse. "If I grow with it, and grow in to and out of that experience, then I have gained something. So why be bitter?" she reasoned.

Merv gingerly broached the subject of Crawford's well-known obsessive/compulsive habits. This he did by quoting another source, gossip columnist Hedda Hopper. Merv tried to relate an example, but before he could finish, Crawford interrupted: "Sure I scrub bathroom floors!"

The next thing Crawford did (according to Hopper) was something her legion of fans would have expected her to do: get down on her knees to scrub the bathroom floor. "Why, Miss Crawford?" asked Merv. "Because I wanted it clean," she snapped.

She rattled off the names of her closest friends among the actors she'd worked with: Clark Gable, Spencer Tracy, and Robert Taylor.

"Is it possible in the business you're in," Merv inquired, "to have, for example, an actor who is a best friend *without* romance entering in?" Crawford said no. "I'll tell you, Merv, I think very often we assume the characters we're playing and in doing that, even off screen, we automatically fall in love with our leading men or co-stars." Crawford said it was always bound to happen, particularly with someone like Gable. The animal magnetism, wonderment, and magic of him, "didn't stop at the end of the picture," she admitted.

Merv asked if Gable (who had died three years earlier) had been the "most exciting man" Hollywood had ever known. "He's *still* the king," answered Crawford.

If actresses *always* fall in love with their leading men, Merv quipped: "wouldn't it have been terrible if she did a picture with Gabby Hayes?" Adela Rogers St. Johns chimed in, noting that Crawford had indeed married *two* of her leading men (Douglas Fairbanks, Jr. and Franchot Tone) so there must be something to her philosophy after all.

The topic turned to contemporary Hollywood, and the new breed of actor less inclined to "dress to the tee," by Crawford's standards. "It's kind of a chore sometimes to get dressed to go out," said Crawford, "but when you're hungry, you get dressed and go out."

Crawford said she refused to go out in slacks, tee shirt, and flat heels. "I'm too proud of my figure, my body, and I have too much self-pride and self-discipline to do otherwise. That's just me."

Crawford's expression turned sour on the current state of movies, commenting that "the magical touch" of yesteryear was gone. Gone, too, was the old Hollywood studio system. "We were trained, *really* trained," she affirmed proudly. "One day we'd do a bit part in one picture, and the next day we'd start a starring part. We never knew. I used to steal scripts all the time, just steal them off the desks while everyone was at lunch."

Merv asked if studios controlled the private lives of the stars. Were they told who to be seen with, what to go to, what to wear? "Not who to be seen with," Crawford explained, "but we were told what picture to do." She said that MGM studio chief Louis B.

Mayer rarely made mistakes, but when he did, he was the first to admit it. "And that to me is greatness," she said.

Crawford talked more about her tour for *Portrait of Joan* than the book itself. "One interesting thing I found in 12 cities," she observed, "were the twelve-to-sixteen-year-old kids that would come up. How they got the money to buy the book, I don't know. But they had seen all the films on television, and they had never heard of me before. A whole new world, for them and for me, and I'm so grateful."

"You should have called your book *Gratefully*," St. Johns mused.

Merv asked Crawford if there had been any "unrealized" film projects in her career. Was there ever a certain character that she longed to play? "Yes, but I didn't get it," Crawford admitted. "Norma Shearer got it!" It was, ironically, a work scripted by St. Johns called *A Free Soul*. "I'd never been so heartbroken in my whole life," St. Johns admitted. "We had Clark Gable, Lionel Barrymore, and I *thought* we had Miss Joan Crawford to play the girl. And we didn't, because Norma Shearer was married to [MGM executive] Irving Thalberg!" Crawford: "She said it; I didn't!" The audience snickered.

Merv asked Crawford if she ever had to "campaign" for a role. "I've wanted to do a picture with Bette Davis since 1942 when we were at Warner Bros. together, and I didn't stop until we did *Baby Jane*," said Crawford. "It took a bit of doing, but we did it."

She continued: "They had a property called *Ethan Frome*, which I thought would have been wonderful for Bette and me, with Ray Massey, who was also at Warners at the time. I didn't give up. She [Davis] left the studio and had a baby…went to another studio. And all of a sudden, I found a script and sent it to Bob Aldrich, whom I had done *Autumn Leaves* with. He was doing *Sodom and Gomorrah* (1962) in Rome and said, 'Not good enough!' All through [the filming of] *Autumn Leaves* (1956), I had talked about wanting to do a picture with Bette; I thought the chemistry would be right. So I sent him another script, and he said, 'Not good enough!' And finally, he found *Baby Jane* and we did it!"

Referring to the famous scene in which the depraved Baby Jane serves up a roasted rat, Merv quipped, "I guess you'll never enjoy eating dinner with her again."

To which Crawford triumphantly replied: "*I* do the cooking now!"

The next day, March 8, saw the appearance of another iconic motion picture actor, Bert Lahr, who had played the Cowardly Lion in *The Wizard of Oz* (1939). Lahr's talents extended well beyond that of his most celebrated role. He was a veteran of vaudeville, burlesque, the Broadway stage, radio, and dozens of Hollywood motion pictures. Oddly, Lahr made not a single reference to the role that earned him cinematic immortality. He talked instead about his current work in S.J. Perelman's *The Beauty Part*, a Broadway hit in which he played five roles.

Lahr said the show had earned great reviews, but had fallen victim to interim booking. He explained: "Interim booking means that you get a theater with the proviso that another show has been booked for it; and you can play up to the time that the other show comes in." Lahr lamented that *Beauty Part* could not secure another theater. "This is a hit show," he said sadly, "it got 99 percent rave notices. But it will close."

A show with great reviews, and it's a failure. "That's a familiar story around this studio," said Merv, echoing his own dilemma.

During Lahr's segment, a young photojournalist from *Life* magazine, Yale Joel, discreetly shot a series of still photographs. "They're doing a picture story here," said Merv matter-of-factly. (One of Joel's candid stills of Lahr chatting on the panel would appear in Griffin's 1980 autobiography, *Merv*.)

There has long been a conviction in the television industry that the more sophisticated a show is, the longer it takes for it to click. The Griffin show had indeed found an audience. According to surveys, that audience was limited to intellectuals and college students, a demographic that didn't make up the bulk of the daytime viewership.

The Griffin show still wasn't bringing in the numbers NBC had expected. *Password* continued to dominate the 2:00 p.m. time slot. (For the record, *Password* would continue flourish on CBS's daytime schedule. Like many other popular game shows, it would return in various updated versions throughout the years.)

Though Merv was acutely aware of the weak ratings, he continued valiantly on the same path, hoping the numbers might improve. They didn't. Ironically, the network execs that had initially envisioned the show with a nighttime flavor were now complaining that it was "*too* nighttime" for daytime consumption. Apparently, talk before dark was not NBC's cup of tea. Despite the legion of hardcore Griffin viewers, the program simply wasn't showing any signs of commercial growth.

"We were in that bullpen in case Carson didn't work out," Shanks points out. "But obviously he did and they no longer needed a bullpen at NBC."

Though Griffin's ratings weren't spectacular, his paycheck was. He was taking home more than double what the network had initially offered him. According to *Making the Good Life Last*, as Griffin and his lawyer, Roy Blakeman, were in negotiations with NBC, the star flatly rejected the network's offer of $8,000 a week. Griffin demanded, and received, $18,000 per week. Three months later, with the network not earning adequate revenue from the show, cancellation became imminent, good reviews notwithstanding.

"We were very disappointed with the cancellation because we thought we had a terrific show," says Bob Shanks. "We thought we were red hot, but we weren't, according to the ratings."

The NBC execs did make soothing noises about keeping Griffin exclusively theirs. There would be much talk in the press about the network offering a new deal for either Griffin, or his company, Milbarn Productions. In the meantime, loyal Griffin viewers had learned that the show would be gone by April Fool's Day, 1963. As it turned out, Merv's NBC finale would air on Friday, March 29, 1963, one year after Paar had departed *The Tonight Show*. Frank Simms announced the lineup: Shelley Berman, Milt Kamen, and Adela Rogers St. Johns. Berman and St. Johns had been on the series opener the previous October, and Kamen had since become a regular.

Viewers at home could barely hear Simms's introduction over the thunderous applause in the studio. When he announced, "And now, here's Merv," everyone in Studio 6-B stood up. They cheered and whistled for more than a minute as the host stood before them, obviously basking in the enormity of the moment. It was a preview of the emotionally charged greeting Carson would receive three decades later on his final *Tonight Show*. Merv wasn't a retiring veteran. He was a 37-year-old newcomer whose program had only been on for six months. The reception he received from the studio audience that day was nothing short of incredible.

"As you may have suspected, this is our final day," Merv began firmly. "No tears; lots of happiness. Somebody once said 'We shall return.' And we shall! You'll see!" The audience roared in approval.

"Now, I'm not kidding myself," he continued, "I've been on shows before that went off the air, but I must say that this is one show—as we all leave the studio today with everybody that's associated with it—this is one group of people that will walk out of here with their heads in the air! No sneaking out the back door!" His voice resonated strength and determination. "We're all darn proud of this show and we're going to miss it."

Griffin said it would take too long to acknowledge each of the 75 people who had put the show on the air each day. "They know who they are," he declared firmly. "And they know how much I appreciate it and how much I love them." There was one person who *did* warrant a special note of thanks.

"This show is headed by a very bright and talented young producer by the name of Bob Shanks. He runs the whole shootin' mess!" Griffin said that his "right-hand man" had recently been stricken with a temperature of 105°. "I don't know if it was really a virus, or whether he got nervous the last week," he said, adding that the ailing producer had "limped into the studio."

Today, Bob Shanks believes his "condition" was more than a bit exaggerated. "I was very sick that day," the producer recalls, "but I don't think it was a 105° fever!"

Griffin then thanked the thousands of viewers who had written letters to NBC, protesting the cancellation.

He said the network had also been bombarded by 12,000 telegrams and countless phone calls over the past several days.

"One light note," Merv concluded. "I'm *not* out of work." He pulled out a telegram and read it: "The White House Correspondents

Association and White House News Photographers Association are entertaining President Kennedy, leaders of government, diplomatic corps, and the news world at their annual traditional dinner, May 24, here at the Sheraton Park Hotel. The entertainment committee would consider it a great honor if you would serve as master of ceremonies for the show following dinner. Since this is entirely a nonprofit affair, the pay is stinky but we guarantee a 100 percent rating. Please say yes and please a great many people! Signed, the Entertainment Committee of the White House Press Dinner."

"I shall be there!" Griffin promised. Then he launched into a song appropriate for the occasion: "A Most Unusual Day."

Seated at his desk for the last time (on NBC, that is) Griffin thanked Frank Simms. Then he brought out Shelley Berman, who had been his first guest six months earlier. "Before I came on," Berman intimated, "We disconnected every phone at NBC so nobody can call you!" (This was the catalyst for a series of gags about telephones, owing to Berman's recent TV special during which an errant telephone rang when it wasn't supposed to.)

Berman did a funny piece of material he intended to perform on an upcoming *Perry Como Show*. The bit, about the differences between neurosis and psychosis, went over big with the studio audience. Next came Adela Rogers St. Johns, who had also been on the series opener; she grabbed a few laughs with Berman.

Merv was about to introduce Milt Kamen when comedienne-singer Kaye Ballard suddenly and unexpectedly walked onto the stage. Ballard, still a few years way from sitcom success with *The Mothers-in-Law*, was a good friend of Merv's and one of his favorite guests. "I just came here to say good-bye and I love you. And think everybody here is great," she said tearfully. After Ballard left the stage, Merv assured everyone that the star, then completing a run in the Broadway musical *Carnival*, wouldn't be out of work too long. "I think she'll be on *The Art Linkletter Show* that's on opposite us today," he said jokingly.

More than 50 years after Merv's NBC swan song, Ballard still has memories of the mood in the studio that day. "It was a wonderful little show that had been canceled," the actress recalls, "and it was sad."

Comedian Milt Kamen was the last official guest on the NBC program. He had been a popular attraction on the show, offering reviews of current movies and bantering with Merv in his trademark style. "I just found out that the show is going off," he said. "I'm worried about *you*," he told Merv, "but what's going to happen to *me?*" After the comic ran out of prepared material, he got serious. "I just want to say that, for me, it's been a tremendous pleasure working on this show. Merv, as you can see, gives a great deal of credit to everybody. And everything that everybody does, he makes quite a thing out of it. Actually, I've been working with Merv now 26 weeks [along with] many other people working with him. And it certainly hasn't been working *for*, it's been working *with*. It was a terrific experience. He's a very nice man." Once again the audience applauded fervently.

As the show drew to a close, St. Johns said to Merv: "Before I go, I've got to say one last thing. I don't think any human being has ever made as many friends as you've made. And I thank you for letting me share it on this show." Then Berman added: "Everything I've wanted to say has been said, by everybody that I've talked to around this country. I will say this. I despise some weird system, which will take great performing, and a fine artist, and throw him off television for a small period. I think it's a mistake. Shame on television!"

Merv said many of the viewers who had written him wanted to know his "personal feelings" about the cancellation. In response, he said: "You know, we're in a business and there are rules that you play by. I play tennis. I don't agree exactly with the rules of tennis. I don't agree with the rules of a lot of games. But we're all in *this* game; and if there are rules that you play by, those are the rules you *must* play by until they are changed. I've had a marvelous time here these 26 weeks. And this may sound like a very strange statement, because there's been a lot of discussion about it in the press, and the press taking NBC to task, and my sponsors, and I must say, I love them all."

He continued: "I said this the day of the cancellation, NBC *did* give this show an opportunity. They gave it 26 weeks and no other television network did that. And I'm proud of every day, in these past 26 weeks, and NBC for taking the chance. So there are many thanks in many different directions. I leave you right now with a gift to all of you from me—a song."

The orchestra had been augmented to include violins, adding an elegant dimension to Merv's soft rendition of "Lost in the Stars." He played the final scene the way Sinatra might have done it, with hat, raincoat, and suitcase in tow. It was a dramatic finale, punctuated by low-key lighting and artistic camera angles. Suddenly, the screen went black as a voice coldly announced: "Produced in color in association with the NBC Television Network." Merv was gone, but he would be back. Soon.

On April 1, 1963, two half-hour soap operas took over the time slot previously occupied by Griffin. *Ben Jerrod*, which filled the first half hour, lasted less than three months. *The Doctors*, which followed in the second half hour, caught on immediately and would run for nearly 30 years.

For many days after Griffin's departure, thousands of letters continued to flood NBC's New York offices. The number of pieces ultimately topped 100,000—an unprecedented reaction for a daytime program of such short duration. Even so, the network remained resolute in its decision and simply forwarded the sacks of mail to Griffin's home. A journalist from *Life* magazine photographed the host, posed on the floor in front of his TV set, buried in the mounds of letters that had swamped the network. If *The Merv Griffin Show* wasn't a winner in the ratings, it was certainly a winning indicator as to the appeal of its star. Millions of loyal viewers had grown fond of the raven-haired host with the blue eyes and broad smile. Millions of viewers wouldn't forget him.

Soon after the White House Correspondents dinner, Griffin would be back on network TV. On June 12, 1963, *The New York Times* reported that NBC had signed Griffin to host an audience participation program called *Shopping Spree*, to be produced by Milbarn. Seven weeks later, a *New York Post* feature with Julann Griffin revealed that Merv would indeed be back on NBC in the fall, but in a new game show called *Word Spree*. In the meantime, Merv had signed on to host *Celebrity Talent Scouts*, the summer replacement for *The Red Skelton Show* on CBS.

Merv's debut as emcee of *Scouts*, which aired on July 2, 1963, was not without some embarrassing rough spots. "Although badly briefed on his guests," wrote columnist Kay Gardella in *The New York Times*, "he nevertheless used an intense I'm so interested stare as a coverup, and then immediately gave himself away when he was obviously at a loss for a sharp follow-up question."

His biggest *faux pas*, according to Gardella, was asking Liza Minnelli—the daughter of Judy Garland and film director Vincente Minnelli—how she got "involved" in show business! And if that question wasn't bad enough, Griffin asked Minnelli if she knew what she wanted to be—after mentioning the stellar reviews she'd received in connection with the Broadway musical *Best Foot Forward*.

From the weekly exposure on *Scouts* emerged two summer stock gigs. The first was *The Moon Is Blue*, presented at the Bucks County Playhouse in Pennsylvania (where "established house records" were broken, according to *Variety*) and at Northland Playhouse in Detroit. Following that tour, Griffin tackled Neil Simon's *Come Blow Your Horn*, in Warren, Ohio. Though Griffin found stage acting artistically stimulating, what he really wanted was to be back on television.

While fulfilling his summer stock commitments, NBC came a-calling. Recognizing the drawing power Griffin held over a large sector of the daytime audience, and his track record as a game-show host, the NBC execs put an enticing offer on the table. *Word Spree* had morphed into *Word for Word*, a game show in which players would be required to make as many words as possible from the letters in one big word.

As much as Merv loved games and game shows, he would love this quizzer even more; the network management not only wanted him to emcee it, they wanted him to *produce* it. The simple premise of the game didn't matter. Merv had been in television long enough to know that the production companies not only reaped the bulk of the profits, they also exercised artistic control, the key element affecting the outcome of any artistic endeavor. With this offer, he could put the lessons he'd learned on *Play Your Hunch* to good use.

Tony Garofalo recalls: "After the cancellation of his NBC [talk] show, I worked for Merv on *Word for Word*. Merv was a groundbreaker with that show, which marked the beginning of his great business acumen. Merv was one of the first, if not *the* first to package his own show. I don't think any other TV personality had done that."

Word for Word, which debuted on September 30, 1963, was no more successful in terms of rating points than *The Merv Griffin Show* had been. Once again, NBC didn't give Griffin a strong enough "lead in" for the mid-afternoon time slot. The ratings were lackluster, and after only one season on the air, the program vanished. For Griffin, however, the ax of cancellation was less painful the second time around. His attention was now focused on his burgeoning organization, and the development of a revolutionary project soon to be pitched to the NBC brass. It was a game show with a clever twist, unlike anything that had ever been done on radio or television.

What's the Question? required its contestants to coin a question after they had been given the answer. In his autobiographical works, Griffin credits Julann with suggesting the gimmick for this brainchild. It was Merv, however, who remained possessed by an unwavering intensity to sell the concept to the network.

Peter Barsocchini, who would join Merv's staff in 1976 as a booker, and rise to the rank of producer, recalls the genesis of the program that would eventually be known the world over as *Jeopardy!*

"Merv had a deal with NBC, but he didn't have a show," recalls Peter Barsocchini. "And he was trying to come up with something different."

Julann Griffin adds: "We were coming back from Ironwood, Michigan where we had visited my parents. We were on the plane back to New York. Merv was always interested in games. I never was, so he would play games with my sisters and do crossword puzzles and that sort of thing. He took out a pen and paper and started to make musical notes. And I asked him, 'what's that for—another game?' He said yes, and I told him, 'I'm sick and tired of all those people jumping around and doing pantomimes. They're so silly. Why don't you come up with a game that's intelligent for a change?' And Merv said, 'You can't do that because the FCC will suspect you of giving people the answers.'

He was referring to *Twenty One*, when Charles Van Doren had been given the answers. So I suggested, 'Why not have a show where you *do* give the answers—deliberately. You give the contestants the answers and they have to come up with the questions. And he said, 'Like what?' 'Okay,' I said, 'the answer is five thousand, two hundred and eighty. He said, 'How long is a mile?'

"Then I said, 'The answer is 52 Wistful Vista.' He said, 'What is the address of Fibber McGee and Molly?' They were famous on radio, and that was their address.

'The answer is Kathy Fiscus,' I said. And he answered, 'What is the name of the little girl who fell in the well in the 1940s?' Everyone had been listening to the radio to find out if she had been saved. I kept giving him answers and he kept coming up with questions. And by the time we got off the plane in New York, we had a show."

In their Manhattan apartment, Merv and Julann tinkered with the format, printing questions and answers on index cards, and affixing them onto to a large poster board. With everything finally in place, Merv was now faced with the nerve-wracking ordeal of selling the concept to NBC. The first presentation before the execs was not successful. The game itself was deemed way "over the head" of the average viewer. Moreover, it required a technical wizardry beyond the perimeters of live television production. In other words, it was a show too big for the small screen.

"The reason it was rejected was because they thought it was too difficult," recalls Julann. "So we had to dumb-down the questions a little."

Merv spent weeks modifying the entire game, adding "Double Jeopardy" and "Final Jeopardy" to the format. After much tweaking, he pitched the results to NBC president Mort Werner. Though Werner played along with the other mock contestants, he didn't get any of the answers right. He, too, thought the game was too cerebral for the average viewer. Grant Tinker, who would later produce *The Mary Tyler Moore Show* during his marriage to Moore, thought otherwise. Tinker, who was one of Werner's assistants, convinced his boss to pick up the show. Consequently, *Jeopardy!* joined the NBC daytime schedule on March 30, 1964 with Art Fleming as its host.

"People loved it right away and it really worked itself up," recalls Julann. "People in the colleges started to take their lunch breaks when it was on so they could watch it. I know that Nixon, in the White House, would take his lunch at a certain time to watch *Jeopardy!*

The show became very big and, eventually, we made the questions difficult again.

One of the reasons it's lasted so long is the writing. There are just so many rivers and mountains, and you can't come up with new geography for the questions. And that show has been on for so many years."

The new venture would be the first show produced under Griffin's eponymous company. The NBC edition of *The Merv Griffin Show* and *Word for Word* had been the product of Griffin's "Milbarn Productions." Episodes of *Jeopardy!*, however, would bear the credit title "Produced by Griffin Productions."

How does Julann Griffin feel today about her participation in the creation of a major chunk of Americana? "It's like having a child that grows up and leaves home," says the former actress. "I'm not connected to it anymore. But if I stop and think about it, even IBM, with Watson Cognitive Thinking, is linked to *Jeopardy!* It's amazing how many 'strings' have been attached to *Jeopardy!*, and how the show has affected the world. It's mind-blowing to think that you can get an idea, work on it, and bring it to fruition, and it will live in a way that grows. It's like yeast; it just keeps growing and growing. And if it's good, you can feel good about it. It's also made me realize that the only things you should concentrate on are the good things. The things that you want to grow. And if you hang on to the bad stuff, that will grow, too."

7. THE WESTINGHOUSE ERA BEGINS

By early 1965, Merv Griffin had settled into a mutually profitable business relationship with NBC. *Jeopardy!* had gained acceptance and evolved into an unadulterated hit. Buoyed by the success of his inspired creation, Griffin began developing another gamer, *Let's Play Post Office*, which he would sell to the network later in the year.

Even with the rapid expansion of his production company, a disappointment lingered in Griffin's professional life. Having experienced the prestige and exhilaration of hosting a national talk show, there was nothing he wanted more than a second bite at the apple. The weeks he'd spent at NBC, on *The Tonight Show* and his own series, had been a vital training phase. The lessons he'd learned, combined with the success of his company, boosted his self-assurance. Griffin knew he was up to the task. All he needed was another chance to prove it. The opportunity would materialize faster than he could have anticipated.

In mid-January 1965, Chet Collier, the executive producer at the Westinghouse Broadcasting Company, reached out to Griffin's lawyer and agent with an enticing proposal. Westinghouse, through its Group W division, was interested in reviving *The Merv Griffin Show* for daily syndication.

Westinghouse was not unfamiliar with the variety/talk format. In 1962, the company syndicated a well received, but relatively short-lived, series starring former *Tonight Show* host Steve Allen. After a scant two seasons on the air, Allen quit the program over creative differences. He would return to the format in 1968, with yet another incarnation of *The Steve Allen Show*, this time for Filmways Productions. To fill the void left by Allen, Westinghouse hired Regis Philbin, a boyishly appealing but largely unknown personality who had been hosting a local talk show in San Diego since 1961.

Philbin was a natural for the variety/talk route. Subsisting on a budget that was nearly nonexistent, Philbin learned how to accentuate what little he had to work with. His major attribute was a relaxed, easygoing style—much like Merv Griffin's. Like Griffin, Philbin managed to attract an impressive array of guests. Major film and television stars, as well as prominent politicians, found a warm and comfortable atmosphere on Philbin's local chatfest.

Group W brought Philbin to Los Angeles and launched him in a far more polished series. Debuting on October 26, 1964, *That Regis Philbin Show* primarily adhered to the same formula the young host had mastered in San Diego. The big problem, however, was that Westinghouse pitted Philbin against *The Tonight Show*, a move that some critics dubbed "career homicide." Philbin was very good at what he did, but he was no match for Johnny. A mere 20 weeks after Philbin had said hello, he was saying good-bye. His 100th episode on the Westinghouse network would be his last. "You're about to see one of television's newest faces become one of television's oldest faces, right before your eyes," said a bittersweet Philbin.

Despite the support of loyal viewers, some critics contended that Regis was simply "too nice" for the late-night battleground. "I'll tell you why I can't believe that," Philbin protested. "You mean to tell me that there are *no* nice people watching late night television?" The audience applauded enthusiastically.

Philbin thanked his executive producer, Chet Collier, for giving him and the show a chance. "You have a lot of guts, but no brains, Chet!" yelled Philbin. He was, of course, joking. A graduate of Boston's Emerson College, Chester Collier ventured into the infant television industry in the 1950s, eventually landing an executive position with Group W Productions. Collier not only recognized talent, he knew how to nurture it. Chief among his accomplishments was the ability to cultivate small-budgeted programming, like *The Mike Douglas Show,* into syndication gold. In fact, it was Collier who had hired Douglas, at the meager salary of $400 a week, at KYW-TV in Cleveland. Years later, Collier would hold powerful positions with Metromedia, CNBC, and, finally, Fox Broadcasting.

With the departure of Philbin, Collier embarked on a search for a well-seasoned personality that would prove bankable. Like many execs entrenched in the production of talk shows, Collier had heard about the blizzard of mail that drenched NBC when it canceled *The*

Merv Griffin Show in 1963. Thus, the name Merv Griffin was at the top of Collier's list of possible candidates.

Up until 1965, Group W's crowning achievement in the variety/talk field had been the daily syndicated *Mike Douglas Show*. Like Griffin, the dark-haired, blue-eyed Douglas was a former big-band singer and actor whose career had been revitalized through daytime television. Douglas launched his series in Cleveland in 1961. Two years later, Group W began syndicating the program to other stations around the country.

As enticing as the Westinghouse offer sounded, Griffin remained skeptical when he heard the word "syndication." In the mid-1960s, the television syndication business was not the fertile field it would be in years to come. The market consisted largely of old movies and former network TV programs. Yet not all syndicated shows were repeats. As far back as the 1950s, several action/adventure series (e.g., *Highway Patrol, Sea Hunt, Whirlybirds*, etc.) had proven enormously successful in first-run syndication. The sixties would see the syndication business rapidly expanding with a wider assortment of programming. *Death Valley Days* and *Exercise with Gloria*, for example, were both syndicated favorites of the period.

There was another major point of concern: the number of Westinghouse stations across North America was alarmingly sparse. Even worse, the company didn't own outlets in New York or Los Angeles, the two most important markets in the nation. As much as Griffin wanted the gig, he realized that a second failure in the talk show arena would spell the end of his career—at least in television.

"At that time, a company like Westinghouse wasn't allowed to own more than five stations," says Albert Fisher, who first encountered Griffin at the Seattle World's Fair in 1962. "And Westinghouse only had outlets in Philadelphia, Pittsburgh, Baltimore, Boston, and San Francisco."

Westinghouse Broadcasting stretched back to the 1920s, when it began its existence as Westinghouse Radio Stations, Inc. Rechristened Westinghouse Broadcasting Company in 1954, the organization adopted the more familiar "Group W" appellation in 1963. "Group W Productions was a division of Westinghouse Broadcasting which was then headed by a man named Don McGannon," says Fisher. "And Westinghouse Broadcasting Company, or WBC, was of course, a division of Westinghouse Electric Corporation."

The parent company operated out of Pittsburgh, Pennsylvania while Westinghouse Broadcasting remained headquartered in New York, with sales divisions maintained in Chicago and Los Angeles.

Don McGannon would later be instrumental in the enactment of the FCC's Prime-Time Access Rule, which, in turn, would have a major impact on Griffin's production/packaging empire. Even in 1965, McGannon's Group W was regarded as a significant player independent of the three major networks. Despite the paucity of stations in Group W's lineup, McGannon remained confident that the Griffin show could be sold to numerous "independents" and network affiliates. These stations would be outside the terrain of the five Westinghouse-owned outlets.

Syndication meant that the show would be sold separately to each individual station with no network affiliation contracts, no rules as to the number of stations required to sell the show, and no artistic interference. Group W and Griffin Productions would jointly produce the program, with ownership and creative control resting solely in the hands of the star. Good money *and* creative control! Merv liked that.

One of the more attractive aspects of syndication, as opposed to "networking," was the scheduling factor. Each station could broadcast the program in the time slot that was best for that particular market. Some cities would see *Merv* in the late-afternoon; others could catch it as an early-evening or late-night entry. Another plus was the fact that the new show would have a 90-minute format (although some stations would run a 60-minute version). The additional half hour would provide more time for the development of fresh talent and a more relaxed atmosphere. Banking on his own instincts, Griffin signed on with Westinghouse.

On February 23, 1965, *The New York Times* reported that the new *Merv Griffin Show* would be televised on all five Westinghouse-owned stations. Interestingly, the paper reported that the company had "tentative plans" to produce the program in California, despite the fact that Griffin was campaigning to keep it in New York. This came as no surprise to those close to Griffin, who had recently purchased a sprawling 28-acre farm in Califon, New Jersey, as a weekend retreat. The Griffins also maintained a plush apartment at Central Park West in New York City, a mere cab ride away from the hub of television production. Griffin won out. The show would be produced in the Big Apple. The target start date was early May.

Endeavoring to promote its newest star, the Group W executives had Griffin co-host *The Mike Douglas Show* in April of 1965. "The execs at Group W were very much attuned to both shows," says Fisher. "When the show started, Les Arries was in charge of operations. Chet Collier, who would become the executive producer of *The Merv Griffin Show*, had succeeded Arries. However, Collier played no creative role in the production of the show whatsoever. Toward the end of the run, Tad Reeves succeeded Collier.

"Before we went on the air in May of 1965," Fisher recalls, "Merv, Bob Shanks, and all of us associated with the program conceived it as being a late-night talk show to go head-to-head in competition with Johnny Carson on NBC. ABC had Les Crane who would be succeeded a few years later by Joey Bishop. But Crane and Bishop were minor competition. The juggernaut, obviously, was Carson."

With NBC's strong lineup of stations, *The Tonight Show Starring Johnny Carson* ruled the late-night roost. In 1963, during his first year on the program, Carson was pulling in an impressive 40.9 percent of the late night audience. Only once did Jack Paar ever top that figure; it happened when he walked off the show in 1960. Viewers who had been accustomed to the tempestuous Paar now became addicted to the more laid-back Carson. The disparity between the two hosts was radical. One NBC exec summed it up thusly: "Paar brought us an anxiety neurosis. Carson brings us a tranquilizer."

Carson restructured the program to suit his puckish on-air persona. His boyish midwestern charm served him well, particularly when he'd let loose with a bad-boy *double entendre*. Unlike other comedians, Johnny was often funnier when a joke had bombed. His "recoveries" were usually funnier than the scripted material. He might repeat the punchline, pretending that the audience hadn't heard it; deliver a masterfully executed double take; or, when all else failed, simply lapse into a soft-shoe routine. Carson had other endearing mannerisms: swelling out his chest confidently; straightening his tie fastidiously; tapping pencils like drumsticks; and rubbing his eyelids nervously when amused, or annoyed, by a guest. Years later, Griffin would take delight in pointing out that his esteemed rival possessed roughly 26 perceptible "peccadilloes."

ABC was eager to cash in on this late-night programming bonanza. As early as 1964, the network had attempted to lure viewers away from Carson with a stylistic alternative called *The Les Crane Show*. Because Crane has the distinction of being the first network competitor of *The Tonight Show*, his name remains an omnipresent footnote in television history. However, unlike *Tonight*, the Crane show would concentrate on topics rather than celebrity guests. The host, a former jet pilot turned radio announcer, took an interactive approach, aided by the shotgun microphone he aimed at audience members as they asked questions. Even in the mid-sixties, it was jarring to witness a television emcee pointing a weapon-like apparatus someone. "Each time he points this mike into the audience, it looks as though he's about to shoot a spectator," wrote Lawrence Laurent in his *Washington Post* essay, "Les Crane's Show Lacks Controversy" (November 24, 1964).

Despite its wide range of subject matter and technical innovations, *The Les Crane Show* failed to click with late-night viewers. After ABC fired Crane, the network revamped the package into an entertainment-oriented series called *Nightlife*, presided over by a succession of rotating personalities ranging from former *Today* host Dave Garroway to singer Pat Boone. When this approach failed, Crane was rehired. Comedian Nipsey Russell, in the traditional role of announcer/sidekick, lent a touch of style to the rapidly declining program. In a last ditch effort to boost ratings, ABC moved the show from New York to Hollywood and began booking big-name talent. But nothing seemed to work. By November of 1965, *Nightlife* was history. ABC turned the 11:30 p.m. time slot over to its affiliates.

Reviving *The Merv Griffin Show* after a two-year dormancy required astute planning so as not to repeat the mistakes of the past. After his experience at NBC, Griffin remained convinced that a traditional television studio wasn't the ideal venue for a variety/talk show; he wanted the new program to embody the energy and spontaneity of Broadway. Griffin and his producer began checking all the available facilities in the theater district. After much scouting, they finally found one that looked good—an ex-legitimate house called The Little Theatre on 44th Street, next door to the landmark Sardi's Restaurant, between Broadway and Eighth Avenue. The Griffin show would be the only television program to originate from that famous stretch of property affectionately known as Shubert Alley.

In his autobiography, Merv would claim that he had the theatre converted for television use. It is worth noting that the facility *had* been used for broadcasting long before Griffin's tenancy there. A venerable landmark since 1912, The Little Theatre had been home to Johnny Carson during his tenure as host of ABC's *Who Do You Trust?* from 1957 to 1962. Today the property is known as the Helen Hayes Theatre, although an engraved marker above the main entrance memorializes the original name of the building.

"It's important to remember that back then," says Fisher, "the print media was the big thing, especially for us. Publications such as *Time, Newsweek*, and *TV Guide* were huge at the time, and I had to deal with all the major columnists. Walter Winchell was still around, but he was on his last legs. Earl Wilson was very big, so was Leonard Lyons. I kept up a daily friendship and working relationship with the columnists that were based in New York. We were right next door to Sardi's, which was a hangout for all these columnists. They would be there every day at lunchtime. They'd make the rounds in the main dining room. Vincent Sardi would seat all the celebrities in one area and that's where I'd sit. The columnists would go from table to table, getting information for their publications. It was like going around in a circle. In fact, that's where the phrase, 'the inner circle' came from."

Fisher says it was often a challenge to generate publicity for the Griffin show. "That's because it wasn't on a major network. But Westinghouse began to expand beyond its five stations fairly quickly.

"Jack Rhodes was the guy who headed sales for Group W when we started to put the show together in May of '65. In the beginning,

I don't think it was on more than 20 or 25 stations because it was difficult for the company to sell Merv as a late-night show.

No major NBC or ABC affiliate was going to buy the Griffin show and air it in late night. Those networks already had their own late-night shows, and there was no way their affiliates were going to replace them with our show."

Group W and Griffin Productions embarked on a masterfully combined publicity campaign. As a result, the path for the newly revived *Merv Griffin Show* looked rosy. "But Johnny still controlled late night," says Fisher. "He was carried on well over 150 stations even in the mid-1960s. There was no NBC station that *didn't* carry Carson. So that made it all the more difficult. But Merv was steadfast. This was a thing with him. He wanted that late-night slot; the slot held by the king."

Griffin would be obliged to get involved in various promotional activities to sell the program to potential markets. He would visit the cities where it was important to bolster the ratings. The show would be taken to Boston, San Francisco, Pittsburgh, Denver, and, more frequently, Los Angeles.

As part of the requisite public relations campaign, Griffin would tape a week's worth of shows in every major market within the Westinghouse network—except Philadelphia. "Merv would never go to Philadelphia," Fisher recalls, "because the Douglas show originated from there. There was a real competitive thing going on, more so on Mike's part. It's my personal opinion that Mike may have been resentful that Merv had come into the fold at Westinghouse. Before Merv came on board, Mike had everything to himself. Westinghouse had been his turf. Then Merv came in with all this hoopla, and when he began encroaching in the daytime area, the competition intensified."

Fisher recalls one incident that genuinely irked the usually good-natured Douglas. "When Mike would do personal appearances, people would call him 'Merv.' I knew Roger Ailes, Mike's producer at the time, and he told me that Mike would really get pissed when people would confuse him with Merv."

Fisher believes the higher production values and prestige of the Griffin show may have been a factor in the rivalry between the two hosts. "But in fairness to Mike, it is like comparing apples to oranges," observes Fisher. "Each week, Mike had a co-host for the entire week and his show would rely heavily on music. Mike didn't do the serious interviews that Merv would do, nor did he offer the variety of guests that Merv had. Obviously, I'm prejudiced. But to this day, I feel that ours was a far superior show, artistically. And in many ways, even superior to the *Tonight Show*, except for the fact that nobody ever came close to doing what Johnny achieved in comedy, or topping him in popularity."

In 1965, *The Merv Griffin Show* and *The Mike Douglas Show* would be airing on the same stations within the five-city West-inghouse network. As both shows expanded beyond the West-inghouse terrain, the company went to great lengths to ensure that they would never be aired opposite each other. At the same time, the company's publicity machine played up the fact that both hosts were largely appealing to female viewers. An early Group W ad featured publicity shots of Mike and Merv, sporting huge smiles, accompanied by the line: "Your wife is seeing other men!"

"One of the things that Merv insisted on, even before the show went on the air, was that the couch and desk, which is the traditional *Tonight Show* setup, be situated as close as possible to the audience," Fisher recalls. "That was done to achieve intimacy. Obviously, they had to accommodate for the cameras getting around. But I think if Merv had had his 'druthers,' he'd have seated himself in the audience! He knew the audience was vital to the quality and energy of the show."

Certain guests would be invited to sit behind the desk next to Merv, ostensibly functioning as a co-host. This practice, a carry-over from the old Paar show, was not necessarily an indicator of a guest's status. Occupying that coveted spot carried a degree of prestige. "Sharing the desk with the star of the show could make someone look and feel like the star of the moment," says Fisher.

As head of publicity, Fisher trumpeted the fact that the Griffin show was now a component of the theater district. The slogan "Our Man on Broadway" would appear on all press releases, print ads, and still photographs. "Part of my job would be to distribute various materials with the promotion kits, which also included trailers, slides, and graphics," says Fisher. "And Westinghouse would handle its own five stations, based on the materials I would provide." Fisher also recalls that the publicity materials had to be "customized" for each station that carried the program, with special attention focused on major markets, such as Los Angeles and Detroit. "They weren't Westinghouse cities," says Fisher, "but rather places we needed to cater to."

A methodical plan for distributing the broadcast tapes was devised. Immediately after each show, the master tape would be duplicated in order to procure a "safety" copy. After that, the two-inch, reel-to-reel videotapes (the industry standard at the time) would be sent to individual stations via a manual delivery service! The distribution procedure was known as "bicycling," an industry term dating back to the dawn of movies, when film prints were rushed from theater to theater by bicycle. Since the Griffin show would be playing in multiple cities simultaneously, a large number of copies, or "dubs," had to be made of each episode. "This process sounds archaic in comparison to modern procedures," explains Fisher, "but this is how filmed and videotaped television programs were syndicated way back in the pre-digital 1960s."

One of the few initial drawbacks at Westinghouse was the company's decision to videotape the show in black-and-white. As late as 1965, many first-run programs, especially those not broadcast in prime time, were still being shot in monochrome. This was definitely a setback, especially considering that the NBC *Merv Griffin Show* had been produced in color.

On the other hand, the new series would have the benefit of the new 90-minute format with an expanded role for the show's on-camera announcer. At NBC, Frank Simms had handled the announcing chores and would occasionally banter with Merv and some of the guests. Simms didn't interact significantly with Griffin like Hugh Downs had done with Paar, or as Ed McMahon was doing with Carson. With a running time of only 45 minutes (sans commercials), there was hardly any time for tomfoolery on the NBC show. Griffin now sought a personality who could bring a quirky element to the show. He needed someone with whom he could trade quips, share an occasional song, and indulge in the lighthearted buffoonery that has since punctuated all variety/talk shows. In short, he needed a sidekick. Griffin knew exactly who to call: that magnificent "gentleman's gentleman," Arthur Treacher.

Merv, recalling the wonderful interview he'd done with Arthur on *The Tonight Show* in 1962, remained convinced that the veteran actor should be his *aide-de-camp*. Whether or not Treacher had been considered for the NBC series is not known. It's unlikely that the actor would have accepted the offer, since he'd landed a comfortable part in Moss Hart's Broadway production of *Camelot*. Nevertheless, in 1965, the 70-year-old character actor was Griffin's first and only choice. What better way to open a show than with a classy English accent?

At one of the first meetings prior to the show's debut, Merv informed the Westinghouse brass, and his reps from the William Morris Agency, that he wanted Treacher. The room fell completely silent. Everyone present, except Griffin, contended that Treacher was definitely the wrong choice. From the executives' perspective, the amusing banter between an aging movie actor and an exuberant ex-band singer was a one-night joke.

The higher-ups may have been reminded of the fact that Jack Paar's first announcer on the *Tonight Show* had been a veteran character actor: Franklin Pangborn. A familiar face in many films in which he played fussy and flustered comedic roles, Pangborn couldn't cut it as an announcer. After a few weeks, NBC replaced him with the more conventional Hugh Downs.

The execs didn't share Merv's enthusiasm about opening the show with a British accent, nor were they pleased about Treacher's advanced age. The big question everyone pondered was: Could "hip" young viewers relate to a man who was alive when Queen Victoria was on the throne?

Treacher's reputation as a respected thespian apparently meant little to the Group W bosses. Throughout the planning process, Merv made it abundantly clear that the show's announcer *had* to be Arthur Treacher. It would be Arthur or no one.

"Hiring Arthur was entirely Merv's idea," admits Bob Shanks. "I wasn't against it, but I was dubious about it—at the start. But Merv wanted him and said, 'I really get along with this guy; he's sassy

and not afraid to take the mickey out of me. He'll be wonderful.'
And he was right, because Arthur was an inspired choice. Merv
did things like this repeatedly. He was very spontaneous in the
decision-making process, which made him great to work for."

Arthur Veary Treacher was born in Brighton, England on July
23, 1894. He was the son of a moderately successful Sussex lawyer.
Young Arthur received his education in several boarding schools
where he was, by his own description, a "desultory pupil." Arthur
had accepted an apprenticeship at his father's law firm, J. K. Nye &
Treacher, but quickly realized that briefs and torts were not his cup
of tea. He quit the job and enlisted in the service shortly after the
outbreak of World War I. While Arthur didn't follow in his father's
footsteps by pursuing a legal career, he would do so by achieving
the rank of captain of artillery in the Queen's Westminster Rifle
Corps. (The elder Treacher had served admirably with the Sussex
Volunteer Artillery.)

In 1919, with his military service completed, Treacher embarked
on a theatrical career, taking a job as a chorus boy on the London stage. He had aspirations of becoming a leading man. "But I
found out that to be a leading man, you have to keep trim and stop
drinking," he said. "I thought that would be as dull as the law, so I
became a comedian."

Treacher would spend several years honing his comedic skills before
winning a supporting role in the musical review *Great Temptations*,
which opened at the Winter Garden in New York City in 1926. The
show, which ran from May to November of 1926, also featured an up-
and-coming deadpan comedian by the name of Jack Benny.

A succession of minor roles would keep Treacher steadily
employed. He began to make a name for himself, owing largely
to successful runs in George K. Arthur's *The Sport of Kings* (1930),
and Philip Merivale's production of Dickens's *A Tale of Two Cities*
(1931), both of which were presented at the Hollywood Playhouse.
After that, it was back to Broadway where he played Crabtree opposite Ethel Barrymore's Lady Teazle in *The School for Scandal* (1931).

Treacher's towering height (six feet, four inches) and British
hauteur made him a natural for character roles in motion pictures,
which had just been revolutionized by the arrival of sound. He

made his screen debut in Paramount's *Battle of Paris* (1929), an early Gertrude Lawrence musical directed by the highly esteemed Robert Florey.

Between assignments on Broadway and regional theater, Treacher would appear regularly in features and shorts, turning up in such delightful (but now forgotten) oddities as *California Weather* (1933), an RKO comedy short with Ruth Etting.

At MGM, Treacher was cast in a role that would solidify his stage and screen persona for the duration of his career. He played Jimmy Durante's inveterate butler in MGM's farcical comedy, *Hollywood Party* (1933). Featured in the cast was Lupe Velez, the "Mexican Spitfire," best remembered for the hilarious egg-breaking scene she shares in the film with Laurel & Hardy. Between takes, Velez did her best to impress Treacher by bragging that her boyfriend's height rivaled his. "Really?" said Treacher, in a tone resonating utter disinterest. This exchange was overheard by one of the film's directors, Allan Dwan, who told Treacher to play the role of the butler with the same impeccable air of haughtiness. The die was cast, and Treacher's interpretation of the imperious butler would remain a prototype for years to come. Many film historians rightfully attribute the classic butler line "You rang?" to Arthur Treacher. In the mid-1960s, the idiom would be popularized by "Lurch" (Ted Cassidy), the Frankenstein-like butler on TV's *The Addams Family*.

Treacher's next screen assignment was Columbia's *The Captain Hates the Sea* (1934), for which he received critical acclaim for his role as Major Warringforth opposite Victor McLaglen. It was during the making of this film that Treacher would meet the love of his life, Virginia Taylor, the young actress hired to stand in for one of the film's stars, Alison Skipworth. Treacher and Taylor would marry six years later in Las Vegas.

Today, Arthur Treacher's best-remembered screen roles are the ones he played opposite Shirley Temple: *Curly Top* (1935); *Stowaway* (1936); *Heidi* (1937); and *The Little Princess* (1939). An accomplished song-and-dance man, Treacher does a wonderful side-by-side routine with Temple in *Princess*, one of the film's most memorable sequences. Twenty-five years later, Treacher would reunite with Temple for an episode of her short-lived television series, *Shirley Temple's Storybook.*

Treacher had made an indelible impression as a servant in three of the four films he made with Temple, so he was the natural choice to play "Jeeves," the ever-resourceful gentleman's gentleman (or "valet") popularized in the writings of P.G. Wodehouse. At Twentieth Century-Fox, the same studio where he'd worked with Temple, Treacher received top billing in two features: *Thank You, Jeeves* (1936) and *Step Lively, Jeeves* (1937).

Attempting to escape the typecasting through which he'd earned fame, Treacher returned to the Broadway stage. As luck would have it, he wound up playing a butler in the B.G. DeSylva musical *Panama Hattie* (1940–42), starring Ethel Merman in the title role. The play prospered at Broadway's 46ᵗʰ Street Theatre where it ran for an astounding 500 performances.

In 1943, it was back to the Winter Garden for a long run in *The Ziegfeld Follies* with Milton Berle and Señor Wences. It was also in 1943 that Arthur Treacher became a U.S. citizen. With an unwavering interest in American politics, Treacher relished discussing Calvin Coolidge and Harry Truman, the two presidents he admired the most.

Arthur Treacher also possessed keen business acumen. In the early 1940s, he suggested that autograph hounds should pay a nominal fee for the privilege of obtaining an actor's signature. His method would have had the box-office attendants selling stamps for 10 cents apiece (or 12 for a dollar, for the true bargain hunter), which could be exchanged for an actor's John Hancock. The proceeds would benefit the actor's relief fund. Although the Theatre Authority responded with unmitigated enthusiasm, nothing ever came of it.

Maintaining a balance between stage and screen work, Treacher's (by now) famous butler persona can be seen in such light fare as *Irene* (with Anna Neagle, 1940); *In Society* (with Abbott & Costello, 1944); *Delightfully Dangerous* (with Jane Powell, 1945); and *That's the Spirit* (with Jack Oakie, 1945).

After more regional productions, Treacher landed back on Broadway for a two-year run in *Caesar and Cleopatra* (with Sir Cedric

Hardwicke, 1949). He was also a radio personality on NBC's tongue-in-cheek jazz series *The Chamber Music Society of Lower Basin Street.*

Treacher remained a steadily employed thespian well into the 1960s. It was on the small screen, just prior to joining the Griffin show, that Treacher made his final appearance as an imperious butler on CBS's *The Beverly Hillbillies* in 1964. His two back-to-back episodes on the sitcom were followed by a small but memorable role as Constable Jones in Disney's *Mary Poppins* (1964).

One day in early 1965, Treacher received the phone call that would change his life. "Merv always enjoyed talking about the first time he'd met Arthur," says Albert Fisher. "He was so taken with him that he knew immediately that if he ever got his own talk show, he wanted Arthur to be the announcer. And Arthur, in his usual manner, said something like, 'You're a dear boy.' Then he dismissed it. But as soon as Merv got the show, Arthur got the call. His agent, Abe Newborn, of the General Artists agency, told him: 'We've just received a call for your services that will change your life.' And Arthur knew immediately that the offer was from that dear boy, Mervyn."

Early publicity photographs of Merv and Arthur often elicited humorous comments from critics and viewers. One photo shows Arthur straightening Merv's tie, as he towers over him on the set. (Griffin was five-feet, ten.) "He *still* looks like the butler in those old Shirley Temple movies," said one observer. "He looks like he could be Merv's babysitter," said another.

Treacher would be the perfect sidekick, thanks to his outspoken frankness and icy disdain. He would offer a balanced counterpart to Merv's low-key, leisurely demeanor. Virtually everyone who worked with Treacher on the show speaks of him with sincere affection and respect.

"Arthur and I would often go next door to Sardi's around 3:00 p.m., before the taping," recalls Albert Fisher. "Arthur had a routine where he'd arrive at the office early in the afternoon. Merv had his suite on the top floor of the building; the rest of us would be on the second and third floors. And Arthur would come in, kiss all the girls, and make the rounds. He'd come into my office and we'd chat, except for the times when he had a rehearsal for a song with Merv or one of the guests. But if he didn't, we would go to Sardi's for some raw oysters and Guinness stout. Arthur would often regale me with incredible stories about his early days in the theater."

One of Treacher's favorite stories involved a man who would have made a captivating guest on *The Merv Griffin Show*—if he'd lived into the 1960s.

As Fisher tells it: "Back in the 1920s, Arthur was doing a play in Chicago that had been running for several months. Al Capone had taken up with one of the chorus girls in the show. And, at least once a week, he would come to the theater, then take the girl out to dinner afterwards. Arthur said everyone knew when Capone was coming in because the first two or three rows of the theater would by occupied by bodyguards. Capone would always sit in the middle. This went on for weeks.

"One night, after the show, Arthur had gone with some friends to a nearby restaurant. And while they were seated, they looked over and saw Capone at a table with the young lady. Arthur said to his group, 'Now there's a chap I'd really like to meet. He's very interesting and quite a legend.' And his friends began telling him he should go over and introduce himself. They had suggested this half-heartedly. But Arthur got up and headed toward Capone's table. He was roughly halfway there when several men from two other tables rushed over and intercepted him. Capone had bodyguards stationed everywhere to prevent strangers from approaching him.

"Arthur explained that he was an actor in the show and merely wanted to say hello to Mr. Capone. With that, one of the guys instructed Arthur to remain exactly where he was. The guy went over to yet another table and whispered in another man's ear. And then *that* guy went over and whispered something in Capone's ear. The whole thing could have been a scene in a *Godfather* movie, with Capone giving a hand signal indicating that it was okay for Arthur to approach his table.

"Capone graciously welcomed Arthur and invited him to sit down. 'What are you drinking?' he asked. Arthur said, 'Drinks aren't allowed. They're illegal!' Capone looked at him slyly and repeated, 'What are you drinking?' Needless to say, they had several rounds of drinks together. And when they were through, Arthur thanked him and said, 'It's getting late. I've got to get going.' Capone asked Arthur if he lived far from where they were. 'I'll have one of my drivers take you home,' he offered. And Arthur vividly recalled the ride in one of those cars you see in gangster movies—a big, black limousine with thick bulletproof glass. Sitting in the back of the car, he could also see the tip of a Tommy gun partially exposed under the passenger seat. The driver dropped Arthur off at his apartment. And that was Arthur Treacher's meeting with the legendary Al Capone."

The Griffin show was a boon to Treacher during what was essentially the ebb of his career. "He was thrilled to be on that show," says Fisher. "Arthur always said that it was an amazing thing that had happened to him at that phase of his life, to be himself instead of playing a role. To the best of my knowledge, Merv never imposed any restrictions on Arthur. I think the only thing he told him about being on the show is that he should be himself. And Merv always knew what would work best for the show."

Of his employer, Treacher once said: "I have come to the conclusion that he is a dear little fellow with a dear little wife and a dear little son. They have a dear little company called Griffin Productions, with a dear little subsidiary called Anthony Productions, named for the dear little son, which pays my dear little salary, which is indeed very dear and very little."

Treacher would be the first person on stage just before the tape started to roll. "Other announcers did warm-ups," says Fisher. "But Arthur did what we called a *cool*-down. He'd come out and greet the audience: 'Now look,' you all know what you're expected to do. When the dear boy comes out, it would be very polite if you would give him some applause. But if you don't want to, that's fine, too.' Then, he'd go over and sit down as the orchestra waited for its cue."

Each episode of the new *Merv Griffin Show* would open with the same musical theme used on the earlier NBC version: an exceptionally bright tune called "Hello, Hello." (The 1965 Griffin album *A Tinkling Piano in the Next Apartment* identifies the song as "Merv's Theme.") "The two of us wrote it," recalls Julann Griffin. "The song actually had lyrics, but we never used them. But it was mainly

Merv's. He'd sit at the piano and go click, click, click. He would have a ball creating a song and was wonderful at it."

Merv would use "Hello, Hello," in various rearranged versions, as his intro for many years. "He stopped using it after we divorced because my name was on it," recalls Julann. However, Merv quietly reintroduced the tune, in a radically updated version with synthesizers, during his last season on the air in 1985–86.

Even the most ardent viewers of *The Merv Griffin Show* would likely attest that Mort Lindsey was the program's *only* orchestra leader during its Westinghouse period. Griffin and producer Bob Shanks wanted Lindsey as far back as the NBC days. "I waited a long time to work with Mort Lindsey," said Griffin. "Every time the chance came, he was busy conducting for Pat Boone or Eddie Fisher or mostly with Judy Garland, not to mention the scoring of motion pictures."

 By the time the Westinghouse deal was on the table, Lindsey had already been signed to conduct for Al Hirt on CBS's *Fanfare*, the summer replacement for *The Jackie Gleason Show*. With Lindsey contractually obligated to another program, Shanks had to look elsewhere for an orchestra leader. The job ultimately went to a Broadway denizen and jack-of-all trades named Colin Romoff.

Bald-headed and goateed, Romoff was the quintessential Broadway conductor. Among his gifts was the ability to compose musical and vocal arrangements with equal panache. In the fifties and sixties, major artists recorded several of Romoff's stylish compositions. Nat King Cole performed Romoff's "Look Out for Love," "Sing Another Song (And Then We'll All Go Home)," and "Something Makes Me Want to Dance With You (with lyrics by Danny Meehan). Jack Jones recorded "Travelin' On," which was essentially a successful "treatment" of the old standard "Gotta Travel On." Several of these songs were later used as "walk-on" or "incidental" cues on the early Griffin show.

Romoff's finest work was accomplished on Broadway. Though his credits weren't exceptional, they were impressive and varied. He'd composed music and lyrics for *The Ziegfeld Follies of 1957*; served as pianist for *Say, Darling* (1958–59); and tackled the musical and choral directions for the Richard Adler musical *Kwamina* (1961), which ran a mere 32 performances.

In 1962, Romoff signed on as musical director of NBC's *The Andy Williams Show*. The producers were unquestionably appreciative of Romoff's reputation and talent. The only problem, however, was that Romoff could never warm up to the task of working in a television studio. The hectic pace of the electronic medium, with its cumbersome headphones and unceasing cues from the director's booth, were major annoyances to him. Romoff walked away from what he regarded as an unrewarding experience at end of the Williams show's first season in 1963. He returned to his natural habitat—Broadway.

Romoff spent the next several months conducting the orchestra for Carol Burnett's starring vehicle, *Fade Out – Fade In* (1964). Following that assignment, he turned up as an actor in director George Roy Hill's film *The World of Henry Orient* (1964), an underrated coming-of-age comedy starring Peter Sellers in the title role. Romoff would round out the year with a dual assignment in *I Hear Music* (1964), a showcase vehicle for opera singer Jo Sullivan. Romoff not only conducted a quartet, he got to display some serious acting and singing chops. Writing for the *Long Island News and Owl*, Jules W. Rabin observed: "Romoff, a music teacher of some repute, is a miracle worker as sometimes comedic, sometimes singing partner to the lovely new lady [Sullivan]." Romoff's next major engagement would be *The Merv Griffin Show*.

It seems odd that Romoff, a serious conductor with a strong disdain for television, would leave the theater for the chaotic pressures of a daily variety/talk show. Nevertheless, he accepted the job in good faith, having come aboard with impressive credentials and good reviews.

No one connected with the Griffin show remembers if Merv had intended to spotlight his orchestra leader in an "on camera" role, as he would for the new announcer. It soon became apparent, however, that no discernible rapport existed between Romoff and Griffin. The conductor seemed to lack the requisite charisma to share any spontaneous moments with the star. On *The Tonight Show*, for example, orchestra leader Skitch Henderson would occasionally banter with Johnny

Carson and ad-lib bits of "shtick" here and there. Similarly, on *The Jackie Gleason Show*, the Great One would grab laughs whenever he acknowledged his flamboyantly attired orchestra leader, Sammy Spear. Years later, Carson would do the same thing with his third orchestra leader, Doc Severinsen.

"Romoff was a very talented and interesting guy," recalls Bob Shanks, "but his chemistry with the show wasn't good and he just didn't work out."

Chemistry notwithstanding, the musical component of the show was beginning to fall into place neatly. Griffin hired some of the best jazz soloists and "side men" in the business. Many of them had performed on the road with the big bands of the 1940s.

The Griffin orchestra boasted several great sax players: Dick Hafer, Roger Pemberton (who would also contribute many songs and arrangements to the show's library), Richie Kamuca, and Shelly Russell (a.k.a. Shelly Gold). The trumpet men were Danny Stiles and Bill Berry. (In fact, Danny Stiles had been delegated the responsibility of selecting the personnel for the orchestra.) Bob Brookmeyer, the trombonist, would remain with the show until 1967, when Bill Watrous replaced him. Art Davis played the bass, and Jake Hanna manned the drums. Mundell Lowe was the featured guitarist, and Colin Romoff conducted from the piano.

Each edition of the show would open with one of television's most distinctive announcements, delivered by Treacher: "Now hear this! With a *what ho* and a *cheerio*, from the Little Theatre off Times Square, it's *The Merv Griffin Show!* The company for your delectation includes. . . . " He'd name the guest stars, including himself as, "your *veddy* obedient servant, Arthur Treacher." He would then command viewers to "look sharp now, here's the dear boy himself, *Merrrrvvyynnn!*" Arthur's intro was most likely his own creation, says Albert Fisher. "I am sure the 'dear boy' thing was something Arthur came up with on his own," says Fisher. "It just sounds so much like him and it was very endearing. It worked well for the show."

Griffin would run down the aisle, having entered the theatre from the lobby, and shake hands with a few folks in the audience as he headed towards the stage. Jack Benny didn't think much of this gimmick. "Why do you run?" he once asked the stunned host. "You've *got* the job!"

Debuting in most cities on May 10, 1965, the Westinghouse version of *The Merv Griffin Show* got off to a winning, though remarkably hectic, start. The first hour of the 90-minute premiere featured some amusing patter with Carol Channing, then starring in *Hello, Dolly!*, at the St. James Theatre, right next door to Merv's studio. Someone thought it would be cute to have Channing make her entrance on roller skates, and she did, with admirable aplomb. Channing presented Merv with a cache of offbeat gifts: a thousand sticks of chewing gum; a pewter mug hand-crafted by Sammy Davis, Jr.; and a skateboard. Not to be outdone, Merv grandly demonstrated his prowess with the skateboard.

There was also an amusing bit by puppeteer Larry Reeling, who manipulated a stringed "Dolly" figure. Channing, visible in the shot via double exposure, watched in amazement. At the end of her segment, Channing skated her way back to the St. James Theatre for that evening's performance. The gimmick of having a live camera outside the Broadway studio was amusing, though hardly new, and it established the freewheeling atmosphere that would define the new program. Channing would revisit Griffin three months later on the night of her final performance in *Dolly*, without her skates!

Nothing on that first show broke any records. There were light and zany moments aplenty, thanks to a potpourri that included comedians Dom DeLuise and Woody Allen, actor Danny Meehan and the "Beyond the Fringe" comedy quartet (who provided a film clip of their two-hour special seen in England), topped off by the vinegary wit of Arthur Treacher. Stage director Philip Burton, the foster father of actor Richard Burton, rounded out the last third of the program, which ended with a brief chat with nationally syndicated reporter Merriman Smith. When it was over, everyone connected with the show ventured next door to Sardi's for a mega celebration.

Reviews of the Westinghouse curtain raiser were filled with superlatives; the word "formidable" used liberally to size up Griffin as a competitor for Carson and Crane. In fact, the *New York Herald-Tribune* said that Griffin was "the first real competition for

Tonight since NBC put Johnny Carson in the driver's seat." Interestingly, the same publication had less than positive things to say about Merv's vocal abilities. "Once a singer, he's apparently out of practice," noted the reviewer. "For openers, he struggled through 'Once in a Lifetime' and just barely made it."

Kay Gardella of the *New York Daily News* predicted that NBC might "rue the day it ever introduced him [Griffin] to nighttime viewers as a sub on *The Tonight Show.*"

Variety opined: "If there is room for three of them—Griffin, NBC's *Tonight* and ABC-TV's *Nightlife*—Griffin should hang in there better than the previous Westinghouse attempts in the format."

On his second outing, Griffin hosted two familiar favorites: the urbane Walter Matthau (who would later star in the movie *The Odd Couple*) and sitcom actor Phil Leeds. Hats were raised respectfully at the conclusion of that one, also.

Brimming with confidence, Merv began to weigh in on the "high standards" he intended to maintain. He promised that the new series would offer "not just interviews with kooky blondes with off-beat parts in Broadway shows, or showcasing corny comics with routine gags. We want to entertain with interesting persons who have something to say; a variety of guests, some good controversy—but no causes."

In comparing Griffin with Carson and Paar, New York's *Newsday* observed that: "He [Griffin] can raise an eyebrow, do the double take, and sit wide-eyed with the best of them." In the same article, Griffin reiterated his commitment to conversation instead of comedy, noting that Steve Allen's Westinghouse show had "too many sketches." Additionally, unlike Jack Paar, Griffin vowed to keep his personal opinions to himself. "I don't want people coming on fighting with me," he said.

The first five shows were in the can. In reviewing them for the *The New York Times,* Jack Gould noted that Griffin seemed to rely too heavily on stage performers for conversation, which challenged him to work "very hard to get the talk going." Gould also suggested that the lighting and settings needed prompt correction, as the picture on the home screen appeared "too cluttered."

In the earliest episodes of the Westinghouse Griffin show, the backdrop behind the desk and sofa consisted of an ample row of severe-looking wooden panels. Such a motif might have been appropriate for a doctor's reception room, but it was hardly conducive to lively conversation on a variety/talk show. "It wasn't a very attractive set," recalls Fisher, "and it didn't photograph well." From the beginning, the wooden panels presented such a distraction that a sheet of industrial carpet had been masked over the section behind Merv's desk, allowing for a smoother look. Art director Tom Trimble gave the set a complete makeover in late 1965.

Trimble had been a busy man at NBC, designing various sets, including those used by Paar, Carson and Griffin. He would have good reason to be proud of the *Merv Griffin Show* set he designed at the Little Theatre, which consisted of a series of industrial-type fabrics, draperies and textured wallpaper, all of which photographed beautifully in black-and-white. The new set also lent itself better to the lighting effects used for certain songs and comedy routines.

The early Westinghouse entries feature an opening sequence depicting Merv, in his convertible, racing through Manhattan at night, arriving at the theatre just before showtime. The filmed portion would end at the point where Merv reaches the lobby door. From there, the cameras would pick up the "live" shot of him entering the theatre and running up the aisle. This was a clever opening, but it presented two problems. The first one involved continuity. Merv would wear a different suit for each show, and what he wore on any given day didn't always match what he had worn in the filmed opening. The filmed portion, of course, *always* showed him in a dark suit, while the live pick up would occasionally reveal him wearing a different shade or style. (For the record, Griffin's wardrobe on the early episodes was credited to Andrew Pallack.)

The second problem: the filmed opening conveyed the notion that the show was a nighttime series. This looked somewhat odd in the markets where *Merv* aired in the late afternoon.

A new intro was created, consisting of a montage of clips showcasing the various superstars that had appeared on the program. After that opening became stale, a simpler and livelier visual would open the show. The camera would simply pan the audience, capturing the faces of the most enthusiastic spectators (mostly tourists), as they waved and applauded during Treacher's opening announcement.

Griffin didn't indulge in "scripted" sketches or zany characters as Carson did. At the top of each show, Merv and Arthur would simply banter, sing a song, or resort to 'question cards.' Before tape would roll, the audience members would write innocuous questions on the cards. The questions would then be given to the writers who would come up with saucy retorts for Merv to read on the air as "spontaneous." One night, a man asked if he could visit the control room. "No, no," Merv snickered. "Not during drinking hours!"

Merv and Arthur would also involve the studio audience in amusing little games. One recurring feature was a bit in which an audience member would have to identify which staff member did which job. Four or five production people would each hold up a card with a job title emblazoned on it: producer, writer, publicist, stage manager, etc. Each professional would be holding the wrong card. It was up to the "contestant" to match the right card with the right person. It was akin to *What's My Line?*

Merv would also tap into his musical talents when bantering with the audience. On one occasion, he instructed his director, Kirk Alexander, to select the faces of several unsuspecting folks in the house. He would then sing a popular song that best described that person's physical characteristics. The first "participant" was an old woman whose head was draped in a kerchief. Merv offered, "Baby, It's Cold Outside." Next, the camera zeroed in on a bespectacled gent as bald as a cueball. With that, Merv belted out a few bars of "I've Got a Lovely Bunch of Cocoanuts." "I don't think he liked that one," Merv noted a moment later. "But you always sing that when a man is wearing glasses!"

Merv and Arthur would also take contemporary rock-and-roll songs and re-adapt them into dramatic readings. The dour-faced Treacher, delivering the more risqué sounding lyrics, always gener-ated gales of laughter.

The biggest laughs on the show were frequently the result of Treacher's sardonic ad-libs. There was never a shortage of sass when Arthur was in the picture. Though he seemed the epitome of the taciturn, English gentleman, Arthur was, in fact, an outspoken observer and critic. Thus, if a guest exhibited even the slightest lack of refinement, "Mr. Treacher" was capable of putting that person down with *one* line.

One night singer Robert Goulet was subjected to Treacher's caustic asides.

Goulet: Hi, Arthur!

Treacher: Why are you chewing, old boy?

Goulet: Because I've got gum in my mouth.

Treacher: Why do you have gum in your mouth?

Goulet: Because I have bad breath.

Treacher: We've put up with that for years, you know...

Griffin would dismiss such embarrassing moments with a simple sentence: "Don't mind Arthur."

If someone on the panel bored Treacher, he'd either turn his back on that person and chat with the audience, or fall asleep. Or, at least *pretend* to fall asleep. "I can't help it," Treahcer told writer Jerry Tallmer in the *New York Post*. "I think I can say some of the things to some of the people that he [Griffin] can't afford to say, and I think he wants it to be like that."

In an interview with Ira Peck in *The New York Times*, Treacher said, "I'm not really grouchy, but I'm irritable with idiots, you know, and I'm awfully angry with people who come on [Mervyn's] stage and they have their little joke to do and it's all written up on a card, and they worry and fret about it when all they do is come on and say the thing that's written there. Then I tell them, 'Now come on, get on with it.'"

Despite his irascibility, Treacher knew where to draw the line. In the same *Times* interview, he admitted: "I don't interrupt everybody all the time. I think that's wrong. I think that if some poor somebody wants to be exposed for eight minutes, they shouldn't be interrupted by an old man who's gone through it all."

Ranking high on Treacher's list of dislikes (which included pompous people, bratty kids, sloppiness, and modern art), were certain female comics. Treacher dismissed many of them as crude and offensive. When Welsh singer/actress Tessie O'Shea playfully planted her legs on Treacher's lap one night, he immediately brushed them off and told her she was being vulgar.

Totie Fields was one of the few comediennes that Treacher liked. He and Fields would often indulge in a routine in which they'd sit next to each other, and, look straight ahead without uttering a word. Treacher was tall and lanky; Fields was short and plump. Seated side by side, they appeared equal in height. As they slowly stood up, Treacher would suddenly tower over the diminutive Fields, who looked no taller standing up than she did sitting down. The visual impact never failed to generate chuckles.

One night, after doing this bit for the umpteenth time, Fields burst into a few bars of "On the Good Ship Lollipop," an obvious reference to Treacher's screen work with Shirley Temple. The audience ate it up.

Treacher was willing to participate in the songs or quirky comedy bits featured in the opening segment of the program. However, there were times when he'd flatly reject certain demands of his services. Bob Shanks recalls that: "A couple of times he balked at me and said, 'No, old chap. I'm not doing that!' And I'd try to placate him. 'Okay, Arthur, how about. . . .' I don't even remember what it was, and he'd repeat, 'No! I'm not going to do that!' It was probably something silly. But I loved Arthur."

A reporter once asked Treacher if he was, in any way, scared of Mr. Griffin. "Not a bit," answered Treacher. Indeed, Treacher would actually bristle at the man who signed his paychecks. Feeling a bit brazen one night, Merv said, "You were at the Battle of Bunker Hill, weren't you, Arthur?" To which Treacher icily replied, "Stop being an ass!"

On another occasion, when Treacher didn't receive payment on time for a promotional spot he'd filmed for Griffin Productions, he reported the matter to his union. Treacher didn't do this out of malice. He simply wanted to teach the 'dear boy' a lesson. "In show business, you must *always* be on time with your money," he told his stunned employer. From a financial perspective, Treacher saw little difference between acting in movies and appearing on a talk show. He applied the same credo to both. "It's marvelous," he told *Newsweek* in 1969. "You say the words, get the money and go home." According to the magazine, Treacher was going home with $2,000 each week.

Despite his on-camera testiness (or because of it), there is no doubt that Arthur Treacher enriched *The Merv Griffin Show* during his tenure on the program. On television, the veteran actor came across as the most colorful conversation piece since Tiffany lamps. Treacher's acerbic wit earned him a new generation of admirers, mostly college-age people, who waited for him after the show to get his autograph. His delightfully cranky disposition, and willingness to express disdain in the face of pretension, generated a respectable amount of fan mail from viewers. More often than not, Treacher would answer his correspondents personally.

"When the show was over, unless there was some special event going on, Arthur would immediately get in a car—he had a driver—and go home to his wife, Virginia," recalls Fisher. "The Treachers lived in a nice apartment in Douglastown, Long Island."

Away from the cameras, the Griffins and the Treachers cultivated a close friendship. "Arthur was a character and a good guy," says Julann. "Merv adored him. And I think Arthur was a father figure to Merv. When we had our farm in New Jersey, Arthur and Virginia would come out and visit us on the weekends. We built a little cottage next to the house and called it Treacher's Corner. Arthur would perform the dance routine he had done in the movie with Shirley Temple. He was always wonderful."

Although Arthur's peers called him by his nickname, Pip, the younger staff and crew invariably addressed him as "Mr. Treacher."

The year 1965 would be as pivotal for Westinghouse Broadcasting as it was for Griffin. The small broadcasting conglomerate was about to weather through a station reversal, or "swap," in which the NBC affiliate in Philadelphia, WRCV-TV, would move back to Cleveland, effectively becoming WKYC-TV. Simultaneously, the Westinghouse station in Cleveland would relocate to Philadelphia as KYW-TV. As part of the deal, Mike Douglas and news anchorman Tom Snyder (the future host of NBC's *Tomorrow* show) would also relocate to Philadelphia. After the move, the Douglas show would gain substantial prestige as a cherished attraction in Philly's multi-cultural landscape.

This swap of stations was in fact a reversal of a switch that had been made a decade earlier between NBC and Westinghouse.

"When we'd gotten off the ground in May," recalls Albert Fisher, "Mike Douglas was still originating in Cleveland, his show's home base. But when Douglas relocated to Philly, the move had a profound effect on our show.

"The Westinghouse station in Philadelphia, which also happened to be an NBC affiliate, couldn't give up Johnny Carson in the 11:30 p.m. time period. That meant that Westinghouse's own station couldn't carry Merv in the time slot that he was *supposed* to be on.

"Jack Rhodes told Merv, 'We can't put you on in late night. But let's try you out in late afternoon as a lead-in to the six o'clock news.' And, as I recall, Merv was really negative about that and didn't want to do it. However, they told him if he didn't, he'd lose Philadelphia, one of the major markets in the country. The end result was that they tried it in Philly, as a late-afternoon show, and it took off like crazy."

"Group W had been selling Mike Douglas mainly as a morning show," remembers Fisher. "And both Westinghouse and Merv quickly got the message that in the cities where the Griffin show couldn't be sold in late night, it could be very successful as a lead-in to the six o'clock newscast."

Indeed, local stations depended on their early evening newscasts to generate much of their advertising revenue. Therefore, it was essential that a good late-afternoon program kept viewers tuned to the same channel for the news.

The marketing of *Merv* as a late-afternoon entry made all the difference in the world, or so it seemed, in getting broader exposure in the sales department. "That affected the way that we promoted the show," says Fisher. "And it also affected some of the bookings on the program, too. We were not appealing to late-night viewers, but rather to a predominantly female daytime audience. And it kept expanding as we picked up more and more stations,"

On June 19, 1965, Westinghouse president Don McGannon announced that Westinghouse had finalized the ownership exchange of its radio and television stations in Cleveland for those owned by NBC in Philadelphia. The exchange of ownership complied with a ruling of the Federal Communications Commission, and became effective at 5:00 a.m. on June 19, 1965.

The call letters KYW-TV, used by Westinghouse in Cleveland, would be transferred to to the station in Philadelphia. The NBC station in Cleveland would use the call letters WKYC-TV. Both stations would operate on Channel 3. McGannon also announced that the new Philly station would be affiliated with NBC, and would therefore carry *The Tonight Show Starring Johnny Carson*. Additionally, Philly audiences would soon be seeing *The Merv Griffin Show* on KYW-TV, Channel 3, at an hour "still undetermined." As it turned out, *Merv* was added to KYW's daytime schedule in July.

Each talent coordinator on *The Merv Griffin Show* had a specifically focused agenda. Larry Holofcener and Jean Meegan handled the literary and political bookings. Tony Garofalo, along with Alan Foshko and Paul Solomon, took charge of scheduling the singers, comics, and stars.

Indeed, the move to Westinghouse had been a boon to the fledgling career of Tony Garofalo, who had started with Griffin as a production assistant and was now promoted to talent coordinator. "What was fun about being a talent coordinator at Westinghouse was the situation where someone would drop out and we'd be short a guest and would have to call somebody and beg and beg and beg," says Garofalo. "And from where we were, right on Shubert Alley, I could run over to the theaters and try to ask Gwen Verdon, Betsy Palmer, or whoever was appearing, to make an appearance."

On more than one occasion, Bob Shanks had to make some last minute phone calls. "We always had a bullpen, meaning people who we could get at a moment's notice. There was Rocky Graziano; Aliza Kashi, an Israeli girl who was pretty and funny; we'd put her on, and about four or five others, including Carmel Quinn and Monti Rock, III, who I knew could be reached at home," the producer recalls. "A couple of times the show had already started and we were short a guest. I'd call Rocky and say 'Can you get over here? We'll send a car for you right now.' And I explained that I'd had a guest that had bombed out."

Last minute cancellations are a nightmarish occurrence for any talk-show producer, and Shanks certainly had his share of close calls. Fortunately, Sardi's proved to be as reliable a source for replacements as it was for excellent cuisine. In desperation, Shanks would venture next door for the sole purpose of snatching a guest star at the eleventh hour. "I had to do that several times when people didn't show up for one reason or another," the producer admits. On one occasion, Shanks found himself *two* guests short. There was an impending sense of panic backstage. As the producer was making phone calls in search of replacements, a booker informed him that Ginger Rogers was in make-up. No one told the star that she was actually scheduled to appear the *following* night. Comedian Dick Shawn would fill the other void. Luckily, one of the bookers had noticed him standing in the back of the theater. As it played out, the two substitutes provided Griffin with one of the liveliest shows of the Westinghouse period.

For rank beginners, landing a spot on *The Tonight Show* can prove seemingly impossible. Usually, by the time a young comic or singer makes it to the guest chair, he or she has endured years of "seasoning," succeeding or failing in various venues on the way up. It's a process in show business known as "paying one's dues."

Merv wanted fresh young talent on the show. Thus, when word got out that the Griffin show was holding open auditions each week, the studio became a hot spot for rookie performers, especially the stand-up comics working in the local clubs and bars.

"This was a practice that I had actually started with Paar," says Shanks. "And Paar was sympathetic, being from the midwest as I was, and having gone through the audition nightmare in New York. And so I thought, why not just hold open auditions once a week? I'll be there at 1:00 p.m. and everybody will get 15 minutes on a first-come-first-served basis. That's the way we found Leslie Uggams, Lainie Kazan, Bert Convy, and Renee Taylor."

Tony Garofalo, who conducted the auditions, also remembers the process: "We became widely known for holding open auditions which proved to be a good opportunity for up-and-coming talent. I was auditioning the singers and comics that were on frequently. The whole process was so different back then. Not like today where you have people just coming on to plug something. They'll go from one show to someone else's show. They just get whomever the P.R. people have in town. It was different and more exciting back then."

"Every Thursday was an 'open' afternoon," explains Albert Fisher, "which meant that anyone could come in and walk onto the stage for an afternoon audition. Tony Garofalo would handle that, and if I wasn't busy, I'd go down and watch."

Anyone means anyone. "And 90 percent of the time, you saw God-awful stuff," says Fisher. "But sometimes you'd see a real winner. That's how David Soul (later famous as half of the *Starsky & Hutch* team) got on the show." Fisher recalls that Soul came on as "the Covered Man." The young artist sang with his face covered by a mask because he wanted to be known for his singing rather than his matinee-idol looks.

"We'd also go to nightclubs to check out the new acts," says Garofalo. "I'm sure *The Tonight Show* still does this. That's how we found Richard Pryor working in a little place in the Village."

"Little Richie Pryor," as Merv would introduce him, began life as Richard Franklin Lennox Thomas Pryor, in Peoria, Illinois, on December 1, 1940. His grandmother, who operated a brothel, raised him. A junior high school dropout, Pryor served in the U.S. Army. After a succession of nondescript jobs, he entered show business and moved to New York where he broke in a stand-up act. Greatly influenced by Lenny Bruce, Dick Gregory, and Bill Cosby, Pryor began making the rounds of numerous clubs. By 1965, he'd found steady work in small clubs in Greenwich Village such as the Café a-Go-Go. That's where someone on Griffin's staff (no one remembers exactly who) caught his act.

Bob Shanks has vivid recollections of Pryor's audition for the Griffin show: "A guy named Peter Paul was managing Richard and brought him to my office. So I saw him perform in my office where he did a little routine right there. And I told them that this audition was being done on a whole different level. It was like a one act play or novella. I began to interview Richard myself and within days he made his national debut on the show. And all of this happened within the first couple of weeks of the show's debut in '65."

Contrary to popular belief, George Carlin didn't make his TV debut on the Griffin show. "George had been part of a team with Jack Burns for a while," recalls Bob Shanks. "I'd put them on with Paar in 1960. And then, in 1962, George came on as a single. I thought he had logged more appearances on Merv's show, but his obit said that he had been on it 29 times. I told him, 'Anytime you want to come on, let me know.' Years later, when I was doing the *CBS Morning Show*, George called and said, "Where and when do you want me?"'

"Carlin and Pryor were undoubtedly the two biggest comedy names on the Griffin show during the Westinghouse era," says Albert Fisher. "Both were young and inventive, but very different from one another. Richard's material was, by and large, all based on life experience. George's material, on the other hand, was scripted stuff that he had invented. Fisher points out that the famous routine Carlin did on his first Griffin show—the one about a tough American sergeant addressing a Native American Indian tribe that was fighting the cavalry—had been performed in clubs. "It was a funny, inventive routine." says Fisher. "Carlin was very good at doing voices and dialects. And he did this routine with a typical 1940s Brooklyn accent, addressing the braves: 'Get your birch bark and fill out this application . . . Put down your last name first, and your first name last, so that if your name is Running Bear, it's Bear Running!' Fisher says that Carlin saved his best-remembered character, the perpetually stoned "Al Sleet, the Hippy Dippy Weatherman," for his second or third appearance on Griffin. "This, too, was scripted material that he had done on all the shows, including *The Tonight Show*."

Once a comic had finished his or her routine, and had joined the panel, Merv was wise enough to let the talent bask in the moment. Tempting as it may have been, he never attempted to top a performer with ad-libs or double takes. In most instances, Merv acted as a foil or straight man. If the comedian was a success, so was the show, he reasoned. Griffin would adhere to this credo all through his career as a talk-show host.

Bob Shanks, following up on the favorable response to young performers on the show, would frequent as many venues as possible in search of the next George Carlin or Richard Pryor. "I often went to clubs and saw new talent, like blues musician B.B. King down at the Village Gate. My wife Ann went with me all the time and she enjoyed them as much as I did. And so we were always in the clubs, going to see comedians. That's how I had found the Smothers Brothers at the Blue Angel, and Streisand at the Bon Soir. They had all appeared on the Paar show."

Like its competitors, the Griffin show retained a "do not use" list of performers who, for one reason or another, had not worked out satisfactorily. With Merv, however, virtually every one of those personalities would be given a second chance.

Griffin was known to speak enthusiastically of the numerous "firsts" to appear on his show during the Westinghouse period. "The list included Julie Christie, Lord Bertrand Russell, and Lily Tomlin, to name a few," remembers Fisher. "And there were quite a few discoveries, such as a young actor named Reni Santoni, and the talented singer Gilbert Price."

The audition process for the Griffin show became a widely-known phenomenon on Broadway. Although the "tryouts" were limited to professionals, a few desperate wannabes resorted to elaborate, if not bizarre, methods to get a crack at the big time.

The Griffin production offices were situated on the second and third floors of the Little Theatre. The offices were accessible via an alleyway that also provided access (from the street) to the stage area. This alleyway served as an entrance for performers, staff, and crew; it was also used for the delivery of scenery and technical equipment.

One day an unusually large crate, addressed to "Mr. Bob Shanks," was delivered to the theatre. The staff and crew looked at the parcel dubiously, wondering what could possibly be inside. "When they told me about it, I refused to open it," recalls Shanks. "And it sat there for quite a while."

The gigantic parcel sat in the alleyway shared by Griffin and the adjacent St. James Theater, where *Hello, Dolly!* was still playing. Before long, Griffin's people were ordered to remove the crate from the alleyway because it was obstructing the fire exits.

"We didn't worry about bombs in those days," says Shanks. "And I told them, 'You guys open it, if you want.' But I just knew there was something wrong about this. And there was. Inside this huge box was a guy sitting at a spinet piano. And out came this kid, who auditioned on the spot—but *didn't* get on the show!"

The "instant audition box" wasn't the only unorthodox method of introduction the producer encountered. Shanks recalls an incident that had occurred at Griffin's NBC offices: "I came back from lunch one day and was told that a man had called, saying he'd be willing to settle out of court for $70,000! And my response was '*WHAT?*' I knew we didn't have any lawsuits pending, or even in the works. So I called this man who turned out to be a comedian. He had been trying to get through to me and couldn't. I told him that he had indeed come up with a clever way of getting noticed—and we did set up an appointment. But I didn't book him, not because of the prank he had pulled, but because his act wasn't funny. But he *did* get my attention."

The task of auditioning talent for the Griffin show could be just as grueling for the producer as it was for the amateurs. "When the auditions were over," says Shanks, "I usually went home and had a dry martini."

Talent coordinators also work under intense pressure. The job of guest procurement is practically the same today as it was in the sixties. Bookers for major talk shows are faced with the challenge of coming up with three or four fascinating people, five shows per week throughout the year. Although they generally seek famous or well-known personalities, the bookers will occasionally invite a "civilian," someone who is not in show business or recognizable to the general public. These are individuals who have unusual abilities or inspiring stories to impart, and their contribution to the show will outweigh the fact that they are not professionals. Merv welcomed a number of such offbeat guests over the years. One memorable booking featured a fellow who claimed he could consume more doughnuts in a minute than anyone else. A competition was held, and, sure enough, the young man prevailed. As for the other participants, it was hard to tell if they were experiencing stagefright or an upset stomach!

The cancellation of Merv's NBC series was due to persistently low ratings. The weak numbers were attributed, at least in part, to the show's intellectual veneer—the very thing that had appealed to so many critics and college students. The bulk of viewers that *didn't* tune in were drawn to the game shows, soap operas, and lightweight variety offerings. By the mid-sixties, however, a multitude of social and cultural changes had already unfolded, sparked in no small measure by the civil rights movement and the escalating war in Vietnam.

There was a counter-culture movement brewing in America, evidenced by the growing number of protests that were making headlines. Griffin remained convinced that daytime audiences were now ready for stimulating conversation balanced with lively entertainment—all within the landscape of the variety/talk format. He sought to prove himself correct on the Westinghouse show.

Though Griffin could tackle serious topics and offer a dissenting opinion here and there, he did so without being offensive. Some guests, however, would push him to the limits.

On May 31, and June 1, 1965, Griffin welcomed Pulitzer Prize winning columnist and writer Westbrook Pegler to the program. Born in 1894, Pegler had been a prolific columnist since the 1930s, and was widely known for his vehement opposition to almost every aspect of the American way of life, including democracy. He was brutally critical of virtually every U.S. president during his lifetime (regardless of party affiliation), going so far as to resort to vile name-calling. Pegler also held a virulent disdain for members of the U.S. Supreme Court.

King Features Syndicate, a subsidiary of the Hearst Corporation, had published Pegler's newspaper column for decades. In 1962, when Pegler turned his venom on the Hearst executives, the company fired him. Consequently, Pegler found a venue for his work in right-wing publications such as *American Opinion*, a product of the John Birch Society.

Though no video footage of Pegler on the Griffin show is known to exist, viewers who watched him remember how he had spewed a repugnant amount of anti-Semitic nonsense. "He was definitely an anti-Semite rightist," says Bob Shanks, "and he was terrible." The producer recalls a severe backlash resulting from Pegler's two interviews. "I caught hell from the head of one anti-defamation league for even putting him on," recalls Shanks, "and I had to write him a letter about the First Amendment."

Merv's opening remarks on the program taped on June 2, provide a good indication of what Pegler said, and of the direction in which the show was heading.

Speaking extemporaneously, Merv said Pegler's two segments were "uproarious," and had sparked criticism from the press, and thousands of angry viewers who had sent letters and telegrams threatening to picket the theater.

"Let me, if I may, *not* apologize for having him on," said Griffin stoically. "Let me just discuss with you the kinds of things we heard. The biggest complaint was that the man now is senile." Merv assured viewers that after sitting next to the man for two nights, and listening to his comprehensible diatribe, he was anything but senile. "He was as crackling and bitter in his criticisms as he was in the 33 years that he wrote his column, and won a Pulitzer Prize," Merv contended. "I do *not* agree with him on most everything he says." Merv could barely get his words out before the studio audience burst into applause. "I also feel as the emcee of this show, and the questioner of a guest, I often sit here night after night and listen to opinions. And I may disagree. But I think my role as emcee is to question these people and allow them in this medium to expose themselves to you, either good or bad. But to question them always so I can get the most out of them, and that you at home can make your own decisions."

Griffin said there had been "all kinds of emotions" in the theatre the previous night, evidenced by hissing and booing. "But that's good," he reasoned, "Because your brains were ticking and maybe you didn't realize it, but you were thinking about what you believe in. I believe in a democracy. Mr. Pegler does not believe in a democracy. And in a democracy we have divided opinions, and it is fair that both sides are allowed to present their opinions."

Merv said it would be very easy to book the show with "carbon copies" of popular beliefs. "We could have a lot of smiley, happy people on, drinking tea, laughing and giggling here every night. And it would be dull, I assure you. Our purpose is to bring on people. Interesting people with interesting things to say, whether we agree with them or not, but allow them to say what they believe in. And we plan to continue that, because that's television at its

best. It really is. When you can photograph people and they're saying things, and you sit at home and decide whether they're right or
wrong. You're the audience. So, if you want us to, we will continue
with unusual bookings on this show. And I hope you do."

The audience cheered; the ratings soared.

Griffin had always maintained that if the guests couldn't come to
him, he'd go to them. Better to jet around the world, if necessary,
rather than wait for certain personalities to visit the United States.
In keeping with this policy of traveling to talent, Griffin and his
staff flew to England in June 1965 to film a series of interviews.

Bob Shanks recalls an era in television that predates the use
of satellites and overseas cut-ins. "In order to get the European
stars, and have a competing edge on Carson," observes Shanks, "we
would tape two shows on Thursday night. We'd leave New York
Thursday night, arrive in Europe on Friday morning, tape a string
of interviews from Friday to Sunday morning, then fly back to New
York on Sunday night and do the show on Monday."

Griffin had filmed several "remote" sequences for his earlier NBC
series. With the expanded format at Westinghouse, there was even
more of an incentive for global journeying. Griffin announced that
he'd make one trip each month during 1965, solely for the purpose
of collecting a cache of archival treasures.

In May, Griffin and crew journeyed to Cannes, France, where
they managed to land an exclusive with "Agent 007" himself, Sean
Connery. The interview, during which Connery sang "There is
Nothing Like a Dame," was shot at the Cannes Film Festival. It
was during this trip that Griffin also scored a one-on-one chat with
John Lennon. It was Lennon's first talk show ever. Griffin's cam-
eras also caught up with Jane Fonda and her then-husband, Roger
Vadim, at their new farm on the outskirts of Paris.

In June, Griffin was in London, shooting segments with director Otto Preminger, and performers Carol Lynley, Michael Caine,
Leslie Caron, Georgia Brown, and Bob Hope. Before leaving, he
had also arranged for an exclusive interview with British philoso-
pher and Nobel laureate Bertrand Russell.

Shot on 16mm film, as opposed to videotape, the interview took
up the better part of a day at Russell's residence. Like the other

segments in this category, the footage would be edited for presentation on the show, interspersed with the "live" guests in the studio.

Griffin knew that the 93-year-old Russell was an outspoken pacifist. He also knew that in the wake of the Cold War, and the escalating war in Vietnam, a provocative dialogue with Russell was bound to create sparks.

Griffin asked Russell if the conflict between the United States and the Soviet Union would ever be settled. Russell said it would, but "most likely by the extermination of all combatants on both sides." This set the stage for a debate about war and peace. Griffin asked how world peace could be achieved. The first step, Russell said, would be for the United States to "give up aggressive war, give up the habit of invading peaceful countries and torturing them." Russell charged that the United States was indeed waging an aggressive war in Vietnam. Griffin was stunned; he asked if they might be protective skirmishes. "No!" Russell said fervently. "Ordinary Americans believe that they are conducting a protective war, protecting non-Communists against these wicked Communists. And that is not the case. They're conducting a war against people who were, until they were attacked, entirely in favor of neutrality. And now they've learned what American troops are." Russell then talked about the atrocities carried out against the Vietnamese people by American forces. He described, in vivid detail, the effects of Napalm.

Griffin tried to focus on the positive aspects of American life. He asked Russell if he admired America for its freedoms of speech and religion. Russell charged that America had actually *infringed* on those rights. Communism was a religion, he contended, insisting that the U.S. government had made it a "criminal act" to be a Communist in America.

The Russell interview aired on July 5, 1965, a time when American support for the war was at an apex. At the beginning of the film, the studio audience listened pensively. However, as it progressed, some people in the audience began to fidget; others expressed disapproval by booing. Merv grew uneasy.

The 30-minute Russell piece was separated by three commercial breaks. It was at the end of the second portion that Russell had made his most biting criticisms about American involvement in the war. As the filmed image of Russell faded from the screen, it was replaced by the "live" shot of Merv at the desk. It was an uncomfortable moment during which some viewers were too angry or stunned to react to what they had just heard. A disturbing silence filled the studio.

"One man's view, Lord Bertrand Russell of England," Merv said softly, obviously distancing himself from the man. "We'll be back with the final segment of his remarks right after this commercial break."

It was one of those tense situations in which a talk-show host gauges the impact of what has just transpired. As rough as it was for Griffin, it would be downright devastating for Colin Romoff.

It's the job of the musical director of any unscripted TV program to select the music to be played on the air. If something unexpected should occur, it's also the musical director's job to make a quick modification of the musical choices. In the aftermath of so much anti-American rhetoric, it would have been prudent for Romoff to "tinker" on the keys, or play no music at all, at the commercial break. Instead, he cut in with an inappropriate, brassy ditty that could have done justice to a circus act. Even worse, he cued the orchestra to begin playing *before* Merv finished his lead-in to the break. A scowl crossed Merv's face as the picture faded to the commercial-break slide, or "bumper," as they're known in television. It's unclear what happened next, but Romoff's abrupt disappearance from the show suggests that he had departed on less than amicable terms.

In fairness to Romoff, it's important to note that he had his back to Merv and couldn't readily detect any visual cues that might have prompted him to play something different. Rob Sinclair, a musician and TV historian, contacted Romoff via e-mail in the 1990s, delicately inquiring about his hasty exit from the Griffin show. Sinclair says, "He wrote back to me and said, 'It's a long story. I'll tell you later.' But later never came. I reminded him several times: 'Still looking forward to your e-mail!' However, I never got anything back from him."

Sinclair also reached out to Mundell Lowe, the guitarist in the orchestra, who had taken over as leader for a two-month period after Romoff left. Lowe told Sinclair that Griffin and Romoff had "gotten into a very heated argument."

When Romoff left, he took his musical arrangements with him, leaving it up to his successors to procure suitable charts for the five tapings each week.

Colin Romoff would continue to compose and conduct over the next two decades, occasionally coming up with a gem, such as "Crazy Butterfly," brilliantly rendered by jazz singer Nancy Wilson in 1968. After decades of being actively involved in the New York music scene, Colin Romoff died in 2003.

One question about the orchestra on the Westinghouse *Merv Griffin Show* looms in the minds of historians. How is it that Merv Griffin, a former big-band singer, musician, composer, and unabashed lover of music, never featured his own orchestra on the show?

"Merv was so used to hearing that great music every night and probably didn't realize that the people at home were only getting these little snippets of music at commercial breaks," Sinclair observes. "It probably never occurred to him that the home audience might like to hear an entire arrangement."

There were, however, two occasions on which the band was featured on the Westinghouse series. The first performance resulted when Merv had come down with a bad cold that prevented him from singing. The second time was when John Barbour filled in as host of the program, and specifically requested that the band be featured.

Before Griffin could grapple with the task of finding a new orchestra leader, he had a certain degree of damage control to deal with. The filmed interview with Bertrand Russell had set off a furor in the press, with some critics suggesting Griffin was a traitor. Some viewers sent nasty letters to the studio, expressing disapproval for giving air time to someone so "anti-American."

Art is supposed to stir controversy. That's exactly what Griffin's interviews with Pegler and Russell had done. Henceforth, no critic worth his salt could dismiss *The Merv Griffin Show* as a mere amalgam of showbiz fluff. "Television *has* to offend somebody sometime," says Bob Shanks, "or there can be no redeeming programs at all." Griffin may have still looked like "the boy next door," but it was becoming more and more apparent that he had outgrown that perceived image.

In addition to making noise, *The Merv Griffin Show* made music. Superb music. "Merv had wanted Mort Lindsey from the beginning," Shanks recalls, "and as soon as he became available, he would take over as the show's new musical director." But before Lindsey could do just that, Mundell Lowe, who had recently played in the *Today Show* studio band, replaced Colin Romoff.

In the summer of 1965, Lowe ran into Jackie Cooper, who was then West Coast vice president of programming for Screen Gems, the television subsidiary of Columbia Pictures. Cooper offered Lowe an assignment in Los Angeles, and Lowe would go on to compose many recognizable themes for television programs produced in Hollywood by Screen Gems.

Even after Mort Lindsey had finally joined Griffin in late August, Lowe retained his place in the orchestra. When Lowe left Griffin for his stint in California with Columbia Pictures, guitarist Jim Hall replaced him.

Morton Lippman was born on March 21, 1923 in Newark, New Jersey. His parents were Russian immigrants. "Mort," as he was affectionately known, had earned a doctoral degree in music at Columbia University. His first major credit was as a pianist for NBC Radio, a position he held from 1946 to 1949. Mort then moved up to a musical director's position at CBS for its popular *Rate Your Mate* program. From 1950 to 1954, he worked as a conductor/arranger for Arthur Godfrey's radio series as well as its TV counterpart on CBS.

Lindsey also achieved a respectable degree of popularity with teenagers, thanks to a deejay gig at WABC Radio. His program, *The Boy Next Door*, which was heard from 1955 to 1957, offered as much rock and roll as rhythm and blues. From his perspective as a successful DJ, Lindsey took exception to the ensuing furor over rock and roll and its effect on American teenagers. In 1955, he said: "It is my opinion that kids who are spending their time listening to and taking an interest in records are not going to be involved in juvenile delinquency. It's the ones out on the street I worry about."

The Boy Next Door would ultimately be praised as one of the more popular platter-spinning stanzas of the day.

Lindsey's work in television was steady but varied. Aside from his work with the enormously popular *Arthur Godfrey Show*, Mort also conducted for the lesser-known (and now forgotten) *George Skinner Show* on CBS during the mid-fifties.

In 1957, Lindsey was hired to serve as musical director of the quartet featured on *Tonight! America After Dark*. Unfortunately, the erratic atmosphere of that disjointed mess led to much hiring and firing. As a result, Lindsey was let go after the first 13 weeks of the show. He joined *The Pat Boone Chevy Show* in 1958, and after two seasons, conducted for an NBC special titled *Paris a La Mode* (1960). From there, Lindsey would solidify his place in show business history by leading the orchestra for Judy Garland's legendary performance at Carnegie Hall on April 23, 1961. Lindsey would also serve as conductor/arranger for Garland's variety series, *The Judy Garland Show*, on CBS during the 1963–64 TV season. Lindsey had also contributed the arrangements for Garland's album, *Judy Garland at Carnegie Hall*.

In 1968, Lindsey took home an Emmy for his work on the Barbra Streisand TV special, *A Happening in Central Park*. He would eventually work with Liza Minnelli, Elton John, Rod Stewart, Willie Nelson, and other iconic performers.

Like other orchestra leaders on the talk-show circuit, Lindsey paid close attention to the "walk-on" cues—those 10 or 20-second ditties that greeted guests as they walked through the curtain. Lindsey used a multitude of classic "standards" for this purpose. Comedians were almost always introduced with the very snappy "Put On a Happy Face." Major film stars or directors were often greeted with a booming rendition of "Hooray for Hollywood." Glamorous women were treated to "You Stepped Out of a Dream,"which dated back to *Ziegfeld Girl* (1941), the film in which Lana Turner sauntered down a magnificent staircase. On the other side of the coin, the dashing leading men made their entrances to "Everybody Loves a Lover," a song popularized by Doris Day in 1958.

Oftentimes, a tune was selected to suit the profession or personality of the guest. For instance, "I Think I'm Goin' Out of My

Head" was the appropriate cue for the renowned psychologist, Dr. Joyce Brothers, while "Diamonds are a Girl's Best Friend" would do equal justice for the abundantly jeweled Zsa Zsa Gabor.

Lindsey also relied on several of his lesser-known compositions for the walk-ons. His slow-paced, moody instrumental called "Electronic Quail," originally written for the Tony Curtis film *40 Pounds of Trouble* (1962), was reserved for sultry female guests (like Jayne Mansfield) as well as the elongated commercial breaks. Tough guys and movie villains frequently made their entrance to Lindsey's "Bernie the Butcher," an intimidating piece made all the more menacing by a succession of pounding drum embellishments.

Certain stars, of course, have always had their own theme songs. (Think Bob Hope and "Thanks for the Memory.") Unless there was a problem with performance rights, almost every guest associated with a particular composition would be introduced with the orchestra playing it grandly. One curious exception was vaudeville comedian and actor George Jessel, a frequent visitor to the Griffin stage in the 1960s and early '70s. There was a straightforward reason why Jessel, the Toastmaster General of the United States, made his entrances sans music.

On one late-'60s segment, Jessel was treated to a few bars of "My Mother's Eyes," a song he'd recorded in 1929 with a soft and soothing resonance. Lindsey preferred the tune with a very upbeat, Dixieland jazz tempo. When Jessel complained, rather vociferously, that the song wasn't played properly, Lindsey came up with a simple remedy: no walk-on music at all for George Jessel!

Though Merv didn't feature the band on the air, he did pay tribute to his "musicianship" in another medium. In 1966, Dot records released *Merv Griffin Presents Mort Lindsey and His Orchestra*, an album of 12 instrumental renditions of standards, including "The Shadow of Your Smile," "Strangers in the Night," as well as a few lesser known tunes familiar to viewers of the show.

The interviews with Westbrook Pegler and Lord Russell had sparked considerable criticism, and the resultant publicity put *The Merv Griffin Show* solidly on the map. The next episode to stir the pot (though with far less bravado) would air on September 2, 1965. The bookers had landed a commitment from Captain

Mitsuo Fuchida, the Japanese naval captain who had planned the attack on Pearl Harbor. Fuchida was already seated in the guest chair when his introduction commenced, a prudent move on Griffin's part, since the audience might have hissed if the former captain had made the customary entrance through the curtain.

"Over 20 years ago, it would have been impossible for this man to sit before an American audience," said Merv. He asked the audience to extend "patience and interest" in his next guest who should be heard. With the intro complete, the interview began without any hissing—or applause.

Although there was an interpreter on the panel, Fuchida, now a middle-aged man with glasses and thinning hair, responded to questions in a thickly accented voice. He recalled how he had meticulously planned the attack of December 7, 1941, and how he had been subsequently "decorated" by the Japanese Emperor, Hirohito. Fuchida said his mission had been one of "absolute duty," and that he held no contempt for the United States. He also said that the bombing of Hiroshima actually wound up saving a half million lives.

What made Fuchida's appearance so compelling was the fact that, after the war, he had been called to testify against the Japanese military for crimes of war. Several years after the war, Fuchida became devoted to God and, in 1952, toured the United States as a member of the Worldwide Christian Missionary. He died in 1976, at the age of 73, from complications of diabetes.

On September 14, 1965, comedian-turned-activist Dick Gregory came on to talk about a recent incident in which he'd been shot during a race riot in the Watts section of Los Angeles. According to press reports, the riot stemmed from alleged police brutality following the arrest of a black man falsely accused of drunken driving.

With a fertile comedic mind, and keen sense of social awareness, Gregory drew much of his material from current events. He would soon establish himself as one of the new breed of "progressive" black comics along with the likes of Nipsey Russell and Bill Cosby. He is credited as being the first major comedian to expound eloquently on the black experience, not only in nightclubs, but also in books, on college campuses and popular TV programs such as *The Ed Sullivan Show*. Gregory once said, "This is the only country in the world where a man can grow up in the ghetto, go to the worst schools, be forced to ride in the back of the bus, then get paid $500 a week to tell about it."

On the Griffin show, Gregory made several observations that remain relevant more than a half-century later. "When 22 million people, be they black or white, start hollering 'police brutality," said Gregory, "then it's time to start listening to twenty-two million people and [start] going in."

Gregory talked about living conditions in American cities. He warned of similar occurrences in the future if American legislators continued to ignore the problem of poverty.

"It's going to be a whole lot of Watts all over this country up north if we don't go in and start solving the problem," he said passionately. "Not only the problem of the Negro, but the problem of the poor white man who also lives under the same conditions, but he's had better ways of expressing his than the Negro has had. And the minute his channels are cut off, and the way his channels are going to be cut off, is by seeing the Negro walk out, and through a civil rights organization, or through bricks, advance the cause.

"Unless you advance the cause and bring the type of attention where they will go in and start solving the problem, you have white people that live in the ghetto; they'll be next unless we sit down and solve this problem, which is not a Los Angeles problem, a Mississippi problem; it's an American problem. And until we wake up and start solving these problems as American problems, we're in trouble."

Gregory said the solution to the problem would not be achieved through emotions. "It's like one big cancer," he warned, "and we're not going to solve any problem by cursing the cancer. We've got to bring in the [right] type of minds and get to the cure. And if we don't do that, the whole country's in trouble."

The hot topics of the sixties weren't limited to politics, social injustice, and civil unrest. The decade would witness several controversial breakthroughs in science and medicine, ranging from the introduction of the birth conrol pill (in 1960) to the first human heart transplant (in 1967).

Sharing the panel with Dick Gregory was Dr. Robert Ettinger, a physics professor whose seminal book, *The Prospect of Immortality* (1962), dealt with cryonics: freezing a dead body and then thawing it after science had effected a cure for the cause of death. The term "freezing" has long since been replaced by "vitrification." Ettinger called the process cryopreservation. The orchestra greeted him with "We're Having a Heat Wave."

In his advocacy for what would come to be known as the "immortalist movement," Ettinger offered to furnish information about cryonics to any interested party. In 1965, no one had actually been subjected to the process. "But a great many people, hundreds, perhaps thousands, have indicated and made arrangements for this treatment of their bodies after death," said Ettinger. "Most of them are very healthy so far."

If there was any element of shock in this discussion, it was Ettinger's assertion that some people get buried *before* they are actually dead. "It is our custom, every day, to bury people, or at least prepare them for burial, while they are really still alive," he alleged.

He continued: "If a physician believes he can no longer help the patient, and he says, 'you're dead,' he ships them off to the embalmer, in spite of the fact that at that moment, the man is still 99 percent alive. His heart has stopped, maybe some of his other organs are not in very good condition; he may even have some general debility. But, nevertheless, most of the cells in his body are still alive. This poor devil whom we call a cadaver would, if medicine were more advanced, be called a *patient*."

All of this led up to one big question: How could we apply the techniques of future medicine to people who are dying today? "The answer is simple," said Ettinger. "We *freeze* them!"

Merv asked if the patient would be the same age at the time of thawing.

"After thawing, they will be in the same *slightly* dead condition they were in when they were frozen."

Dick Gregory asked how all this would affect the insurance industry.

Ettinger: "This is going to be a tremendous boon to the insurance business because now, in addition to carrying life insurance to provide for our families after we are temporarily dead, we must also carry additional life insurance to pay for the cost of this freezing and storage."

Arthur Treacher raised the question of possible opposition from religious leaders.

According to Ettinger, the clergy had been "more enthusiastic" than any other group, with only one denomination (he didn't disclose which) expressing disapproval. (This made perfect sense, since most religious doctrines concur with the unconditional preservation of life.)

"I'll bet the funeral directors aren't too thrilled with this," Merv quipped.

"This isn't to cut them out," Ettinger said, "because they are going to be the ones who will process the bodies." An eerie silence ensued as several still photographs were shown. "This looks very much like an ordinary coffin," Ettinger said cheerfully. "Except that there's a transparent plastic window. This means that, if you wish, you can make periodic trips and visit grandpa and *look* at him."

Another photo depicted several odd-looking chambers. "These people are kept of course at very low temperatures, much colder than an ordinary refrigerator." "You come up with one body," Merv warned, "and I'm leaving the show!"

Thoroughly stimulating and articulate, Robert Ettinger was the type of guest talk-show hosts pray for. He would make more appearances with Griffin (including a befitting 1970 "theme show" exploring what life might be like in the 21st century) and publish another eyebrow-raising book, *Man into Superman* (1972). As one would expect, following his death on July 23, 2011, at age 92, Ettinger's body was cryopreserved.

Shortly after this mind-boggling discussion about death and dying, the time was ripe for some provocative dialogue about life and living. Enter *Life* magazine author/editor Albert Rosenfeld, who appeared on October 10. Rosenfeld had written a compelling analysis of the dilemma society would soon face in the wake of "startling" new advances in science.

"We're going to talk about babies," warned Merv. "There's something your mother *didn't tell* you! There are new ways of conceiving babies and growing them!"

Rosenfeld had been invited to discuss the then-delicate subject of creating human life other than through conventional means. The orchestra greeted Rosenfeld with several bars of "You Must Have Been a Beautiful Baby." The audience giggled.

"We've had Mr. Ettinger on," said Merv. "He wants to freeze us and wake us up a hundred years from now." Rosenfeld laughed. This episode wouldn't be about death; it would focus on recent developments that would reshape humankind's vision of life.

They began by talking about the "new way" of making babies. "What's wrong with the old way?" asked comedienne Mimi Hines, also on the panel. "There are a number of new ways of doing this," Rosenfeld responded. "One way—and nobody has done this all the way through—is to take a human egg, put it in a glass, artificial womb and introduce sperm into the setup; fertilize the egg, and than a baby will begin to grow."

The gasps in the studio audience were almost palpable. No other daytime talk show, much less a *variety*/talk show, had dared to tackle such an intimate subject.

Rosenfeld continued: "Now this has been done only experimentally in very early stages, but it's assumed that in the long run, people will be able to do these things. And once they know how to do them, the tendency is for anyone who wants to make use of it can start doing it."

Rosenfeld predicted that humankind would be someday control its own evolution. "These subjects wouldn't have been speculated about outside the pages of science fiction," he said. "I don't know what the science fiction writers are going to find to write about. But it's hard to imagine anything now that is *not* being seriously proposed by scientists and universities."

Merv asked what the scientists were "closest to," in terms of new treatments and procedures. The answer was: transplanting organs into people from living donors or cadavers, perhaps mammals, and the use of artificial materials. "How soon a lot of this begins to take place on a large scale will depend on how interested people are in pushing it," Rosenfeld offered in conclusion.

Rosenfeld was, of course, hinting at the prospect of human cloning. He played it safe, though, keeping his comments very nonspecific. Perhaps he was concerned that such a discussion might trigger a religious, moral, ethical, or legal backlash. (Not that this would have been bad for the show!)

With the onset of the cold and flu season in New York City, persistent coughing could be heard throughout the theater as the editor/author spoke. "Well," said Merv resolutely, "I hope they'll be able to cure some of these coughs here in our audience." The onslaught of coughs may have been the result of nervousness *and* boredom. Nevertheless, since cloning, test tube babies, bionics, and organ transplants have become realities as opposed to science fiction, Rosenfeld's less-than-stellar delivery is historically significant.

One of the most noteworthy bookings on *The Merv Griffin Show* occurred in October 1965. Trendsetting visual artist Andy Warhol was seen on Griffin's couch, but not heard. Warhol was a booking that Bob Shanks clearly remembers because it was one he hadn't supervised. "One of the staff came to me and said, 'He doesn't talk.' And I said, 'that's fine. Tell him he doesn't have to. We can work with that.' And so Andy came on the show and didn't say a word. But, of course, I had to warn Merv about it, so he would be able to play it that way and not get nervous or crazed." Shanks had encountered a similar problem several years earlier, during a Jack Paar taping in London. Peter Sellers had been scheduled to appear, and the actor claimed he had nothing to say. Shanks had him do the show anyway, sans dialogue. The silent bit "worked beautifully both times," recalls the producer.

Many important personalities were eager to chat with Griffin, especially if they had a product to promote. The producer and talent coordinators would always go the extra mile for certain Hollywood stars. Joan Crawford was one of them.

Crawford had done well for Merv's daytime show on NBC in 1963. Bob Shanks now wanted her on the new show.

In the late afternoon hours of November 9, 1965, Shanks hired a limo to transport the iconic movie queen from her Manhattan apartment to the Little Theatre.

He says, "I'd been courting her for a long time to come on, and finally, she agreed. Just as I reached her apartment building, the lights went out. And the men there, at first, thought it was just *that* building. So did I. And I thought, hell, I'll have to *walk* up. And I did—all 14 flights! Then we found out as we looked around, it was dark everywhere. Around 10:00 p.m. Joan began getting calls in, but I couldn't get a call out from her apartment. Finally, the phones began working before the lights came back on. I had let the limo driver downstairs go, because we obviously weren't going to make it back to the theater. And once I knew it was a universal blackout, I knew there would be no show. I said, 'I've got to phone my wife, Joan.' So, I did. And she said, 'Let me get on,' dramatist that she was. The two women had a nice conversation."

Shanks also got to converse with the veteran actress for several hours. "Of all the men in your life," Shanks said to Crawford as they waited for the lights to come back on, "Who was the best? Clark Gable?" It didn't take Crawford long to come up with an answer. "They didn't call him the *king* for nothing," she said.

Aside from bringing the eastern seaboard to a virtual halt, the blackout had another amazing effect: a marked increase in the birth rate nine months later!

On December 12, 1965 Griffin brought his entire staff and crew to his alma mater, the College of San Mateo, for a star-studded special edition. Videotaped in the college's spacious auditorium, the bill included Carol Channing, Phyllis Diller, Mahalia Jackson, artist Walter Keane and announcer Arthur Treacher. Sadly, no copies of this on-campus cavalcade are known to exist. This is truly unfortunate, since people who saw this entry remember it as an exceptionally fast-paced show, with lively musical performances by Channing and Jackson, and a memorable stand-up routine by Diller. The culmination, however, was an appearance by San Mateo Chamber president William Burkdall, who bestowed an "honorary citizenship" award on Merv at the end of the program.

"After the taping, we all went to a party at the home of Walter Keane," recalls Albert Fisher. "He was the famed artist who painted all those kids and animals with big eyes." He had also been a guest on the San Mateo episode.

"Phyllis was there with her husband and had gotten into a big argument with Keane's wife and stormed out. Years later, Keane's wife claimed to have been the actual artist of her husband's iconic works," says Fisher.

Fisher would work with Diller many times, on various shows, over the years. "She was a class act," he says, "both on screen and off."

With 1965 nearing its end, it was time for *The Merv Griffin Show* to celebrate Christmas. Bob Shanks got Treacher to don a Santa Claus outfit for the musical episode, which aired in most cities on December 25. The staff had put together a Christmas show on Merv's NBC series. Sadly, the master tape for that holiday extravaganza no longer exists. But its Westinghouse counterpart is still extant—and a joy to behold. Merv had a soft spot in his heart for the Yuletide season, and it shows in this entertaining hybrid of songs and personal reflections.

Treacher began the program thusly: "With a *ho, ho, ho,* and a *cheerio,* from the Little North Pole off Times Square, it's *The Merv Griffin Christmas Show!* We have a spirited cast for you!"

As he continued his announcement, a dusting of snowflakes trickled over his head. "You're in higher spirits than anyone, aren't you, Arthur?" observed Merv. "My dear little fellow," Treacher retorted, "will you please be quiet until I've introduced you?" "Well, you'd better hurry up," snapped Merv, "because I'm running out of snow." With that, the camera panned back to reveal Griffin holding a tray of prop flakes, which he began sprinkling with increased vigor. "Obviously, once more, Westinghouse has spared no expense," said Treacher, referring to the cheesy manner in which the "snow" was being dispensed. "We were lucky to get this," said Merv, "it's defrosting day at the refrigerator division!"

Aside from several brief interviews, most of the program was devoted to Christmas songs sung by a pre-*Brady Bunch* Florence Henderson, Barbara McNair, Jimmy Boyd ("I Saw Mommy Kissing Santa

Claus"), Earl Wrightson, and Griffin protégé Steve Perry ("Another Rainy Day"). Griffin and Henderson teamed up for a delightful rendition of "Winter Wonderland," and the entire assemblage offered a medley of popular carols. To wrap up the night, Merv showed a filmed segment featuring a department store Santa greeting a group of unenthusiastic toddlers; then he read a humorous (but poignant) list of wishes for the coming year. As charming as all the interludes were, it was Treacher who stole the show with his warmhearted renditions of "Santa Claus is Comin' to Town" and "Rudolph, the Red Nosed Reindeer."

8. IS THIS SHOW A HIT?

The Griffin show had become a mecca on Broadway. Mounds of publicity had been generated by the open auditions that the young comics and singers were flocking to each week. Locals, tourists, autograph hounds, and even the out-of-town muggers (according to Merv), were lining up at the Little Theatre to behold the daily galaxy of stars. The demand for tickets to *Merv Griffin* tapings had increased sharply. Those who were lucky enough to get seats usually went home with a favorable impression of what they'd seen. The show that some initially saw as a mere furrow on the Westinghouse brow had evolved into an unmitigated hit.

Unfortunately, none of this excitement was reflected in the all-important Nielsen ratings for New York City. From its debut in May 1965, to early January 1966, *Merv* had been floundering on WPIX-TV, Channel 11, owing to the fact that the station scheduled the show at 11:00 p.m., opposite the local newscasts on the other channels. Everyone connected with the program knew it *had* to be a hit in the nation's biggest market if it was to survive. On January 17, 1966, WPIX moved the Griffin show to the 10:00 p.m. slot, hoping for a bump in the ratings. It didn't happen. Once again, cancellation jitters were in the wind.

Griffin lamented his concerns to Al Krivin, an executive with Metromedia Television. Almost immediately, negotiations got under way to move *The Merv Griffin Show* over to New York's Metromedia station, WNEW-TV, Channel 5. A deal was consummated, and, on May 16, 1966, it was good-bye Channel 11, hello Channel 5.

Channel 5 put Griffin on at 11:*10* p.m., immediately after it's own 10-minute newscast. Wisely, the station also embarked on an effectively successful media campaign. "That deal effectively saved the show," says Albert Fisher. "And that's when it skyrocketed."

One night Merv decided to explore the balcony. "I've never been up there," he said, "not even in the daytime." Realizing that ordinary folks were often the funniest of all, Griffin had several tourists stand up and tell jokes. Unlike NBC's *The Tonight Show*, neither Griffin Productions nor Group W offered free dinners or prizes to the participants for their "performances." Nevertheless, a genuine sense of adulation became apparent as Griffin worked the aisle. One lady couldn't contain her enthusiasm. "We like you better than Johnny Carson!" she yelled. "That's not nice," snapped Merv, quickly distancing himself from the woman. "He's very good."

Indeed, Johnny was good, but interrelations between the Carson and Griffin camps were anything but. The two hosts didn't hate each other, but they weren't exactly buddies. Because both talk masters were based in New York, their respective staffers were engaged in a battle, not only for the top singers and actors, but also the red-hot comedians. The tense situation was reported in the *New York Daily News* on January 27, 1966. According to the periodical, Bob Shanks contended that NBC had pressured certain comedians—Jack E. Leonard, Myron Cohen, Milt Kamen, and Professor Irwin Corey—to stay off the Griffin show. In response, *Tonight Show* producer Art Stark said he was unaware of any such actions. "As far as putting the arm on anybody, that's just silly," said Stark. "Of course, if its publicity they want, that's another story."

Stark also said that since Griffin's show followed Carson's in some markets, it made sense *not* to book the same guests on the same night. Stark did admit, however, that he'd warned certain performers they might not get on *Tonight*—*if* their appearance risked an overlap with Griffin. "Otherwise, I don't care," he said.

Some showbiz insiders believed an unwritten law existed at the *Tonight Show*: if you score big on Carson, you must remain loyal to Carson and not go on Griffin—even if you got your start with Griffin.

Not long after this story surfaced, *New York Sunday News* columnist Ben Gross asked Griffin if his show and Carson's were in competition, and if he, Griffin, wouldn't book guests who appear on the *Tonight Show*. "That's not so at all," said Griffin, "although we definitely are in competition. Besides, in addition to long established names, we have offered talent who are our own discoveries, as far as TV goes."

When it came to singers, Griffin could have named a cluster of protégés: Aliza Kashi, Bruce Scott, Jaye Kennedy, Eloise Laws, Gilbert Price, Ronnie Dyson, Steve Perry, Emily Yancy and Julie Budd.

Griffin also regarded Richard Pryor, George Carlin, actor Reni Santoni, and comic/actor Sandy Baron among the major talents he heavily promoted. "Regardless of their reputations, they work for scale, only $265 a show," Griffin told Gross. "But despite this, even the biggest stars love to appear. We telecast from the Little Theatre and often such names as Beatrice Lillie, who have been dining at nearby Sardi's, will actually come on and visit us completely unannounced."

Beatrice Lillie's "unannounced" visit to Griffin's couch was the result of a last-minute cancellation. Bob Shanks had to come up with a suitable substitute—*pronto*. "I remember going next door to Sardi's, and there was Bea Lillie having dinner with somebody," Shanks recalls. "She was a British star who was doing a one-woman show on Broadway. I told the headwaiter that I had to talk to her. So I went over to her table and said, 'Bea, I need you next door on the Griffin show—*now!*' She said, 'I can't. I'm having dinner.' I assured her that I'd pick up her tab for *that* dinner, and pay for another one after the show. So she came over, did the show, and was absolutely wonderful. And then, she went back to Sardi's and had dinner!"

No one on Griffin's staff had to beg or barter for big-name stars when the show presented the Annual 44th *Photoplay* Awards. This special edition of the show, seen on March 9, 1966, included an appearance by Photoplay publisher Frederick A. Klein, and would mark the beginning of a black-tie tradition on the Griffin show. (In 1963, the prestigious awards were presented on *The Tonight Show*.)

There was a considerable amount of raucous ad-libbing from the comedy team of Marty Allen and Steve Rossi, which turned out to be a blessing since the evening would see its share of flubs.

Robert Vaughn, then starring on NBC's *The Man from U.N.C.L.E.*, was on hand to receive the "Best Actor of the Year Award." That's when the first *faux pas* occurred. Merv asked Vaughn about his "co-star," J. Carrol Naish. Obviously taken aback, Vaughn said, "I don't know him." Vaughn then mentioned that his co-star was Leo G.

Carroll. Merv quickly recovered from this minor mistake with his typical *élan*.

Next, Patricia Morrow and Christopher Connelly (*Peyton Place*) were introduced as the "Most Promising New Actors." Connelly, then 24, already had his trademark raspy voice and was obviously nervous; he kept whispering his responses into the desk microphone.

Joan Crawford made a splashy appearance to accept the award for the ailing Dorothy Malone (also featured on *Peyton Place*). Marty Allen pretended to faint at Crawford's feet. She loved it. Crawford said that the last time she'd been scheduled to appear, the Eastern Seaboard blackout thwarted her plans. She also recalled, with unabashed pride, how Bob Shanks dutifully climbed 14 flights of stairs that night to inform her that the taping had been canceled!

After reading a message from Malone, Crawford did her obligatory public relations bit for Pepsi-Cola. Arthur Treacher brought out a champagne bucket on a silver tray, which held a large bottle of the popular soft drink—and a single glass. As each guest sampled the product from the same glass, Merv said, "I'm sorry we don't have enough glasses to go around, but this is awfully expensive stuff." With that, Crawford clutched the bottle, took an enormous swig, and garnered the biggest laugh of the evening. Playing the good butler to the hilt, Treacher escorted the veteran star down the aisle and out of the theater.

Next up was John Wayne, recipient of the Gold Medal award. In accepting the award, Wayne said he felt relieved. "When I first heard about this, I thought they said *Playboy* magazine," said Wayne. "And I don't pose that way!"

Wayne talked about his earliest visits to Manhattan as a young man. Then Merv, in yet another gaffe, did his best to steer the conversation toward politics, knowing that Wayne and Vaughn were "on opposite sides of the fence." When that effort failed to produce sparks, Merv began talking about Ronald Reagan, who was then running for governor of California. He asked Wayne: "Are you getting ready to run for something?" To which Wayne replied: "Outta here!"

Wayne and Griffin both assumed the segment was over. Wayne walked up the aisle, making a hasty, but gracious, exit. After the commercial break, Merv said: "This kind of show is a very strange, because it is not scripted and very strange things happen at times. But when John Wayne was sitting here, he suddenly indicated to me, which you can spot immediately, that he'd accepted his award, thanked *Photoplay*, and us, for a very pleasant evening. I thought that he had to go, and I said goodnight. And somebody tells me he's still standing backstage. I'm gonna get him back out here." Wayne returned to the guest chair, with a drink in his hand. It would have been better to let Wayne's spot end the way it originally did. After relating a few uninteresting anecdotes, it was clear that the actor only had enough chat in him for one segment. At the next commercial break, the panel lapsed into total silence, something very unusual on the Griffin show. The heavily edited version of this episode that has aired on cable TV does not contain Wayne's "comeback" segment—and it's just as well.

Actress Peggy Wood was the final guest, accepting an award for *The Sound of Music* (1965) as Best Picture. Not since Peter O'Toole's appearance in 1963 did Merv experience such an awkward exchange. Wood had to correct him twice as they talked about the various aspects of her career. Merv asked the actress if she wanted to redo her entrance so they could start all over. In response, Wood recalled a rather "inept" interviewer she had once encountered. "He was just as unprepared as you are," she told the stunned host, who concealed his embarrassment with that "Ooops, what-have-I-done?" expression.

Merv thought it was a good time to show a clip from *The Sound of Music*, enthusing about what a "wonderful" movie it is. One again, Wood managed to trip up her host by getting him to admit that he actually hadn't seen the picture. It was one of the very few times in which Merv could have used some guidance as he began to introduce a scene from the movie. Just when it appeared as though things couldn't get worse, the clip that had been selected didn't feature Ms. Wood! The moment wasn't lost on Marty Allen, who suggested that Wood return someday with *another* clip. To which Wood sarcastically replied: "And by then he [Merv] will have seen the rest of it!"

There were plenty of laughs on the *Photoplay* Awards show of 1966. Unfortunately, too many of them were unintentional.

In 1966, George Carlin was still the clean-cut, ostensibly conservative master of stand-up comedy. Though his career was in full swing, Carlin found that he couldn't get booked on *The Tonight Show* because of an exclusivity provision in his contract with Anthony Productions, one of Griffin's ancillary companies.

On June 14, 1966, Carlin filed an arbitration suit against Anthony, claiming that his contract with the company precluded him from appearing on the Carson show.

The syndicated Griffin show had been a vital source of exposure for Carlin. But like all comics, Carlin knew that *The Tonight Show* was *the* venue that could catapult him to the top.

The problem stemmed back to 1965. Carlin's reps had entered into a negotiation phase, during which the comedian would perform on the Griffin show, and other programs to be developed by Anthony Productions. According to Carlin, he had rejected the "exclusivity" provisions in the agreement with Anthony. To prove his case, he cited the numerous shows he'd appeared on during the negotiations: *The Mike Douglas Show, The Hollywood Palace, Kraft Summer Music Hall*, and others.

However, when the time came for a *Tonight Show* appearance on June 1, Griffin's people notified NBC that Carlin was "exclusively" theirs. Carlin, of course, disputed the claim, and sought $350,000 in damages.

In his arbitration pleadings, Carlin demanded that Anthony Productions "cease and desist" in interfering with his career; provide a written declaration stating that he was never under contract to Anthony, and that NBC and other producers be notified accordingly. Another demand required Anthony to publish a notice in trade papers acknowledging Carlin as a free agent.

In addition to counsel for both parties, an attorney from the American Arbitration Association participated in the dispute, with the American Federation of Television and Radio Artists ("AFTRA") acting as "ex officio" party as well.

The dispute was settled before any proceedings got started. On June 23, *Variety* reported the disposition of the case: "George Carlin, Merv Griffin Settle Tiff Sans Arbitration."

According to the settlement terms, Anthony had to notify NBC that Carlin could accept any job in television. As a result, Carlin was immediately slated for a *Tonight Show* appearance on June 29. The outcome of the $350,000 demand for damages was not made public. It was also reported that the Carson and Griffin shows paid union scale. With agent's commissions factored in, NBC paid $320 while Griffin's show paid $265.

Four years would pass before George Carlin would be invited back to *The Merv Griffin Show*, proving once again that old wounds heal, and that business sense takes priority over personal reactions.

During its brief life on NBC, the *The Merv Griffin Show* had tackled a few topics ultimately deemed "too sophisticated" for daytime audiences. That was in 1962. By the mid-sixties, the issues that would define the decade were plastered on the front pages of newspapers and blared over the daily TV and radio newscasts. In the wake of the civil rights struggle, the women's movement, and mounting opposition to the war in Vietnam, the "counter culture" revolution was fully in the wind. Students were dropping out of school. Young men were burning their draft cards, and young women were burning their bras. Both sexes were experimenting with drugs, LSD included, as a form of self-expression and escape. These topics demanded exploration and analysis. One of the more provocative voices that would accomplish this was Mort Sahl.

Known for his wickedly funny, satirical take on the political scene, Sahl had been performing in nightclubs since the 1950s. A brilliant iconoclast, Sahl poked fun at many "sacred cows" with the hope of effecting a change for the better. A familiar face on the talk-show circuit, Sahl would make periodic visits to every incarnation of the Griffin show. On the July 18, 1966 edition, Sahl said, "In Los Angeles, in addition to political candidates, we have strange pressure groups, and we had a hearing on fluoridation of the water in Los Angeles, attended mostly by little old ladies in tennis shoes, and a woman got up and said, 'I don't want fluoridation of my water, and not only that, I have it on good authority that the Communists are going to put LSD in municipal water supplies!' And some kid stood up in the back of the auditorium and said, *"Promises! Promises!"*

Dr. Timothy Leary appeared on the Griffin show at a time when America's attitude towards drug use was still influenced by the reasoning of the 1950s. Leary was not a medical doctor, but rather a clinical psychologist who had practiced as a psychotherapist, with years of research to his credit, in the treatment of mental illness.

In the summer of 1966, Leary was still in the process of appealing a 30-year jail sentence he'd received for smuggling marijuana from Mexico. He told Griffin that he'd begun experimenting with LSD some six years earlier. He said he'd "come to the sorry conclusion" that psychology wasn't doing much to solve the emotional or mental problems of the human race. It was an anthropologist friend that had informed Leary about certain "sacred mushrooms" that grew in the mountains near Mexico City. The anthropologist gave Leary a sampling, and he consumed seven of them. Leary said he had learned more about psychology, the human mind, and "the human situation" in the five hours *after* having ingested the mushrooms.

Leary boasted that, "more and more young people, college students and graduate students, are using psychedelic drugs."

Normally unfazed by the most outrageous remarks, Merv shot Leary a surprised look. "Why, doctor?" he asked indignantly. Leary said that "creative and adventurous people" had been using these plants and drugs for thousands of years. "LSD is nothing new," Leary declared. "Wise men, medicine men, shamans, and philosophers have been using drugs which open up the mind for thousands of years."

Leary said that 15 to 20 percent of young people were using the drug to explore their consciousness, "trying to find out more about their mind using these chemicals."

"But aren't the majority of them doing it for kicks?" asked Merv. Leary paused for a moment. "I don't think so," he said. "The pleasure you get from LSD is being tuned in. You're turned on to your own nervous system. You're turned on to your own body. You're turned on the incredible wisdom that lies inside every cell in your body. It's the ecstasy that a scientist gets when he suddenly has something to open up to."

Merv listened politely, but quickly cited a case in which a boy thought he could fly and attempted to jump out a window. Merv argued, "It doesn't work because it doesn't have the same effect on every human being." On that point, Leary agreed, admitting that there were "deep philosophical questions" that needed to be asked before using the drug.

"Then shouldn't it be done under the care of a doctor?" asked Merv. Leary said no, explaining that LSD was not a drug, like penicillin for instance, that's used for the purpose of curing a medical illness. "LSD is an instrument," he argued, "like a microscope."

Time had run out, but Griffin wanted Leary to explore the topic further.

The following day, July 19, Leary picked up where he had left off. But now the panel also included talk-show host David Susskind (*Open End*).

Once again Leary stated, emphatically, that psychedelic drugs are not like heroin, or even alcohol. He regarded them as "instruments that expand consciousness, they speed up the mind." He advocated the use of the substance without medical supervision, claiming, "There's no evidence that psychedelic drugs affect the physiology of the brain."

Merv turned to Susskind. Leary had been a guest on Susskind's show, *Open End*, multiple times. "I have an absolute dichotomy about him," said Susskind. "As a man, I like him. As intelligence, I respect him. But I think his advocacy of this permissiveness with this drug, total freedom with this new and potentially fascinating and dangerous drug, is arrogant and irresponsible."

The audience applauded loudly. With that, Susskind turned to Leary and said, "I'm always worried when I have the crowd with me, Tim. I *must* be wrong!"

Nevertheless, Susskind continued: "Many doctors of great reputation, all over the country, have admitted at one and the same time that the drug has fascinating possibilities." He cited a few examples. In Canada, for instance, the drug had proven to be a cure for alcoholism. And in Boston, habitual criminals had been given LSD over a period of time and the rate of recidivism dropped to almost nothing. "But those were carefully superintended scientific experiments," Susskind cautioned. "It is a drug with dangers and possibilities we are only beginning to sense and I think it would wrong, criminal, and irresponsible, for people to have access to this drug, to be encouraged to use it, to take flights into fantasy."

The segment was one of rare instances in which a guest, Susskind, seemingly took over the show in Merv's presence. When Leary had had enough, he barked at Susskind: "You don't know what you're talking about. You've never even *taken* LSD!"

Time had run out. At the close of the episode, Griffin said he was obligated, in accordance with FCC regulations, to provide a qualified expert with an opposing viewpoint regarding the use of LSD.

The next day, July 20, brought Dr. Henry Brill to Griffin's panel. "We've invited the foremost expert in psychiatric drug therapy in the New York area to come on the show and talk about the uses and abuses of LSD," said Griffin. He began by asking Brill if the drug was dangerous. "I think it's decidedly dangerous," said Brill. "The free and general use of LSD means that people would regulate their own dosage, the frequency of the dosage, and it's been thoroughly demonstrated that this is a highly dangerous procedure. It can produce acute psychotic states; it can produce long-term psychosis, and conduct disorders. Even if LSD, eventually, were to be demonstrated as a good treatment, it still would have to be in skilled medical hands."

Brill said the drug had been under "experimental examination" for a long time. "There are some indications that are favorable, but there are many that are *unfavorable*."

There had been wide speculation that the drug could cure alcoholism. Brill pointed out that alcoholics could be cured with and without LSD. He said most of the cases he'd observed had been conducted within a clinical setting wherein some of the patients had experienced a good deal of anxiety. "I'd say that most of the people I've seen did not want to have it again."

As the subject drew to a close, Brill said there were "well established cases" in which people had actually developed mental illness from the use of LSD. He said that after more than 20 years of clinical experimentation, the drug "still remains one of the doubtful ones." According to Brill's observations, experts with vast experience in the field were still very doubtful as to whether the drug had a proven therapeutic effect, in spite of a tremendous amount of work that had been done. If ever there was an example of the Griffin show's diverseness, the July 20 episode was it.

Prior to Brill's interview, buxom actress Jayne Mansfield had dominated the stage with four of her five kids (including toddler Mariska Hargitay, future star of *Law & Order, Special Victims Unit*), her husband Matt Cimber, and their four rambunctious dogs. "Welcome to the Griffin kennel," quipped Henny Youngman. Pandemonium erupted several times during the taping, as the out-of-control canines snapped at everyone on the panel, including the kids. Commotion notwithstanding, Mansfield calmly sang "Diamonds Are a Girl's Best Friend." And she danced, the frug (pronounced "froog"), epitomizing yet another craze of the decade.

A former Playboy Playmate, Mansfield had achieved success in the 1955 Broadway production of *Will Success Spoil Rock Hunter?*, as well as the 1957 film adaptation. Though Mansfield's screen career was short-lived, her sultry performances in films like *The Girl Can't Help It* (1956), *The Wayward Bus* (1957), and *Too Hot to Handle* (1960) ensured her reputation as Hollywood's blonde bombshell of the era, second in popularity only to Marilyn Monroe. And like Monroe, Mansfield would die tragically.

On June 29, 1967, the actress was killed in a car crash after a performance in Orleans Park, Louisiana. Three of Mansfield's children were in the back seat of the vehicle at the time of the accident. Fortunately, the children survived, though they sustained injuries.

The Mansfield appearance remains an enduring legacy of the Westinghouse *Merv Griffin Show*, and is included in its DVD collection.

Many of Merv's 1966 entries would mix sophistication with spasmodic silliness. More and more offbeat personalities, booked strictly for laughs, were making their way to the Griffin stage. Brother Theodore, the German-American monologist and comedian, was one of several guests falling into this category. Theodore's shtick consisted of dispensing a series of meaningless ramblings in a menacing baritone. Theodore, who would later appear on David Letterman's show, described his act as "stand up tragedy."

Rip Taylor, the wonderfully flamboyant actor/comedian known as the King of Confetti (he sprinkled himself and everything around him with the stuff), would enliven the program many times through the years.

There was also Professor Irwin Corey, an underrated comic genius by any standard. With a pair of worn sneakers and unkempt hair, which contrasted with his formal attire, "The World's Foremost Authority" would wander on stage and deliver a monologue in polysyllabic language that made no sense. He used big words haphazardly. Though Corey's appearances were well received, he was usually seen at the program's end. Griffin would joke that Corey would be on last so they could roll the credits over him!

Perhaps the wildest of all was Broadway and Hollywood actor David Burns (*Hello, Dolly!*). Burns never failed to show up in an outlandish costume (e.g., a suit of armor), bearing one or more bizarre props. One night, he came on dressed in a Confederate Army uniform, armed with an old-fashioned Flit bug-spraying device. Suddenly, and without warning, he began tossing rubber chickens all over the place. Soon, there were chickens everywhere, behind the couch, on the desk, in the orchestra, and in the audience. Burns said he was setting the stage for a friend who, according to his laconic description, was in the fried chicken business. A moment later, the camera focused on Colonel Harlan Sanders, of Kentucky Fried Chicken fame, sitting in the middle of the audience. Someone in the balcony threw one of the bogus birds on the stage. "Don't do that!" snapped Merv, obviously baffled and annoyed.

No one, including Merv, seemed to know who Colonel Sanders was. Yet everyone in the theater was clearly enjoying the free samples of fried chicken Sanders had provided. Several folks were caught on camera licking their fingers, a testament to the "finger-lickin' good" slogan for which Sanders became world famous. "What's happening to my show?" Merv moaned as the unrestrained antics continued.

Things also spiraled out of control during the taping on August 1. The guest lineup included Jerry Lewis, Richard Pryor, Dagmar, the Everly Brothers, and comedian Charlie Callas.

The second half of the program evolved into an ad-lib fest, commencing with Lewis' Q&A session with the studio audience. "When do you plan to retire?" asked an elderly man in the balcony. "When it takes me as long to stand up as it took you," Lewis shot back.

Since childhood, Richard Pryor had been in awe of Jerry Lewis, referring to him as "the God of comedy." With that, Lewis placed his hand on Merv's head, in mock anointment. "Am I Jewish now?" asked Merv. "One more little job and you're in," said Lewis. The in-house audience cracked up at Lewis's obvious reference to circumcision, and so did the host.

Later, the voluptuous Dagmar took a seat next to Pryor, who began sweating profusely. Realizing that Pryor was "feeling the heat," Merv cooled him off with a glass of water, which he poured over the comedian's head. Within seconds, Lewis, Griffin and Pryor were spitting water all over each other, but with remarkable precision so as not to douse the other guests.

Water can trigger undesired responses in people. Griffin looked over at Lewis, whose hands were suspiciously hidden under the desk. "Whatever I'm doing," the comedian told Merv, "you won't see it."

Dagmar had been expected to sing. But as she belted out "Teach Me Tonight," the trio kept up the water works, completely upstaging her performance. The last guest of the night was comedian Charlie Callas. Fortunately, his act was brilliant enough to live up to, if not outshine, the zaniness that preceded him.

"Is this show a hit?" asked comedian Jack E. Leonard on a 1966 telecast. "*Big* hit!" Merv answered, his eyes twinkling. Not only was the show performing well, it was actually winning its time slot in several key markets.

"It's 90 minutes of verve with Merv," declared one Chicago affiliate in its ad campaign. With its longer format, the show could book extensively, offering as many as eight guests per episode. It was usually an eclectic mix. Shanks equates the booking of a talk show to planning a party. "You want to put people together who might enjoy meeting each other, but seldom get a chance to," says the producer. "And they may hate each other on sight, which creates sparks and can make for a terrific evening. We had that especially in the daytime because there was no interference and it was pure art."

Thus, it wasn't uncommon to see the demure English ballerina Dame Margot Fonteyn sitting next to Jack E. Leonard or Moms

Mabley. You might catch the ultra-square Henny Youngman ("Take my wife, *please!*") sharing the panel with the flamboyant singer/musician/personality Monti Rock, III. "Combinations like that drive me into sheer happiness," says Shanks.

Accurately described by *Vanity Fair* as one of the architects of the sixties, Monti Rock, III was born Joseph Montanez, Jr., to a Puerto Rican family in the Bronx, on May 29, 1942. He'd first gained national attention as a celebrity hairdresser in New York, a gig that would land him on Carson's *Tonight Show*.

More than a half-century later, Rock vividly recalls his on-air escapades with Griffin and Carson. "Johnny was the greatest straight man I ever worked with," says Rock. "I would do a joke and he would get it. He just *knew*, and he understood it because he created the phenomenon that he had become." Rock, who made his *Tonight Show* debut in 1963, would chalk up an additional 83 appearances with Carson, which would span into the 1980s.

Rock got his first shot on the Griffin show in 1966. "On Merv's show, I played it dumb. If you look at the tapes, I'm *always* playing it dumb. Like, why am I here? It was a reality show, without reality. Reality was taking one martini, and I'd have six minutes. It was like vaudeville."

As an interviewer, Rock says Griffin could be a bit "condescending" at times. "Merv was the master of how to make money through his brilliance and knowledge of television," says Rock. "His genius was in the spin-offs. Look at the wealth of shows he created."

Rock credits Arthur Treacher for getting him booked on Griffin. "I loved Arthur," says Rock. "He and his wife Virginia just absolutely got it. He was definitely a character, but an honest one. Merv, Arthur, and Bob Shanks used to hang out at Sardi's. I would be sitting there too, with my mink coats and little dogs. I was like the male Zsa Zsa Gabor. Arthur had seen me at Sardi's first, and thought I'd be good on the Griffin show. I'd already done the Carson show, and they thought I was a one-time wonder. Then Johnny suspended me. And when Johnny suspended you, they wouldn't call you back. Everybody wanted to be on the Carson show, and I wanted to be *off* it. So Griffin got me. Arthur kind of adored me because he knew I was trying to have a film career."

It's ironic that one of Rock's most distinct reminiscences involves Treacher. The Westinghouse execs had initially been dismissive of Treacher for, among other things, being too old to click with the "hip" generation. Yet it was the seventy-something sidekick who envisioned a marketable potential in the twenty-something performer. Rock would go on to become one of the giants of '70s disco. His 1975 album, *Disco Tex and His Sex-O-Lettes*, sold millions of copies. Rock would also appear in several movies. He played a DJ in *Saturday Night Fever* (1977), and turned up in *Sgt. Pepper's Lonely Hearts Club Band* (1978), in addition to roles in a handful of Broadway shows.

"The talk show thing had been kind of a career for me," says Rock, who attributes much of his Griffin-related success to Bob Shanks. "Bob had this great sense of a producer, and a way of bringing you back, and knowing what was good for the show. In this business, certain people will have empathy for you. Bob Shanks was one of them. I did Joey Bishop's show, and Mike Douglas's. And I made myself, Monti Rock, into a business. I made hit records and movies. But I didn't understand the power of television back then. 'They'd ask, what are you famous for?' And I'd say, 'I'm famous for being famous.' But I eventually got tired of being a talk-show guy."

Rock has reinvented himself multiple times over the years. He has attained iconic status in Las Vegas, where he is still entertaining audiences. Drawing from his experiences with the talkers of yore, Rock has advice for anyone who thinks they'd be a "natural" on any of today's mouth marathons.

"On a talk show, you're there to entertain, to be reality," says Rock. "You must learn to embellish, to be entertaining, to be vaudeville. You have to have the audience relate to you in some way. And they *have* to like you. The key words are *personality* and *fascinating*. You have to be fascinating, or at least interesting. And if you can't be, then you should stay off television."

In 1966, Griffin Productions was packaging more than 12 hours of programming each week. In addition to *The Merv Griffin Show*, the company also produced *Jeopardy!* and, as of September 27, 1965, the new quizzer called *Let's Play Post Office*. Created by Louise Adamo, and hosted by the genial Bill Wendell, *Post Office* required its contestants to identify a famous person based on a fictitious letter he or she might have written. Despite having the (by now) well-established *Jeopardy!* as its lead-in, *Let's Play Post Office* failed in the ratings and was quietly dumped by NBC on July 1, 1966.

Whether you work in front of the camera or behind it, success in television can be as overwhelming as failure. The typical workday for production people on a talk show begins long before airtime, and ends long after the studio has gone dark. Everyone on the team settles into a planned routine. At *The Merv Griffin Show*, the producer's day would officially begin at 10:00 a.m. Bob Shanks would be in his office conferring with the associate producer (Tom O'Malley, later replaced by Bob Murphy), the talent coordinators (Larry Holofcener, Jean Meegan, Tony Garofalo), the publicist (Al Fisher), and the production assistant (Corky Wylde). The purpose of this meeting was to discuss who was available, and who had dropped out, etc. These "booking meetings" were something of a butual assessment of talent—who was great, who came off as boring, who looked promising, and so forth.

Shanks would then meet with the writers to review the notes to be used for each guest. Possible jokes and "ad-libs" for Merv to use in his opening monologue would be discussed and evaluated. This meeting was followed by lunch, which was hardly a leisurely interlude. Lunch consisted of business meetings with agents, public relations people, and talent. Shanks would later check in with the production crew (the director, assistant director, and technical director), attend to phone calls, the mail, auditions, and last-minute rehearsals. By 5:00 p.m., Shanks would again meet with the talent coordinators—this time with Merv—for a "run-down" on that night's taping, and to discuss any last-minute changes or problems. The producer would have one final pre-show meeting with the star at 6:00 p.m. At 6:30 p.m., Merv would be on stage. By 8:00 p.m., the show was over, but not the working day. There would always be a post-show discussion as to what had worked and what didn't. There was also a meeting with the censor. Occasionally it would be necessary to bleep any unacceptable language or references (including unauthorized "plugs") from the audio track.

"When the show was over," says Fisher, "Merv never fraternized with any of the guests. Nor did he do that before the show. He wanted things to be spontaneous." Fisher recalls that after the cameras shut down, Griffin would leave the stage, take the elevator to the third floor, get out of make-up and into the street clothes. "And within 30 minutes of the end of taping, he'd be on his way home," recalls Fisher. "Bob Shanks would stay in the office long after the show was over, but Merv had a chauffeur waiting to drive him to his apartment at Central Park West."

Merv and Bob Shanks both lived in the same apartment building. "Bob and his wife Ann got us the apartment," recalls Julann, "because we had been living on the East Side. It was wonderful living at Central Park West. And there were some great people living in that building, famous and non-famous."

There were times when Griffin couldn't go home immediately after the taping. Such was the case when Marlon Brando appeared on the program. The iconic star of such films as *A Streetcar Named Desire* (1951) and *On the Waterfront* (1954) was not known to make appearances on the talk-show scene. "But," says Fisher, "Merv and Brando had been roommates back in the fifties. So he came on and did a good interview with Merv. Afterward, Bob Shanks, Merv, and I took Brando out on the town, and got royally drunk with him. We started out at Sardi's and then made our way up and down Eighth Avenue." One can only imagine the looks on the faces of pedestrians who caught a glimpse of that quartet in such a state of inebriated bliss!

Though Merv didn't usually socialize with guests, he did encourage a sense of camaraderie among those who worked for him. Like many other productions based in New York City, *The Merv Griffin Show* had its own baseball team, a component of the Broadway Show League. "Every guy on the staff played," recalls Fisher. "Arthur Treacher was our bat boy and cheered us from the bleachers. Merv and Bob Shanks would pitch. We played two or three seasons, as I recall, but we rarely won a game. It was great fun, though. I still have my team shirt. I've kept it all these years, even though it no longer fits me."

9. ODDBALLS AND HEAVYWEIGHTS

One of the more significant, but seldom acknowledged, bookings on Merv's Westinghouse series was Herbert Khaury, known professionally as Tiny Tim. "Tony Garofalo would walk over to 42nd Street, where Tiny was working in front of Ripley's Believe It or Not," recalls Albert Fisher. "Tiny would be right on the sidewalk, strumming his ukulele, and singing songs from years gone by. We could literally grab him, bring him over to the show, and put him on immediately. You didn't have to prep him or anything. He was what he was. The allure of Tiny wasn't because he was a novelty act; it was because he was so bizarrely naïve. He addressed everybody as 'Miss' or 'Mister' and was terribly embarrassed if anyone ever mentioned words like 'penis' or 'breast.'"

Plucked out of obscurity and thrust into the national spotlight, Tiny Tim made his debut on the Griffin show in 1967. Unfortunately, the long-haired, hook-nosed falsetto failed to click with Merv or the audience. "Merv just didn't know what to make of him," says Fisher.

Carson's people became aware of Tiny through his successful appearances on NBC's *Rowan & Martin's Laugh-In*. "And, of course, when Johnny put him on," says Fisher, "and staged his wedding on *The Tonight Show*, it became, and still is, one of the highest rated shows. Not just in late night, but one of the highest rated shows, period."

An offbeat personality who *did* click sat in the front row in the studio as opposed to the guest panel. Diminutive and elderly, Lillian Dorothy Miller, known as Miss Miller (even though she was alternately referred to as "Mrs." Miller, despite the fact that she was never married), was a typist of the U.S. Army quartermaster in Philadelphia. Off duty, she had achieved a degree of celebrity by attending the tapings of numerous television programs. Her earliest appearances were on Jack Paar's *Tonight Show* in the late '50s. Miller was following the footsteps of Mrs. Sterling, an elderly woman who sat in the audience during Steve Allen's tenure on *Tonight!*

Far more interactive on camera than Sterling had been, Miller would come to be known as "the famous audience." Paar was keenly aware that Miller liked the attention and "giveaways" from the show. One night he decided to needle her a bit. "Tell me," he said smugly, "why do you come here every night?" The old woman looked up and said, "Because I'm lonely, Mr. Paar." No one laughed. "That response not only stopped Paar, it stopped everything—cold," recalls Bob Shanks.

Miller would attend *Tonight Show* tapings well into the Carson era. When she became a regular fixture at Merv's theatre, Bob Shanks dubbed her "the Golda Meir of studio audiences." Like Jack Paar before him, Merv would bounce wisecracks off Miller, occasionally at her expense. Occasionally, a guest on the panel would acknowledge her presence as well. Merv would roll his eyes, knowing that a long-winded response was sure to follow. Oftentimes, Merv cut her off. "That's four lines you've spoken, Miss Miller," he'd warn in half jest. "One more and we'll have to pay you!"

Miller's most memorable participation on the Westinghouse Griffin show involved the Tony-winning producer, David Merrick (*Hello, Dolly!*). Merrick was known to be contentious, and his unpredictable rancor ensured numerous return visits to the program. One night, Merrick got into a snit with fellow guest Phil Foster about the competency of stage actors. Merrick grandly stormed off the set, only to return minutes later to aim more verbal fireworks at Foster. Then he stormed off again. It was one of those highly charged moments on which talk shows thrive. Merv loved it.

Merrick knew that Griffin's talents were uniquely suited to multiple facets of the entertainment business, including the Broadway stage. In September 1967, Merrick offered Griffin a role in the weekend matinée performances of his new play, *I Do! I Do!* Griffin was flattered, but the rigors of hosting five, live-on-tape programs per week compelled him to decline. Unlike his actors, Merrick wasn't used to rejection. Viscerally offended, he swore off *The Merv Griffin Show* forever. There was talk around Broadway that Merrick's actors weren't allowed to appear on the program either.

Merrick was known for his outrageous publicity stunts. Bob Shanks recalls how the producer would locate people with the exact same names as prominent theater critics in New York, like Clive Barnes. "He would bring these people in to see one of his shows, and then write wonderful blurbs of what the *critics* had said," recalls Shanks. "So, we decided to have Mrs. Miller do this for us."

If Miller had aspirations of moving up a notch on the talk-show totem, they would be realized the day she became the official theater critic for *The Merv Griffin Show*. She would be given free tickets to various Broadway shows, and would then be required to critique each production she'd seen. Not by coincidence, Miller's first assignment was Merrick's *Keep It in the Family*, a play that had been panned unmercifully in its out-of-town previews. Griffin expected Miller to concur with the pros. "But the problem was that Miss Miller liked everything," says Albert Fisher. "There wasn't anything she *didn't* like. If she had seen a garbage truck unloading, she would have liked that, too."

Everyone stood by with bated breath to hear Miller's verdict on *Keep It in the Family*. "It was one of the loveliest I've ever seen," Miller said sweetly. "Needless to say," Fisher recalls, "the whole joke backfired."

Despite the unexpected thumbs-up from Miller, Merrick remained furious. "I had to take him to lunch to calm him down," remembers Bob Shanks. After this unforgettable incident, Merrick and Griffin were never the same toward each other. Merv was better off not having worked in *Keep It in the Family*. The play fizzled out within a week of its opening.

By mid-1967, Griffin could boast that his show was pulling in a 65 share in Detroit, where it aired at 9:00 a.m. The show was also an early morning hit in Miami, where residents could kick off the day with Merv before heading out in the leisurely resort town. In other markets—Los Angeles, Indianapolis, and Toronto—Griffin was pulling in respectable ratings in prime time. The show seemed to be doing its briskest business in cities where it aired at 4:30 p.m., like Philadelphia.

Only in four markets, one of which was New York, was Griffin pitted against Carson in the coveted late-night slot. Then, in

June 1967, Merv's flagship station, WNEW-TV, announced that it would be moving the Griffin show from late night to the 8:30–10:00 p.m. time slot. Station VP Mel Bailey announced that the program had reached "a new peak in popularity," and was therefore deserving of "prime time exposure when even more people will be able to enjoy it." It was a wise move. In 1967, some 1,995,000 sets were in use during the 11:30 p.m. time slot; at 8:30 p.m., that number was a far more impressive 3,698,000.

Merv's NBC series had offered a mingling of showbiz and literary giants. At Westinghouse, another element would be added to the blend: the political "heavyweight."

One such personage was Dr. Martin Luther King, Jr., who paid a visit to the Griffin stage in July 1967. King's appearance occurred while the series was still being videotaped in black-and-white. Looking at the tape today, the dimly lit set (courtesy of lighting director Dave Clark) and intermittent cigarette smoke evoke memories of the old Mike Wallace interview series, *Night Beat*.

The Atlanta-born King relaxed in a swivel chair at center stage, sandwiched between Merv and actor/activist Harry Belafonte. "Merv had always wanted Dr. King on the show," recalls Albert Fisher. "He and Bob Shanks had been working a long time to get him to agree to come on. The appearance really came about because of Harry Belafonte, who had been close friends with Merv when he first moved to New York in the 1950s. And, of course, Belafonte had been very close to Dr. King, so he was the only other guest to participate in the interview."

All through the sixties, violent demonstrations and riots were an all-too-familiar occurrence in American cities. "In Chicago, some of the blame was put on you," Griffin told King. "And still, you have never advocated violence. I know now you are absolutely against it. Why do they blame you?"

King said the blame was due to a wrong analysis of events, history and circumstances. "It so happens that many demonstrations that I lead end up in violence, in the sense that we, who are demonstrating, are *inflicted* with violence," said King. "And I always say that you can't blame non-violent demonstrators, who are demonstrating for their constitutional rights, when violence erupts." Blaming the non-violent demonstrators would be like blaming the robbed man for the evil act of robbery because his wealth had precipitated the act, King said.

King expounded on other current events: The resultant progress of the civil rights movement, and how the black community had been affected by it; how segregation was now a thing of the past; and the urgent need to deal effectively with the ongoing problem of poverty in American cities. King also commented that American involvement in Vietnam was unjust because it worked against the "self-determination of a people."

Many people connected with the Griffin show rate King's appearance as the most poignant in the history of the series. The King interview encompassed the last third of the 90-minute show. "We had a beautiful lunch with him prior to the taping," offers Bob Shanks. "The liquid in his eyes told you of the decency in the man."

According to Fisher, Merv was also profoundly impressed by King's eloquence. "There is a Spanish term that Merv would fre-quently use to distinguish a star from a superstar: *duende*. In this case, he used it to refer to the certain qualities in a man that are truly indefinable. And Merv believed that Dr. King had *duende*."

On April 4, 1968, at 6:01 p.m., shortly after tape had begun to roll at the Griffin show, King was shot and killed as he stood on the third-floor balcony of a Memphis motel. His interview at the Little Theatre would mark one of the high points of *The Merv Griffin Show*, and remain one of the most talked about (and frequently requested) segments of the series.

Shortly after the King interview, the Griffin show prepared to make the long-awaited switch from monochrome to color. Full color broadcasting, in network prime time, had begun at the start of the 1966–67 TV season. Even so, much daytime programming continued to be produced in black-and-white. With the upswing in color TV sales, coupled with surveys confirming that color shows generated higher ratings, virtually all-first run programming switched to color by late summer/early fall, 1967.

"That was one of the things where, as publicity promotion and PR director, I had to do a really big push on the fact that the show was going to color," says Albert Fisher. "It meant changing all our graphics, logos, and publicity materials that were supplied to the press and local stations. I still have the film we shot promoting the move to color. In one of the promos, a young couple is seen running down 44th Street, in the heart of Broadway, with multi-colored balloons in their hands. And they release all the balloons in front of the marquee of the Griffin show. There's a time in June when the sun goes down right in the middle of 44th Street, and we had filmed this promo just when that had happened. You saw a big yellow ball setting in the sky, with the young couple running in slow motion. The effect was stunning. And *I'm* the guy in the couple!"

The switch to color would result in another revision of the set. The basic pieces of furniture—Merv's chair, the "hot seat," and the couch—were retained. But the rust-colored fabric on the panel behind Merv's desk (which photographed gray in monochrome) was replaced with lightly textured strips of Japanese rice paper. The grayish panel behind the guest sofa was replaced with a series of multi-colored, honeycomb-like cells. To further accentuate the use of color, Merv began wearing shirts in bright shades of blue, yellow, and green.

On October 3, 1967, two months after the show began broadcasting in color, Senator Robert F. Kennedy sat behind the desk next to Merv.

Like the King interview, Kennedy's appearance would come to be regarded as an archival treasure. However, what viewers never knew was that the Bobby Kennedy interview (which Griffin would regard as his finest up to that time) almost didn't happen.

"I had a phone at my seat in the front row which would blink if I was needed," recalls Bob Shanks. "If the control room or backstage needed me, they could call. And the light began to blink while the show was going on. One of our bookers was Jean Meegan, who had been a wonderful AP journalist. But the call wasn't from Jean; it was from someone she told to call and inform me that Kennedy was at the theater, but was going to walk.

"Broadway theaters always have an aisle that goes from the front of the theater to the back, to the outside of the theater, primarily for fire purposes. And that's where Jean was, with Kennedy. And I said, 'Do whatever you can to keep him there, short of anything physical. Try to get people between him and the door to the street, just to make a little obstacle. And off I went. I met him in the aisle that went from the street to the backstage area. 'Hello, Senator,' I told him, 'we are delighted you're here.' And he said, 'Well, I'm leaving. I don't feel that I'm going to be good tonight.' He was cranky and felt that his hair looked bad.

"And I said, 'Bobby, you are here. You've got to do this. I'm going to pester you until you do it. And you know you're going to do it sooner or later. You meant to do the show or you wouldn't have gotten this close.' He said, 'I don't know.' Finally, I told him, 'Look, just to make it special, we've hired a terrific make-up man for you.' He kind of looked at me. And I said, 'It's the guy who did Nixon's make-up on your brother's first televised debate!' [On that broadcast, JFK's fresh-faced appearance scored points while Nixon's washed-out look was said to have cost him votes.] Bobby laughed. 'You bastard! Okay!' And he went to make-up and did the show."

Kennedy had been campaigning heavily in his bid to win the Democratic nomination for the presidency. Despite his "bad hair," he managed to reflect eloquently on the events that had marked the summer of 1967, a time of riots, and unprecedented contempt for authority via demonstrations, both peaceful and violent.

Kennedy said that while he couldn't speak in generalities, he expected the situation to grow "more critical." He said that ongoing violence in the world was at least partly responsible for some of the civil disobedience on the part of young people. Also, the fact that government had grown so large and "impersonal," made the individual feel like a "small cog" in a big machine.

"I think that for young people, the Peace Corps made a difference," said Kennedy. "Because then you can see your effort, compassion, intelligence changing the lives of people around the globe who desperately needed help. The civil rights movement of the early 1960s was that, also. But now, with the advent of 'black power,' many of those involved in civil rights movements, where one race turns against another, one part of the population turns against another part of the population, you don't know where you belong in all of it, what you can do, and what role you can play. It seems to me that that has a tremendous effect on our country."

He referred to the situation in Vietnam as "a difficult war—no matter whether one supports it or is opposed to it — it's difficult to explain and it doesn't have universal support." Merv asked if there would ever be a solution to the war. "I think that's very difficult," Kennedy said thoughtfully. "Obviously, if anybody has an easy solution, I'd think they'd come forward with it."

The senator also said it wasn't just the war that was causing young people to revolt. "We have to understand that with all of our promises and all of our statements," he explained, "that the life of the individual, the boy or girl or man and woman, living in the ghetto, now, in 1967, is worse that it was in 1960. The unemployment rate is greater, the housing is worse; the opportunity to obtain adequate or satisfactory education is less. Only two out of five Negro men in the ghetto have a job that pays more than $60 a week. Three out of 10 boys and girls who live in the ghetto get through the twelfth grade, and they have a 50/50 chance of having the equivalent of an eighth grade education.

"So we're turning all of these people out onto the streets, who are unequipped, untrained, unskilled, who can't find jobs, live in houses that are filled with rats, and are illegitimate themselves, or are from broken families."

As Kennedy spoke from the heart, Merv wanted to know what Kennedy's parents had said or taught that had resulted in the family's long-standing dedication to public service. The senator said his father had instilled in him and his brothers the philosophy that their family had been "extremely lucky." And since money wasn't a problem for them, the Kennedys had an obligation to repay the nation that had been so good to them. "We should continue to try, throughout our lives, in some way, to do something on behalf of those less well off than we were," he said.

Not long after Senator Kennedy's appearance, the staffers had scheduled the matriarch of the clan, Rose Kennedy, for a rare in-studio appearance. Bob Shanks had taken a crew to Brookline, Massachusetts, where JFK had been born and raised, to film the Kennedy residence. "She wasn't with us for that," Shanks recalls, "but she allowed us to film the place. I cut the film and sent her a copy. She loved it, and that gave her a sense of what it would be on the air. She could talk over the film and provide a tour.

"Around the same time, Joan Rivers had phoned me and said, 'Bob, there's this comedian you've got to have on. He's the funniest man alive right now. His name is Rodney Dangerfield.' 'I've never heard of him,' I told her. 'You will,' said Joan, 'He's fantastic.' So I booked Rodney for his first appearance on Griffin, the day Rose Kennedy was on. And Rose was just wonderful that day; she had come to talk, and she did. She ran two segments over what we had scheduled and we had to bump Rodney. And he took it very hard. But we became friends. I'd go to his club and he'd say, 'That's Bob Shanks, the producer of *The Merv Griffin Show*. He's the guy who bumped me the first time I was on Griffin!'"

The next major political figure to occupy the hot seat would be the presumptive Republican presidential candidate.

Richard Milhous Nixon had filmed a "remote" interview for the Griffin show in January of 1966. Though he wasn't running for office at the time, his answers were guarded nonetheless, particularly with respect to the burning issue of the day—the war in Vietnam. "At a time when negotiations are taking place, or when they're being talked about," said Nixon, "this is the time when all those who do not have knowledge as to what's going on, should be silent." "Fine," agreed Merv. "We'll get off the subject."

Now, nearly two years later, as the presumptive Republican candidate, Nixon was eager to appear on a national talk show to discuss the war and other issues. He would do just that at the Little Theatre on December 20, 1967.

After the usual exchange of hellos, Merv thanked the former vice president for not imposing any rules or restrictions on the impending interview. The audience snickered. "No!" retorted Merv. "This happens, and Mr. Nixon very kindly waived any idea of what my questions might be, and I appreciate that, sir."

That sounded good on television, but it wasn't the scenario Griffin would present in his 1980 memoir. Nixon's people had indeed attempted to finagle, if not control, the entire segment. First, they requested an "advance look" at the questions that would be asked.

Griffin said no, reminding them that Mr. Nixon had agreed to an "unconditional" interview.

They also requested that Griffin toss out "setup" questions to which Nixon could respond with witty comebacks. In their efforts to humanize themselves in front of audiences, especially those in entertainment venues, politicians sometimes hire comedy writers to help them come off as clever and witty. For this purpose, Nixon hired Bob Howard, a seasoned writer who had also worked for Griffin and would do so again later. It was Howard who suggested the setups, to which Griffin also said no.

On the air, Nixon said he knew it wouldn't have done any good to impose rules in the first place. "Let's just relax and enjoy it," he said cautiously.

By the late-1960s, the prerequisites for American presidential candidates had expanded beyond the scope of political ideology. Merv commented, "You *must* be a rich man, you *must* have plenty of children at home, a great smile, a winning way . . . almost able to do a commercial," said Merv. "Can a poor boy ever be president ever again?"

"I suppose we might find out, but I'm not sure, " Nixon smiled.

The tone suddenly grew serious as Merv said, "You must be aware of an undercurrent with politicians, people in our business, even comedians, who refer to Richard Nixon as a loser. You have that stigma because of losing two big contests." The room fell silent. The question, of course, was fueled by Nixon's unsuccessful attempt at winning the presidency in 1960, and California's gubernatorial election in 1962.

Nixon survived the awkwardness of the moment, stating firmly that the "stigma" could be overcome simply by winning something. He pointed out that many great leaders in history—Lincoln, Churchill, and Roosevelt—had all lost elections before winning the big ones.

Focusing on the impending 1968 election, Nixon said that for the first time in history, what happens in America could determine the fate of peace and freedom in the world. "I would put it this way," he continued, "The task of the next president is peace abroad and peace at home."

Nixon said he wanted America to have "the best man possible" in the White House. "You don't really know until a man has been in his most recent battle, whether he is the man who has that extra bit which is going to make the difference when the great decisions are made. I want this country to have its best man," Nixon avowed. "And only if I can prove I'm the best man am I going to become a candidate!"

Amid thunderous applause and cheers, Merv cut to a commercial. But when the show resumed, the subject of Vietnam surfaced powerfully. Nixon said he disagreed with Russia's proposal to halt the bombing of North Vietnam as a method of getting the enemy to the negotiating table. Instead, he strongly advocated the continuation of air strikes because the enemy, in his estimation, was in pursuit of victory rather than peace.

Nixon's characteristic blandness was tolerable because he was expounding on the burning issue of the day. As long as the conversation focused on the war, the interview remained compelling. After acknowledging "the boys who are valiantly fighting the war," Nixon took a jab the boys who were protesting it. The audience applauded.

All was going well, until David Susskind, also on the panel, entered the conversation. Merv sensed that Susskind was itching to broach the subject of the impending campaign. In a blistering moment, Susskind asked Nixon how he expected to get elected president, given the fact that Democrats traditionally outnumber Republicans. "You can't become president of the United States unless millions of disaffected Democrats vote for you," Susskind reasoned, "and to those people you are *anathema*." Nixon took the question in stride, commenting appreciatively that in 1960, many disgruntled Democrats had switched over to vote for him. But in rebuttal, Susskind cited a study claiming that those votes had come from "religious bigots." (Nixon's Democratic opponent, John F. Kennedy, was Roman Catholic.) Restraining his anger, Nixon said that Susskind's remarks were a "slander" on the Democrats who had voted in that election.

In what can best be described as a righteous snit, Nixon delivered an extemporaneous response far more substantive than most of his meticulously prepared speeches. In the process, he made the persuasive argument that the "crossover voters" were not religious bigots, but in fact a sector of the electorate strongly in cohesion with his party's ideology. More applause.

Susskind kept it up: "But why now, when not two other times?"

Nixon coolly pointed out that in 1960, a time when the Republican party was weaker, it ran a virtual "a dead heat" that wouldn't have been possible without winning a substantial number of Democratic votes. "Let the record also show," Nixon continued, "that I did *not* win those states in which most of the religious bigots are supposed to be located. I didn't win any of the states of the so-called solid South."

Over the years, writers have erroneously reported that the former vice president stormed off the show during a commercial break. According to Griffin himself, Nixon had wanted to do just that. Wisely, he persuaded Nixon to remain on set until the end of the segment, making the situation "look good" for everyone.

There was no question that Nixon loathed the outcome of the interview, going so far as to request that it be edited, if not "pulled" (not shown) altogether. Griffin said no. As it turned out, some pundits opined that the tense exchange actually benefited the presumptive Republican candidate. The show went on the air as planned.

Years later, Griffin recalled that of all the politicians he'd interviewed, only two listened to his questions: Nelson Rockefeller and Bobby Kennedy. Nixon? "Before I'd even finish a question," Griffin said, "I could hear his mental filing cabinet click open and a folder come out with the answer."

Some months later, *candidate* Nixon was back on Merv's turf, though not as a guest on the program. As much as Nixon disliked Griffin's show, he liked Griffin's studio. He booked time there to produce a series of campaign promos.

Bob Shanks vividly recalls the filming of the Nixon spots, since he nearly got arrested because of them. "The Secret Service guys were there," the producer recalls. "And I was used to going to the office every day. I was the boss—right? And suddenly these guys in black suits start coming up against the building. I was enraged!"

It took a few moments for the harried producer to explain who he was before being permitted to enter his own office.

Albert Fisher, the show's publicity man, wasn't aware of any Secret Service on the premises. "That's why they're called the Secret Service," he says wryly. Fisher does recall "tight security" at Griffin's theater for the appearance of Nikolai T. Fedorenko, the Soviet ambassador to the United Nations.

"Merv had met Fedorenko at a party given by the famed attorney and politician Henry Dorman," Fisher recalls. "They were seated next to each other at dinner, but Merv hadn't caught his name. And so, he leaned over and said, 'I'm terribly sorry, but I didn't hear your name when we were being introduced. My name is Merv Griffin.' The other guests at the table, including Walter Cronkite, became silent as they waited to see the reaction of the guest of honor. The ambassador leaned back in his chair, and out of the vest pocket of his impeccable, custom made, three-piece suit, pulled out a business card which he flipped in front of Merv. Emblazoned on it was the name, Nikolai T. Fedorenko. And Merv said, "Mr. Ambassador, my apologies! Of course I know who you are.'

"Everyone kept a close eye on Fedorenko, waiting to see if he might get angry. Instead, he patted Merv on the shoulder and said, 'Griffin! I like you! I watch your show. Why you never have me on?' To which Merv replied, 'Oh, Mr. Ambassador, we'd be delighted to have you on any time you want.'

"Merv came in the next day and recounted the entire story to Bob Shanks and the staff," says Fisher. "But no one really thought anything would come of it because Fedorenko had never done any American television. Not even *Meet the Press*. But a short time later, Bob got a call in the middle of the afternoon from Fedorenko's press agent. He said, 'The ambassador will be at your studio tonight at 6:15 for the 6:30 taping!' No plans, no pre-interviews, nothing. Of course, we had to inform our other guests what had happened and reschedule them for a later show."

Merv opened the show cold. After Arthur had done the intro, Merv walked out through the curtain and sat at center stage. Fisher recalls Griffin's opening remarks: "This man has never been on American television, and we are deeply honored to have so important an official from the Soviet Union to be with us. So, please give a warm welcome to His Excellency, Nikolai T. Fedorenko."

Fisher says he can still see the surprised look on Griffin's face when the curtain parted and out came Fedorenko, with loads of books under his arm. "Of course Merv asked him what the books were for," Fisher recalls. "And the ambassador explained that in watching the show, he noticed that authors *always* brought along their books to plug. So Fedorenko brought along his books. The volumes were written in Russian and available only in Russia. The interview turned out to be a riveting one."

In his capacity as publicity director for the show, Fisher recalls much criticism for giving airtime to a Communist official (perhaps even greater than the backlash after Lord Russell's interview in 1965). "But I also think we got more coverage out of that interview than any other," says Fisher.

10. THE ESCALATING LATE-NIGHT WAR

In 1967, Carson's *Tonight Show* was commanding $17,000 for a one-minute commercial spot. Today, advertising rates on late-night television are approximately 10 times that figure. All was going well for NBC until the American Federation of Television Artists (AFTRA) threatened to go on strike. At issue were better contracts for on-air news reporters in the major markets, and the mandatory retirement age at 65, for staff announcers. The three major broadcasting networks—NBC, CBS, and ABC—could not come to terms with the union and a strike commenced on March 29, 1967. As a result, NBC re-played old *Tonight Shows* from late 1966, an action that Carson regarded as a breach of contract. Carson quit the program.

While the late-night star languished in the Florida sun, many members of the press speculated that he was using the strike as a means to procure a better deal from NBC. As Carson's reps hammered out a more lucrative deal for their client, the folks over at ABC were mounting a strategic return to the late-night arena.

After the demise of *The Les Crane Show,* ABC turned the post-11:00 p.m. time slot over to its affiliate stations, most of which played old Hollywood movies. Still, many within the network hierarchy believed there was enough room at the top of the mountain for another late-night star. All they needed was a host capable of making the treacherous climb. ABC went a-hunting for a bright, witty, congenial host who might at least *equal* Carson in popularity. Recalling comedian Joey Bishop's track record as guest host of *The Tonight Show* (on which he got his pal Frank Sinatra to make a rare appearance), the network signed him.

Glum-faced, but perpetually witty, Bishop had been a favorite guest of both Steve Allen and Jack Paar on their respective versions of *Tonight.* In fact, it was Paar who made the frequently quoted observation that Joey looked like an untipped waiter. In addition to his guest shots on various variety, game, and talk shows, Bishop starred as a talk-show host in a weekly sitcom, *The Joey Bishop Show*, seen in various formats and on different networks from 1961 to 1965. Bishop's trademark catchphrase was: "son of a gun!"

When Paar first hinted that he might soon relinquish *The Tonight Show*, Bishop's name turned up on NBC's list of possible replacements. But when Carson finally accepted the network's offer, which he had initially rejected, Bishop merely became one of the 17 performers who served as guest host during the spring and summer of 1962.

By the late-sixties, Bishop was a veteran comic who knew the rigors of show business inside out. He knew taking on Carson would be a daunting, if not futile, challenge. The money was good ($25,000 a week), and the prestige of hosting a late-night talk show on a major network was hard to resist. To produce the Bishop show, ABC hired Paul Orr, who had produced the Paar *Tonight Show*. Thirty-five-year-old Regis Philbin, a skillful interviewer in his own right, was relegated to the role of Bishop's announcer/sidekick. Johnny Mann led the house orchestra, in a refurbished studio on Vine Street in the heart of Hollywood.

Amid much anticipation, *The Joey Bishop Show* debuted live on April 17, 1967 with guests Debbie Reynolds, Danny Thomas, and an unknown singer named Brenda Arnau. The big draw of the evening was then-governor Ronald Reagan. From the beginning, the show exuded a "homey" ambience. Philbin came up with his own attention-grabber for announcing Bishop each night. "And now, ladies and gentlemen," he would intone, "It's time for Joey!" Bishop would then breeze onto the stage to a jazzy theme song as the audience sang, *Joey—Joey, Joey!* He'd do a brief monologue followed by a droll exchange with Philbin and, on occasion, the folks in the studio audience.

On the surface, Bishop's program resembled a carbon copy of *The Tonight Show*, with the host sitting behind a desk with several office-like chairs to his right. But that's where the similarity ended. As a comic, Bishop's quick-wittedness was appreciable, and he delivered every punchline with deadpan splendor. As an interviewer, he lacked the adroitness of a Jack Paar or a Merv Griffin. Bishop's conversations, laden with non-sequiturs, often came off as low-key. When an interview would begin to fall flat, he'd turn to the pre-show notes or take questions from the audience.

Bishop thought he had the right formula to make the midnight magic work. He contended that a late-night talk show should be overheard rather than heard. The comedian had done surprisingly well during his first few nights on the air, largely due to the curiosity factor. One week later, Johnny Carson made a strategically planned return to *The Tonight Show* with a lineup that included comedian Buddy Hackett, the folk-singing group Peter, Paul and Mary, and a Mighty Carson Art Players sketch. Bishop attempted to counter Carson's return by bringing Jack Paar out of "retirement." Though the combination of Paar and Bishop sounded good, the throne at ABC wasn't big enough for two kings. The former *Tonight Show* host completely usurped Bishop by asking *him* questions, and then telling old stories about his time on the late-night circuit. This made Bishop appear lackluster and not in control of his own turf.

On April 26, 1967, *The New York Times* confirmed that Carson had defeated Bishop in the ratings race. In reviewing the late-night competition, the paper said Paar had inadvertently drawn attention to Bishop's plight as a host who is ill at ease with guests. The ratings for the evening told the story: Carson won a 41 percent share of the audience; Griffin, on the Westinghouse network, chalked up 16 percent; and Bishop, 12 percent. The CBS station, which showed an old Rock Hudson movie, came in second with a respectable 22 percent.

It was predicted that Merv Griffin would likely reap the biggest bonus of all because his show aired as a pre-bedtime entry in most markets. Merv also beat the competition with regard to the handling of guests and for the offering of fresh faces from the New York stage.

By this time, it was patently obvious, even to the most casual of viewers, that late-night television had become big business. The post-11:00 p.m. time period had become a battleground on which a high-stakes competition was escalating. This was a remarkable shift from the days when NBC had to cajole its affiliates into carrying late-night programming.

Owing to the phenomenal success of *Tonight*, the variety/talk show became one of the most duplicated formats on the tube. The late-sixties would see a stream of various chatterboxes presiding over network and syndicated programs. It was as if someone had published a manual titled, "You, Too, Can Host a Talk Show."

Between 1967 and 1969, Alan Burke, Bill Dana, Woody Woodbury, Al Capp, Allen Ludden, Dennis Wholey, Ed Nelson, Della Reese, Rosey Grier, Joan Rivers, and Pat Boone all had short-lived careers as TV talkers. Most of these diverse personalities barely made it through a season. During this same period, several hosts demonstrated that they indeed had the chops. The granddaddy of the art, Steve Allen, returned to the fold via syndication. Dick Cavett inaugurated his first chatfest in the daytime on ABC.

The Tonight Show clung tight to its command over 35 percent of the viewing audience. That meant that Carson remained in first place, with Bishop lagging far behind in the ratings race. One source claims that only one in five late-night viewers watched Bishop, while one in three watched Carson.

Throughout this escalating late-night war, CBS hadn't fired a single shot. CBS's affiliate stations subsisted with dozens of Hollywood movies the network had purchased in "package" deals from the major studios. By early 1968, however, many of the titles in the CBS library had already been treated to multiple airings. With Hollywood turning out fewer feature films, the cost of obtaining the more recent ones had skyrocketed. It essentially boiled down to supply and demand. The local stations weren't satisfied with the paltry revenues earned from movies that had been shown four or five times. On the other hand, the network was disgruntled because it wasn't reaping any remuneration from the local airings. Consequently, the CBS affiliates in the major markets began clamoring for some form of "original" late-night programming. Since television was now permitted to tackle adult subject matter (particularly late at night), the possibility of something more sophisticated than an old western seemed intriguing.

The CBS research department began conducting surveys to determine what type of programming would be acceptable to the network's affiliates. Some station execs expressed interest in something different and exciting, like a Vegas-style extravaganza. Others, however, favored a traditional late-night variety series in the same vein as *The Tonight Show.*

As the months passed, the bulk of the nation's viewers remained glued to NBC. At CBS, the execs kept an eye on ABC to observe how well, or how poorly, Bishop was competing against Carson. NBC and Carson had nothing to worry about.

CBS put out its feelers for a host who was already known to the viewing public, a pre-tested personality who could win over the viewers and rake in a healthy share of the revenue. In short, they were looking for a name brand.

Several possible candidates were approached. One of them was Jack Paar. Though Paar had quit a weekly prime-time variety series in 1965, he was still turning out an occasional network special. He rejected the offer instantly. Mike Douglas was also considered. Douglas was blissfully secure in his little studio in Philadelphia, and he, too, said no. It was at this time that the network became keenly aware of that other successful daytime talker—Merv Griffin.

11. THE BIG EYE WANTS A PIECE OF THE PIE

During the first weeks of 1968, Griffin and company were happily preoccupied with a new pet project. Merv, who attributed much of his success as an interviewer to his Irish sense of humor, had given his stamp of approval for a St. Patrick's Day special.

Filmed in color (especially green, according to the ad campaign), the one-hour program would emerge as a visually stunning hybrid of location segments and studio performances. In Ireland, Merv visited the homes of producer-director John Huston and actor-balladeer Burl Ives. Huston recited "Come Back to Erin" and Ives offered a soothing rendition of "The Song of the Wandering Aengus," written by Irish poet William Butler Yeats. Added to the mix was John Wayne, recalling the making of *The Quiet Man* (1952), in an interview shot on location in the U.S. The segments produced in New York featured fast-paced musical acts by the Clancy Brothers and Tommy Makem, Sandy Duncan, Ella Logan, Jimmy Joyce, and the McNiff Irish Dancers. In several cities, *Merv Griffin's St. Patrick's Day Special* aired back-to-back with the 90-minute talk show.

Three months later, the Irish Leprechaun, as one critic described Merv, could have used a four-leaf clover in his pocket for the next chapter in his career. "His contract with Westinghouse was up for renewal," recalls Bob Shanks. "The show was a hit and was being seen on about 150 stations. Merv wanted a million dollars a year more. And he was entitled to it."

By June 1968, Griffin was already a multi-millionaire, having done exceedingly well with his thriving enterprises. "America's Boy Next Door" was the owner of six production companies with two hit shows on the air: his own daily talkathon and the enormously popular *Jeopardy!*. Not every Griffin production was a winner. Two game shows, *Reach for the Stars* and *One in a Million*, both failed miserably during the first half of 1967. Despite their cancellations, these programs further enhanced Merv's reputation as a reputable producer/packager of game shows, and he would continue to develop new ones.

Westinghouse Broadcasting reaped the benefits of Griffin's mass appeal to daytime audiences. Indeed, *The Merv Griffin Show* had contributed handsomely to the amazing success of Group W, which, at one point, raked in over $10 million a year in profit. "But Westinghouse was used to making toasters and refrigerators," says Bob Shanks. Even Merv once joked that his bosses paid him in pop-up toasters.

The producer recalls the non-productive negotiation meetings with Don McGannon, the head of Group W Productions: "McGannon fumed, 'A *million* dollars more? That's more than the president of Westinghouse makes.' And I told him, 'that is what you pay for talent. If you had a ball team, that's the price you'd have to pay, and there would be no negotiating. If you don't go forward with this, there will be no Merv Griffin Show. We're not talking about a replaceable part on an assembly line. It's called *The Merv Griffin Show* because there's only one man who can do it—Merv Griffin—and he's worth the money."

The company's cavalier attitude toward one of its biggest money-makers came as a surprise to Shanks, whose best pep talks proved futile. "Never could talk them into it," says the producer, "and they wouldn't pay him what he wanted. And I think Merv's agency, the William Morris people, spread the word within the industry, and ultimately to CBS, because it was known that they were looking to get into the talk show business. And the next thing you knew, we were head to head with Johnny."

In his principal volume of autobiography, Griffin recalls, with great zeal, how he instructed his lawyer, Roy Blakeman, and agent, Sol Leon of the Morris agency, to demand an incredibly huge salary from CBS. At 43, Griffin wasn't interested in adding the pressures of network television to his already-demanding schedule. He'd had enough of that at NBC. Nevertheless, the prospect of taking on Carson was an enticing one that kept nagging at him. Griffin had always wanted to shine in the late-night spotlight. In a dexterous move, the star came up with an unfathomable demand: *double* the amount of Carson's *Tonight Show* salary. (Various sources claim Carson was then earning roughly $40,000 per week.)

With a "they-can't-afford-me" stance," Griffin expected the CBS bosses to laugh their heads off, and when the laughter subsided, along with the offer, he could tenaciously resume negotiations with Westinghouse. That would never happen. Amazingly, CBS had agreed to his terms.

On August 6, 1968, *The New York Times* confirmed what many within the television industry already knew: "Merv Griffin Show Will Move to CBS in 1969." According to the story, the network had finally resolved to compete in the 11:30 p.m. time slot after having procured "unanimous clearance" from its affiliate stations. Ironically, three years earlier, when the proposal for late-night programming had been put to a vote, most of the affiliates flatly rejected it, preferring to stick with old movies. Now, however, the managers of those stations had apparently realized what Pat Weaver knew in 1950: there was big money to be earned in those "golden" midnight hours. The article also disclosed some interesting stats. When the Carson, Bishop, and Griffin shows aired in New York City from April to June 1967, Carson averaged a 33 percent share of the audience, Griffin averaged 17 percent (not bad for a non-network show), and Bishop averaged 10 percent.

The *Times* also reported that CBS president Thomas H. Dawson said his network had acted "very quickly" when it became known that Griffin had not reached an agreement with Westinghouse. "We are convinced that Merv Griffin guarantees us late-night supremacy," Dawson said. In the same article, another CBS exec, Michael Dann, commented that there would be no change in format to the new Griffin show. "He [Griffin] seems to be doing very well the way he is," Dann said.

Griffin was indeed doing very well. He had not only landed one of the most lucrative contracts in television history, he also managed to secure creative control of his show. "That's the beauty part," Griffin told *TV Guide*. "CBS requested we not change it too much, and we won't."

There was one other enticing aspect about joining the network: topicality. In syndication, *Merv* had played on a delayed basis, which meant that the tapes were aired several weeks after they had been recorded. Under this system, caution had to be exercised with regard to guests promoting certain "plugs" for upcoming appearances, as these would most likely be outdated by the time they were heard on the air. On CBS, however, the shows would be seen a matter of hours after they'd been taped, thereby allowing for fresh discussion of contemporaneous events and issues.

For the most part, the CBS network was delighted with the acquisition of *The Merv Griffin Show*. Yet there were some within the network hierarchy with lingering doubts about Merv's prowess as a late-night contender. This stemmed from reports claiming that in markets where Griffin had been pitted against Carson, the undisputed winner had always been Carson. This was not surprising, considering that *Tonight* had been a nightly addiction for the past 14 years. Questions loomed in the minds of several execs. Could a host who had charmed millions of viewers in the daytime work the same magic at midnight? Would people actually switch channels, abandoning Johnny in favor of Merv?

With the contract signed, the CBS publicity machine went into full gear, touting Merv Griffin CBS's answer to insomnia in the forthcoming three-way contest.

The press approximated the midnight hours on TV to a multi-million-dollar game. Those magical numbers called ratings would determine which network would win the bulk of the advertising revenue, estimated to be in excess of $50,000,000 per year. What it actually boiled down to was the popularity of each host and the drawing power of his guests.

Though Griffin's negotiations with Westinghouse had ended on a sour note, the star still had nearly a year's worth of shows to host for the company. Several "specials" Griffin hosted during his last year with Group W were lively and well received. The first of these, produced outside the studio, was a musical comedy revue with the Big Apple as an exhilarating backdrop. *Merv Griffin's Sidewalks of New York*, as it came to be titled, was another special done for Westinghouse syndication, apart from the talk show series. *Sidewalks* headlined Merv and Arthur with guest stars Dionne Warwick, Joel Grey, who was then starring on Broadway in *George M*, and the musical group The Union Gap. Dick Shawn and Renee Taylor did an uproariously funny bit as hippies; even Arthur dressed up as a hippie! The one-hour special was shot entirely on location at Central Park, the Plaza Hotel, the Staten Island Ferry, Greenwich Village, and even the S.S. United States, as it pulled out of the harbor past the Statue of Liberty.

Perhaps the most elaborate, and best remembered, of the Westinghouse/Griffin specials in 1968 was "Give a Damn." Airing during the month of July, the program was essentially an outdoor concert taped on the streets of Harlem with live performances by Gladys Knight and the Pips, Spanky and Our Gang, and James Brown. Muhammad Ali, Godfrey Cambridge, and Mayor John Lindsay also contributed to the show's energetic and "feel good" ambience.

"Give a Damn was actually Mayor John Lindsay's campaign, not something done exclusively for *The Merv Griffin Show,* says Albert Fisher. "It was a city program to promote awareness and consciousness of equal rights and respect for everyone."

It was a project designed to heal wounds. "American cities were burning after the King and Kennedy assassinations," recalls Bob Shanks. "John Lindsay called us and said, 'What can you guys do to help me keep the lid on this city?' And we all agreed this would be a good thing to do.

"James Brown had been on the Griffin show several times. I called and asked for his help. 'James,' I said, 'We're going to do this show in Harlem and I need your advice to avoid making mistakes. We want you, of course, and we'd like you to close the show. Now who else should be on?' And he mentioned the last person I would have thought of—John Wayne! James said that black people admired Wayne for his values, and the fact that, in his movies, he's a lone man struggling against the system. So I went to Merv and said, 'You've got to make *this* call yourself!'"

Wayne, who had previously been on Merv's show several times, was now ill and unable to come to New York. Wayne suggested that Burt Lancaster, a native New Yorker, would be a perfect alternative. "Wayne even offered to phone Lancaster," says Shanks, "and he did."

Lancaster gave totally of himself that day. "He got there early," Shanks remembers, "and went into the audience of 20,000 people, climbed up fire escapes, and was wonderful the whole day."

Despite the unrelenting summer heat, the crowd roared enthusiastically through all the musical performances. As the show began to wind down, everyone kept a sharp eye for James Brown, the closing act of the night. "We'd started at noon and now it's 10:30 and it's been a great day," recalls the producer. "No incidents, not a single fistfight, nothing. But Brown hadn't shown up. So I phoned him: 'James, where are you?' Well, he didn't like this and he didn't like that." The main thing Brown didn't like was John Lindsay. According to Merv's autobiography, Brown believed that the mayor had once snubbed him. It took several minutes of sweet-talk for the singer to change his mind. He eventually agreed to do the show. There was one proviso: a fleet of police cars with flashing lights and blaring sirens would have to accompany Brown's limo, affording him the most spectacular entrance possible. "No fool he, James was the consummate showman," says Shanks. "I was annoyed at him that night. But, nevertheless, we pulled it off and he was great. He came down Third Avenue—and the crowd went crazy. He performed well over an hour and it was fantastic."

After "Give a Damn," another musical special would have seemed anti-climactic. In October, Griffin and company decided that the best route would be a scenic one. Assisted by cameraman Michael Wadley, associate producer John Rhinehart, and a crew of more than a dozen, Griffin ventured to Boston for the filming of "Sidewalks of New England." Ten days of shooting in historic locations, such as the Old Granary Burying Ground, resulted in a fast-paced hour's worth of footage, aired in most markets during November. With the lovely fall foliage as a backdrop, the production focused on popular sites like Pier 4 and Mt. Snow, with performances by Paul Revere and the Raiders, along with the always-dependable Arthur Treacher. When it was over, Merv turned his attention to taping the last round of talk shows for Westinghouse.

Liza Minnelli had made one of her earliest TV appearances on Merv's NBC show in 1963. "And her mother, Judy Garland, came on as a guest in 1967," recalls Albert Fisher. "I had seen Judy at the Palace, which was one of those rare, truly great show-business experiences. Mort Lindsey was her conductor, so a number of us were able to go to her opening night. And to see her now, at Merv's show, and have some words with her, was quite special."

Garland's personal problems were well known to her intimate friends and associates. "She had been under a financial strain," says Fisher, "and I understand she had stayed at one of the hotels in New York City where her bill remained unpaid. We had read in the newspaper that Judy had been kicked out of that hotel because she didn't have the money to pay the bill she had run up. We got hold of her and offered her the opportunity to do these shows."

In the twilight of her career and, as it turned out, her life, Garland needed to work even though she was not in the best of health. In December 1968, Merv invited her to guest host the show while he vacationed in Switzerland. "She would be the substitute host in exchange for, not only a fee, but a suite at the Plaza Hotel," says Fisher. "Then she asked for a fur coat, and other perks, and we did a thing to promote the fur coat that she would wear on the show."

When showtime finally rolled around, Garland was nursing a case of cold feet.

"I was giving her what we called the star entrance," recalls Bob Shanks. "I was bringing her in from the rear of the theater, through the audience, up to the stage. But she wanted to escape onto 44th Street. I said, 'Judy, you can't do that.' And Mort began to play the theme. So I said, 'Judy, come here. I want to dance with you. It would be the honor of my life to dance with you to Merv's theme. Then, Arthur said, "Here's Judy!' And I opened the door and she went up the aisle and did the show."

As a special surprise, the bookers arranged to have veteran actress Margaret Hamilton, who had played the Wicked Witch of the West in *The Wizard of Oz* (1939), sitting in the front row of the theater.

"You're my favorite witch," Garland told the diminutive actress. "Well, I'd *better* be," said Hamilton, who was appearing in the musical, *Come Summer*, which, coincidentally, starred Ray (the Scarecrow) Bolger. "Did you bring your broom," Garland smirked. "It's a New York broom called a *bus*," snapped Hamilton. Though the reunion was brief, it was made all the more memorable when Garland asked the aging actress to re-create a bit of her immortal characterization. In her best I'll-get-you-and-your-little-dog-too vigor, Hamilton let out a cackle as good as any she delivered in the classic film.

As Garland settled into the host's chair, Arthur briefly assumed the role of interviewer and asked her about the making of *Oz*. Garland said, "I guess it was a very good picture!"

"It keeps on going," Arthur chimed in. He asked Garland if she continued to see any of her fellow cast members from the film. "I see Ray Bolger, and I just saw Miss Hamilton," Garland beamed.

"Margaret had to do a skywriting in the picture," Garland winced. "She was in her green makeup and black hat and was on her broom, writing *Dorothy go home . . .* or something. And they did this with a broom that had a motor, and they took this poor lady who was standing in—or *flying* in—for Margaret Hamilton. And she had to be lifted *thousands* of feet in the air to do sky writing on a broom. It was pretty tricky. Well, the broom blew up and that was the last we saw one of her stand-ins. People dropped like flies on that movie. (As legions of *Oz* buffs certainly know, Hamilton herself sustained serious injuries when her facial makeup ignited during an early scene in the film.)

Also on the panel that day were actor Van Johnson, film critic Rex Reed, and the irrepressible Jackie "Moms" Mabley.

Moms had always been one of Merv's favorite guests. Born Loretta Mary Aiken in 1894, the magnificent Miss Mabley had broken into show business as a teenager, eventually working her way up to headliner status in the black vaudeville houses of the 1920s. Her nickname stemmed from the motherly qualities she imbued to the struggling young performers (regardless of their color) breaking into show business. Enormously popular on the "Chitlin' Circuit" (the venues in which African-American artists could work during the era of segregation), Moms would go on to become one of the most highly paid entertainers at Harlem's Apollo Theater during the 1930s. She also appeared in a sprinkling of films, beginning with *The Emperor Jones* (1933). Her greatest success, however, would be realized through years of nightclub work and recordings. Deemed "racy" by the standards of the 1950s, her stand-up act included an abundance of jokes about sex, as did her comedy albums, which had proven enormously successful.

With her matronly house dresses, frumpy hats, and ancient slippers, the raspy-voiced Moms had endeared herself to mainstream audiences of the early 1960s. Her triumphant 1962 act at Carnegie Hall was followed by a string of successful appearances on *The Ed Sullivan Show* and, later, *The Smothers Brothers Comedy Hour*. On television, Moms's uproariously funny take on the black perspective had always been well received, even with suburban white viewers. With a style that was poignant as well as hard-hitting, Moms would influence the careers of Bill Cosby, Eddie Murphy, and Whoopi Goldberg. She would eventually play Cosby's aunt on his first sitcom, *The Bill Cosby Show*, in 1970.

On the panel with Garland, Moms wisecracked about her pseudo-boyfriends and -husbands, as well as her feigned infatuation with younger men. She said she wanted Van Johnson as a Christmas present. "All I want is *you* in my *stockin'*," she told the actor in her raspy voice. "From there on, I'll take care of everything."

Johnson asked Mabley if she would be playing the Apollo. "Moms don't play the Apollo no more; they have too many shows," she responded. Mabley claimed she was now working for Merv Griffin exclusively. "I'm the den mother on *The Merv Griffin Show*," she declared boldly. "That's all I need. He's the greatest man I've ever found in show business. And I'm gonna stay with him until he leaves. And when he leaves, I'm goin' with him!"

"Where's he going?" Garland chirped. "He's going to CBS," said Moms, "and I'm goin' with him."

For those who didn't keep up with the latest buzz in the business, this was the first inkling that Griffin would soon be leaving his roost at Westinghouse for the more prestigious network.

Following that bombshell, Garland and Treacher paired up for a rendition of "If You Were the Only Girl in the World." Though Garland wasn't up to the task of conducting a cohesive interview, she nevertheless wowed the audience with a solo rendition of "Just in Time." Time, in fact, was running out for the show *and* Garland. No one realized it at the time, of course, but Garland had just completed her last appearance on American television. She died in London on June 22, 1969.

December 1968 would mark the passing of another Griffin regular—the delightfully urbane Tallulah Bankhead. On stage and screen, the Alabama-born actress exuded style, fortitude, and a larger-than-life presence. In private life, she was diminutive (five feet, three inches tall), sultry and wildly uninhibited. She once said, "I'm as pure as the driven *slush*." Bankhead's most distinctive characteristic was her gravel-toned voice, with which she addressed everyone as "daaahling."

After years of stage productions on both sides of the Atlantic, Bankhead attained iconic status, as evidenced by her Broadway triumph in Lillian Hellman's *The Little Foxes* (1939). Bette Davis played Tallulah's role in the 1940 film adaptation. Three decades later on the Griffin show, Davis, who had reprised several of Bankhead's roles in movies, recalled meeting the tempestuous star at a party one night. "She was very loaded," Davis told Merv, "And she said, '*You* played all the parts I've played, and I played them *soooo* much better!' And I said, Miss Bankhead, I couldn't agree with you more."

Bankhead lit up the silver screen, too. In George Cukor's *Devil and the Deep* (1932), Bankhead gets top billing over Gary Cooper, Charles Laughton and Cary Grant, such was her fame at the time. Being a true southern belle, she'd been in the running for the role of Scarlett O'Hara in *Gone With the Wind* (1939). Bankhead, among others, lost out to Vivien Leigh. Nevertheless, she would achieve great acclaim as the foreign correspondent in Hitchcock's *Lifeboat* (1944), a role that won her the New York Film Critics Circle Award.

Merv and Tallulah shared a long and somewhat anomalous friendship. They had first worked together on Tallulah's acclaimed NBC radio series, *The Big Show* (1951). Four years later, when Tallulah needed an opening act for her Vegas engagement, Merv was only too happy to oblige. After each nightly performance, the pair would go out on the town. They hung out together, got drunk together, and gambled together—the latter activity producing truly spectacular results.

"Merv loved Tallulah," recalls Julann Griffin. "He once walked in to see her after a show they'd done. She said, 'come in, dahling.' And there she was—on the john! She carried on a conversation with Merv, while sitting on the john. He loved that."

Bankhead's candor and unpredictable wisecracks made her a natural for the talk show circuit. She brazenly wore her derision on shows hosted by Steve Allen, Jack Paar, Johnny Carson, and Mike Douglas. Her talents were also seen to optimum advantage on variety programs, including *The Andy Williams Show* and *The Smothers Brothers Comedy Hour*, as well as two episodes of *Batman* in which she guest-starred as the Black Widow.

In January 1968, Bankhead made her last visit to the Griffin show. Bankhead had always been the consummate professional, but she now seemed somewhat distracted. "As the time for Tallulah's spot grew nearer, I went looking for her," recalls Bob Shanks. "I found her downstairs, talking in one of the dressing rooms. We were ready to bring her out as the next guest, but I couldn't get her to break away. Tallulah would talk to *anyone*. I said, 'Tallulah, do you want to be on the show or not?' She did, but I still couldn't get her upstairs." Finally, the producer had to grab the loquacious actress by the arm and forcefully escort her to the set.

On the panel with Bankhead was Margaret Truman, the only child of former President Harry S. Truman and former First Lady Bess Truman. The discussion eventually focused on the reluctance of certain women to reveal their age. With not the slightest trace of deceit, Truman admitted that she was 43. "Oh, please, *dahling*," Tallulah snapped. "People are eating!" Obviously, Ms. Truman must have been experiencing a bad day, since she *was* only 43 at the time!

Tallulah Bankhead died of pneumonia on December 12, 1968.

In the spring of 1969, Merv Griffin's image seemed to be everywhere—on magazine covers, newspaper columns, TV supplements, commercial ads, and even a few public service announcements.

With its hefty investment in Griffin, the CBS network sought to collect some equally substantial dividends. To showcase its new star, the network saw to it that Merv would appear on several of its popular series and specials. In March, he did a guest shot on *The Red Skelton Hour,* singing and dancing his way through "I've Got a Lovely Bunch of Cocoanuts," and "acting" in a weak sketch that parodied his own show.

In early May, the wire services circulated publicity photos of Merv holding TV's most coveted prize: the Emmy. He'd been tapped to co-host the annual Emmy telecast, portions of which would originate from New York's Carnegie Hall. The other portions would be telecast live from the Santa Monica Civic Auditorium, with Bill Cosby presiding.

In late June, Merv was back up on the big screen, albeit briefly, portraying himself in the Ivan Tors production of *Hello Down There* (1969). The film, which had gone into production two years earlier, was completed at Tors's studio in Florida where his *Flipper* and *Gentle Ben* TV series were shot.

Hello Down There is a wacky farce about a marine scientist named Fred Miller (Tony Randall), who sets out to prove that he and his family can live comfortably — 90 feet below the surface of the ocean—in the experimental "home" he has designed. His high-tech invention, the Green Onion, is reminiscent of the saucer-like craft inhabited by the Robinson family on CBS's *Lost in Space*. Taking the plunge with Miller and his wife are their two energetic teenagers, who perform in a "groovy" rock band that features a fresh-faced Richard Dreyfuss.

Merv, who hadn't been in a film since *Phantom of the Rue Morgue* (1954), was accorded "special guest star" billing in the film's animated opening titles. He was in good company. Janet Leigh is pleasantly tolerant as the matriarch of the Miller clan; Jim Backus (*Gilligan's Island*) is effective as Miller's grumpy boss; and there's first-rate support from Roddy McDowall, Ken Berry, Arnold Stang, and Charlotte Rae.

Aside from the usual perils of the deep, the aquanauts face a series of slapstick-laced threats from greedy prospectors, a hurricane, and even the U.S. Navy! The most frustrating challenge occurs when the kids are offered a gig on *The Merv Griffin Show*, but can't get to the mainland because their transport sub has been wrecked. In typical *Merv Griffin Show* style, the enterprising host dispatches himself and his crew to the Green Onion. Resplendent in his familiar dark blue suit, striped tie and TV makeup, Merv introduces a "special song" from a "special place" in the world. The cleverest line is so subtle it almost goes unnoticed. "You're my favorite TV star—*Johnny!*" says Backus' character to the slightly haughty Mr. Griffin.

Despite its clever premise and top-notch cast, *Hello Down There*, released by Paramount Pictures, was not a winner at the box-office. The film received limited distribution upon its release, but would resurface in 1974 under the title *Sub-A-Dub-Dub*. In no way did Merv's cameo role present any challenges to his acting prowess. It did, however, serve as a worthy publicity device at the time when he was on the threshold of launching the biggest television show of this career. Moreover, the film showcased the host in a medium other than the one in which he was now identified exclusively— television.

As the weeks rolled by, plans to move *The Merv Griffin Show* from Westinghouse over to CBS progressed swiftly. CBS stood firm in its decision to originate the show from its Studio 5, located on West 52nd Street—an area that was depressing, according to Bob Shanks. "The studio was close to an unemployment office," notes Shanks. "And what star wants an audience of people who might have just come from an unemployment office?" Merv, who never liked the starkness of a television studio, rejected the facility instantly. The past four years had demonstrated how a tiny facility in "Shubert Alley" had generated an almost palpable energy—something essential for the making of good conversation. Griffin's mind was made up; the program *had* to originate from a theater, preferably one in Manhattan's Times Square sector.

It was Westinghouse, not Griffin Productions, which held the lease on the West 44th Street landmark. That lease still had two years to run with options. The marquee above The Little Theatre would soon bear the logo of *The David Frost Show*, Westinghouse's replacement for Griffin. Ironically, on July 1, 1969, Merv appeared on the Frost show as a good-will gesture to the new host in command of his former base of operations. "The word around Rock Row," wrote columnist George Maksian, "is whatever Merv wants, Merv gets." He was correct.

The star and his producer embarked on a mission, fastidiously checking all the available theaters on Broadway. It didn't take long for them to find one they liked. "The people who loved us were the Shuberts," says Shanks, "because CBS wound up spending a fortune refurbishing the Cort Theater on 48th Street."

The CBS brass balked vigorously over the two million dollars it would cost to convert the ancient theater into a modern television facility compatible with the other CBS studios. Nevertheless, Merv stood his ground; he sent the network a letter of resignation, which he intended to implement, if a deal to lease the theater wasn't consummated. Once again, management acquiesced to the demands of their new star. Now that *The Merv Griffin Show* had a found a new home, it needed new production offices.

On one of his periodic inspections at his new "home," Merv noticed an old, unoccupied, four-story building 50 feet west of the Cort Theater. The property could serve a dual purpose: convenient office facilities *and* a restaurant/bar where the Griffin gang could hang out between shows.

"I had to take the lead in the deal," says Bob Shanks, "because if Merv had done so, they would have doubled the asking price. We bought the building, which was in my name for about 24 hours. Our offices were set up there, and our restaurant, Pip's, would be on the ground floor."

By spring 1969, CBS had expanded its well-saturated publicity campaign to include a series of TV commercials featuring none other than Miss Miller. Because of her appearances in the filmed ads, Miller lost her amateur status and was required to join the American Federation of Television and Radio Artists union. In the commercials, Miller came across as eccentric (which she was, of course), but nonetheless sincere.

The ads, slated to appear regularly over the coming months, would be puzzling to younger viewers who had not the slightest notion who Miller was. It didn't matter. The 60-second spots conveyed the intended message: Merv was unquestionably the *nicest* of the three hosts to dominate the late-night terrain. In one spot, Miller displayed her collection of Merv treasures, including a recording of Treacher's now-famous intro. "If you want to see what makes me so crazy about Merv," she cooed, "watch his new show on CBS and you'll go crazy, too." Each commercial ended with Miller's catch-phrase: "Give the kid a break . . . *please!*"

An affectation resulted from these commercials. "I began getting random calls from Mrs. Miller," Shanks recalls, "and she'd be complaining that no one had come to do her hair that day." Miller thought that because she was now working for a star, she should be treated like one. She demanded transportation to and from the studio. On one occasion she complained that her car had arrived late. The producer went to the trouble of ensuring that Miller's driver arrived on time to get her to the studio. He spotted her on camera that night, sitting in the audience—of the *Carson* show.

With the big move to CBS only a few months away, the Griffin entourage faced two dilemmas. First, a temporary announcer had to be found. Seventy-four-year-old Arthur Treacher, who had a long history of cardiac ailments, had undergone bypass surgery in mid-April. His recovery was complicated by a leg artery aneurysm and a subsequent attack of hepatitis. Because he wouldn't be able to return to work until the CBS opener in August, a substitute was urgently needed.

Whenever Treacher had been unavailable in the past, Frank Gallop, best remembered for his work on *The Perry Como Show* and *The Kraft Music Hall*, took over the announcing chores. This time, however, Shanks hired veteran TV announcer Johnny Olson (*What's My Line?*, *The Price is Right*), to serve as guest announcer from April 14 to April 22, 1969. On April 23, former middleweight/welterweight Rocky Graziano served as the announcer, and would continue in that role until the end of the Westinghouse run. Graziano had been one of those I'm-available-whenever-you-need-me personalities. He lived close to the studio and had an affable on-camera countenance.

Born Thomas Rocco Barbella in 1919, Graziano ranked among the top knockout boxers of all time. He was included in Bert Sugar's book, *The 100 Greatest Boxers of All Time*. Graziano's 1955 autobiography, *Somebody Up There Likes Me*, was the basis for an Oscar-winning film released under the same title. However, when Graziano eventually hung up his boxing gloves, he turned his sights to entertainment. In the 1950s, he co-hosted *The Henny and Rocky*

Show with comedian Henny Youngman (another Griffin stalwart) and appeared regularly on *The Martha Raye Show.* His other notable TV credits include *Miami Undercover, Car 54, Where Are You?* and *Naked City* (the latter two being programs filmed in New York City). On the big screen, Graziano played an ex-boxer in the hit film, *Tony Rome* (1967).

As the fill-in announcer for the Griffin show, Graziano was the antithesis of Treacher. Many announcers, particularly those on talk shows, employ the same verbiage in their intros, effectively putting their personal stamp on what is to follow. Treacher had always opened with: "Now hear this," delivered in his clipped British accent. Graziano's approach was earthier. He opened with: "*Hey, you!* From 'da Little Theatre off Times Square, it's 'da *Moiv Griffin Show!*" Strangely enough, this intro became an accepted feature, adding yet another layer of quirkiness to the lively program.

The other weighty problem involved a choice of venue. Griffin had to pack up his belongings at the Little Theatre, since the facility was about to be turned over to *The David Frost Show,* which would replace Merv on the Westinghouse network beginning on July 7, 1969.

Making the move with Griffin to CBS were Treacher, Shanks, director Kirk Alexander, musical director Mort Lindsey; writer Bob Howard, and talent coordinators Jean Meegan and Tony Garofalo. One unfortunate loss, however, was Albert Fisher. "I wanted to move out of the area of publicity, and be more involved in the creative side of television," explains Fisher. "And when the Griffin show was ending at Westinghouse, Tad Reeves asked me if I would stay and produce pilots for the replacement shows, including John Barbour, Dennis Wholey, and David Frost. And my deal was that whichever of these pilots that got accepted, I would go on board with the staff of that show. And *The David Frost Show* was the one that got accepted. But when Frost got the job, he told Group W, 'Here's who I want to work on my show.' He wanted all the people he had worked with in England and he brought them over. Obviously, he was the star, and there was no way I could fight or finagle that. Frost did well, but I don't think his show ever caught on the way Merv's did. Merv wound up getting a smaller audience on

CBS, with a smaller number of stations, than he'd had at Westinghouse. But he made a hell of a lot more money!"

The last installment of the Westinghouse *Merv Griffin Show* aired, in most cities, on Friday, July 4, 1969. At the outset, Merv told the studio audience that they were about to witness the taping of Griffin show number 1,061. Unlike the NBC finale, the final Westinghouse episode contained no laudatory speeches or emotional farewells. This finale was the result of progression as opposed to cancellation. There were no "blockbuster" guests. The lineup included actress Lynn Redgrave, comedian Rodney Dangerfield, Reverend Billy Graham, singers Julie Budd and Aliza Kashi, and guest announcer Rocky Graziano.

It was an unremarkable finale to a remarkable chapter in American television. When the curtain came down that night, everyone connected with the show was confident that a bigger and better *Merv Griffin Show* lay ahead—on a different channel.

Critics and viewers were now eagerly awaiting Griffin's CBS opener, which promised to be the biggest talk-show event of the year, if not the decade.

Merv and his writers (from left): Pat McCormick, Dick Cavett, and David Lloyd at NBC, on day one of the The Merv Griffin Show, *Oct. 1, 1962. Credit: Ann Zane Shanks, Courtesy of Bob Shanks.*

Merv at the New York World's Fair with his future publicist, Albert Fisher, 1964. Credit: Albert Fisher.

Carol Channing laughs it up with Merv on his first Westinghouse show, May 10, 1965. Note the pewter mug on the desk, a gift from Sammy Davis, Jr. Credit: Albert Fisher.

Announcer/sidekick Arthur Treacher joins Merv for an impromptu song at the beginning of a 1965 show. Credit: Albert Fisher.

A nervous Richard Pryor gets some backstage bolstering from Albert Fisher just before his debut, May 1965. Credit: Albert Fisher.

Richard Pryor engrossed in semi-serious conversation as Arthur Treacher and Dody Goodman look on, 1965. Credit: Albert Fisher.

Merv belting out a tune with his conductor/arranger/pianist Mort Lindsey, 1965. Credit: Albert Fisher.

The College of San Mateo, Merv's alma mater, is the venue for this special edition of the show, December 12, 1965. Note the laudatory signs held by several enthusiastic attendees. Credit: Albert Fisher.

Phyllis Diller convulses Carol Channing and Merv during the San Mateo taping. Credit: Albert Fisher.

Carol Channing greets "The Queen of Gospel," Mahalia Jackson, in San Mateo. Credit: Albert Fisher.

Merv and Jerry Lewis engaged in some high-spirited storytelling, 1965. Credit: Albert Fisher.

Joan Crawford takes a swig of her favorite soft drink during the 44th Annual Photoplay Awards, 1966. The young actors are Christopher Connelly and Patricia Morrow of TV's Peyton Place. *Merv looks thrilled. Credit: Albert Fisher.*

John Wayne on the Photoplay Awards presentation, 1966. Credit: Albert Fisher.

Former V.P. Richard Nixon about to tape a "location" segment, January 1966. From left: Nixon, producer Bob Shanks (back to camera), Merv, and Albert Fisher. Credit: Albert Fisher.

Arthur looks displeased as Merv checks out some "mod" sunglasses, 1966. Credit: Albert Fisher.

Insult comic Jack E. Leonard, a familiar fixture on the Griffin stage in the 1960s and '70s. Credit: Albert Fisher.

The legendary Groucho Marx in April of 1967. Marx would make his final television appearance on Merv's show in May 1976. Credit: Albert Fisher.

*The delightfully eccentric and unpredictable Tallulah Bankhead in
1967, the year before she died. Credit: Albert Fisher.*

*One of the high points in the Westinghouse series: Merv's interview
with Dr. Martin Luther King, Jr., 1967. Harry Belafonte is seated at
right. Credit:©Albert Fisher/Fisher Media Productions.*

August 1967. Merv has good reason to look happy. His show is a primetime hit in New York, and has made the long awaited switch from monochrome to color. Credit: Albert Fisher.

Heavyweight champ Muhammad Ali, 1967. Credit: Albert Fisher.

*A pleasantly distracted Merv surrenders the spotlight to Moms Mabley
and exercise guru Debbie Drake, 1967. Credit: Albert Fisher.*

Jazz trumpeter/singer/actor Jack Sheldon, 1967. Sheldon would join Merv's orchestra as a regular in 1970. Credit: Albert Fisher.

Ethel Merman and Marty Allen demonstrating the latest dance moves, 1967. Credit: Albert Fisher.

Monti Rock III capturing the attention of Totie Fields, 1967. Credit: Albert Fisher.

Vincent Price obviously enjoying one of his host's wisecracks, 1967.
Credit: Albert Fisher.

Comedian Shelley Berman taking over the guest seat, much to the
displeasure of its female occupant. Berman has the distinction of being
Merv's first guest on the 1962 debut. Credit: Albert Fisher.

Senator Robert F. Kennedy making his only appearance on the Griffin show, October 1967. Credit: Albert Fisher.

A backstage, post show recap with Bob Shanks, Merv (back to camera) and Senator Robert F. Kennedy. Credit: Albert Fisher.

The lovely French singer Genevieve is charmed by special guest Mrs. Rose Kennedy, 1967. Orson Bean is seated on Merv's left. Credit: Albert Fisher.

July 1968. A member of the Joe Tex Band (left) gets the Harlem edition of the show rolling as Merv, Mayor John Lindsay, and workers from the Mayor's "Give a Damn" campaign observe thousands of residents present for the taping. Credit: Albert Fisher.

Richard M. Nixon in December 1967, shortly before he announced his candidacy for the presidency. Credit: Albert Fisher.

Future talk-show superstar Joan Rivers, 1968. Credit: Albert Fisher.

Muhammad Ali, one of Merv's special guests on the Harlem "Give a Damn" special, 1968. Credit: Albert Fisher.

The fabulous Zsa Zsa Gabor, a talk-show stalwart since the heyday of Jack Paar, looks for her cue near the end of a commercial break, 1968. Credit: Albert Fisher.

*A pre-*Sanford and Son *Redd Foxx, 1968. Merv would make a cameo appearance as himself on Foxx's hit series in 1975. Credit: Albert Fisher.*

Totie Fields exuding her usual exuberance, 1968. Credit: Albert Fisher.

Norman Mailer generating some laughs, 1968. Credit: Albert Fisher.

The irrepressible Charo on an early 1968 appearance. Credit: Albert Fisher.

Merv at bat for The Merv Griffin Show's baseball team, 1968. Credit: Albert Fisher.

The Brooklyn Bridge is a perfect backdrop for daredevil Merv in this publicity still for the "Sidewalks of New York" special, 1968. Credit: Albert Fisher.

Producer Bob Shanks, Albert Fisher, Arthur Treacher, cameraman Michael Wadley, and Merv atop the RCA Building, shooting footage "Sidewalks of New York," 1968. Credit: Albert Fisher.

Art Linkletter, one of Merv's erstwhile competitors, promotes his latest book, I Wish I'd Said That, *1968. Credit: Albert Fisher.*

Merv and the inimitable Moms Mabley in 1968. The following year, Moms would help launch Merv's new series on CBS. Credit: Albert Fisher.

Jack Benny during a commercial break, 1968. Benny could never understand why Merv would run out at the beginning of each show. Jack to Merv: "Why do you run? You've got the job!" Credit: Albert Fisher.

Judy Garland, filling in for Merv in December 1968, is reunited with her former conductor, Mort Lindsey. Credit: Albert Fisher.

Margaret Hamilton, the Wicked Witch of the West in The Wizard of Oz, and Judy Garland in their last photo together, 1968. Credit: Albert Fisher.

The famous audience, Miss Miller, 1969. Credit: Albert Fisher.

Christine Jorgensen, the first person to attract world attention following sex reassignment surgery, in a lighthearted moment, 1969. Credit: Albert Fisher.

Arthur Treacher and Bob Hope showing off their distinctive noses, 1969. Credit: Albert Fisher.

One of the official "Our Man on Broadway" portraits.
Credit: Albert Fisher

Merv and his first producer Bob Shanks shortly before the move to Hollywood, 1970. Credit: Author's collection.

Salute to Stars of the Silents, January 1971. From left: Betty Blythe, Charles Rogers, Betty Bronson, Richard Arlen, Beverly Bayne, Viola Dana, Minta Durfee Arbuckle, Merv, Eddie Quillan, Jackie Coogan, Carter DeHaven, Neil Hamilton, Chester Conklin, Babe London, Lillian Gish, and Vivian Duncan. Credit: Judd Gunderson, Copyright ©1971 Los Angeles Times. Used with Permission.

Making a grand entrance atop Tanya the Elephant at Caesar's Palace in Las Vegas, 1972. Credit: Author's collection.

Burt Reynolds, Merv, Florence Henderson, Bob Newhart, Ginny Newhart 1973. Credit: Author's collection.

Merv in Philadelphia to promote his book, From Where I Sit: Merv Griffin's Book of People, *November 1982. Credit: Author's collection.*

A very upbeat Merv, backstage before airtime, in 1986. Credit: Author's collection.

Merv in Monte Carlo, joking around with Miriam Paar (Jack's wife) in 1978. Among the onlookers: Jack Paar (wearing bandana), Carl Reiner (wearing cap), and producer Bob Murphy (wearing glasses). Charlton Heston (wearing sunglasses) is standing behind the crowd at left. Credit: Don Kane.

Merv's Resorts International Hotel in Atlantic City is the venue for this 1990 performance. The ever-faithful Mort Lindsey is at the piano. Credit: © Cashman Photo.

12. MERV HOLDS CORT

The show ticked its way into expansion mode. In addition to the carryovers from Westinghouse, three new writers were added to the fold: Andrew Smith, Norman Stiles, and Noel Kinglin. Paul Solomon and Tony Garofalo retained their positions as senior talent coordinators. Mort Lindsey, whom Merv regarded as indispensable, made the move also. Because CBS wanted a larger orchestra, Lindsey's aggregation would be augmented to 18 players. Except for a larger, updated set, replete with mod colors and sophisticated lighting fixtures, the show was expected to look and function much as it had at Westinghouse.

The CBS debut was slated for August 18, 1969. A late summer launching had purposely been planned to allow time to correct any "kinks" before commencement of the new season in September. The date would present a booking problem, since many of the major film and TV stars were likely to be on vacation or already back at work before the cameras.

Coming up with five or six top-notch guests five nights a week can prove challenging for any show. The talent coordinators began making phone calls, hoping to wangle an appearance from at least one elusive megastar. "Everybody starts out wanting to get Cary Grant and the return of Christ," Steve Allen told *Newsweek* in 1969. "But soon they settle for Morey Amsterdam. It's not a serious problem."

Several weeks prior to the debut, Griffin told reporters that he wanted Charles Lindbergh and Howard Hughes for his series opener. Everyone knew he was joking. He *had* to be. Lindbergh was elusive, and Hughes was reclusive. *Notoriously* reclusive! Setting his expectations several rungs lower, he invited Mayor John Lindsay, New York Jets quarterback Joe Namath, former movie queen Hedy Lamarr, and author Henry Miller (*Tropic of Cancer, Tropic of Capricorn*).

As it turned out, Griffin's guest list for his CBS curtain raiser included Hedy Lamarr, Woody Allen, Leslie Uggams, Moms Mabley, and former presidential speechwriter Ted Sorensen.

Griffin, who oversaw the most minuscule of production details, threw himself into what he believed would be the biggest show of his career. He did as much work and planning at home as he did at the office. "I loved it because you could hear his brains grinding," recalls Julann Griffin. "I used to tell him, 'Your brains are sounding too loud.'"

Finally, it was August 18. The sweat on Griffin's brow that day wasn't due to the oppressive Manhattan heat; it was attributable to the surge of nervous energy every performer experiences before facing the spotlight. Merv spent most of the day talking with reporters and mulling over last-minute production details, the latter being an area that had always been of intense professional concern. Shortly before tape time (6:30 p.m.), the star and his producer did a quick rewrite of the opening monologue. Griffin would later admit that there was nothing wrong with the initial draft they'd written. Nevertheless, he felt he had to do *something* to soothe his nerves during those anxious moments before the show.

The evening would mark the return of Arthur Treacher, still recovering from cardiac surgery four months earlier. The ordeal had reduced his physical appearance to a pale approximation of its once robust glory. His voice still echoed the Arthur Treacher of old and he opened the show with amazing gusto: "Now hear this, from the Cort Theater off Times Square, it's the *NEW Merv Griffin Show!* Accompanying Merv for your delectation, Mr. Woody Allen, Miss Hedy Lamarr, Miss Leslie Uggams, Jackie "Moms" Mabley, Mr. Ted Sorensen...."

There was no mention of Joe Namath, Mayor Lindsay and Henry Miller. A CBS spokesperson said Namath wouldn't appear because he was "concentrating" on the Jets-Giants game of the previous day. Lindsay couldn't appear because he was an incumbent running for re-election, and his opponents could have demanded "equal time" pursuant to certain laws in effect at the time. Miller, unfortunately, couldn't make it to New York because of unavoidable delays in travel.

As the show began, the cameras—still under the direction of Kirk Alexander—panned the expensively refurbished theater. The audience, consisting of a prosperous-looking assemblage, applauded politely. Unlike today's talk show audiences, there was nary a pair of jeans or tee shirt in the house. As Treacher continued his announcement, all eyes in the theater focused on the blue-speckled curtain; everyone was eager to see how much weight Merv had gained or lost over the summer. Suddenly, the music stopped, the curtain parted, and out walked Miss Miller! "Like I've been telling you all summer," she shrieked, "give the kid a break, *please!*" By this time, it sounded like Miller was begging people to watch the show. After delivering her now-famous catchphrase, Miller took to her seat.

Treacher continued: "Look sharp now my duckies, here's the dear boy himself, *Merrrrrvyn!*"

Sporting a dark blue suit and brightly striped tie, Merv ran through the curtain as he'd done over a thousand times on the Westinghouse show. But this wasn't Westinghouse. This was CBS, the Tiffany network, and Merv was its warrior in a multi-million dollar battle. The most important television show of his career lay ahead of him. He seemed almost as ill at ease as he'd been on that harrowing night in 1962 when he first subbed for Paar. Every comment, question, and joke would be dissected, analyzed, and memorialized by the critics—beginning with the ones occupying the first several rows of the theater.

From his earliest days in television, Merv would gauge his and everyone else's performances by the reactions of non-show biz folk sitting in the studio audience. People who work in television refer to them as "civilians" because they are not connected with the entertainment industry. Merv never made it a point to seat his family members or close friends in the choice seats. He wanted responses that were genuine rather than obligatory. Now, to his unutterable disgust, 50 austere-looking critics were peering up at him from those seats. This was an arrangement the network had made without informing the host or anyone connected with the show. In recounting the CBS opener to *TV Guide*, Merv said, "I looked at them and went right into the toilet."

Merv managed to mask his opening night jitters, but just barely. With his rhythm thrown out of kilter, he nervously called attention to his new "home."

"How do you like the theater? Isn't it beautiful?" he asked, beseechingly. "The minute I walked into this place when we were looking for theaters, I knew I wanted it. It's so right for the audience! Can you see?" The response was less than enthusiastic. "Hey," he groaned, "This is opening night!"

He couldn't wait to broach a subject that had been the source of consternation among the network brass: the cost of refurbishing the theater. "It was a little hard to convince CBS because they had to go for a little bit of loot for this place," he said gleefully. "And they balked at first, but when I showed them the negatives of their Christmas party, they came around."

At this point, the host had no choice but to acknowledge the critics looking up at him. "Let me get the record straight because I know there's a lot of visiting press here," he said earnestly. "There's been much discussion in the papers and magazines about the three-way competition. I think Carson does a great job. Bishop does a great job. We're going to try to entertain you, and there is room for everybody." Then he delivered the punchline: "And may the *best* man win!" (The joke, unfortunately, flew over most of the heads in the theater.)

Unlike Johnny Carson or Joey Bishop, Merv could belt out a tune. He walked over to the band, looked down, and said, "Are you guys in a hole?" That's because a good portion of the players were positioned on the same level as the audience, while others were on stage with Mort. This was a bit unusual for a major orchestra. After a soft rendition of "I'll Never Fall in Love Again" (from the hit show *Promises, Promises!*), he strolled over to his new desk and read a few congratulatory telegrams, including one from Mayor Lindsay. Next came a short presentation depicting how the show is put together, made up of zany clips from silent films. This amusing bit is not included in the DVD release, most likely due to rights clearances for the clips.

The indomitable Moms Mabley was the first guest. A large aspect of Moms's appeal had always been her cogent assessment of the sexes, her comments and observations always coming off as derisively amusing. She frequently chatted about how old, ugly, or stingy her previous boyfriends or husbands had been. Tonight would be no exception. She told Merv that she'd recently married yet again. "I still don't know what happened to your first husband," said Merv, following the routine faithfully. "He's been dead," said Moms. "I know he's been dead," Merv asserted, "but *how* did he get dead?"

Moms: "Well, I didn't poison him!"

Merv: "So how *did* you do it?"

Moms: "He thought he could and he *couldn't!*"

Merv: "Now this first husband…you told me you had him cremated."

Moms: "Yeah, I burned him up."

Merv: "Why'd you do that?"

Moms: "Well, I determined that he *had* to get hot at least one time!"

[Big laugh and applause from the audience]

Knowing of Moms's penchant for blue material, Merv grew visibly uneasy when she said: "Did you hear the one about the man I…."

"Here we go Mr. Tankersley!" Merv interrupted, "We might as well test the whole censorship department tonight." He meant it as a joke, but his words would ring true. In the coming weeks and months, Griffin's producer would have several highly charged dealings with William Tankersley, the CBS censor. Tankersley remained on guard to chop out any of Mom's salty asides—and he did. At one point, as Merv was chatting with Moms just before a break, a harsh edit in the tape became evident. The remaining laughter and applause on the soundtrack left no doubt that something objectionable, at least by the network's standards, had been excised. After the cut, Merv continued: "If you're having trouble with your girlfriend…." then added: "it couldn't help *him!*" We'll never know who the "him" was, or what "he" might have needed help with, because the entire bit remains lost.

Cutting edge material had always been Moms's specialty. Her 1961 comedy album *The Funniest Woman in the World* had been a best seller. "But it's stuff you really can't do on the show here," said Merv nervously, as he picked up the sleeve of her latest recording. Merv felt there was something questionable on the front cover, so he displayed only the back. "Aw show it, Merv!" Moms pleaded. "They ain't gonna hear anything on there that they wouldn't hear on the street!"

Though Moms couldn't perform the "stuff" on *that* record, she could offer a song that had been released on another. It was a recording that had reached number two on the charts in 1968: *Abraham, Martin, and John.* Written by Dick Holler and first recorded by Dion, the folk/rock hit was, of course, a tribute to Abraham Lincoln, Martin Luther King, John F. Kennedy, and Robert F. Kennedy.

Though Woody Allen had not yet achieved major stardom, he'd been a Griffin favorite since the NBC era. Allen's film, *Take the Money and Run,* which he had written, directed, and starred in, had opened that very day. He was concurrently starring in a successful stage adaptation of *Play it Again, Sam,* which was in its seventh month. Allen's casual attire drew fire. "You really spruced up for my opening," said Merv. Then, taking a long stare at Allen and Moms sitting next to each other, he said, "This looks like a meeting of the labor unions."

Allen seemed uncharacteristically subdued. He was eager to plug *Take the Money and Run,* a comedic romp about a totally inept bank robber, played by Allen. In reviewing the film for *New York* magazine, Judith Crist declared that "the golden age of comedy is back, courtesy of Woody Allen," adding that the film was "basically an old-fashioned, rib-cracking comedy, a rarity in our time." Those words confused Merv. He said he didn't understand the direction in which Allen's career was heading. "I've always thought you'd go for the intellectual comedy," Merv reasoned. "The topical, today, protest kind of comedy. And you went the whole other way. You've become America's sex symbol." To which Allen replied, "Yes, but we don't know of which sex I'm a symbol of!"

Realizing he'd hit pay dirt with Allen's retort, Merv began grasping at other subjects that might elicit laughs, such as Allen's childhood. Allen admitted he was an obnoxious kid.

Merv: "Did you do the same things that other boys did?"

Allen: "Yes, but not to the right people!"

The elegantly dressed Leslie Uggams livened up proceedings with two numbers: "Get Me to the Church on Time" and "Didn't We." Uggams, who was under contract to Griffin at the time, would launch her own variety series on the CBS network that fall. Interestingly, Saul Illson and Ernest Chambers, the future executive producers of *The Merv Griffin Show*, would produce Uggams' new variety hour.

Next up was Austrian-born Hedy Lamarr, the sultry star who had caused a sensation in her first film, Gustav Machaty's *Ecstasy* (1933), in which she bared her breasts. The film, which was shot in Prague, was also widely noted for a scene in which Lamarr's character experiences an orgasm, indicated solely by the expression on her face shown in close-up. Lamarr went on to fame playing exotic roles in hit films including *Algiers* (her American debut, 1938); *Boom Town* (1940), with Clark Gable; *Ziegfeld Girl* (1941), with Lana Turner and Judy Garland; *White Cargo* (1942), with Walter Pidgeon; and *Tortilla Flat* (1942), with Spencer Tracy and John Garfield.

"That's a great name for a movie star—Hedy Lamarr," said Merv, as he welcomed the actress to the panel. "It was formerly Hedy Lipshitz, I think," quipped Allen. "Don't attack me," said Lamarr, jokingly. "Well, on the other hand…are you *willing* to be Miss Lipshitz?" retorted Allen in a Grouchoesque delivery.

"You really came over here with a bang," said Merv, obviously referring to Lamarr's notorious nude scene. "What they're doing now in movies is something you did some years ago." Griffin was, of course, referring to *Ecstasy* (1933).

"Well, I didn't know there were zoomar lenses back then," Lamarr explained defensively. The young actress thought the swimming sequence, which required her to be nude, would be shot from a great distance. With the use of a special lens that could zoom in close, the film's most controversial scene was created. (Lamarr's recollection might explain why the fuzzy quality of the swimming scene is incongruous to the rest of the film.) "Besides," she smiled, "that didn't sell the picture anyhow." The inference was that the young actress didn't know her breasts would be visible in the final cut. Merv asked if the scene *wasn't* supposed to be in the movie. Lamarr said she didn't think so because it wasn't in the script. "But then," she added, "so many things aren't."

Merv plugged the book, *Ecstasy and Me*, which he assumed had been written by the actress. "Don't talk about that," Lamarr protested. "That's *not* my book." Lamarr emphatically stated that she was writing a book of her own. Merv appeared stunned for a moment, but shifted gears immediately. Since he couldn't talk about the book, Merv refocused on *Ecstasy*, asking if the film had hurt Lamarr's image in Hollywood. "I don't know," she answered laconically. "What's an image? What's your image, Woody?" she asked. "The same as yours!" Allen replied smugly.

Though Lamarr was past her prime, she had aged well. She was lovely to look at, but her interview lacked the sparkling repartee Merv needed for his premiere episode. Even worse, she had thrown Merv a major curve regarding the book, forcing him to improvise. Although his mind was racing furiously to keep the conversation moving, Merv didn't miss a beat on camera and abandoned his planned line of questioning. Instead he simply said, "Tell me something I didn't know about you." "I want to be a very simple, *complicated* person," said Lamarr, matter-of-factly. With that, Merv cut to a commercial.

Ted Sorensen dominated the last portion of the show, traditionally reserved for authors, lawyers, scientists, and other non-showbiz types. Sorensen had served as advisor, counsel, and speechwriter to President John F. Kennedy. He had assisted in the writing of Kennedy's inaugural address in which the newly elected president said, "Ask not what your country can do for you; ask what you can do for your country." However, there has always been some debate as to who composed the famous line, Sorensen or Kennedy.

Sorensen was about to embark on a political career of his own. [The following year, he was unsuccessful in his attempt to run for U.S. senator for New York.]

Sorensen said he'd been to Israel and Jordan where he held press conferences with the leaders. He said he'd been asked about his views on American policy in the Middle East, and in general. "While I don't like to criticize my government while I'm aboard, I also believe in telling the truth when I'm asked, so I told them." When Sorensen was asked to expound on what he had told the leaders, all he would say was that he had visited some 40 countries. "I've seen all the other systems," he said, "and I wouldn't trade ours for any of them." This response generated applause, but didn't answer the question that had been posed. Instead, he launched into a spiel about how it was *not* "old-fashioned" to be patriotic. "In any event, I think the best patriotism is to try to make your country better."

On the subject of the war, Sorensen said: "I think that we've done what we had to do. We have prevented a communist military conquest of Vietnam. Having done that, we really ought to get out. And get out more quickly, in an orderly way and stop this killing. For young men to be sent over there now and give their lives— most of them you know are only 18, 19 years old—is going to affect us for the next generation."

As the audience burst into applause, Merv interjected: "But the big question is, how do you get out?" Sorensen paused and looked at Merv. "On *boats*," he said impishly. The audience laughed. Merv didn't.

Sorensen continued: "We can't just withdrawal in one day. We can't look like it's a disorderly sort of thing, and let a lot of people be slaughtered. But we can certainly move a lot faster than we're moving and I wish we would."

Merv asked the question everyone had been waiting to hear: "Being a close friend of President Kennedy's, how would he view where we have gone in this country, at this moment? Would he have been disappointed? Would he be pleased?" Without hesitation, Sorensen said: "I think he'd be pleased with some of his programs and goals that have been carried out. But one of his favorite saying in the campaign was 'we can do better.' The moon shot was one of President Kennedy's ideas and goals, but to spend all that money going to the moon, and have that genius, that tremendous engineering accomplishment, and not be able to make our cities decent places to live in and, and work in, and walk safely in, that's an incredible gap. He would not be satisfied with that."

This one-on-one with Sorensen was an admirable demonstration of Griffin's interviewing prowess, but the segment changed the tone of the entire show. None of the other guests said another word for the rest of the program, making *The Merv Griffin Show* look more like *Meet the Press.*

The show had been running behind schedule all night. When the studio clock (set for "TV time") indicated it was 1:00 a.m, Merv wrapped things up swiftly. "Thank you all for joining us on our opening night," he smiled, "you made it very comfortable and very nice." Merv announced his guests for the following night: Sonny and Cher, Dinah Shore, Tiny Tim, and James Mason. (He would fare far better on his second outing with that enviable line-up.) The music swelled up and the curtain came down.

When the premiere show was over, both network and star were far from elated with the results. An eclectic mix of music, laughs, and politics, the first entry in the Griffin/CBS column in no way measured up to the enormous fanfare that preceded it. A comfortable and nice show would have been fine at 4:30 in the afternoon, but CBS needed a fast-paced blockbuster that would have given Johnny a run for his money. Indeed, money was a key issue. To the network execs that had authorized the expenditures for renovating the theater, advertising costs, and production overhead, words like "comfortable" and "nice" were synonymous with failure.

Many reviewers, who had been expecting something "new" and "different," were less than generous. The *New York Daily News* said that despite the Big Broadway look, "it was just another late-night talk show."

Newsweek complained that the program had "floundered" in certain spots, with Woody Allen's "sex symbol" retort being one of the few bright moments. The publication had no ovations for the other guests, dismissing Hedy Lamarr as "uncommunicative" and Ted Sorensen as "smugly evasive." Moms Mabley and Leslie Uggams weren't even acknowledged.

Time offered kinder words, but not many. "Pleasant personalities," declared the magazine, "but hardly show stoppers."

Some reviewers felt that Merv had indeed established himself as different—from the relaxed, easy going Merv of the past—instead of the competition.

The competition, of course, had attempted to slaughter Griffin in the ratings that night. Joey Bishop sought to win the evening with the Smothers Brothers, then involved in a major skirmish over censorship issues that culminated in the cancellation of their show on CBS. Over the years, many writers have noted that Johnny Carson whipped the living daylights (or *nightlights*) out of Bishop and Griffin simply by booking NBC's top gun, Bob Hope. This is true, but only in part.

The August 30, 1969 edition of *TV Guide* reported that CBS had claimed victory for the evening, citing a New York Nielsen count giving Griffin a 31 percent share of the audience, Carson 25, and Bishop 8. That meant that 31 percent of all viewers watching television at 11:30 p.m. were tuned in to the Griffin show. This came as no surprise, since the "curiosity factor" almost always aids the new kid on the block. The same report also noted that, according to NBC, Griffin eventually *lost* the bulk of viewers to Carson by the end of the night.

Newsweek, in its September 1, 1969 cover story ("Battle of the Talk Shows"), also cited a set of New York Nielsen ratings. According to that source, Griffin won 49 percent of the network audience during the first hour and a half. Carson won 39 percent; and Bishop, 12 percent. This survey confirmed that Carson had won back the audience, *but not until the final 15 minutes* of the evening, by which time the entertainers had finished and Ted Sorensen's political discourse had begun.

The race between Carson and Griffin would largely be influenced by one frequently overlooked fact: NBC had more stations in its lineup than CBS. (ABC, still third in rank, didn't have as many stations as CBS.) That meant that in markets where CBS didn't have an affiliate station, the Griffin show could only score a zero rating. This would become an ongoing source of consternation for Merv who, at this late date, learned that his show was now playing on *fewer* stations than it did in syndication.

The *Newsweek* cover bore flattering images of Griffin, Bishop and Carson. The three leering hosts had not been photographed together. The cover was a composite job depicting Griffin posing next to two TV sets, one atop the other. Bishop's face was superimposed on the top screen, and Carson's on the bottom. This was an ironic configuration, in view of the fact that Carson was the reigning champ in the three-way race.

As the weeks rolled by, the new ratings charts clearly demonstrated that Griffin had toppled Bishop, but not Carson. By early fall, there was no question that Merv would *continue* to beat Bishop, but not Carson. With NBC commanding 220 stations, opposite CBS's 120, the numbers would always be stacked in Carson's favor.

The concern over weak numbers intensified with the approaching November "sweeps" period. Griffin took the show on the road in late October for a week's worth of shows to originate from Hollywood. With a larger pool of celebrities to choose from, the Griffin guest list included Carol Burnett, George Burns, Eva Gabor, Groucho Marx, Tim Conway, Danny Thomas, and Bob Cummings. His next stop was Caesar's Palace, in Las Vegas, where he welcomed Sid Caesar, Walter Matthau, Jack Benny, Cesar Romero, Glen Campbell, Ann-Margret, and Danny Kaye.

No one at NBC was losing any sleep over Merv's Hollywood or Vegas excursions. It did, however, become readily apparent that the ratings for the West Coast editions were significantly higher than their New York counterparts. There was speculation in the press that a plan to move the show to Los Angeles, on a permanent basis, was under consideration. There was also talk that the Griffin show would visit Chicago, Washington, and even London. Initially, Merv wasn't wild about relocating to California. His production company was headquartered in Manhattan, and his beloved farm ("Teetertown") was located in nearby Califon, New Jersey. CBS, which had spent two million to refurbish the Cort Theater, was emphatically against such a plan. Nevertheless, the numbers couldn't be ignored. Griffin and company wasted no time in scheduling a return visit to Hollywood for mid-December.

Back in New York, the show needed a "heavy-hitter" to bolster the sagging ratings. Merv dug into his social register and called Rose Kennedy.

Griffin's viewers had previously been treated to a glimpse of the Kennedy aristocracy. The 1967 segment had been one of the high points in the Westinghouse series. Everyone connected with the show now hoped that a follow-up with Kennedy would lure viewers away from Carson.

For her second appearance on the Griffin show, taped on November 12, 1969, the 79- year-old matriarch wore a simple, but elegant, pink dress. (Weeks earlier, she had submitted a sample of the fabric to the director, thereby allowing him to gauge its suitability for the cameras.)

Kennedy seemed genuinely moved by the warm greeting from the audience as she took her seat next to Merv at center stage. She smiled approvingly when Merv announced that she was indeed a grandmother—with 28 grandchildren. "When you're all together as a family," he asked cheerfully, "what do you talk about?" Kennedy said that the family method for talks and debates stemmed back to the time when she was raising her own brood. She'd learned, early on, the importance of grouping the children separately when it came time for discussions, which were strongly encouraged. "The older ones could discuss more advanced subjects than the younger ones," she explained, "and the older ones do better at talking, so the younger ones never get a chance and that's very bad." The rule in the Kennedy household was to separate the kids into groups, based on age, thereby giving everyone an equal chance to participate on his or her own level. "And that's very important," she added, "Because when they go out, they're confident and able to talk and be articulate."

"It sounds like there's no generation gap in your family," Merv smiled. "The young are listened to." "Yes," Kennedy replied, "but they *must* participate. The more things they're interested in, the finer human beings they are, because they never get bored and they never get *boring*."

It came as no surprise when the subject shifted to JFK. Merv asked if there had been a moment in his life when he seemed to signal an interest in politics or, more specifically, a desire to live in the White House. Kennedy explained that it was only "natural" for him to have political ambitions since both sides of his family had been active in government. "These things all go back a long time," she said solemnly. "And Jack, I remember, *was* interested. He couldn't understand why a governess who we had would rather be under the queen—she was a Canadian—than under the President of the United States. That interested him, even as a little boy."

Kennedy added that she'd always believed her children might fare better in the business sector. Her husband, Ambassador Joseph P. Kennedy, maintained that they should "devote themselves to public service and government."

Roughly four months prior to this interview, U.S. Senator Edward M. (Ted) Kennedy dominated the headlines after his car had plummeted off a bridge at Chappaquiddick Island, Massachusetts. After he swam safely to shore, the female passenger he left behind, Mary Jo Kopechne, died in the vehicle. The resulting scandal from this tragedy stemmed from the fact that Kennedy didn't report it until many hours after it had occurred. The senator pleaded guilty to leaving the scene of an accident and causing injury. Kennedy was sentenced to two months in jail. The sentence, however, was ultimately suspended.

It was too hot a topic to ignore. Merv had been friendly with the Kennedys for years. He knew that the mere mention of "Chappaquiddick," as the scandal came to be known, could cause a rift in his relationship with the family. On the other hand, avoiding the subject altogether would make him appear inept as an interviewer, and obsequious to a powerful political dynasty.

Merv played it cool. "Senator Teddy has been going through an acute personal struggle at the moment," he said casually. "What is his mood?" Rose Kennedy responded guardedly: "I believe he'll always devote himself to government service, and he will always do it in one capacity or another. I don't know what the future will bring, but that is his firm resolve which, of course, I cooperate very sincerely."

As the segment drew to a close, Merv asked: "What sustains you?" Smiling through many wrinkles, Kennedy cited the title of the Irving Stone novel *The Agony and the Ecstasy*. "We've had great ecstatic moments, and we've had tragedies," she said eloquently. "But the ecstasies and the triumphs are greater than the tragedies."

Although the Kennedy interview was indeed a "prestige" booking, it had no impact on the ratings registered during the sweeps period.

The numbers were not improving. Not only was Merv getting trampled by Carson, he was trailing behind David Frost, his successor on the Westinghouse network. In New York, *The David Frost Show* had taken over Merv's old time slot, 8:30 to 10 p.m., on WNEW-TV. According *The New York Times*, the first week of December 1969 saw Frost fetching a 6 rating and a 9 share in prime-time, compared to Griffin's 4 rating and 14 share in late night. A year earlier, when Griffin held the 8:30 p.m. slot, he had garnered an 8 Nielsen rating—two points *higher* than Frost was now getting.

Frost was also reaching 150,000 more homes each night than Griffin. Even more distressing: Frost's rate card indicated that commercial minutes on his syndicated series cost $1,550 to $2,220, while the CBS was peddling the Griffin show in the $500 to $1,000 range.

"Networks get nervous very quickly and they can be weird," says Bob Shanks. In his autobiography, Merv would recall a series of nagging memos and phone calls from network execs, all brimming with suggestions on how the program could be "improved."

For starters, the CBS bosses wanted a steady stream of big-name stars. Scrounging around for "biggies" five nights a week proved more challenging than anyone had anticipated, particularly with Carson and David Frost vying for whichever superstar happened to be in New York. Soon, Dick Cavett would be another constituent to be reckoned with.

During the last quarter of 1969, Joey Bishop came to the realization that his show wasn't going to make it. Nothing he tried seemed to work. Not even Paar-like drama. Some months earlier, announcer Regis Philbin walked off the show because he felt he'd been criticized for being a detriment to Bishop. This pumped up the ratings, but only for a few nights until the wandering announcer returned.

On November 26, 1969, Bishop opened his show with the usual fanfare. He'd kept mum about his intention to throw in the towel. In fact, even Regis Philbin and Johnny Mann said they'd learned of their boss's decision to quit only hours before they went on the air. Bishop began his monologue by talking about the pressures associated with network television. He noted that affiliate stations maintain the right to carry or *not* carry a show. If a show loses enough cities, it's reflected in the ratings, and survival becomes very difficult without a solid line-up of stations, he explained. Bishop also revealed some sobering stats: Bishop was carried by 125 cities; Griffin had 152 cities, and Carson had 209.

Bishop said that he, like Merv and Johnny, tried to give the audience the best show possible. Reiterating the pressures of the three-way race, Bishop thanked his network, sponsors, staff, and crew. He said that if he could think of anything else to say, he'd ask either Johnny or Merv to let him say it on their show.

Bishop didn't stick around for the rest of the evening. He would leave the remainder of the show in Philbin's hands. He blew a kiss into the camera and walked off the stage. Although Bishop had another month's worth of shows to do, he wisely assigned them to a succession of guest hosts, including Philbin.

As Bishop's gabfest slowly fizzled out, the folks at *The Tonight Show* were planning an event that would bedazzle the American public and warrant a chapter in the annals of late-night television.

Although Tiny Tim had made his national debut on the Griffin show in 1967, he owed his stardom to *Laugh-In* and *The Tonight Show*. In September 1969, Tiny stunned Carson's viewers with the announcement of his engagement to 17-year-old Victoria Budinger, whom he invariably referred to as Miss Vicki. Realizing the potential publicity value of such a spectacle, Carson offered to present the wedding on a special segment of *The Tonight Show*.

On December 17, 1969, the stage in Studio 6-B was restructured to resemble an ornate English church, tastefully decorated with thousands of tulips, an obvious reference to Tiny's signature song, "Tip Toe Through the Tulips with Me." A minister presided over the ceremony, which was conducted in surprisingly good taste, and identified the groom under his given name, Herbert Buckingham Khoury. When it was over, Carson toasted the newlyweds with champagne. Joining in the traditional gesture were guests Phyllis Diller, Florence Henderson, and veteran singer Nick Lucas, who had recorded "Tip Toe" four decades earlier. The bride and groom, however, preferred milk and honey. The wedding was the second most talked about television event of the year; the first was Apollo 11 moon landing.

Over the years, various sources have reported that Merv's crew watched the wedding on backstage monitors at CBS. Yet no one has ever explained how this could have been possible. The Griffin show was taping in Los Angeles that week, so Merv's people would have been working at Studio 43 in Television City. *The Tonight Show* was taped at 5:30 p.m., and went on the air at 11:30 p.m., as did Merv's show. The actual wedding portion of the program didn't commence until after midnight. Why would Merv's crew be watching television in the studio at that hour? Had they been working overtime that night? Or did the CBS crew somehow gain access to the NBC taping as it transpired earlier in the evening? It didn't matter one iota if the Griffin team had tuned in, because nearly everyone else who was watching television at that hour *did*.

Two nights later, Merv poked fun at the *Tonight Show* triumph. "I'm very proud to tell you that tonight, there's going to be a wedding on our show," he said proudly. "Tonight's the night you've all been waiting for. The night when that falsetto singing star, Big Steve, gets married to lovely 14-year-old Miss Jaynie." The audience went crazy.

The curtain parted to the sound of somber organ music and a church-like set, resembling the one used on the Carson show. Waiting at the altar was Steve Allen, sporting a long, black frizzy wig and a hooked proboscis large enough to rival Tiny's. Steve's wife, Jayne Meadows, costumed in a baby-doll outfit to satirize the youthful Miss Vicki, took on the role of the bride. Comedian Jack Carter played the minister, and the proud papa givng the bride away was none other than the delightfully grumpy Arthur Treacher.

"Dearly beloved," Carter began, "we are gathered here in Studio 43, in the sight of cameramen, stagehands, and sensation seekers, to join these two, uh, *people*—in a long-term contract, two years firm with options." When that dialogue registered only a mild chortle, Carter ad-libbed, "Dearly beloved, we are gathered here to *increase our rating!*" The audience laughed and applauded.

Virtually every nuance of the "real" wedding was parodied, right down to the milk and honey toasting ritual. It was a very funny, fast-paced sketch, penned by Allen. In fact, the bit was so well received that Merv would replay a portion of it on his New Year's Eve show, broadcast live from the Cort Theater.

With most celebrities out of town, or otherwise unavailable, on New Year's Eve, Merv decided to try something different. "I haven't been on live television since 1962," he said excitedly, referring to his now-forgotten stints on *The Tonight Show*. The audience would be permitted to get up and dance, but Merv cautioned that no drinking would be allowed. The crowed booed. Merv offered a solution. "During the commercials," he said, "The band will turn in your direction and breathe at you."

Merv, who rarely got political in his monologues, took jabs at a few politicians, beginning with the vice president. "We wanted to have the world's biggest noisemaker here," he announced. "But as you know, Spiro Agnew is in Asia." The crowd cheered. "Mayor Lindsay wanted to be here, but he couldn't make it because he's home melting down his supply of 20-cent subway tokens." (New York City had recently discontinued use of the coins on its public transportation system.)

To commemorate the old year going out, Arthur dressed up as "Father Time" and indulged in some innocuous chitchat with Merv. It was a prophetic role for Treacher, since the network was, by this time, clamoring to put the aging announcer out to pasture.

Following the old man was the New Year "baby," an adorable toddler named Billy Berry. His dad, Bill Berry, had been with the Griffin orchestra since the earliest days at Westinghouse. Berry had begun as a trumpeter and switched to cornet. Though many of Berry's original compositions had been performed on the show, Mort was especially fond of one song called "Come to Me," which was frequently played during commercial breaks. Bill Berry would be one of several musicians to make the move to Los Angeles with the Griffin show in the coming year.

A versatile musician/composer/arranger, Berry would eventually form his own big band, Bill Berry's L.A. Express, which could be heard at jazz concerts, festivals, and on several albums for Concord Records. He died in 2002.

Though the show largely consisted of videotaped highlights representing Merv's four-and-a-half months with the network, there were two "in-house" guests who sparkled that night. Eloise Laws sang, "Get Together," and the perpetually vivacious Hermoine Gingold dedicated a poem to Arthur.

At midnight, the camera switched to the Allied Chemical Building to the strains of "Auld Lang Syne." A new decade was born; 1969 had given way to 1970. At that moment, *The Merv Griffin Show* certainly looked like the liveliest of lively parties, marked with noisemakers, vigorous applause, and dancing in the aisles. It was undoubtedly one of the most unconventional episodes in the history of the program.

Merv and his staff screened many hours' worth of tape to select the best vignettes for the occasion. These included Tommy Smothers recounting his experience of being canceled by CBS; Gene Kelly tap dancing to "Hello, Dolly!"; Carol Burnett guiding Merv through some unlikely exercises ("You're rotten!" she told him); a hilarious bit with Merv and Totie Fields bouncing on a trampoline; and a remarkably lithe Danny Kaye demonstrating an exaggerated "entrance" on a runway.

Other interesting highlights included a rare segment with Max Yasgur, the farmer who had leased his land for the Woodstock Music Festival four and a half months earlier. Yasgur showed a film clip of the "clean-up" in the aftermath of the legendary event. There was also British actress Katie Drew-Wilkinson talking about her role in the controversial production, *Oh! Calcutta*. (She commented that being on a talk show was "more scary" than appearing nude on a Broadway stage!)

Like any good variety retrospective, there *had* to be moments with kids and animals. The offspring of various staff members modeled clothes. (Billy Barry and Merv's 10-year-old son Tony were also featured in this segment.) Merv sang "If We Could Talk to the Animals," while a band of critters stole the spotlight.

Several of Merv's serious moments in 1969 were likewise represented. These included interviews with Rose Kennedy, Mrs. Martin Luther King, and Dr. Christian Barnard.

During the penultimate commercial break, Merv allowed some of the young people in the audience to come on stage and demonstrate some of the more trendy dances. To top off the evening, Arthur offered a rendition of "It Was a Very Good Year."

"We've all brought in the seventies together," said Merv at the close of the show. "And we all hope and pray that they'll be the answer to all of our dreams. May they be peaceful and may they bring all of you individual success and happiness. God bless you all."

If there's any misfortune connected to this edition of *Merv*, it's the fact that it no longer exists. Like most of the CBS episodes, the two-inch master tape was not preserved. The foregoing extracts were culled from an audiotape supplied from a private archive. One can only hope that a good quality dub (or even a black-and-white kinescope) might surface one day. Nevertheless, a nearly complete audio copy affirms that Merv's New Year's Eve show came off as a happy celebration consisting of live performances, nostalgic clips, audience participation, and the bustling energy of Times Square. Was this robust sampling an indication of good things to come in the new decade? Would the show eventually jell into an enviable late night institution with ratings that lived up to the network's expectations? These were the important questions in the minds of the creative forces behind *The Merv Griffin Show*.

A new player had entered the three-way contest. On December 29, 1969, ABC launched the first late-night edition of *The Dick Cavett Show*.

In 1960, 24-year-old Dick Cavett was living in New York City, making the rounds as an actor. While supporting himself as a copy boy for *Time* magazine, Cavett read that Jack Paar was in search of fresh material for his nightly monologues. A lifelong devotee of comedy, Cavett penned a few jokes for the late-night star. To make himself look "official," Cavett placed the written material in a *Time* envelope and headed for NBC. Cavett knew exactly where to find Paar—on the sixth floor of the RCA Building where the *Tonight Show* offices were located. When Cavett spotted Paar, he handed him the envelope. Later that night, sitting in the *Tonight Show* audience, Cavett heard several of his lines uttered by Paar as ad-libs. Paar encouraged Cavett to contribute more material. In due course, Cavett was hired as a talent coordinator for one of the hottest shows on television. He eventually graduated to writer.

Griffin had hired Cavett as a staff writer for his NBC show in 1962. Unfortunately, when Merv got the ax 26 weeks later, Cavett found himself out of work. He would write material for Jack E. Leonard, Groucho Marx, Johnny Carson, and Jerry Lewis.

In 1964, at the suggestion of his friend Woody Allen, Cavett broke in a stand-up comedy act at New York's The Bitter End. He began performing stand up routines on Merv's show, and later did the same on Carson's.

Cavett was becoming a very familiar face on the tube. In 1966, ABC signed the young comic for hosting chores on the youth oriented *Where It's At*, and Groucho Marx showcased him on NBC's *The Kraft Music Hall*. In March 1968, ABC signed Cavett to host *This Morning*, a talk show with the flavor of late-night television. After morphing into *The Dick Cavett Show*, the program disappeared in January 1969, only to return in May as a prime time entry, seen three times a week. By the end of December, Cavett found himself in competition with two of his erstwhile employers—Griffin and Carson.

As the new late-night contender, Cavett brought style, substance and an unrestrained energy to the late-night landscape. Many of his programs offered rare, in-depth interviews with legendary figures like Marlon Brando, Katharine Hepburn, Fred Astaire, Noel Coward, Laurence Olivier, Orson Welles, and Groucho Marx. Many of Cavett's broadcasts remain historically significant. Among the most memorable is a young John Kerry fiercely engaged in a debate about the Vietnam War.

Unlike Griffin or Carson, Cavett would occasionally preside over several near-pugilistic interludes. One of the best remembered is the skirmish between Gore Vidal and Norman Mailer. The dispute was the result of Vidal's scathing assessment of Mailer's book *The Prisoner of Sex* (1971). John Simon and Mort Sahl got into a similar argument. Actor Chad Everett made sparks one night after making certain comments about his wife that were deemed sexist by Lily Tomlin. Best of all was a 1970 airing in which former

Georgia governor Lester Maddox angrily walked out on Cavett and Truman Capote amid a heated debate over racial segregation.

Despite the excellence of his shows, Cavett would soon be facing the same problem that had plagued Joey Bishop: low ratings and station defections. Merv, too, had this problem when several CBS affiliates began to balk publicly about his persistent low ratings. Taking into account the revenue lost at 11:30 p.m., several CBS stations sought to air *Merv* in late afternoon time slots. A few stations wanted to drop the show completely. Initially, the network denied these requests, enforcing the contractual stipulation to air the show in the 11:30 p.m. time slot. Later, however, the network softened its stance, at least partially.

On January 21, 1970, *Variety* reported that CBS would allow stations in Atlanta, Cleveland, and Providence to air Griffin at 4:30 p.m. As far back as early 1969, when the network was still marketing Griffin, some stations had requested permission to air the program in late-afternoon time slots. Those stations, however, were required to show cause as to why the earlier airings should be authorized.

Barely six months into his new contract, Griffin was already longing for the good days at Westinghouse. He expressed his troubles to TV critic Rex Polier of the Philadelphia *Evening Bulletin*. "Philadelphia was the first major city to put me on at 4:30 p.m. when I was with Westinghouse," Griffin told Polier. "It gave me a 60 percent share of the Greater Philadelphia audience at that time.

"Right now, Johnny Carson, Dick Cavett, and I are fighting over 110,000 homes in San Francisco at 11:30 p.m. At 4:30 p.m. in San Francisco when I was with Westinghouse, I used to draw 300,000 homes. I've never wanted to be known as 'Mr. Midnight.' Let that 'Prince of Peace' over at NBC be known as 'Mr. Midnight' if he wants to."

Griffin was cognizant of the fact that certain affiliates were primed to recapture the substantial audience he'd commanded on the Westinghouse network. "I will be happy to have up to 12 stations carry my show at 4:30 p.m. if they want to," he told Polier. "What I will insist upon is that I be shown the same night in New York, Los Angeles, and possibly, Chicago.

"The reason for New York and Los Angeles is that when you put your talent on for a $265 scale fee, they expect to be seen that night in New York and Los Angeles. They don't like the idea of being seen on a delayed basis in those cities at 4:30 p.m. the following day."

Not all of Griffin's numbers were bad. By early 1970, Merv Griffin Productions was doing so well that a number of companies approached the star about the possibility of "going public." As it turned out, MGP remained a non-public company. The company had roughly 300 people on its payroll, and gross billings from $7,000,000 to 8,000,000 per annum. Griffin, the sole owner of the company, also owned five radio stations (AM and FM); a company called Teleview Racing Patrol, Inc., which provided taping facilities for several east coast racetracks; the jai alai and dog races in Miami; and the daytime game show *Jeopardy!*, in its sixth season on NBC.

Aside from these diverse interests, Griffin had another ongoing enterprise—an eatery on the ground floor of his building called "Pip's."

"Arthur Treacher's nickname was Pip," recalls Bob Shanks, "and we agreed to name our restaurant after him." Patterned in the style of a classic English pub, Pip's opened its doors in February 1970. The place was popular, "but there were too many cooks," says Shanks. "Vincent Sardi came on board as a consultant and he had the right idea. He told us to make it a Joe Allen's with simple burgers, and *bigger* burgers. But Merv and I wanted four-star food and we began hiring various chefs. It had been set up as a limited partnership, much like a Broadway show. My wife Ann had raised $300,000 to get the restaurant open. And everybody who had given us money wanted to be on the show; they were given little plaques in return for their investment. But before we knew it, we were going out to California. If the show had stayed in New York, we would have been okay with just the bar business alone. Ann and I tried to run it for about six months or so, but it was a disaster. We knew we were in trouble when Malachy McCourt, whom we had brought on to run it, called to report that, the night before, someone had stolen all the fixtures. Merv and I had a discussion about the situation and he wanted to sell the place, so we knew it was over. But Pip's was fun while it was there."

As the months rolled by, the battle wasn't strictly over ratings. The three major late-night talk shows (plus David Frost's syndicated program) were all produced in Manhattan. And the producers and bookers of each were clamoring for whichever superstar happened to be in town. Sometimes the unavailability of major celebrities resulted in appearances by offbeat (but thoroughly captivating) personalities. A good example was Willie Sutton ("Slick Willie"), the infamous Depression-era bank robber who, after serving his time behind bars, put his professional "skills" to good use as an anti-robbery consultant. He gave a compelling interview on a panel shared with Zsa Zsa Gabor (who kept a watchful eye on her jewelry).

Another controversial personality to sit on Merv's couch was Christine Jorgensen, generally acknowledged as the world's first transgendered person. Jorgensen appeared on the show to plug the release of her biopic, *The Christine Jorgensen Story* (1970). Despite a few scattered snickers from the audience when she walked out on stage, Jorgensen's segment went smoothly and came across as respectful and informative.

The staff concocted creative ways to showcase some of the more obscure celebrities, mostly the older ones who had long faded from the public eye. Knowing how much Merv loved games, the staff devised one called the Mystery Guest. Merv would be allotted five minutes to identity someone (usually a retired actor) based on clues supplied by Arthur Treacher. One evening the guest was a woman who had been pelted in the face with a grapefruit, courtesy of James Cagney, in the film *Public Enemy* (1931). "There's a certain breakfast fruit she isn't particularly fond of," said Treacher. With that, Merv knew it *had* to be actress Mae Clarke. Years later, Clarke said she enjoyed playing the "game," admitting that it was actually contrived. Griffin knew who she was all along. Clarke, however, wanted to be on the show, and the show was in need of a willing participant, so the bit was mutually fulfilling.

Another gimmick that should have been exploited more frequently was audience participation, along the lines of "Carson's Stump the Band."

Griffin would play the "elimination" or "poll" game that required the entire house to stand up. Then, depending on what Merv said, certain folks would have to sit down. For instance, one night he said: "All those not carrying a picture of [Vice President] Spiro Agnew, sit down." Ninety-five percent of the participants sat down.

"All of those living east of the Mississippi sit down." A good number plopped down in their seats. "If you *cannot* recite the exact words to "The Star Spangled Banner," sit down." Two women remained standing.

With the mike planted in her kisser, the first woman began to sing the national anthem in a sultry monotone. "You don't have to do it *sexy*," Merv sneered. "We all know better!" As the audience began howling, the woman became nervous and wasn't able to finish what she had started.

Merv then turned to the only woman still on her feet. "Don't palm it off on me," she said in protest. "Well," snapped Merv, "you stood up. You *have* to do it!"

When the woman refused to play along, Merv asked her why she was still standing. "I don't know how to sit down," she said. The sheer ridiculousness of that statement aroused great laughter, although to this day no one knows why. Was a suggestive remark or gesture edited out of the tape? All we saw was Griffin retreating to the stage, shaking his head.

No one, including Griffin, and certainly not the censor, knew what anyone on the show might say or do. Occasionally, a word, a potentially libelous reference, or an unauthorized plug, would have to be bleeped for broadcast. At Westinghouse, Griffin's concerns with censorship were practically nonexistent, but it was a different story at CBS. The network's Standards and Practices people kept a sharp eye (and ear) on everything going out over the air. Griffin would frequently receive nagging memos about off-color remarks made by a guest, or any subject matter considered too "blue." In compliance with applicable FCC regulations, the network also paid close attention to any solicitous remarks for pet charitable causes or messages made on network time.

On December 31, 1969, *The New York Times* reported: "C.B.S. Keeps Pleas for Peace Off Air." According to the article, Carol Burnett and Elke Sommer had, on separate episodes of the Griffin show, urged viewers to write letters to Mrs. Martin Luther King on behalf of peace. At the time, both women were members of an organization called "People for Peace." The Burnett segment aired on Christmas night. (What better time to make a plea for peace?) The segment with Sommer aired a few nights later. It was later reported in the *Times* that "pleas" had been snipped out of both broadcast tapes with no explanation.

An audio recording of the Burnett interview still survives. "These are bands that we have been wearing," said Burnett, explaining that the adornments were to be worn through the holiday season in support of a "non-party organization."

"And, in other words, if you are for peace—we all are—to kind of even show it, and say *yes* you are, in hopes that some good might come. It couldn't *hurt!*" The audience applauded.

Burnett, a CBS superstar at the time, did not make an issue over the matter. Sommer, however, was reportedly distressed over the censorship incident. Griffin would later tell *TV Guide* how "the network censors snipped whole sentences and paragraphs out of our tapes, making some of the conversation unintelligible."

The excising of "Pleas for Peace" was mentioned briefly when Griffin welcomed FCC commissioner Nicholas Johnson to the program on March 17, 1970.

Johnson began his term with the FCC in 1966, when he was 32. Not only was Johnson the youngest person ever to serve on the commission up to that time, he was also the most controversial, earning a reputation as a "dissenting" commissioner. An attorney and author, Johnson's book, *How to Talk Back to Your Television Set* (1967), had been a widely-discussed topic within the broadcast industry and in colleges. Unlike the stuffy bureaucrats or authors who typically occupy the last 20 minutes of a talk show, Johnson came off as personable, informative, and upbeat.

Johnson expounded on something that many viewers at the time were unaware of: the airwaves belong to the public. He explained that licenses issued to TV stations in the United States have a duration period of three years, after which a renewal must be applied for. "And it is only to be renewed if the station has been serving the public interest," he noted. "The public not only has a right, but an obligation to participate in that election, and to vote, and tell the FCC which of their stations have been doing a good job, and which, they think, might do better."

Television advertising, in particular, was of major concern to Johnson. "Look at the commercials that are on your program," he told Merv. "How many of them are designed to help people? And how many of them are designed to sell people products that they don't need, don't want, are over-priced, or can possibly contribute to their disease or death?"

Asked what television *should* be, the commissioner said: "responsible" as well as "entertaining." Merv invited "Nick" Johnson back for two more appearances.

If the CBS censor had headaches from the utterances on Griffin's show up to this point, he would have a migraine on the night of March 27, 1970.

It was Good Friday, and Merv opened the show with several light jokes about the impending holiday. He even got Treacher to dress up as the Easter Bunny. "Are you a male or female bunny?" Merv asked. "At my age," Treacher grumbled, "it really doesn't matter!"

The lead guest that night was 57-year-old Virginia Graham, whose razor sharp outspokenness had always aroused excitement on talk shows. "Virginia Graham had been booked on the show that night to represent the values of middle-America," says Bob Shanks.

Graham, who held a master's degree in journalism and had authored numerous articles and books, had just completed a long run with her syndicated TV series, *Girl Talk*. "If you were on the air now," Merv began, "I know what you'd be saying about this feminist movement." Merv noted that he had "them" (the feminists) in his theater almost every night. "Yes," said Graham, "I noticed you had Lysol back there and I hope it works."

Graham said she'd be willing to serve a sentence if she could line up those women and force them to look at themselves in the mirror. "What are they striking for?" she exclaimed, "equal *wrongs?*" According to Graham, there was nothing wrong with being a woman except for that time of the month when she wasn't "too crazy about it."

"Being a woman is a fantastic thing," Graham continued, "because you always have a man to blame it on." Merv pointed out that Graham was a bad example, since she was a successful businesswoman and performer, in addition to being a wife, mother and grandmother. "You've everything going for you," he told her. Graham boldly pointed out, as if anyone cared, that she had become a wife and mother "in that order."

The subject turned to sex, which Graham regarded as a bodily function to be performed in private. "That's why the latrine is in the back of the house," she said, "it's not attractive in the living room."

"I didn't ask about that," said Merv. "No," said Graham, "but we always get around to it." She continued: "Anybody that has sex in front of a group because they're excited at the fact that other people are revolted by their defiance. That's not sex. That's *half* sex! Now, half sex is better than none, but it's without love."

Graham attributed the current incivility of young people to the current situation in Vietnam. "Some of the young people of today, whom we shall meet later," Graham said firmly, "I don't agree with too much." Merv knew precisely what Graham was getting at. "Abbie Hoffman is coming out later," he chuckled, to a roar of applause.

A buzz of uneasiness filled the studio. Merv ignored it and introduced Mark Frechette and Daria Halprin, the young attractive stars of Michelangelo Antonioni's *Zabriskie Point*, a documentary-style film about campus unrest that turned out to be a disappointment at the box office, but did play successfully in art houses.

Graham questioned the methods by which the children of the community were being raised in this "new way" of living. Her sharp-tongued inquisitiveness failed to liven up the conversation. Merv cut to a commercial.

When the show resumed, viewers at home were startled by a network announcement: "Ladies and gentlemen, before we continue with the next part of *The Merv Griffin Show*, here is Robert D. Wood, president of the CBS Television Network."

In a videotaped appearance, Wood stated that Abbie Hoffman, the "self-proclaimed revolutionary," was about to join the other guests on the recorded program. "During the actual taping last night," Wood explained, "Mr. Hoffman wore a shirt made of an American flag. And as you will hear him point out, this use of the flag raises serious legal problems." Wood said that because of the possibility of violating laws pertaining to desecration of the flag, and the likelihood of offending viewers, Hoffman would be seen, but his use of the flag as a garment would be "masked" by electronic means. "I hope you agree," Wood concluded, "that this is the best procedure for meeting our obligations as responsible broadcasters."

In his meticulously prepared intro, Merv cited some factual data about the "self-styled revolutionary" who was about to walk out. Hoffman had authored two books, *Revolution for the Hell of It* (1968) and *Woodstock Nation* (1969). He had been the subject of "an enormous of amount controversy" since his arrest on conspiracy charges for inciting to riot at the 1968 Democratic National Convention. Hoffman and six other protestors had already achieved a negative fame in American history books as the Chicago Seven.

If the high volume of applause that greeted Hoffman was any indication, he had a horde of supporters sitting in the audience. The orchestra played "Chicago" as Hoffman took the guest seat.

"You didn't give Virginia Graham a kiss," said Merv, obviously trying to get the sparks flying as soon as possible. He needn't have bothered. Hoffman attacked Graham instantly. "I thought what she said about women was very degrading," said Hoffman. The studio audience cheered. "And since I'm not a woman, I can't discuss that."

Hoffman asked if he could take off his coat. "It's warm in here," he said, ditching his jacket. Since Hoffman had worn the flag shirt on prior occasions, everyone knew what he was about to reveal. The audience began to snicker.

As striking as the network's disclaimer had been, the method by which Hoffman's offending attire was "masked" was far more compelling, and, in some ways, amusing. "The network censor simply blued-out the flag shirt on Hoffman," explains Bob Shanks. "So while Hoffman was on camera, you saw his face with a torso of blue!"

A man chatting on a television talk show, with his body obliterated by an electronic blue grid, was a bizarre spectacle. Some viewers who had tuned in late (and missed Wood's warning) thought something was wrong with their TV sets; others suspected that Hoffman may have been sitting there naked. But as innovative as the blocking technique was (for its time), it wasn't perfect. When Hoffman moved his arm beyond the confines of the blue grid, a glimpse of Old Glory could be seen. "The technology wasn't quite there yet, so it was rough-edged," explains Shanks, "and we only had a short time to deliver the tape for broadcast."

The studio audience responded enthusiastically to each utterance Hoffman made. He pointed out, after the titters in the theater had died down, that 50 people had been arrested for essentially doing what he'd just done on national television.

Hoffman also took delight in noting that several weeks earlier, two of his heroes, Roy Rogers and Dale Evans, had worn replicas of the same shirt without any legal repercussions. "It all depends who you are," he said, before launching into a dizzying diatribe condemning patriotism and capitalism.

"Where did you go wrong, Abbie?" asked Merv, more amused than angry.

"I think I went wrong in 1960," Hoffman confided, "when I looked up the House on Un-American Activities, then went south to Mississippi, and got shot at a few times, arrested a few more times, then went on trial a few times for shirts and things like that, and possession of loaded automatics which you never saw. Then finally ended up in Chicago, on trial for conspiracy [for] intention to cross a state line with a certain state of mind."

Hoffman joked that he wouldn't be arrested for wearing the flag shirt on this occasion because he was "protected by Merv," whom he regarded as "the ultimate anti-ballistics measure."

Halprin asked Hoffman how the Chicago experience had changed him personally. "It intensified everything I ever understood about law, and how it has no relationship to justice," said Hoffman. "It's only there to keep the people in power *in* power." More applause. He also noted that he was currently involved in a number of pending actions involving freedom of speech and expression.

In view of all the charges that had been leveled against his guest, Merv asked, "What would be your plan for America? What would you like our system to be?"

In his five-minute response, Hoffman mumbled much about free speech without offering anything of substance.

"But answer me once and for all," reiterated Merv, "what do you *want* for America? You're obviously anti-capitalist. What do you want the country to be, Abbie?"

"A little island in a whole sea of humanity called the world, the planet," Hoffman said, without "a nationalistic concept." He then brought up the subject of the war.

"The basis for all of your anger and protest is the Vietnam war, isn't it?" said Merv.

"No," answered Hoffman.

"I don't think the Vietnam War is some sort of accident where, say, John Kennedy rolled over in bed and said to Jackie, 'Let's get involved in Vietnam.' I *think* that's what they call it—getting involved—the genocide of 500 million people. So I don't think it's an accident. No, I think its part of an intrinsic foreign policy that's imperialist."

Merv leaned toward Hoffman and said, "Do you mind if I bring a guest out who has views absolutely opposed to yours?"

"I'm here already!" Graham snapped. Half the audience cheered; the other half booed. The next guest was Tony Dolan, a college senior and member of the editorial board at Yale University, and frequent contributor to *The National Review*. Merv introduced Dolan as a right-wing conservative who would represent "the other side of the coin."

"Are you boys going to be all right?" Merv asked, devilishly. "I have water here to throw on either one of you."

Dolan said that Hoffman wasn't taken seriously on college campuses. "That's a lie," Halprin interjected. Then Hoffman defended himself: "A lot of people come up to me and say, 'We're behind you!'

And I say, 'You ought to be in *front!*' To which Dolan responded: "Most of them are *above* you, I'm afraid."

Dolan said that the "oppressive racist society" that Hoffman frequently spoke of could be disproved with facts. The moans in the audience grew louder.

"Let him make his point," said Merv firmly. Dolan asked which group had used "storm trooper tactics" to bust up meetings, thereby preventing the other side from being heard. "The conservatives? Hardly!" said Dolan. "It's the Hoffmans and the far left," he said.

This sparked a free-for-all discussion about the current state of race relations in the United States. Dolan said that life in America for blacks had improved over the last decade. The audience grew uneasy. "Nobody's interested, as is evident, in hearing that," said Dolan, noting that "the point is to kind of liberate yourself if you're a spoiled little rich kid and you've had an unhappy childhood, take it out on America and see if some white reporter will stick a microphone in your mouth and tell you how rotten this country is, so he can turn to his audience and say, "See what you did.' That's the point behind all of this rhetoric."

Though Dolan was far more articulate in expressing his arguments, the audience seemed to favor the iconoclastic Hoffman. Graham, out of camera range at the end of the sofa, could be heard mumbling as the exchange between Hoffman and Dolan grew more and more tense. Caught in the crossfire, Merv called for a commercial. As the camera panned the panel, Graham called attention to her indignation by plopping a few Alka-Seltzer tablets (one of the show's sponsors) into a glass of water.

"Virginia, Abbie—don't fight during the commercials," Merv cautioned after the show had resumed. What viewers were seeing was a prime example of the "planned chaos" that Jack Paar frequently talked about.

"I can't stand this any more," Graham fumed. Even so, Merv insisted that Dolan be given the opportunity make his point— uninterrupted. He did, directing his rebuttal to the people in the audience who had applauded Hoffman. He said that in pre-war Germany, "the educators were just the way they are today, they said the students were taking over schools and busting up classrooms

and meetings and not letting people be heard." Dolan got no farther. A man in audience shouted, "THAT'S A LIE!"

Merv asked the man why he thought Dolan's comment was a lie.
"It's a lie because the fascists in Germany were taking over...." The
man got no farther. Dolan responded as another voice in the audience erupted, followed by another, making it painfully obvious that
Merv was losing control of the show.

"I want to apologize," said Graham in her shrill. "I was wrong.
I want to congratulate *you*," she told Dolan. "How else could the
world see a self-portrait of such destructive idiocy?"

Mark Frechette chimed in. "I'd like to say something here," he
demanded, cutting Graham off. "There's been a lot of talk about
revolution, that we have to avoid one or it's going to be violent.
And it hasn't occurred to anyone that there's going to be revolution
whether Abbie Hoffman is here or...."

"No," Graham shouted at Mark, "there's going to *evolution!*"

Mark Frechette got the last word. "This country is in need of
much more than a face-lifting," he said, looking directly at Graham,
who had bragged earlier about her recent cosmetic surgery. The
crowd went wild. Enraged, Graham leaped out of her seat. "You
need a sock in the behind," she screamed at the young actor. "You
need a *back*-lifting!"

Laughter filled the entire studio.

"This sounds like our dinner table at home," Merv quipped.
"*Merv!*" Graham cried, "the twentieth century degenerate parents
of these children, as so labeled, are the ones discovering the cure
for cancer, for TB, for muscular dystrophy, for cerebral palsy. They
never cared in all their lives about that. But we're the ones that are
finding the cure while they're tearing down the prisons, the hospitals, the banks that gave us the money to find the cure for cancer;
they're *bombing*."

The house went ballistic. "Virginia Graham discovered the cure
for cancer," sneered Hoffman. "She's a running ad for it!"

"Yes, I did Mr. Hoffman!" Graham cried. "I *did* discover the
cure—*because I was cured!*"

The next 20 minutes saw the conservatively attired Dolan and
the electronically obscured Hoffman drawing potent fire over social

injustice and racial prejudice. As the stage grew hotter and hotter, Merv's expression became one of boredom. "Virginia," he said reassuringly, "you and your husband are in this next commercial."

"Oh, thank God!" Graham whined.

Merv read the intro: "Now here's an opinion from someone who doesn't think men's underwear has to be *white!*" Those words garnered the biggest laugh of the night.

In what can best be described as verbal free-for-all, Griffin wisely allowed the sparks to fly until the last minute of the program. "We're out of time," Merv announced, with Dolan and Hoffman still going at it. And they *kept* going at it. "We have to go!" yelled Merv. "*Good night!*"

"When it was over," Shanks recalls, "we all breathed a sigh of relief." In the hours after the taping, the CBS brass scratched their heads as to what should be done about the 90-minute imbroglio that had just taken place. One exec suggested withholding the episode and playing a rerun in its place. Another exec wanted to "burn" (electronically erase) the tape altogether. "Over what?" Shanks recalls asking. "I told them, 'You can't *not* run this show. Last week you had Roy Rogers and Dale Evans on in American flag shirts. Is there a double standard?'"

Although the Hoffman episode made for good water cooler conversation the next day, no benefits, in terms of ratings or publicity, were derived from it. There were reports alleging that Hoffman and Dolan had gotten into a fistfight either during or after the taping. "If there was a fight," says Shanks, "it didn't happen at the Griffin show." In fact, Hoffman invited Shanks to his apartment to have dinner and watch the show.

"Here was this long-haired, radical guy living in this *bourgeois* apartment," the producer recalls. "Merv did not go; just the staff and I went and it was amazing."

The censorship debacle would provide one more memorable moment for Merv, one in which he would have the last laugh.

The following Monday, Merv began his monologue as usual. With his nose in the air, he scoffed about the way the network had "tampered" with his show. He assured the audience that such tactics would not be tolerated in the future. As he rambled on about the "control" he would exercise henceforth, the blue grid popped on the screen. It eliminated the top half of the picture, then the bottom half, causing Merv to dart swiftly so as not to be cut off by the electronic monster. The blueness eventually occupied most of the screen, except for a tiny spot at the bottom, allowing just enough space for the bemused host to peek through and finish his rant!

It was a funny bit, but no one at the network was laughing. A few days later, CBS president Robert D. Wood invited Merv to lunch. "Merv asked where they'd be going for lunch, and Bob said, 'I'm not going to tell you. Just trust me and we'll have a great lunch.' He came by and picked up Merv up, drove to LaGuardia, got on the CBS plane and took him to Anthony's Pier 4, in Boston. It was a great restaurant, which Merv loved. And I thought that was such a classy thing to do. Bob Wood was a good guy. You have to remember that he was in a tough spot, too. Merv had creative control of the show, so they couldn't just walk over him," says Shanks." Wood and Griffin exchanged thoughts about the Hoffman show, and no blood was drawn.

Of the hundreds of shows Griffin hosted at the Cort Theater, the Abbie Hoffman episode is the one that is requested most often by fans and historians. It is most unfortunate that the original tape, like the others in the series, does not exist. So far, only an audio recording has come to light. It's the next best thing to having the video (most of which was electronically obliterated anyway).

Not long after the Abbie Hoffman incident, Bob Shanks had yet another crises to deal with. "Merv got sick an hour before the show and couldn't go on," recalls the producer. "I had to find a suitable sub-host—fast!" Luckily for Shanks, Garry Moore was working in Manhattan, hosting the syndicated reboot of *To Tell the Truth*.

Shanks: "I found out that Garry had just left New York for his home in the suburbs. So I told someone to get a hold of the New York State Highway people, explain the situation to them, and have the people at the toll booths be on the alert for Garry and to stop him. They did, and Garry turned around, drove back into the city and did the show!"

One of the more serious difficulties Bob Shanks faced during this period was network interference. The standards and practices department was routinely monitoring the number of pro-war and anti-war statements uttered on each show. To maintain a balance, nagging memos would be issued to the producer, and star, demanding that more conservative, "pro-war" guests be heard on the program. "Okay, find me some," Shanks wrote back. The persistent nagging was disconcerting. "We'd gotten a little of that at Westinghouse, but more at CBS," says Shanks. "At that time it was difficult to find such guests, unlike today where you have hundreds of articulate right-wingers, all trained and schooled in the Heritage Foundation. In those days, you had [columnist] William F. Buckley, and a conservative journalist named M. Stanton Evans, and maybe one or two others. But you couldn't keep having the same two or three people on. So I told them to find me some conservatives and I'd put them on."

The Merv Griffin Show had always courted controversy. By early 1970, network intrusion and censorship, stemming from a succession of vociferous guests, began to hamper the program's fluidity. This was particularly galling, since the success of Merv's Westinghouse show had been largely attributable to provocative interviews with the likes of Norman Mailer, Jimmy Breslin, Gore Vidal, and others. It was the success of the Westinghouse show that had sparked CBS's interest in Griffin. Now, however, Griffin was being called on the carpet for doing precisely the kind of show that had solidified his reputation as a credible broadcaster.

Bob Shanks recalls one disagreement he had with the censorship department concerning an appearance by author Joe McGinnis. "He'd written a book about Richard Nixon that had quoted him swearing, which apparently Nixon did quite often," the producer recalls. The book in question was *The Selling of the President 1968* (later reissued under the title *The Selling of the President*), which had been hailed as a "masterpiece" by the *The New York Times*.

There was an interesting connection linking Griffin, Nixon, and McGinnis. As noted earlier, Nixon had filmed a series of commercials at Merv's theater during the 1968 presidential campaign. One day while McGinnis was at the theatre interviewing Merv for a *TV Guide* piece, Nixon and his crew also happened to be on the premises, rehearsing on a closed set. Intrigued by the "live" image of Nixon flickering on a dressing room monitor, McGinnis asked if there was any way he could get an introduction to the Republican candidate. Without hesitation, Griffin got the young journalist cleared through the Secret Service with little or no trouble. (After all, it was *his* theater!)

Within a remarkably short span of time, McGinnis had managed to ingratiate himself to an extent that permitted him full access to Nixon throughout the campaign.

After the election, the Nixon camp expected to read a glowing account of the campaign journey, and the new president, penned by the highly trusted Joe McGinnis. What they got, however, was an unflattering expose detailing how Nixon's public persona had been shrewdly remolded and sold to the American electorate. The cover of the book said it all: Nixon's face on a pack of cigarettes, like any common commodity that had been manufactured and marketed.

On the panel with Merv, McGinnis recalled an incident that had occurred during the making of the meticulously scripted campaign commercials filmed at Griffin's theater. Like the others in the series, this particular piece depicted the candidate responding to questions that were supposedly "spontaneous." The issue was law and order in the classroom. Nixon had given an answer that one of his aides deemed "too strong" and likely to offend certain minorities. The aide asked Nixon if that was the response he *really* wanted to give on the subject. According to McGinnis, Nixon told the aide (after the cameras had been switched off), "That's *exactly* it. It's just a matter of law and order. And these damn Negro, Puerto Rican groups out there, they run around hitting teachers over the head. *Goddamn it*, they have no right to teach in our schools."

The utterance of "goddamn" triggered a response from the censor. "A CBS rep told us, 'You can't say that word on the air,'" recalls Bob Shanks. "And I said, 'Wait a minute; this is a direct quote of the president swearing. It's not Joe McGinnis or Merv Griffin talking. This is a journalist with good credentials and he's quoting the president. You *have* to let this go on!' The rep mumbled something under his breath, blah, blah, blah. But I finally won that one. We called his boss and he said, 'You're right, there's a distinction here.' I used to love things like that, and felt very sorry for the poor kid at

CBS who was assigned to our show. Those shows were nightmares for the Standards and Practices people."

Nixon was said to have loathed the book. Although McGinnis made no mention of Merv Griffin within the 278 pages of *The Selling of the President*, Mr. Nixon eventually traced his initial encounter with the author back to that momentous occasion at Merv's studio.

Not surprisingly, *The Merv Griffin Show* was not seen in the White House during Nixon's residency there. There would be one exception, in September 1970, when the president's daughter Julie, and her husband, David Eisenhower, appeared on the program. Merv would later recall, on the air and in print, how the president had phoned him to express approval of how well the interview had gone.

President Richard M. Nixon would soon be the subject of yet another biting segment of *The Merv Griffin Show*.

On May 4, 1970, the Ohio National Guard opened fire on a group of unarmed college students at Kent State University that had been protesting the U.S. invasion of Cambodia, announced by President Nixon on April 30. Four students were killed, nine were wounded, and one was left paralyzed. The tragedy would mark a significant milestone in the escalating opposition to American involvement in the war in Vietnam.

On May 14, outspoken essayist Gore Vidal appeared on the show. Merv knew the booking would be an electrifying one, since Vidal had strongly criticized the president a week earlier on *The Tonight Show*.

The witty "Paul Revere of the talk shows," as Merv described him, was greeted by a few hisses as he made his way to the guest seat. "I see Mr. Buckley has his people here," said Vidal, dryly. He began by saying he'd seen the April 30 press conference, and concluded that Nixon didn't represent anything except his desire to be president.

Merv asked Vidal if Nixon would have all ground forces out of Vietnam by 1971. "Of course he's not," Vidal answered. "He's going to stay there as long as he can unless we stop him." There was scant applause.

"There's a nice movement afoot which I throw out to all of you, and that is to impeach him." This suggestion was met with an equal number of cheers and boos. "Where there's life, there may *not* be Nixon," Vidal concluded. He also said there was a plan in the state of New York to have a referendum in the November election which would, in effect, bind the New York delegation in voting for Nixon's impeachment.

Though Griffin was no big fan of Nixon, he asked if there might be better ways in letting the president know of such mounting disapproval.

"It's very difficult to let him know *anything*," Vidal said indignantly. "I think that came out when those kids were killed at Kent State, and the cold way that he reacted. He sort of said, 'Well, they had it coming to them.' And this whole sense of just not knowing anything that's going on." Vidal reasoned that an impeachment proceeding was what it would take to get Nixon's full attention. "He would hear *that*," Vidal said firmly.

Merv looked at the studio audience and saw what he considered to be "a good, young representative cross section" of our country.

In an attempt to gauge public opinion, 100 seats in the theater had been equipped with an electronic voting mechanism. Merv would ask a series of questions to which the selected audience members could vote yes or no; if they had no opinion on subject, they could simply abstain. The results would be registered on a stadium-like scoreboard affixed to the side of Merv's desk.

Merv asked the first question: *"Do you agree with President Nixon's decision to send troops into Cambodia?"* Thirty-four answered yes; Fifty-six answered no; 10 abstained. There was thunderous applause, but Merv interpreted the response as "rather close."

"Do you think the National Guard was justified in opening fire on Kent State students?" Thirty-two voted yes; 55 voted no; 13 abstained.

"Do you think peace demonstrators are unpatriotic?" Twenty-four voted yes; 55 voted no. (Merv noted that 21 audience members hadn't voted on this issue.)

"Do you think the government is out to destroy dissident groups like the SDS [Students for a Democratic Society] *and the Black Panthers?"* Fifty-three voted yes; 30 voted no.

"Do you agree with [Vice President] *Spiro Agnew's speeches?"* Twenty-five said yes; 57 voted no.

Vidal was permitted to ask a few questions:

"Would you like to see [New York Mayor] John Lindsay president?"

Twenty-two said yes; 60 said no. That result garnered the biggest applause of the night. "Okay, John, we're working on that," Vidal promised.

Finally, Vidal asked: *"Would you like to see a new political party, which represented peace and the saving of the environment?"*

Sixty-one voted yes; 17 voted no.

Nixon's penchant for tape recording was not limited to telephone calls and conferences; he also videotaped certain TV programs off the air. His immediate predecessor, Lyndon B. Johnson, had had videotape equipment installed in the White House for the purpose of recording his speeches and then using the playback mode for self-analysis. Nixon used the same equipment. Roughly a decade before home video recording became commonplace, the president would have selected news and talk shows taped in order to monitor what was being said about him.

Consequently, a color video copy of the foregoing Gore Vidal segment exists today solely because of Nixon's diligence. CBS, like the other two major networks of the era, did not preserve the master tapes of programs that weren't likely to be replayed.

Nixon and Vietnam weren't the only topics that generated sparks, but the conversation would almost always shift to one of those subjects, if not both, particularly when there was a "generation gap" on the panel. Such was the case on June 5, 1970, when actor Tony Randall got into a gentlemanly but nonetheless stirring debate with singer/actor/bandleader Rudy Vallee.

At 50, Randall was a veteran of numerous hit plays and movies; he would soon embark on a TV adaptation of Neil Simon's *The Odd Couple*. Vallee, whose career stretched back to the 1920s, had recently starred in the stage and film versions of *How to Succeed in Business Without Really Trying*. A hardline conservative, Vallee was now making the rounds on the college circuit.

When Merv asked the 69-year-old former crooner if the kids were asking any serious questions, he responded with a disparaging estimation of young people in general. "I don't think we should pay too much attention to the opinions of our young college boys and girls," said Vallee. "For the simple reason that when I was 18 or 19, no one paid any attention to me—and I didn't know anything. I didn't know my rear end from my elbow and I don't feel that they do." Half the audience applauded; the other half hissed.

"If you have a real serious illness you don't ask a first year medical student or an intern to diagnose or operate on you. You get a *man* with years of experience and thousands of operations. A boy 18 or 19, rough and tumble of life, knows nothing about it. He's never done an honest day's work. No experience in law, or medicine, or military. How could he be able to tell our military leaders what to do when he knows nothing about the art of the military science?"

Mildly incensed, Randall expressed an opposing view. "He's the one who has to go and do the dying, of course."

Vallee said he understood completely, having served in the U.S. Navy and the Coast Guard. "But I still feel that at 18, 19, or 20, a boy who hasn't had experience . . . there's no substitute for experience!" "I disagree entirely," Randall countered.

According to Vallee, a "wet-behind-the-ears" kid would be incapable of making military decisions. "Napoleon did," said Randall. "And Alexander the Great was twenty-one when he conquered the world," said Merv.

"Well," said Vallee, "if anyone had asked me at eighteen or nineteen, I would have said, 'why do you ask my opinion? I don't know anything.'"

"But the world has changed since you were eighteen or nineteen," Merv interjected. "In what way?" Vallee asked. "Well, for one thing" Merv smiled, obviously aiming for a punchline, "We now have cars!"

When the laughter subsided, Randall recalled that during his time on the campaign trail with Eugene McCarthy, he'd witnessed thousands of college people working fervently to help get McCarthy elected to the Senate. "Now there's an example of what kids are doing today, that they didn't do before," said Randall. "They're that much more sophisticated, educated, and able. They were good citizens working the way citizens *ought* to work."

Vallee remained unconvinced. "But they know *nothing* about life!" he shouted. "They've had no experience, Tony!"

"So far," Merv interrupted, "Look at what's happened with the guys who've had experience!" The crowd cheered.

Vallee then turned his venom on the Los Angeles police academy. "They're not teaching the policemen well at the academy in L.A., and I want to correct that. I think I can do a real good job."

As several people in the audience began hissing at Vallee, Randall came to his defense. Even after some mild mud slinging, actors stick together.

Controversy and chaos alone does not a good talk show make. The programs are essentially entertainment vehicles, and Merv, the consummate entertainer, was at his best when he assumed the role of master showman.

In a fervent effort to pump up the ratings, Merv would continue to take the program on the road during the crucial sweeps periods. Although the ratings on these programs had always been consistently higher, they were nowhere near the figures needed to topple Carson.

With the show failing, the CBS brass was no longer suggesting changes; they were *demanding* them. "They felt they had to do something," recalls Bob Shanks. That "something" would begin with a series of dismissals. The first casualty on the team was Merv's longtime director, Kirk Alexander, who had been with the program since its inception in 1962. For reasons known only to them, the CBS execs wanted Alexander gone. "Kirk was a competent director," says Shanks. "So why did they want to get rid of him? Why did they want to get rid of me?" asks the producer. "We'd both had five successful years with Merv on the Westinghouse show. And *that* was the show CBS had bought. After they'd bought it, it wasn't what they wanted. Treacher and I used to talk about this. They knew it was a no-win situation, but they kept hoping. Treacher would say, 'That little man is never going to be beat Carson.' Then, the network brought Fred Silverman into the picture and he began firing all of us."

The Griffin show had lost a good director in Kirk Alexander. His skill in picking up the crucial shots, via the three-camera setup, remains remarkably vivid, even in today's high-tech world. Alexander was well liked, not only by the members of the Griffin crew, but also by members of the show biz community. (Albert Fisher remembers that Alexander's talent as a director was exceeded only by his culinary abilities.) Replacing Alexander in the director's booth was the equally competent Dan F. Smith.

Unlike Alexander, Smith had a prior association with CBS, having served as associate director on two of its most successful game shows, *What's My Line?* and *I've Got a Secret*. Moreover, Smith had prior experience with talk shows, having directed the ill-fated late night *Joey Bishop Show* in Hollywood.

Not long after the firing of Kirk Alexander, Bob Shanks would receive his pink slip. July 31, 1970 would mark his last day as producer of *The Merv Griffin Show*. In the penultimate segment of the last Shanks-produced Griffin show, Merv called attention to the man who persevered with him through thick and thin since that first harrowing experience on the Paar show. "Bob discovered, from the beginning, the Smothers Brothers, when he was the associate producer for Paar, and convinced Jack to put them on. When he became my producer in 1962, the first one he put on the show was Woody Allen, and then people like Tiny Tim, Bob Newhart, José Feliciano—and *Dick Cavett!* [Laughter and applause from the audience] And Bob has guided my career for the last eight years. This is his last night with me as my producer. He's leaving us and it's the saddest night I can remember. But he knows that I'm terribly grateful for all the people he's discovered. It's an incredible role that he's played. He's a great producer and I'm really going to miss you, Bob!"

Happily, many of the producer's proudest achievements in broadcasting were ahead of him. After leaving Griffin, Shanks produced the PBS series *The Great American Dream Machine*, which he describes as an "ambitious mélange of everything from hard investigative reports to low-comedy blackouts." The program won Emmys two years in a row.

As a programming executive for ABC, Shanks would ultimately create *Good Morning America* and *20/20*. He also oversaw the network's late-night "Wide World of Entertainment" package, which rotated Jack Paar's comeback attempt, *Jack Paar Tonite*, with *The Dick Cavett Show* in 1973. His decades of experience in broadcasting spawned several books, most notably *The Cool Fire; How to Make It in Television* (1973), praised by *The New York Times* as "the best account we have about the television industry." In the book, Shanks admits that his exit from the Griffin show did indeed "hurt." At the same time, however, he notes that he and his former boss had done their "equal best" over the course of time by remaining personal and professional friends.

In 1978, Griffin invited his former producer back to the show—as a guest. Shanks had penned a successful novel titled *Love Is Not Enough*. His subsequent writings include movies for television, such as *Drop-Out Father* (1982), a well-received comedy that starred Dick Van Dyke in the title role. In 1986, Shanks authored yet another invaluable guide for aspiring hopefuls: *The Primal Screen* (subtitled "*How to Write, Sell, and Produce Movies for Television*"). Veteran TV producer David L. Wolper described the tome as "A perfect inside television story—from a television maker on the inside."

Today, Bob Shanks looks back at his years with Griffin with nostalgic fondness. "Merv and I stayed friends, and years later, he asked me to run his production company," recalls Shanks. "It was a tempting offer, but I didn't want to relocate to Los Angeles."

A year had come and gone since that awkward opening night in August 1969. Griffin's ratings were still nowhere near what CBS had expected. It was now painfully evident that if Merv wanted to remain in the late-night game, he'd *have* to move the program to Los Angeles—at his expense. CBS president Bob Wood flatly rejected the proposal, solely because the network had shelled out that exorbitant sum to refurbish the Cort Theater. The subject of the theater exacerbated a rift that had been brewing between Wood and Griffin. The pair began to take shots at each other in public and in print.

Merv, it seemed, had begun to make more noise in the press. On August 5, 1970, *Variety* reported that the host had flown to London to meet with Saul Illson and Ernest Chambers, the producers of *The Smothers Brothers Comedy Hour*. It was Griffin's hope that the well-respected team might be able to breathe new life into the ailing late night show.

Upon his return to New York, Merv told journalist Tom Mackin that negotiations with Illson and Chambers were under way. In

Mackin's column on August 11, 1970, Griffin spoke effusively of several "wild ideas" he had for revitalizing the show. At the same time, he hinted at moving to the West Coast, noting that the new producers preferred working in California.

Several weeks earlier, CBS president Bob Wood had told *TV Guide* that it was the network's decision to keep Griffin in New York. "We have this elaborate facility, we spent a ton of money on it, and we just can't walk away from it," said Wood.

Merv addressed the same issue in his interview with Mackin: "Bob Wood says we can't move out there until they get some more money out of the theater he says I forced CBS into buying for the show in New York. His words were, 'That theater is stuck in my throat.'"

One of the "wild ideas" Griffin had in mind involved getting rid of his desk. "The other night, Zsa Zsa Gabor came out wearing a million dollars' worth of Harry Winston's diamonds," he recalled. "And there I was, greeting her from behind a desk. It was about as exciting as meeting her in an office."

Other changes to be employed on the "probable" move to the West Coast included putting the band up on the stage, thereby allowing the singers to fully benefit from "that great sound right behind them." Griffin promised that the revitalized show would offer more than just talk, leaning more heavily on entertainment. "That's where Illson and Chambers will come in, perhaps as consultants," he told Mackin. The host also disclosed that hiring the producers would be an expense to him, not the network.

Griffin kept pressuring the network for the green light to move west. Then, an unlikely occurrence helped sway the decision in his favor. A portion of a building under construction close to the Cort Theater collapsed one day, making the star's request seem reasonable if not preventative. The network certainly didn't want to be named in any lawsuits initiated by injured people attending *The Merv Griffin Show*.

CBS finally acquiesced to Griffin, but not without making one inexorable demand: Arthur Treacher would have to be let go.

When word leaked out to the press that Treacher would be "retiring" from the show, Merv made it abundantly clear that there would be no replacement for him.

People in show business have coined a pejorative term to identify hard-nosed and unenlightened executives: the "suits." Demographic studies were becoming more and more relied upon in the marketing process of television programming, and the suits were convinced that Treacher's advanced age was a detriment to the show, and that younger viewers were "turned off" by his continued presence on the program.

Actually, Treacher had always scored a hit with the college-age crowd. "He has a big teenage following," Griffin told columnist Ben Gross in 1966. "The youngsters admire his frankness. Why, they lap it up when he tells some of the unkempt girls: 'Go home; take a bath; and dress like a young lady.'"

"That's what they didn't get," concurs Bob Shanks. "The college-age kids loved him because he was so outspoken and honest. Nobody wanted to admit that Merv wasn't going to beat Johnny Carson. So their solution to the problem was: fire Treacher; fire Shanks. The age thing was an excuse they used for firing Arthur. You always fire the coach when the team is losing. And Merv couldn't protect us at that point. The show was wounded and they were thinking about canceling it. And Merv wanted to stay on, which was understandable."

As it turned out, Merv did not have to fire Arthur Treacher. Throughout the years, Treacher had said repeatedly that he had never wanted to live in "a state that shakes." He told Merv to go to California without him.

Even so, for months, rumors circulated within the television industry that Treacher was being forced out of his job. The actor put on the best face possible, both on the air and in the press. As the weeks led up to Treacher's departure, he and Griffin emphatically denied that they were embroiled in a feud.

"They are even trying to drive a wedge between Arthur Treacher and me," Griffin told writer Tom Mackin. "Thank God, they can't do that." Similarly, in an interview with the *New York Daily News* ("Griffin's Show Will Miss Treacher's Performance," July 24, 1970), Treacher said that he'd enjoyed a "wonderful association" with his friend, Merv Griffin. "But I've been in show business for 51 years and now have arrived at the stage when I would like to do some things that have been long been on my mind." One of the things on Treacher's mind was the endeavor he had launched more than a year earlier.

One day in early 1969, Treacher received a phone call in his dressing room from one of the most enterprising figures in show business, Bob Hope. The comedian told Treacher that his brother Fred knew a man named Bob Davis, who was well established in the fish and chips business in London. He asked Treacher if he'd be interested in going into that business with Davis.

Arthur Treacher was very familiar with entrepreneurship. Several years earlier, the actor had attempted to capitalize on his valet persona through a "household help" franchise, Spectrum, Ltd., a/k/a Arthur Treacher's Service System. (The advertising catch phrase: "Call Arthur Treacher Service System.") Filmdom's foremost butler was now set to cash in on the fast-food business. Trading under the legal name Arthur Treacher's Fish N' Chips, dozens of "shops" (as the actor called them) would open in various cities throughout the U.S. and Canada. By mid-1970, it was obvious that the franchise had caught on. One door had opened for Treacher just as another one was about to close.

On Friday, August 14, 1970, Arthur Treacher made his last appearance as a regular on *The Merv Griffin Show*. It was a bittersweet occasion that began with a full chorus of "For He's a Jolly Good Fellow," sung by everyone in the theater.

Merv devilishly suggested that Arthur would remain a welcome presence on the program. "You'll be joining us often, won't you Arthur? The network told me to get that commitment from you right away." To the casual viewer, this seemed like a sincere statement that any boss might make to a retiring employee. Those close to the situation recognized it for what it was—an inside joke intimating just how badly the bosses wanted the old man gone.

It was an odd grouping of guests. Abbe Lane, the singer, flirted unabashedly with the retiring announcer as she murmured sweet nothings in his ear. Comedian Jackie Vernon grabbed a few laughs here and there. The biggest chuckles were attributable to Criswell, a pseudo-psychic well known for his picturesque predictions. Criswell was a carryover from the old Paar show. He is remembered today chiefly for his role in director Ed Wood's *Plan 9 From Outer Space* (1959), a film duly celebrated for its inane plot and laughable production flaws.

In an obvious jest, Criswell predicted that Arthur and Virginia Treacher, who had remained childless throughout their 30 years of marriage, would soon be expecting. "Expecting *what*?" Merv quipped. Griffin's reaction was more of a commentary on Treacher's disdain for kids than it was an aspersion of his virility. Criswell did make at least one accurate "prediction" that night. He told Merv that his show would soon relocate to the West Coast and be seen in a new format. Obviously, Criswell kept up with the latest news in the entertainment columns.

Arthur's departure from the show had been the talk of Broadway and, as a result, several celebrities were expected to "drop by" for a quick farewell. The producers had positioned a camera outside the theater to capture any important arrivals. At various intervals, Merv would cut outside to the "action" on 48th Street. No one was there, except for the occasional passer-by. Nevertheless, one star *did* make a dramatic entrance that night. It was Ethel Merman, who arrived in a limo.

Merman and Arthur had remained good friends since they'd worked together in the Broadway musical *Panama Hattie* (1940). Merv let the two veterans bask in the spotlight as they reminisced sweetly.

Before the end of the night, Treacher relished in telling the audience what he had told reporters. "I am not leaving the theatrical profession," he said resolutely. "I'm going *back* to the theatrical profession!"

As the show ended, Arthur and Virginia Treacher were driven away from the theatre in an elegant horse and carriage. Out of respect for his friend, Griffin would never employ an onscreen announcer for the duration of his talk show career.

True to his word, Arthur Treacher did not retire. But he didn't return to the theatrical profession, either. He would make several return visits to the Griffin show, but there would be no more acting credits on his resume. In his final years, Arthur devoted his time to the expanding chain of Arthur Treacher's Fish N' Chips restaurants, though the extent of his ownership in the company was not known.

On December 14, 1975, Arthur Treacher died of cardiovascular disease at North Shore University Hospital on Long Island. He was 81.

It was Merv's first anniversary with the network. The new producer, Walter Kempley, wanted to mark the occasion by reflecting on the past 12 months with some videotaped highlights. He soon realized that virtually all of the choice clips had already been played on the New Year's Eve telecast. With the exception of the Abbie Hoffman episode, nothing unusual or spectacular had occurred in the months since. In lieu of a retrospective program, the producer sought to create some "new" magic moments with Mayor John Lindsay, actress Elke Sommer, singer Eloise Laws, former middleweight champs Rocky Graziano and Jake LaMotta, comedian Marty Barris, and novelty musician Jack Valenti (not to be confused with Jack Valenti of the MPAA's rating system).

Merv reminded viewers that in the past year, he had completed 257 shows, logged 400 hours on the air, sung 46 songs, interviewed 1,200 guests, and had gotten six laughs. (Seven, counting that last joke.)

It turned out to be a garden-variety show, kicked off with a scripted bit that fell flat. Merv knocked on a series of doors to receive congratulatory comments and gag gifts (such as love beads) from characters appearing in such Broadway shows as *Hair*, *1776*, and *Hello, Dolly!*

Merv to "John Hancock": "Does everybody in 1776 watch my show?"

Hancock: "Half of them do. The British watch David Frost."

Merv: "Get out of here, John."

The next mishap occurred during Mayor Lindsay's segment. Merv thought it would be a cute idea to ask tourists in the audience to reveal what warnings they'd received before visiting the Big Apple.

One woman said she found New York a "frightening" place littered with filthy streets. Lindsay blamed the problem on the people, particularly the "out-of-towners." Half the crowd (most likely the out-of-towners) moaned. When another woman began complaining about the "ladies of the night," Merv cut her off. "This was one of the worst ideas we've ever had," he said, hurrying on to the next segment after apologizing to the mayor.

Elke Sommer came on to publicize her impending tour of *Irma La Douce,* and new film, *Zeppelin* (1970). Eloise Laws sang a few tunes, and Merv put Rocky Graziano to work by having him sing, and tap-dance to, "On the Sunny Side of the Street." Merv also tested his fluency in Italian. Graziano and Sommer began chatting away, sounding like a pair of foreign exchange students. Apparently, Merv had quite a few Italians in his audience that night. Because when Graziano said "stunod" (the Sicilian term for stupid or crazy), everyone roared. Merv thought Graziano had uttered something obscene. "What did he say that they all laughed?" asked Merv. "Oh, he's all right," said Sommer reassuringly. "Then why did our censor run out with a pair of scissors?" asked Merv.

Next, Graziano demonstrated his prowess in the ring opposite LaMotta. More interesting than that, however, was LaMotta's announcement of an upcoming memoir to be published under the title *Raging Bull.* Merv snickered at the title. He had no way of knowing that the 1980 film adaptation would provide not only Robert De Niro with a starring vehicle in one of the best films of his career, it would also result in a *magnum opus* for director Martin Scorsese.

Marty Barris did some fairly routine stand-up comedy. Best of all was an offbeat segment with John "Jack" Valenti, playing standard tunes on an air hose, a handsaw, balloon, and pump.

It had been an abysmal season plagued by low ratings and high turnover. Between early spring and late summer, three colleagues—Kirk Alexander, Bob Shanks, and Arthur Treacher—had said their goodbyes. Of the three, only Treacher had made an exit with any semblance of grandeur. Soon it would be Merv's turn to leave the Cort Theater. Before leaving, however, he was to experience one more vexing incident at the famous landmark.

On August 27, 1970, a half-hour after tape had started to roll, Merv introduced singer Larry Kert, then starring on Broadway in the musical *Company.* Suddenly, something bizarre occurred. Approximately 60 demonstrators, seated in middle of the theater, began blowing whistles, flutes, kazoos, and other noisemakers.

Some held up signs that said, "Stop the Whitewash,"while another sign read, "Tom Jones Rose to Fame singing Black Songs." Several demonstrators tried to take the stage.

Unbeknown to Merv, or producer Walter Kempley, a group identifying itself as the Lovers of Music, was protesting the apparent lack of black jazz artists working in television. The fact that the Griffin show had been targeted seemed odd to those aware of Merv's ongoing support of black performers.

The disruption did not abate. In fact, it got worse. Unable to continue with the show, Merv left the stage shaking his head. He reappeared several minutes later, but only to inform the audience that the program would have to be halted. Following this, the efficient pages escorted all 400 members of the studio audience out of the building without further incident.

The producers later spoke with several of the demonstrators. Andrew Smith, a young writer/associate producer who had recently joined Griffin, told a reporter that the door would always be open to any professional musician to talk with the staff, and possibly appear on the show.

The following day, *The New York Times* reported that a large number of protesters had picketed the outside of the theater while the show was in progress. The group was identified as "militant black musicians and other performers"who were demanding equality for black artists on TV.

A CBS rep told reporters that the first 35 minutes of the program would be seen on the air, and that the remaining two thirds would have to be "re-taped." In other words, home viewers would see the show leading up to the moment where the disruption had occurred, while the remainder would be "new" footage. The patchwork episode wouldn't be available for broadcast until Monday, August 31. In an era long before the advent of electronic video editing, the network most likely needed additional time to physically "splice" the tape together, thereby ensuring the requisite running time of 73 minutes.

Researching the "protest show," as Griffin fans call it, can prove mystifying. Recorded history merely offers a puzzle as perplexing as the incident itself. Merv's autobiography states that he informed the protesters that they had picked a bad night to disrupt the show, since his guests would have included comedian Dick Gregory and the leader of "an emerging African nation." The *TV Guide* listing for that night, August 27, indicates that Gregory had indeed been booked, but there was no mention of the African leader. The other guests were to have been the comedy team of Phil Ford and Mimi Hines, singer Enzo Stuarti, and Dr. Joyce Brothers. As it turned out, the guests who actually were on that night were Dick Gregory, actress Julie Newmar, Enzo Stuarti, and comedian/actor Chuck McCann.

As for the show that ultimately aired on August 31—the one that had supposedly been patched together—the guests included Charo, Jóse Molina, Larry Kert, comedy writer/actress Selma Diamond, soul singers Dean & Jan, and comic/voice actor Dayton Allen.

No video copies of the August 31 episode are known to have survived, but an audio recording remains extant in private archives. There was no mention on the air by Merv, or anyone else, of the incident that had occurred on August 27, and there is no discernible clue as to where the original portion of the show ends, and the "pick up" begins. Knowing that the protesters in the audience were armed with smuggled noisemakers, one would be inclined to listen closely for any restlessness or unusual sounds during those first 30 minutes. Protestors often "telegraph" their intentions (albeit inadvertently) long before they make their move. With the energetic Charo as the opening act, it is impossible to detect any impending disturbance in the audience. Her overzealous performance was probably louder than the protest! This singular incident in the history of the Griffin show can be classified as *un*-planned chaos at its worst.

Merv now began dropping hints on the air that the show might soon move to Hollywood. Throughout the summer of 1970, there had been persistent rumors that CBS, distressed over Griffin's weak ratings, might cut back his program to one night a week, filling the other four with movies and specials. At the same time, CBS president Bob Wood maintained his stance that the Griffin show would *have* to remain in New York because of the network's heavy investment in the Cort Theater. It is not known whether Wood changed his mind, or was overruled. Whatever the case, *The Merv Griffin Show* was indeed moving west—right away.

The formal announcement appeared in the September 2 edition of *The New York Times:* "GRIFFIN TV SHOW MOVING TO COAST." Writer George Gent reported that Griffin had spoken to members of the press the previous day, informing them that the first of the Hollywood shows would be taped on a Sunday evening for airing on either the following Tuesday or Wednesday.

"I'm delighted with the move," said Griffin. "Something had to be done. There are three late-night talk shows in New York and the same guests bounce from one to another. Hollywood will give us a lot of fresh faces."

The Griffin farewell to the Cort Theater was taped on September 3, 1970, and aired the following evening. Merv jokingly recalled the advice he'd received from CBS president William S. Paley. "He said, 'Go west young man!' I think he meant Hong Kong!"

It was an ostensibly confident Griffin who walked out on the stage that night. "You're all waiting for me to say something, aren't you?" he asked the audience. The silence was almost deafening. "We're moving to California," he finally admitted. There was considerable moaning, and even a slight "boo" here and there. "Well, how do you think California feels?" Merv joked. He attempted to explain why the move was necessary, but a barrage of questions interrupted him. "What will happen to this beautiful place?" asked one man. Merv seized the opportunity to take a dig at his bosses. "Well, Mr. Paley, here's the problem," he said, wickedly. By this time, the antipathy between network and star was so widely known that virtually everyone got the joke. "This is, of course, still a Shubert theater, and a very famous one," said Merv. "I would suppose that CBS will try to put it back into shape so it can have a *legitimate* show."

It had only been 12 months since Merv first stepped onto the stage at the Cort Theater. He was now eager to finish his last show there and clear the decks for the much-anticipated move to Los Angeles. His staff invited the best talent available for the New York swan song: actor Victor Buono, singer Dana Valery; Charo ("for the *cultured* crowd," according to Merv), novelist Mickey Spillane, comedy writer Carroll Carroll, and Wallace Ross of the Television and Radio Commercials Festival.

It was an incredibly dull show. The only bright spot during the entire 90 minutes occurred when Ross presented a Clio Award (the advertisers' equivalent of the Oscar) to Miss Miller. That was in recognition of the commercials she had filmed for the Griffin show a year earlier. After accepting the trophy graciously, Miller revealed that while she was filming the promotional spots, she was worried about being late for the show. The *Carson* show. This was obviously a planned joke, but some of Merv's loyalists in the audience didn't take it that way. "It doesn't matter," Merv assured everyone. "We're getting out of town."

Maintaining the best face possible, Merv wrapped up his New York swan song quickly and eloquently. "In these last moments, I want to thank everyone," he said softly, looking into the camera. "It's been an incredible experience working here at the Cort Theater and I'd like to thank everyone who came here through rain, sleet, and snow to give us support. We'll see you from Hollywood, and we'll be back here from time to time. But thank you again and good night." Those words, along with the music and applause, quickly evaporated into the night. *The Merv Griffin Show's* tumultuous tenancy at the Cort Theater had come to an end.

13. TELEVISION CITY

On Monday, September 7, 1970, *The Merv Griffin Show* went on the air at 11:30 p.m., as usual. As the theme music played, the camera panned the orchestra, capturing a modest "HOLLYWOOD" logo depicted above the trumpet section. There was also Arthur Treacher's familiar announcement: "From Television City in Hollywood, it's the Merv Griffin Show! Here he is, the dear boy himself, *Merrrvvv!*"

Regular viewers of the program were momentarily stunned. Had CBS changed its mind about Treacher? Had Treacher changed *his* mind and returned to the show for some unfathomable reason? No. What the network put on the air that night was a rerun of a Hollywood episode from June 15, 1970. In fact, four episodes shown during that week were repeats from earlier in the year. Because the long-awaited green light for the move to the West Coast had come suddenly, there wasn't adequate time for the booking of guests. Also, during the four-day hiatus, the producers had to work fervently to hire replacements for several key positions left void due to the relocation.

"Merv left for California before I did," recalls Julann. "I had to pull up stakes and go after him, and there wasn't too much time for preparation. I had to move everything. And he got mad because I'd packed things up and had given away all the furniture and good stuff. The moving van was full of jars and strings. I was born during the Depression, and, to me, jars and strings were more important than paintings and clocks."

It wasn't until Friday, September 11, 1970, that viewers would see the first "new" *Merv Griffin Show* originating from Studio 43 in Television City.

The premiere edition was introduced by one of television's most glamorous women. "Hello, darlings!" she cooed. "Guess who's on the Merv Griffin Show tonight? Me—Eva Gabor, plus Glen

Campbell, Broderick Crawford, Rona Barrett, and Linda Ronstadt. *And now, here is darling boy, MERV GRIFFIN!"*

The Gabor intro marked the beginning of a clever, though short-lived, gimmick. Each night after the show, the lead guest would tape an intro to "billboard" the guests for that particular edition. The videotaped intro wouldn't be seen, of course, until the show aired on the following night. The studio audience had no idea who the guests would be. When Merv boasted that he'd snagged Glen Campbell ("a treat for the ladies") and Linda Ronstadt ("a treat for the guys") the surprise reactions were genuine.

"We're here!" beamed Merv. "I live in Hollywood now! And we're going to stay here a long time, or until I get a tan, whichever comes first." Griffin had barely gotten past the first few jokes when a visitor interrupted him.

Sam Yorty was not unfamiliar to television audiences, having appeared on scores of local and network programs during his tenure as the 37th mayor of Los Angeles. Yorty would later host a local talk show of his own after leaving office in 1973.

"Whenever we welcome anybody to Hollywood," Yorty smiled, "we do it properly." He read an official proclamation:

"Hear ye, hear ye! Know all men by these presents that on this 11th of September in the year of Our Lord nineteen hundred and seventy, I, Sam Yorty, Mayor of the City of Los Angeles, and Hollywood, in town or out. . . ."

That last line elicited several unexpected guffaws. Yorty was notorious for his frequent out-of-town excursions, which merited him nicknames like "Travelin' Sam" and "Suitcase Sam."

It was officially "Merv Griffin Day" in Los Angeles. The proclamation, endorsed by Yorty, was filled with so much pomp and bombast that the mayor literally lost his place reading it. "Let's just leave it at *whereas*," Merv suggested, much to the relief of the yawning audience. "Yes, that's enough of *that*," Yorty concurred.

The tone suddenly turned serious. The mayor thanked Merv for bringing the show to Hollywood, and he thanked Bob Wood, "one of the leaders of CBS," who had formerly been a director at CBS's Channel 2 in Los Angeles. Yorty claimed he had told Wood that the Griffin show belonged in Hollywood. "But now we've got you," said Yorty, shaking Merv's hand firmly. "And we want to keep you. Good luck, Merv!"

Griffin hinted that Gabor had brought along one of her male co-stars. She did. It was Arnold Ziffel, better known to Green Acres fans as "Arnold the pig." As popular as Arnold was, all eyes remained focused on Gabor's décolletage the whole time the animal wandered around the stage. In Hollywood, female stars are expected to epitomize the glamour and sophistication of the movie industry. Accordingly, Gabor's neckline was cut so low that Merv asked her if the dress was on backwards!

On one of Gabor's previous appearances with Merv, a CBS rep informed producer Walter Kempley that the actress's dress was too revealing. It then became the personal responsibility of everyone within earshot to check out Gabor's dress, remembered Kempley. The rep refused to let Gabor go on, but that didn't stop her. As the actress headed for the stage, the rep grabbed the front of her dress with both hands and pulled it upward. "That'd startle anyone, even a Gabor," said Kempley.

Glen Campbell (whose *Goodtime Hour* would soon be a prime-time hit on CBS), belted out a few tunes, as did a then largely unknown Linda Ronstadt. Though Ronstadt had been recording for several years, major stardom was still a few years away. At 24, she added a touch of youthful vigor to the show. Ronstadt would go on to make many more appearances on Merv's show, Carson's *Tonight Show*, and many others. (Interestingly, when Merv made an appearance on Carson in 1987, Ronstadt happened to be the glittering star on the show that night.)

Much of the pizzazz on the first "permanent" Hollywood episode was sparked by reporter Rona Barrett and veteran actor Broderick Crawford, sparring about the "significance" of actors. Crawford, best remembered for his role as Lt. Dan Matthews in the hit '50s series *Highway Patrol* ("ten-four, ten-four!"), had a new series to plug. As Merv was about to wrap up the show, Crawford blatantly interrupted him, getting in one more plug for *The Interns*, soon to premiere on CBS.

The first Hollywood installment was in the can. In the weeks that followed, the show transitioned into a tightly-structured and edited production, leaving little room for the spontaneity that had marked the New York entries. It was during this early CBS/Hollywood phase that Griffin began a practice that would endure until the end of his talk show career. During the course of an interview, particularly if the guest was a major star or political dignitary, Merv would allow the conversation to extend well beyond the allotted time without pausing for commercial breaks. On CBS, it was imperative that the breaks be taken at designated times. To comply with network orders, an extra measure of post-production editing became necessary. At the end of each show, Merv would tape a few snippets in which he'd look directly into the camera and announce, "We'll be right back after this message" or "Here's a word from your local station." These five-second inserts would then be physically spliced into the tape wherever a commercial break was needed. Because Merv wore a different suit on each show, the process had to be done nightly so his wardrobe would remain contemporaneous.

After the commercial break, the show would resume with one of the familiar graphic slides, or "bumpers," and the interview would pick up where it left off. The process, however, almost always resulted in several minutes of airtime being cut. Thus, a program with a running time of 73 minutes would be truncated to about 68 minutes, sans commercials. Unlike the CBS shows produced in New York, the Hollywood editions did not air the same night they had been taped. Consequently, the editing department had the luxury of additional time to "tinker" with the finished product, much to the dissatisfaction of the producers, guests, and host.

Despite the intrusive cutting, and a delayed airtime of one week, the show seemed to be running smoother than it had during the final days in New York. At least Merv didn't have to worry about the audience interrupting the show with loud whistles or other forms of protest.

Veteran writer Walter Kempley continued to produce the show, with assistance from Lillian Tobinson. The respected team of Saul Illson and Ernest Chambers, who had produced *The Smothers Brothers Comedy Hour*, were now credited as the show's executive producers.

There is some uncertainty as to how Illson & Chambers came to produce Griffin's show, based on information contained in two of Merv's autobiographical works. In *Merv* (1980), he wrote that he flew to England to meet with the producers and ask for advice on how to "fix" his ailing late night program. The producers, known chiefly for their expertise with prime-time variety programs, weren't interested in getting involved with a talk show, according to Merv's account. The host recalls a second meeting with the men several days later at which time he offered them $250,000 a year to produce the show. According to the book, the team not only accepted the offer to produce the show, they began rewriting it practically on the spot. Years later, in *Making the Good Life Last*, Griffin wrote that while he held Illson & Chambers in "high regard," it was difficult to figure out exactly why the network had *made* him hire them.

Dan F. Smith, the director who had succeeded Kirk Alexander in New York, continued his directorial chores in Hollywood. Smith, whose prior talk show experience had been the ill-fated *Joey Bishop Show*, was asked if he knew of any competent talent coordinators who might be looking for work. Smith suggested 42-year-old Donald Kane, a booker who had built a solid reputation in working for Bishop. Kane had been with the late-night Bishop show through its two and a half year run on ABC. "That's where Dan knew me from," says Kane.

Earlier in his career, Kane had been a TV director in Chicago, having worked on the Herb Lyon and Irv Kupcinet programs. He moved to the West Coast because, as he readily admits, "that's where the big opportunities and bucks were."

"Dan was a good director and a nice guy." Kane remembers. "He recommended me and that's how I happened to get interviewed for Merv's show. Dan also recommended a young woman named Betty Bitterman and a couple of other people that got hired."

The other newcomers in the talent coordinator arena included Leonard Friedlander and Donis Gold (Kempley's sister). By this time, Tony Garofalo had taken on the position of senior talent coordinator. Bitterman would eventually work her way up to associate producer and, finally, producer.

Kane and Bitterman were practically hired on the spot. "You have to remember that Merv left New York on Friday and flew to L.A. to tape the first of the new shows on Sunday," says Kane. "They had moved over the Labor Day weekend and had only three days to find a talent coordinator. I was interviewed on Saturday and got hired. 'Okay, you'll start tomorrow,' they told me. It all happened very fast. And I was glad to get it because Griffin paid better at the start than Bishop had paid at the end."

Ray Sneath and Robert L. Savery signed on as stage managers, while the attractive new sets—used for interviews and musical performances—reflected the work of art director Robert Tyler Lee. Dick Carson, who had previously directed *The Tonight Show* for his brother, eventually replaced Dan Smith as director of the Griffin show. Bob Murphy, Merv's boyhood friend and associate producer, moved up in the ranks to producer, replacing Walter Kempley. (Later in the decade, Kempley's name would frequently appear on TV screens as the writer of numerous specials and sitcoms, including one of ABC's biggest hits, *Happy Days*.)

Mort Lindsey had also relocated to the West Coast. A few of the band stalwarts, like Richie Kamuca, Shelly Russell, Bill Berry, and Jake Hanna, likewise remained on board. CBS had entered into an agreement with ASCAP in which the rights to several hundred songs were cleared for use on the Griffin program. It was a bountiful list that Lindsey was able to hand over to his assistants who were assigned the task of re-arranging the charts. The band was in good shape.

With Treacher no longer in the equation, Merv needed someone to joke around with at the beginning of the show. He would find a lively personality in his trumpet player, Jack Sheldon.

Sheldon had been a well-respected jazz trumpeter, with some 20 years of experience, when he signed on with Griffin. Born in Jacksonville, Florida on November 30, 1931, Sheldon graduated from Immaculate Conception High School, and then began playing with several major jazz bands on the nightclub circuit. He would eventually land a substantial gig with singer Julie London, who saw a comedic potential in the boyish trumpeter. London would gleefully banter with Sheldon on stage (much like Merv would do years later) as part of her act.

Sheldon exuded a likable "everyman" quality that made him a candidate for light comedic roles. In 1964, he landed a co-starring role on CBS's *The Cara Williams Show,* playing the star's neighbor in a sitcom about a young couple (Cara Williams and Frank Aletter) that had to conceal their marriage in order to retain their jobs. Though CBS wasn't impressed with the Williams show (it was canceled after one season), the network apparently thought enough of Sheldon to create a series expressly for him. *Run, Buddy, Run,* starred Sheldon as Buddy Overstreet, a hapless character who had the misfortune of overhearing a murder plot that subsequently forced him to keep on the run—hence the title. It was an interesting premise, but Buddy didn't run very long. The program was canceled after only 16 episodes, telecast during the 1966–67 TV season.

Sheldon's acting skills weren't limited to comedy. He turned up in a few dramatic supporting roles in Jack Webb's revival of *Dragnet,* which aired on NBC from 1967 to 1970. Webb knew Sheldon from his professional association with Julie London, Webb's wife. The versatile Sheldon also got a chance to shine in a few movies. One of his major triumphs was the trumpet solo he performed in the film, *The Sandpiper* (1965), which evolved into the hit song "The Shadow of Your Smile." He also rendered a respectable rendition of the title song in Robert Altman's *The Long Goodbye* (1973). Sheldon's next major acting assignment would be a supporting role in Sally Field's 1973-74 series, *The Girl with Something Extra.*

On the Griffin show, Sheldon's on-air repartee with the host usually occurred within the first segment. The two of them would have an exchange just long enough for Sheldon to utter something to which Merv could respond with a witty wisecrack. Occasionally, Sheldon would join Merv on the stage for a duet, and the lighthearted banter that followed usually led into the first commercial break.

Sheldon inaugurated a running gag involving a dummy, positioned in the seat next to his in the trumpet section. The dummy was nicknamed "Bix," after the great jazz cornetist/composer of the 1920s, "Bix" Beiderbecke. Sheldon would ask a question, or make a silly comment, and then look over at Bix and say, "Take it!" (Meaning, *play* something!) The lifeless figure, of course, would never respond. Sheldon would then deliver a swift punch with exaggerated gusto, knocking Bix off his seat. The routine, which became a nightly expectation, was well received, but it eventually wore thin and was discontinued after a few months. It worked long enough to establish Sheldon as a comedic on-screen presence, and the audience would giggle with anticipation as soon as Sheldon would peer in Bix's direction.

Now that he had his "regulars" in place, Merv devised some additional *shtick* to engage in before bringing out the guests. One appealing feature was called "On This Day." Merv would relate several interesting facts about a particular date in history and fortify it with songs or visuals. On his telecast of November 9, 1970, Merv said: "If you were watching my show on this day in 1965, this is what you saw. . . ." The screen faded to black. That's because November 9, 1965 was the date of the eastern seaboard blackout that caused *The Merv Griffin Show*, and everything else, to go dark. While the feature was interesting, it seemed to work faster than sleeping tablets. Consequently, "On This Day" never did catch on.

One night someone noticed that the lining in Merv's suit jacket, a mishmash of wild colors and psychedelic patterns, resembled something one might see on an LSD trip. From then on, Merv would gleefully flash his jacket linings, much to the amusement of the audience. The gimmick would invariably punctuate the opening segment of the show, much like Johnny's imaginary golf swing. Over time, the linings got louder and louder. So did the laughs.

The show now attempted to establish a west coast clique of familiar guests, much like it had in New York. Griffin's staff had no difficulty locating several colorful personalities that fit the bill. There was the perpetually glib Ruben Carson, a Los Angeles writer for television and magazines, who offered his assessments of what was happening in the world of television and the world in general. His initial appearance was so well received that he was invited back for multiple bookings during 1970–71. During one of these appearances, Merv took a mild jab at Johnny, commenting that Ruben was the *only* Carson that would ever appear on his show. (The future, however, would prove him wrong.)

Another captivating guest during this period was 65-year-old Gladys Towles Root, a prominent Los Angeles criminal defense lawyer. Decked out in flamboyant attire, topped with furs and a Hedda Hopper-like hat, Root was a brilliant conversationalist, as colorful as the outfits she wore. She had established her own law practice in 1929, working as defense counsel in a succession of high-profile murder and sexual assault cases. She claimed that she was forced to open her own office because no one in those days would hire a female attorney.

In 1964, Root had been the recipient of an indictment issued by a federal grand jury. It was alleged that Root, who had represented one of the defendants in the kidnapping case of Frank Sinatra, Jr., had fabricated false testimony. Ultimately, the charges against the attorney were dropped.

On the air with Merv, Root was nearly as commanding as she was in court, addressing many of the problems affecting American society. She opined about the war in Vietnam, the military draft, and poverty in American cities, usually taking a liberal stance. After several appearances on the Griffin show, Root began to receive offers to appear on other talk shows as well. She died in 1982, at the age of 77, in a Los Angeles courtroom.

Other "regulars" at Television City included Charo; the delightfully flirtatious Gabors—Zsa Zsa Gabor and Eva, Pamela Mason (the former wife of actor James Mason); Fred "the Hammer" Williamson, a pre-*Family Feud* Richard Dawson (then co-starring as Cpl. Peter Newkirk in the weekly series *Hogan's Heroes*); and actor Joe Flynn, best remembered for his co-starring role in the TV sitcom *McHale's Navy*.

Sadly, Flynn died on July 19, 1974. He had recently made an appearance with Merv. "He died the morning the show aired," recalls Don Kane. "He had taped it three weeks earlier, along with Helen Reddy, and his body was found floating in a swimming pool. We were all shocked to hear of this tragedy," says Kane.

As the show began to jell in its new surroundings, Griffin was hit with the news that more stations were dropping him. Realizing that some significant changes were in order, Merv began to tinker with the format. True to his word, he discarded the desk, chair, and sofa. Henceforth, he would conduct the interviews in much less formal setting, with chairs situated several feet away from the audience, at center stage.

It became readily apparent that ratings and reviews were more favorable when the show focused on one subject. From mid 1970 forward, *The Merv Griffin Show* had begun to tackle topics that would soon become the object of controversy on daytime TV later in the decade. The show seemed to be at its best when it focused on topics that were somewhat titillating.

One of the earliest "self improvement" themes focused on what the average looking person could do to become more attractive. A recurring guest was Dr. Kurt Wagner, the Beverly Hills plastic surgeon whose book, *The Youth Game*, helped debunk the myth that cosmetic surgery was strictly the domain of the rich and famous. The doctor pointed out that in 1970, more and more ordinary folks, including a surprising number of men, had had their noses, chins, jowls, and other body "flaws" corrected. "You must have an ugly waiting room!" Merv told the stunned physician.

In reviewing Dr. Wagner's segment today, one can readily appreciate the advancements in the quality of life for seniors since the early 1970s. The discussion eventually got around to facelifts for 80-year-olds. Wagner said that the procedure could erase years, if not decades, from one's appearance. "Yes," Merv concurred, "but wouldn't it be awful to have a young face, and then go swimming with an old body?" Actress Suzanne Pleshette (*The Bob Newhart Show*) was on the panel. "I don't think you do a whole lot of swimming at 80!" said Pleshette. Merv nodded in agreement.

The irony, of course, is that millions of today's octogenarians indulge not only in swimming, but other activities (including sex) once thought to be limited to the young.

In the early 1970s, America was in the throes of a huge wave of nostalgia. The grisly aspects of the Vietnam War, seen in American living rooms via the network newscasts, sparked a yearning for a simpler time. The Griffin show became very proficient in serving up regular courses of Hollywood nostalgia. One memorable telecast reunited Bob Hope, Bing Crosby, and Dorothy Lamour, who had long been popular favorites in their "Road" pictures.

One segment in particular, airing on September 30, 1970, featured a heart-warming reunion between two of television's earliest stars, Gale Storm and Charles Farrell of *My Little Margie*. There would also be full-length, 90-minute tributes to the famous Hollywood movie monsters, the veteran comedians, cowboys, and crooners.

It wasn't until October 9, 1970, that the staff put together what would be regarded the first official "theme show"—a tribute to Charles Schulz's beloved comic strip, *Peanuts.*

"I think someone along the way must have pitched the idea to Merv about the Charles Schulz show," explains Don Kane, "because it's not one that *he* would have come up with and I know I didn't." Kane says that at the time, he wasn't familiar with the famous comic strip characters. "I didn't follow comic strips, so that particular show didn't mean much to me, but it meant a lot to people who were fans of *Peanuts.*"

Nevertheless, the 90-minute program, which included a clip from the newly-released *Charlie Brown* feature film, was extremely well received, paving the way for other programs devoted to pop culture.

The theme shows accomplished two things: they set the tone of the Griffin show of the '70s, and they provided scores of jokes for Johnny Carson's monologues. Merv himself would later mimic a typical Carson joke: "Merv's doing another one of his fabulous theme shows tonight. He's interviewing 10 Lithuanian proctologists who want to be nuns!" (The reverse of that joke, "ten Lithuanian *nuns* who want to be *proctologists*," might have worked better.)

Though Steve Allen and Jack Paar had occasionally focused on certain themes, Merv was the first to do so on a regular basis with a broader scope of topics.

"Merv liked the idea of doing theme shows and he was good at them," says Kane. "I had found a psychiatrist named Dr. Rader, who did five or six shows for us, along with young kids who were addicted to drugs or alcohol. Those shows were quite successful and Merv appreciated the fact that they revealed the serious side of him."

"I remember when he'd have on specific groups of people, like billionaires," recalls Julann. "He'd come home and say, 'What should I ask them?' And I'd suggest asking them about their schooling.

Half of them hadn't even graduated from high school. That was interesting to me. Another time he came home and said, 'I've got astronauts coming on. What should I ask them?' And I said, 'Ask them if they believe in extraterrestrials.' He did, and that led to an interesting discussion about the incident in Roswell, New Mexico."

Did Merv watch his own show? "No," says Julann, "because he was too busy doing it and thinking of the next one."

Despite the efforts of hardworking staffers, who uncovered stimulating topics and booked interesting people from all walks of life, Griffin would occasionally drift into boredom—even when interviewing celebrities he genuinely admired as friends. "How may times could he interview the same people?" asks Don Kane. "Merv would lose enthusiasm with comics doing the same tried-and-true jokes and routines. Often, he would start the show with one of the minor names, just because he wanted to liven it up with something fresh. He didn't want to start by dragging out someone he had already talked to 25 times," says Kane.

The trick was to keep Merv interested. "And if you could keep him interested with something new or different," says Kane, "the show rolled along pretty well."

One archival-worthy installment during this period was dubbed "The Year 2000," which aired on December 3, 1970. The Griffin show had tackled sensitive subject matter involving human reproduction back in 1965, when *Life* editor Albert Rosenfeld had appeared. By 1970, however, science had advanced significantly. It was time to revisit what lay ahead.

The main guest was Dr. Robert Francoeur, whose book, *Utopian Motherhood*, explored artificial insemination, population control, and other controversial experiments in biological matters. In addition to being an accomplished scientist, Francoeur also happened to be an ordained Catholic priest. He started out rather strongly, pointing out that in 1970, one out of every 200 babies born in the United States had been conceived via artificial insemination. The folks in the audience began shifting in their seats as he explained how some of those births resulted from frozen sperm of fathers who had been dead for years. "These are things that are going on right now while we're in this revolution," Francoeur said.

Francoeur also expounded forthrightly about the 49 women waiting to receive embryo transplants. While this process is well known today, most people in 1970, including Merv, were unfamiliar with the mechanics involved. Francoeur explained it: "A woman, for instance, who has two blocked fallopian tubes and can't conceive a child in the normal way because egg and sperm can't get together, you inject her with hormones so she super ovulates ten or twelve eggs, collect the eggs surgically, fertilize the egg with the husband's sperm in a test tube; incubate them in perhaps a rabbit, and then when they get to be about 120 cells, you implant them back into the woman."

Francoeur said that while no baby had yet been born by this process, he suspected that at least one current pregnancy was the result of embryo transplant. Francoeur predicted that embryo transplants were "around the corner."

The new science would benefit families affected by "sex linked" diseases, such hemophilia. Hemophilia is carried by women but shows up only in men. Thus, for the family in which hemophilia is prevalent, the parents could elect to have only girls.

The real kicker came when Francoeur began talking about bypassing human sexuality, including the act of intercourse. "Simply take a piece of your skin," he explained, "isolate and segregate the individual cells, put them in a special culture meeting to get them back to their embryonic condition, put them in an artificial womb, and then grow your carbon copy, or a hundred carbon copies of Merv Griffin."

"Ah, so there would always be a Merv Griffin on earth," said Merv. The audience snickered. "Yes," Fancoeur said, "and you can train them yourself!"

"*That* would show Carson and Cavett!" snapped Merv.

Francoeur said that asexual reproduction was roughly 20 years in the future.

Merv asked if the use of science as a tool for population control might trigger government involvement. Francoeur said that mass education was the key. "We have to face the basic question: whether mass education will condition the American people, and people around the world, to be able to face up to, and control, their reproduction so that we can have a "livable world in the year 2000."

Griffin reminded the audience that these words were coming from a Catholic priest. "The pope hasn't even seemed to indicate that he's going to approve birth control," said Merv, "let alone things that you and other scientists are suggesting here."

Francoeur: "I think basically the theologians in all the churches are beginning to deal with this. For instance the United Presbyterian Church, in its statement on human sexuality last May, said that we're facing the problem of increasing numbers of people in the senior citizen category, human sexual activity is extended into the seventies and eighties because of therapy, maybe the church ought to consider polygamy for senior citizens. They didn't spell it out that way, but they offered it as one alternative pattern for male/female relationships."

The topic of life extension was the perfect lead-in for Merv's next guest. Apropos of frozen sperm and eggs, a discussion about freezing an entire body seemed par for the course. Who was better qualified to expound on the subject than Dr. Robert Ettinger? The cryonics movement had seen significant developments since Ettinger's appearances in 1965. In the years that followed, two operational storage facilities had been established, one in New York, the other in California. Some 14 patients had now been subjected to "cryonic suspension," the first publicized case having been implemented in 1967. Cryonics was no longer a matter of speculation; it was a scientific reality. In fact, the cryonics society had grown to such proportions that a respectable representation of its members saw fit to attend the taping.

Of the 14 bodies that had been frozen, only 11 remained. "Somebody did thaw out his mother," Ettinger explained, "and two other families thawed out their relatives because they'd changed their minds."

Once again Ettinger elucidated the mechanical aspects of the storage unit, which "works like an old-fashioned icebox." Merv: "Do you have an ice man that comes and delivers?"

Ettinger: "It's analogous to that, yes. In the old days you put in a chunk of ice and when it melted, you put in another chunk. Well, in these storage units, you fill them with liquid nitrogen and when it's evaporated down to certain levels, you recharge it again. This is just once every few months, and there's no question of any catastrophe because of a power failure."

It was a more confident and assertive Ettinger this time around. "Do you catch somebody at the point of death?" asked Merv.

"I think perhaps we ought to put this in perspective," Ettinger said. "And I think I'll say it in a way that will sound the most *unpleasant* to the most people. Our goal is to become not only immortal, but immortal supermen. That is, we are interested in the year 2000, and for that matter the year 3000, not just as a matter of intellectual curiosity, but because we plan to do our very best to be there, in person and in the flesh.

"Now this is a goal that some people will think of as immodest, but we see no reason why we should set our sights any lower."

Merv thought the plan sounded "greedy." He asked how society would feed so many people. "There has to be new life."

With regard to population control, Ettinger predicted that it would become possible for society to expand beyond our solar system. "And there may be periods when there will be population crises. But if those periods occur, we'll just have to ride them out and have the appropriate temporary solution. But what I'm *not* willing to do is kill living people, particularly my own family, for the sake of the unborn." Merv frowned, as did Dr. Francoeur.

Francoeur began talking about family relationships. "For instance," he said, "if the son has taken over a large business and is now acting president of a company, is he going to revive a father who's in the deep freeze?"

Ettinger predicted that family loyalties would actually be strengthened, along with an improved morality. "When people realize that life is not short," he warned, "and they, in person, will have to stick around and face the consequences of their actions and live in the world that they make."

Ettinger pointed out that scientists around the world were laboring on a "cure" for old age, which, according to him, was the worst known disease. Phyllis Diller said there already was a cure for old age—*death*. The audience laughed. Ettinger grimaced.

This particular theme show generated more publicity than usual. One of the more intriguing photos that appeared in newspapers depicted Merv alongside a gargantuan robot dispensing food cubes—the "chow" of the future!

After pondering the possibilities of the future, it seemed like a good time to recount one of the joys of the distant past.

Of the many theme shows Griffin hosted at Television City, the most lavishly produced, and highly acclaimed, was his tribute to the silent-film era. Because the taping ran significantly overtime, and was marred by several inexcusable glitches, an extensive amount of editing was required. Consequently, Merv Griffin's "Salute to the Silent Screen," originally slated for broadcast on December 16, 1970, wouldn't be seen until January 14, 1971.

With appearances by 18 silent film stars and supporting players, the finished product came off far glossier than the typical "clip retrospective" program. The reminiscences of these living links to the infant motion picture industry, combined with a generous sampling of classic footage, would result in an important record to be relished by silent film scholars and aficionados.

The idea was entirely Don Kane's. "I had read a story in the *Los Angeles Times* a couple of weeks earlier about silent motion picture stars being honored," says Kane. "And at the time, Merv wanted to do more theme shows and I thought this might be a good one. So I proposed the idea to him and he said, 'Yes, let's go ahead and do it.'"

Kane had been a frequent patron at the Silent Movie Theater in Los Angeles, which revived oldies like Janet Gaynor's *7th Heaven* (1927), and a plethora of other classics. The manager of the theater had given Kane the telephone numbers of several long-forgotten stars who were now residing at the Motion Picture Country House and Lodge in nearby Woodland Hills. "The silent motion picture stars that I knew of were not necessarily the ones that ended up on our show," says Kane. "The ones I really wanted were either dead or unobtainable."

Kane's dream list would have included Lon Chaney, Sr., Charlie Chaplin, Harold Lloyd, Mary Pickford, Lillian Gish, Janet Gaynor, and Dolores Costello.

Chaney was dead. Chaplin was still active, but living in self-imposed exile in Switzerland. The likelihood of getting Chaplin on an American talk show was nil, so his people were never contacted. Harold Lloyd, another iconic comedian of the silent era, was alive but ailing. Lloyd wasn't contacted either. Dolores Costello said no. Janet Gaynor said no. "Gaynor said she considered herself a star of the talkies," recalls Kane, who reminded the actress that she'd won an Oscar for *Sunrise* (1927), which was indeed silent. "But that wasn't important to her," says Kane. "Her work in sound movies, like *A Star is Born* (1937), is what was important. Maybe she thought doing the show might make her appear old."

Gish was one of the era's megastars who said yes. She flew to Los Angeles from her Manhattan residence the night before the taping. Pickford also said yes—but would only commit to a prerecorded telephone interview that would be played into the show.

The major stars like Gish, Richard Arlen and Neil Hamilton, et al., arrived at the studio via limousine. The residents of Motion Picture Home, however, would make the 30- minute trek from Woodland Hills to Hollywood in a far less glamorous mode of transportation.

"We brought them in by bus," recalls Don Kane. "But we had a very nice buffet ready for them in the studio next to ours, which was the one used by Carol Burnett."

Kane recalls that the veteran "thespians" were delighted to be in each other's company. "And they were all hungry," he says. "We actually held two parties, one before the show and another after it."

The staff of the Motion Picture Home had provided Kane with a list of provisos, most of which had to do with sustenance. "They told us we had to feed them. We were told what to feed them and *when* to feed them. These were elderly people that had to eat at certain times. They really seemed to be enjoying themselves. And after the show, they all mingled again, and had more to eat, along with a little booze, if they wanted it."

Aside from the guests on stage, an aggregation of actors, bit players, stuntmen, and other stalwarts of the era, occupied a good portion of the 500 seats in the studio. Several of them would be seen to good advantage in the film clips that had been selected. For them, this would be a night to sit back and revisit their days of glory without the pressures of "performing" on a network television show. Several hundred fans also showed up for the taping, but were unable to get seats; they had stood on line for hours outside the CBS facility, which was bombarded by klieg lights and chauffeur-driven limousines.

Attired in a three-piece tux, Merv noted the irony of a television *talk* show saluting a medium in which talk was never heard. This would be a rare celebration with one form of entertainment paying homage to another that was long extinct.

The set of chairs normally used for the interviews was put aside. Griffin Productions sprang for an elaborate but not ostentatious set adorned with marquee-style lights and elegant fixtures. The lighting in Studio 43 (Merv's usual studio) was brilliant, yet soft enough to flatter the features of the elderly actors. The guests didn't walk through a curtain that night; they entered the stage via a sliding door in the set that opened electronically. Additional rows of cane-backed chairs were positioned on the left and right sides of the stage, allowing everyone to remain on stage for the duration of the taping.

Merv began his monologue by recalling Bobby Kennedy's appearance on the show in 1967. Kennedy credited his father for instilling a sense of obligation in him, and his brothers, to "give something back" to the nation that had provided them with so much. Similarly, Merv said he felt obligated to give something back to Hollywood, the community from which he would be "drawing" on a nightly basis.

After the monologue, the cameras shifted to Fairfax Avenue, where *Daily Variety* columnist Army Archerd greeted the first arrivals—Lillian Gish, Richard Arlen, Neil Hamilton, and Laura LaPlante. Then it was time for the first round of clips, culled from two of the earliest surviving films: *The Kiss* (1896) and *The Great Train Robbery* (1903). The scratchy black-and-white images were accompanied by a tinkling piano and scattered giggles from the studio audience.

Lillian Gish was the first guest. At 77, Gish was still recognizable as the fragile, pale-skinned waif she had played in the silents. Through the years, her eyes remained radiant, her tones genteel.

She had been touring the college circuit talking about her work with director D. W. Griffith, and the memoir she had recently penned, *The Movies, Mr. Griffith, and Me* (1969). Lillian and her older sister Dorothy Gish (1896–1968) had made their screen debut in Griffith's short, *The Unseen Enemy* (1912), and would later team up in his highly acclaimed feature, *Orphans of the Storm* (1921). In the interim, Lillian had surpassed her own expectations by starring in a string of the director's masterpieces: *The Birth of a Nation* (1915); *Intolerance* (1916); *Broken Blossoms* (1919); and *Way Down East* (1920).

Gish's recollections benefited from a choice selection of film excerpts, topped off by the climactic sequence from *Way Down East*. Gish is seen lying unconscious on an ice floe that is about to be swept over a waterfall. She is rescued in the nick of time by the young hero, played by Richard Barthelmess. The scene remains chillingly realistic because it is *real*. No rehearsals. No stunt doubles. No trick shots.

Merv asked if the scene had been shot in one take. "Oh, I should *hope!*" said Gish incredulously. The actress recalled her consternation over the fact that she couldn't hear Griffith's voice, which was obscured by the noise of the water and crackling ice. Though Gish never lost faith in her director's judgment or expertise, she began saying her prayers nonetheless.

Death, injury or illness can quickly end a production. According to Gish, *Way Down East* marked the first time an actor had been insured for working in a motion picture. Insurance agents, as well as doctors, had been dispatched to the set, Gish said. The agents were there to assess the level of physical risk to be assumed by the actors, and conducted thorough surveys of their family histories. She recalled that Barthelmess, a leading man with considerable athletic prowess, was deemed uninsurable. "Poor Dick had sinus trouble, so he couldn't pass," she said. As it turned out, Gish was the only member of the cast who was able to obtain coverage, despite her perceived fragility.

Even in the earliest days of cinema, the only thing that mattered to filmmakers was getting the desired result on the screen, Gish said. "In those days," she explained, "we thought the film was much more important than we were. We never thought about ourselves."

Lillian Gish continued to appear in films well into the sound era. Her final screen role was in *The Whales of August* (1987), opposite Bette Davis and Vincent Price. She died in 1993 at age 99.

Switching from drama to comedy, Merv introduced a scratchy fragment of film depicting a funny little man sporting a derby hat and toothbrush mustache. Charlie Chaplin, the preeminent film comedian of the silent era, had achieved world fame and enormous wealth through his iconic screen persona known as the Little Tramp. On hand to discuss the artistry of Chaplin were three performers linked to the comedian's early success—Minta Durfee Arbuckle, Jackie Coogan, and Babe London.

Remarkably feisty at 81, Durfee stated, with great relish, that her career in films dated back to 1913. At that time, she'd been married to one of Chaplin's legendary contemporaries, Roscoe "Fatty" Arbuckle. Durfee, who worked in Chaplin's earliest films, said she liked the comedian, but thought he was "strange" in that he wasn't as "outgoing" as the other comics employed at Mack Sennett's Keystone Studio.

A snippet from Chaplin's *A Day's Pleasure* (1919) would serve as an introductory piece for the delightfully rotund Babe London, one of the era's most prolific comediennes. London played a seasick passenger aboard an excursion boat in this rare (but uninspired) Chaplin short. Whether it was due to time constraints, or subsequent editing of the program, London didn't offer much insight about her work with Chaplin. Nor she did mention, even in passing, the other great comedians she'd worked with, including W.C. Fields, Laurel & Hardy, and the Three Stooges.

Best of all the Chaplin clips was an extract from *The Kid* (1921), "a picture with a smile—and perhaps a tear," with five-year-old Jackie Coogan in the title role. Chaplin discovers an abandoned baby boy (born out of wedlock) and raises it in a Dickensian slum. By the time the kid is five years old, he and the tramp are happily entangled in all sorts of urban mischief. The film would catapult Jackie Coogan to major stardom, making him the highest paid child star of the 1920s.

The celebratory nature of the evening precluded any references to controversial matters, past or present. Under different circumstances, Merv might have pursued a more provocative line of questioning, particularly with regard to Arbuckle and Chaplin.

In 1921, Durfee and Arbuckle separated, just prior to a scandal that would shock the film community, and the world, eventually leading to the comedian's downfall. A 25-year-old actress named Virginia Rappe (pronounced Rap-pay) had died after a drunken party in San Francisco, hosted by Arbuckle. Newspapers had a field day as the Rappe story morphed into a *rape* story, with Arbuckle being accused of sexual assault and manslaughter. The prosecution was unable to prove its case against Arbuckle, and the comedian was fully acquitted during the third trial he was forced to endure. His career, however, had been ruined. Nevertheless, Arbuckle was able to regain some footing in Hollywood as a director, using the pseudonym William Goodrich. He was on the verge of a new stardom in talkies when he died in 1933 at age 46.

The British-born Charlie Chaplin had been a controversial figure during the 1940s and early 1950s. Vilified in the American press as a Communist sympathizer, Chaplin endured a series of legal troubles that began in 1943. He was acquitted of violating the Mann Act (the transporting of women across state lines for immoral purposes) and survived a messy paternity suit filed by his erstwhile protégée, Joan Barry. Additional bad press stemming from tax problems, and a steadfast refusal to obtain American citizenship, further tarnished the name of the most universally recognized figure in motion pictures. In 1952, while *en route* to Europe to launch his latest film, *Limelight*, the U.S. attorney general revoked Chaplin's re-entry permit on grounds of "moral turpitude." The comedian eventually settled in Switzerland.

By 1970, any residual antipathy between Charlie Chaplin and the United States government was unknown to a new generation that had discovered the great man's work through television and theatrical revivals. With Chaplin still alive, and active, Griffin wisely avoided any discussion that could be construed as libelous or disrespectful. All he said was: "I'd be curious to know if any of you have ever heard from Mr. Chaplin again."

Durfee said her last communication with Chaplin occurred in 1963, after she'd paid him a compliment during an interview for the BBC. When she happened to meet up with her former co-star in Paris, he thanked her for the "very kind things" she'd said on the broadcast. Durfee jokingly told him: "I didn't tell them you were communistic and that you didn't pay your taxes!" To which Chaplin replied: "I ought to spank you on your little fanny!" On her return to Los Angeles via the Queen Mary, Durfee found a bouquet of flowers and a bottle of champagne in her cabin, courtesy of Chaplin. Attached to the bottle was a note: "Dear Minta: The next time I see you, I'm *still* going to hit you on your *prat!*"

Durfee was still semi-active in show business at the time of her appearance with Merv. She died in 1975 at age 85.

Although Jackie Coogan had never been directly connected to scandal, his name had once been the source of considerable controversy. As a child, he had earned several million dollars, which he expected to receive upon turning 21. He didn't. He wound up suing his mother and stepfather, alleging that they had squandered his fortune. The civil suit resulted in the passage of a California law that would become known as the Coogan Act. The statute requires that a certain percentage of money earned by child actors be placed in a trust fund. Consequently, today's child actors are protected, thanks to the enactment of this law.

In middle age, Coogan would enjoy a renewed popularity as the bald-headed Uncle Fester in *The Addams Family* television series (1964-66). Coogan died in 1984 at age 69.

The western genre was accorded its place in the sun via a montage of clips featuring Tom Mix (*Twisted Trails*, 1917); William S. Hart (*The Return of Draw Egan*, 1915); and an early (unidentified) short subject with Broncho Billy Anderson. Tom Mix died in 1940. William S. Hart died in 1946. Broncho Billy was still alive, but not for long; he died on January 20, 1971. To represent the great cowboys of yesteryear, the show booked 74-year-old Ken Maynard.

Maynard had entered films in 1923 through his friendships with Tom Mix and another contemporary, Buck Jones. Square-jawed and ruggedly handsome, Maynard ultimately became one of Hollywood's most popular cowboys. By the early 1930s, after sound movies had become commonplace, Maynard enjoyed even greater success as a *singing* cowboy, solidifying his "wholesome hero" image. On screen, Maynard had always avoided anything that remotely smacked of adult behavior. "I never made an issue of it, either," *The New York Times* quoted him as saying. "I did it because of all the kids who came to my pictures. I didn't think it was right for them to see drinking and smoking on the screen."

Merv introduced Maynard via a clip from *The Range Fighter* (1926). When it was over, the actor bounded on stage decked out in full western attire, including his trademark white hat. He seemed remarkably lithe, but his words were coming out in a slightly slurred pattern. Maynard, who had worked in rodeos early in his career, explained that he had taken a tumble down the steps that day. "Why didn't you use your lasso?" Merv quipped. With that, Maynard burst into a discourse about his lasso technique, punctuated by a loud and furious "*Yaaaahhooo!*" Merv jokingly asked him to do it again. Maynard obliged. "I think you just broke a few contact lenses in the first row," said Merv, as he cued up another scene from *Range Fighter*.

Merv: "Do you remember that film?"

Maynard: "No!"

There isn't too much a host can do with a one-syllable answer except roll the film and hope for the best. Fortunately, Maynard's memory kicked in when he caught a glimpse of his horse, Tarzan.

The most amusing incident during Maynard's segment was never seen or heard on the air. At one point, the aged cowboy got up to leave the set. Knowing that he was in closer proximity to the men's room from the stage, he decided to take a short cut by exiting through the sliding panel in the set. According to Merv's autobiography, Maynard boldly announced the reason for his quick departure: "I gotta *piss!*" The book does not specify if this utterance was audible only to the host, or to everyone in the studio. Was it said during a commercial or while tape was rolling? Knowing that the sliding panel opened and closed electronically, Merv suggested an alternate route. Ignoring his host, Maynard effortlessly separated the split in the panel and disappeared.

Don Kane remembers Maynard's urgent restroom break, but doesn't recall what was actually said during that maladroit moment. "He might have said 'piss,' says Kane, "and if he had, the word would have certainly been blipped. But I do remember him at that portal, trying to get it opened. Needless to say, they don't make cowboys like Ken Maynard anymore."

It was time to pay tribute to the leading men and women of the silent screen. Buddy Rogers was the first guest in this segment. Rogers, at the time, was still married to the woman affectionately known as "America's Sweetheart," Mary Pickford.

There was much more to Pickford than her starring roles in American silent films. As a screenwriter, independent producer, director, co-founder of United Artists, and co-founder of the American Academy of Motion Picture Arts and Sciences, Pickford helped pave the way for women to gain acceptance in a male-dominated business. Griffin's staffers desperately wanted to include the 78-year-old star in the program, even though it was widely known that she hadn't made a public appearance in years. "So they made arrangements to interview her by telephone before the show," remembers Don Kane. "But she kept saying *'Whoopee! Whoopee!'* right in the middle of the conversation. Merv thought that was hilarious. We all thought she was drunk, which she probably was."

According to Kane, even Lillian Gish thought Pickford had had a drink or two as she listened to the tape played on the air. Buddy Rogers immediately requested that the "interview" be cut out of the show—and it was. Nevertheless, Pickford's contributions to the genre were well represented by a choice selection of scenes from *Rags* (1915); *Pollyanna* (1920); and *Little Lord Fauntleroy* (1921).

Rogers, along with Richard Arlen, had starred in *Wings* (1927), considered the best aviation picture of the silent era and the first film to win an Academy Award for best picture. Rogers remembered that he and Arlen were required to fly the planes themselves. "We didn't have the back process [photography] at that time," said Rogers. "So we had to go up and fly. And I think we had over 300 hours of flying time during the filming. And we had to find our own clouds because we didn't have the back process; and if we didn't have the clouds that day, we just had to sit. We once had to wait 18 days to get the certain clouds that we had started the sequence with before."

Richard Arlen was introduced. Arlen and Rogers had remained good friends through the years.

Merv: "How did you get your role in *Wings?*" Arlen: "Purely by accident," he said cheerfully. "Everybody else had taken a test for it. Buddy *didn't* have to take a test. He was a friend of Jesse Lasky, who was vice president of Paramount!"

Arlen recalled that he was reluctant to try out for the role, until several technicians convinced him to at least "rehearse" for it. He knew he'd be required to cry. "In those days, if you could cry, they thought you were a great actor," said Arlen. "I was pretty bad. But we had an onion. And while I read a letter, I sniffed the onion and the tears just came to my eyes. And they thought, isn't wonderful the way this guy can cry?"

Despite his resourcefulness, Arlen wasn't invited to take the actual screen test. He gave the director, William Wellman, what he called "the long nose" (the classic nose-in-the air hauteur). Later, however, Wellman sent for Arlen. As it turned out, Wellman, who had been in the Lafayette Flying Corps, learned that the young actor had been in the Royal Air Force. Arlen was then assigned the role based solely on his flying ability, but he soon heard that the studio was making a test, for the same role, with another young actor named Gary Cooper. "They'd found out that I couldn't act, in the meantime," Arlen admitted. Ultimately, Wellman realized that all he needed was a couple of guys who weren't afraid to fly an airplane. Arlen got the job.

"Before I introduce my next guest," Merv continued, "I want to show you a very exciting scene from *Nomads of the North,* a film made in 1922. In it, Betty Blythe proved the old adage that a man's best friend is his dog—unless you happen to have a bear."

In the scene, Blythe plays the heroine in distress, with her wrists tied and her hair frazzled, as she's held captive in a cabin at the mercy of the villain (Francis McDonald). As she screams for help (via pantomime, of course), a bear and a dog suddenly emerge from the wilderness. Both animals leap through a window, but it is the canine that comes to the rescue by attacking the villain, thereby allowing Blythe's character to flee.

Unlike Lillian Gish or Mary Pickford, Blythe had never achieved iconic status in silent cinema. But she did enjoy enormous popularity by starring in such hits as *The Queen of Sheba* (1921) and similar "exotic" melodramas. Film scholars and historians are quick to credit her as one of the first actresses to be seen on screen in "various stages of undress." Though Blythe's career spanned well into the sound era, she is remembered chiefly for her work in the silents.

"Ladies and gentlemen," Merv proudly announced, "the heroine of *Nomads of the North*, Miss Betty Blythe." Out walked an elegantly coiffed but somewhat unsteady woman who, at age 77, bore not the slightest resemblance to the heroine in the clip.

Blythe looked happy to be on the program, her face beaming brightly. "I am absolutely in another world," she said softly.

Griffin's staff had been warned that Betty was known to have an occasional bad day. Not wanting to exhaust her, Merv began the interview right where Blythe was standing, just a few inches away from where Ken Maynard was sitting.

Merv: "Miss Blythe, do you remember how long it took you to...."

Maynard: "I know her well."

Merv: "Easy there, Mr. Maynard!"

Merv to Betty: "How long did it take you to shoot that rescue scene? Do you remember?"

Maynard: "But she worked with *me!*"

Merv: "I may have to rescue you *again!*" [Moving Betty away from Maynard]

Unfortunately, Blythe had no recollection of the scene that had just been shown. Even worse, she had not the slightest memory of the director, the leading man, or even the dog. She did, however, remember the bear.

"When did you leave films, Miss Blythe?" Merv asked. "They left me, dear, because I got so old," she said gingerly.

"Betty, I hate to interfere," Maynard interrupted, "but tell 'em how you worked for me and never even *seen* me while you was on the picture!"

Someone apparently told the overzealous actor to pipe down, because an off-camera "*Aw, shut up!*"—in Maynard's voice—is audible on the soundtrack. This utterance would garner the longest laugh of the evening. For the record, Betty Blythe *did* appear in a Maynard film, a low-budget programmer titled *Western Courage* (1935).

Maynard's obstreperousness had everyone in stitches, except Merv, who quickly guided Blythe to her seat—at a respectable distance from Maynard.

As if Blythe's spot wasn't embarrassing enough, Viola Dana, a well-known comedienne, couldn't recall anything about her work in *Children of Eve* (1915) as it flickered on the screen. Dana, however, was enough of a pro to keep the conversation flowing with an anecdote concerning the disintegration of her early films. Merv asked if she had any favorites. "Well, certainly not *this* one!" she said wryly. Slightly perturbed, Merv moved on.

Generous scenes representing the heyday of the silent, full-length feature were played. These included: John Barrymore's *The Sea Beast* (1926); Chaney's *The Phantom of the Opera* (1925); *The Big Parade* (1925); *The Merry Widow* (1925); *Ben Hur: A Tale of the Christ* (1925), and others. After a brief chat with Neil Hamilton (best remembered today for his portrayal of Commissioner Gordon on the *Batman* TV series) the focus shifted back to comedy.

Priceless footage of Fatty Arbuckle, Babe London, Mabel Normand, and Harry Langdon, were interspersed around a rare clip from an unidentified 1928 Sennett comedy filmed in two-strip Technicolor; it featured a raving beauty named Carole Lombard, seen cavorting on a beach with an attractive young couple played by Sally Eilers and Matty Kemp.

Next came a remarkably clear Sennett clip, circa 1914, starring Chester Conklin. In the scene, Conklin enjoys some blandishments from the undisputed diva of the Sennett films, Mabel Normand.

A veteran of some 280 films over a 40-year period, Conklin was the embodiment of American screen comedy. He had entered films in 1913 as a $3-a-day player at the Sennett's Keystone Studios. His character, known as "Walrus" (inspired by a paste-on walrus mustache) caught on quickly and he soon found himself working regularly in a string of hastily made comedies, 12 of which starred

Charlie Chaplin. Conklin had remained on friendly terms with Chaplin, and turned up in two of the of the comedian's masterworks, *Modern Times* (1936) and *The Great Dictator* (1940).

"And here *is* Chester Conklin, ladies and gentlemen!" Merv beamed. The 85-year-old Conklin slowly strolled out, still recognizable as the lovable character from the Keystone era, replete with his original walrus mustache. "You've given every single one of us an awful lot of laughs," said Merv sincerely. "And what a thrill to be able to say thank you in person!" The comedian was genuinely touched by the tribute. For comedy film buffs around the world, this was a poignant and significant moment. Sadly, it would mark Conklin's last major public appearance. He died on October 11, 1971, less than a year after this program had been taped.

The show had been running significantly overtime. With the end quickly approaching, four actors stood in the wings nervously awaiting their intros. One by one, they were introduced: character actor/comedian Eddie Quillan; leading ladies Vivian Duncan and Dorothy DeVore, and Carter DeHaven, father of actress Gloria DeHaven.

When the clock finally ran out, Merv eloquently stated that the silent era could not be adequately summed up in 90 minutes. As he spoke, the orchestra softly played "Hooray for Hollywood." He acknowledged some the greats that had made an impact on the genre, but hadn't been represented in the clips: Colleen Moore, Corrine Griffith, Dorothy Davenport, Vilma Banky, the Talmadge Sisters, Wallace Reid, George O'Brien, Duncan Renaldo, Emil Jannings, and Douglas Fairbanks, Sr. Griffin also gave a respectful nod to many unforgettable films that had not been discussed in detail: *The Birth of a Nation* (1915), *Intolerance* (1916), *The Covered Wagon* (1923), *Beau Geste* (1926), and others.

"You've seen tonight the Hollywood we've all been living on," said Griffin. "This is the glamour that we're all trying to recapture. And there'll never be another time like the silent era, or a place like Hollywood during the silent era, or stars like those of the silent era. Our thanks to the many great stars on our stage tonight, and in the audience, who have made this a memorable evening."

Griffin gave a special acknowledgment to the "extraordinary young man" who had put the show together—Don Kane.

"It was nice of him to do that," says Kane. "But the show still credited Andrew Smith as the writer!"

Kane has vivid recollections of that magical evening. "I thought Lillian Gish's interview had gone very well," says Kane. "But I didn't care for Jackie Coogan." Kane claims that Coogan had demanded a solo interview like the one accorded Gish. "I remember him saying, 'These people aren't important. Why don't you give me more time?' He wanted more airtime because he thought he was as big a star as Miss Gish. And we didn't."

Kane also encountered problems with the CBS editing department. "They cut out quite a bit of the program," he says. "Three guests had been cut out and I had them put it all back. But the show still ran in the 90-minute time period."

Griffin's "Salute to the Silent Screen" scored a hit with viewers and critics. The greatest accolade, however, would come from the American Film Institute, which requested a copy of the program for a special presentation in Hollywood. "Betty Bronson, who had played Peter Pan, was among the guests who attended the screening," recalls Kane. "Merv was there, and so was I. The show was presented mostly for reporters, and that's the only time I ever saw it after it had been edited." Kane believes much of the ballyhoo was attributable to the luminaries who appeared on the show rather than the ancient film clips. "You didn't seen those old stars around," Kane explains, "and by that time, it had been 20 years or more since most of them had worked."

The only known copy of Griffin's "Salute to the Silent Screen" is a black-and-white kinescope film, since the master two-inch color videotape was not preserved. This, however, is not too disappointing because the black-and-white copy exudes the flavor of an old time Hollywood premiere.

Shifting gears from movies to music, Merv struck another nostalgic chord the following week with a "Salute to the Big Band Era." The salute was presented in two parts, airing on January 18 and 19, 1971. Merv, himself a former big band crooner, took delight in reliving a bygone era with his contemporaries while, introducing younger viewers to a sound that had long since faded. In his review for *The New York Times*, Jack Gould praised the program as a "warm, tuneful and entertaining remembrance of the league of forgotten men—the leaders of the Big Bands of Yesteryear."

Mort Lindsey outdid himself in leading in his own orchestra in various tunes that had been immortalized by the guests, among them: Lawrence Welk, Horace Heidt, Les Brown, Vaughn Monroe, Freddy Martin, and Charlie Barnet. (Barnet joined in the performance of the show's closing number, "On the Sunny Side of Life.")

"To shift effortlessly from the champagne horn of Lawrence Welk to the Dixieland beat of Bob Crosby left no doubt of Mr. Lindsey's versatility," said Gould.

Other theme shows during Merv's early Hollywood period celebrated noble professions: "Lawyers," "Medicine," "Football Stars," "Law Enforcement," and "Magicians." Others themes focused on nostalgia: "Vaudeville," "The 1950s," and "Horror," as in horror films, celebrated with special guests Vincent Price, John Carradine, and Lon Chaney, Jr.

Now that his show was part of the Hollywood landscape, Merv paid special attention to the creative forces behind the movies. He began to plan tributes to top producers like Ross Hunter and Howard Koch, as well as veteran directors like David Butler.

Of all the theme shows geared toward nostalgia, Don Kane recalls the "Salute to Tarzan Actors," broadcast on March 2, 1971, as the most problematic. "I had a terrible experience with that one," recalls Kane. Although the show was essentially a celebration of the famous character created by Edgar Rice Burroughs, much of the focus would be on Johnny Weissmuller, the most famous screen Tarzan of all. He had mastered the role in a string of popular movies produced between 1932 and 1948. Kane recalls how Weissmuller had been ostensibly cooperative in the weeks leading up to the show. "I kept calling him to confirm that he'd be coming," recalls Kane. "And he'd say, 'Yeah, I'll be there.' But on the day of the taping, he didn't show up. I had sent him an airline ticket—which he exchanged for a ticket to Acapulco!"

At the last minute, the talent coordinator hastily assembled a floor show with a South Seas flavor. "We got Gardner McKay from the TV show *Adventures in Paradise*, and we put together a show with him. He had brought along a leopard, and we had some Polynesian dancers on the show that did a hula-like dance."

Actor Lex Barker, who played the Tarzan role in movies from 1949 to 1953, made an appearance, as did Ron Ely, who played the role on television in the mid-1960s. "And we wound up doing a South Seas tribute rather than a tribute to Tarzan," says Kane wistfully.

Throughout much of 1970, Merv had been pestered by complaints from CBS about all the "anti-war talk" uttered on his show. The network strove to balance out the anti-war sentiments with equally powerful pro-war statements. Merv would later recall one memo in particular, from a CBS lawyer, complaining that 34 anti-war statements had been made on the show, while only one pro-war statement had been made during the same period. The pro-war speech had come from John Wayne. Merv responded to the memo by saying that if the network could find him a pro-war guest as famous as Wayne, he'd book him on the show.

John Wayne had, of course, been on the Griffin show throughout the years, and Merv had been on location with the actor during the production of *The War Wagon* (1966) and *The Green Berets* (1968).

The interview on the set of *The War Wagon*, shot on 16mm film in Mexico, is notorious for the fact that both men were more than slightly inebriated on camera. (Merv would later recall Wayne introducing him to the wonders of tequila!) The two of them sat there, more or less "winging it," after having offered an incredibly bad rendition of "The Shadow of Your Smile." As their time on camera drew to a close, Merv spoke from heart. "I am going to make a flat statement that I have never made on my show before," he said soberly. "You are my favorite actor in motion pictures."

"You've lost your mind!" Wayne protested. "No, I'm serious," said Merv. "You are not an actor, because the way we're talking now, you are exactly the same on the screen."

Five years later, Merv was on location with Wayne again. This time, however, it wasn't for a film shoot.

On January 24, 1971, CBS aired "The Duke and I; Merv Visits John Wayne" (a title obviously inspired by *The King and I*), in the 11:30 p.m. time slot. Griffin brought his cameras and crew to the actor's ranch in the middle of Stanfield, Arizona. On this day, cattle buyers from all over the country had come to Wayne's ranch to bid for bulls. In other words, it was to be one "big bull auction!"

Wayne said that viewers were about to get a glimpse of something city folks never get to see: a panoramic view of his 22-acre cattle ranch. Merv asked the actor why the appeal of westerns has endured for so long. "Folklore of any country is best understood the world over," Wayne said. "Ours, the cowboy, has represented a hundred years of legend that's been written about in prose, poetry, and song, more than any other country's. I guess it's the most popular folklore in the world and people want to see it. Folklore is about basic emotions; there's no nuance. People can just sit there and enjoy themselves, and they don't have to look at somebody else's problems."

Merv was curious to know what Wayne, an exceedingly "moral" man in private life, would *not* do on screen. "What would you take out of a script," he asked.

"I like to think of myself as moral, but I guess I'm not," Wayne replied smilingly. "I hate pettiness. And anything that's petty, I like to get rid of, or let somebody else do it."

Merv asked Wayne if he had any heroes while growing up. The actor rattled off the names of a few: General MacArthur; cowboy actor Buck Jones, and western star turned character actor Harry Carey.

Their attention turned to Wayne's ten-year-old son, Ethan, who was present for the filming. "When you look at Ethan today," Merv asked, "who might *his* heroes be? The astronauts?" Wayne turned to the boy and asked, "Who are your heroes?" And without hesitation, the kid looked at his father and said, "You." It was the most poignant moment in the ninety-minute program.

Wayne recalled the making of his favorite film, *She Wore a Yellow Ribbon* (1949). He said his favorite director was John Ford, who had also directed Wayne's *life* as much as his movies. "I have respect for him," he said with unwavering sincerity. "I think every young man finds some older man to look up to. My dad had passed on, and I met Pappy and counted him as a big brother. He set a sense of values to my thinking that I think helped me."

When Wayne appeared on the Westinghouse show in 1966, Merv tried his best to goad him into a discussion with another guest whose political ideology differed dramatically. On that occasion, all the actor would say was, "Well, he's on my side, but doesn't know it." Now, in the absence of a studio audience, the two conservatives could take a light-hearted poke at liberals.

"You don't find too many liberals in the west," observed Merv. "Or at least in the cattle business." Wayne, one of the most outspoken Republicans in the entertainment world, said, "The word is radical. I always figured I was liberal. I'll listen to anybody; whatever they've got to say. But these so-called liberals won't listen to anybody but themselves. And they're very articulate, too."

Wayne offered an assessment of the nation's youth. "Actually," he said philosophically, "there are damn *few* kids that are out of line. It's a wonderful generation. I think they care more than we did. And I think they'll help each other more, because we came out of that era where there was a depression, and you start scratching for yourself a little more, rather than worrying about the fellow next door."

The war in Vietnam was tearing the country at the seams; it was the burning issue that dominated every medium. Merv suggested that the war was the main thing separating the generations. "Absolutely not," Wayne protested. "If you got over and saw some of the young kids that are fightin, you wouldn't feel like that."

Wayne, a vociferous opponent of Communism, had previously expressed his stance when Merv interviewed him on the *Green Berets* set in late 1967. On that occasion, Wayne had said: "Those kids know what they're fighting. They're going to fight it there or they're gong to fight it over here. But they're going to fight it and they might as well start now."

With the war still raging on more than three years later, the actor was delighted when Merv told him that on the battlefields of Vietnam, an act of heroism was referred to as a 'John Wayne." "I am very complimented, said Wayne, "whether they mean it as a laugh or not." Merv assured him that it was not.

"The Duke and I; Merv Visits John Wayne" garnered respectable notices in the trade papers. "Griffin's visit to Wayne was an absorbing portrait of an actor unafraid to express an opinion," wrote Tony Scott in *Variety*.

Despite the backdrop of Hollywood and legion of big-name stars, the show's numbers were still in the basement. In an effort to attract a more youthful audience, Merv thought it might be good to have 18-year-old Desi Arnaz, Jr. fill in for him one evening. The network bigwigs instantly vetoed the idea. They couldn't fathom a kid hosting a late-night talk show. Treacher had to go because he was too old. And now Desi, Jr. was unacceptable because he was too young. Merv wondered if there was anything he could do, short of quitting, that would please the suits. For the record, Desi Arnaz, Jr. did *sub* for Merv and did a fine job. The ratings, however, remained stagnant.

Once again, stories began to circulate in the press. The pervasive rumor had always been that CBS was exploring late-night alternatives to Griffin. This time, there was much talk of an "anthology-of-dramas" concept. In other words: late-night soap operas. Another idea was for a "countrified" talk show, packaged by the producers of *Hee Haw*. As these proposals were bounced around, the network cited March 15 as the fateful day for the decision on renewal of the Griffin show. The show survived.

Griffin set out to explore topics that might improve the show's ailing numbers. As he and his staff continued to seek out the new, CBS set out to divest itself of anything old. Or anything that *appealed* to the old. Attempting to change its folksy, rural image, the network began handing out pink slips. Many stars and shows were unceremoniously dumped. A prime example is Red Skelton, whose variety series had been a staple on CBS since 1953. Also gone, or *soon* to be gone, would be many of the network's long-running, family-oriented sitcoms: *The Beverly Hillbillies, Petticoat Junction,* and *My Three Sons*. The Big Eye was about to establish a new look for the new decade.

On January 19, 1971, CBS launched a half-hour sitcom that its producer, Norman Lear, had tried to sell to the networks several seasons earlier. ABC had rejected the first "pilot" episode, made in 1969, because it was deemed too controversial. Based on a British program called *Till Death Us Do Part,* the American counterpart was ultimately sold to CBS as *All in the Family*. It focused on a middle-aged, blue-collar bigot named Archie Bunker, played by a relatively unknown actor named Carroll O'Connor. In the first American pilot, O'Connor's character bore the moniker Archie Justice, and the title of the program was *Justice for All*.

For the first time in the history of American television, a weekly sitcom would grapple with subjects such as racial prejudice, homosexuality, impotence, menopause, death, and rape. As recently as the late sixties, these topics had to be dealt with tactfully within the scope of news reporting or scholastic documentaries. Now they were fodder for a prime time comedy. On the night of the first broadcast, CBS employed extra telephone operators to handle the onslaught of complaint calls that were expected. As it turned out, no one called.

Merv was greatly impressed by the fresh performances and bold writing style that epitomized *All in the Family*. In April 1971, Griffin booked the entire cast: Carroll, O'Connor, Jean Stapleton, Rob Reiner, Sally Struthers, and Mike Evans on his show for a 90-minute salute. How could he go wrong? He'd be probing an embryonic phase in television comedy *and* promoting a new CBS series at the same time. The network's top brass, however, didn't see it that way. The morning after the show aired, CBS president Bob Wood phoned Merv: "No wonder you're doing badly when you keep saluting shows like *All in the Family*, which is going off the air."

True, *Family* hadn't packed quite the wallop as expected in its Tuesday evening time slot, at 9:30 p.m., opposite ABC's *The Mod Squad*. The viewing audience simply hadn't had enough time to discover Archie, much less warm up to him. During the summer of 1971, a series of commercials featuring O'Connor and Stapleton (in their respective roles as Archie and Edith) struck a chord with home viewers. Also, reruns of the series that aired during the summer reached a new audience that had missed the initial broadcasts. By the end of September, after *All in the Family* had returned for its second season in a more desirable time slot—Saturdays at 8:00 p.m.—it surged in the ratings and became the number one program on television.

Merv's faith in *All in the Family* was not lost on Norman Lear, whose writers occasionally made flattering references to either Merv or *The Merv Griffin Show* in their scripts.

It was early autumn 1971. Although the move to the West Coast had resulted in better guests, creative format changes, and intriguing themes, Merv Griffin simply couldn't put a dent in Johnny Carson's ratings. As if the station defections weren't bad enough, a few CBS affiliates moved the Griffin show to late-afternoon slots, while others attempted to drop it altogether. The management of these stations believed it was more profitable to fill the 11:30 p.m. slot with theatrically released features, the very form of programming they were eager to replace two years earlier. There were continued reports that CBS might replace Griffin with talent already under contract to the network.

One day CBS programming chief Fred Silverman dropped by Merv's dressing room with some "advice" on how to improve the ailing show. Silverman, who would later move to NBC where he would clash spectacularly with Johnny Carson, wanted to re-format *The Merv Griffin Show* along the lines of *Broadway Open House*. Irate, Merv bluntly told Silverman that if he wanted a show of that type, he should look up Jerry Lester and Dagmar, sign them, and put them on the air. Griffin not only dismissed Silverman's recommendation, he dismissed Silverman. He practically ordered the exec out of the dressing room. Griffin and Silverman never saw each other again.

Although Griffin was a man who rolled with life's punches, the strain he was under was beginning to take its toll. The press commented that his hair was growing increasingly gray. His weight zoomed upward. He also had to cope with hypoglycemia, a chronic condition in which one's blood sugar level plummets dramatically.

Adding to Merv's troubles during this period was a defeat in court, stemming from a lawsuit involving—of all things—yo-yos. A charitable organization had used Merv's name and likeness on 500,000 yo-yos and pillboxes. The plan was for the charity to sell the items for a dollar, splitting the money with the star. Merv, however, sought a temporary injunction, barring the organization from selling the toys. Understandably, he didn't want his name or picture associated with a charity that was paying him money. A judge ruled against Merv, citing a lack of evidence to warrant the injunction. By default, the co-defendant that had supplied the yo-yos, was prohibited from selling or distributing any more of them. As mundane as the incident was, it found its way into the mainstream press.

The mood in Griffin's production offices was growing tense. Though Don Kane says that Griffin was, by show-business standards, a relatively easy man to work for, there were times when he could get "in a bit of a tether." This was particularly true during the final months at CBS. "There was a time during that period when I had to be honest with Merv," recalls Kane.

The boss had called an emergency meeting late one evening. Says Kane: "We all had to stand around at eleven o'clock at night and hear him go on and on about something that had gone wrong and that *we* had to fix. Finally, he began asking everyone in the room what they thought should be done. Most people wouldn't tell him anything because they were afraid to say anything. And they would hem and haw around. But I didn't do that and would just tell him the truth. He would take it, but he didn't like it. I was never a bosom buddy of his, so if something on the show was really wrong and could be corrected, I'd tell him. And he really didn't want to hear about anything that might reflect upon him—that possibly *he* wasn't doing something right. Like many stars, he only wanted to hear good news."

The ratings during the last quarter of 1971 had remained consistently weak. "It was a troubling time for him," says Julann Griffin. "But in everyone's life there are troubling times, and a time for transition."

Merv Griffin was on the threshold of a major transition. There were persistent rumors in the press, and within the TV industry, that CBS might drop the Griffin show when the star's contract expired on February 15, 1972.

On September 4, 1971, New York's *Daily News* reported that Griffin wanted out of his contract as of December 31. According to the article ("Merv Griffin Asks Out, Beats CBS to the Punch"), the star was considering an offer to move his show to Metromedia.

"We are definitely interested in syndicating a Merv Griffin show," a Metromedia spokesperson was quoted as saying. "But so far, no deal has been made." In the same story, a CBS rep confirmed that Griffin would remain under contract and the decision to pick up his "next option" wouldn't be made until mid-December. The names on the list of possible replacements for Griffin included Bill Cosby, and CBS's hottest variety act at the time, Sonny and Cher.

Griffin's autobiographies, *Merv* and the subsequent *Making the Good Life Last*, offer a different spin on the foregoing events. According to both volumes, Merv, sensing an impending cancellation, began to "quietly" negotiate with Metromedia in the fall of 1971. He'd had lunch with the company's president, Al Krivin, the man who shifted the Griffin show from Channel 11 (where it had been underperforming) to Metromedia's Channel 5 in New York City. In his books, and in contemporaneous interviews with the press, Griffin reported that Krivin was "anxious" to make a deal. As negotiations continued, the host kept mum about the likelihood of any possible return to syndication. The motivating factor for Merv's covertness was a clause in his contract stipulating that if CBS canceled his show, the network would be liable to him for severance pay to the tune of $250,000.

Therefore, at Merv's behest, the staff and crew were kept in the dark about the finalization of the Metromedia deal. The agonizing suspense came to an end on December 3, 1971, when Bob Wood personally delivered the dreaded cancellation notice to Merv's offices.

As Wood spoke, Merv did his best to look utterly dejected when, in fact, he had been hoping all along that the network would dump him. He kept looking down at his shoes, feigning concern about his soon-to-be-unemployed staffers, knowing full well that he had the Metromedia deal in his pocket, and that he'd soon be a quarter of a million dollars richer.

"I was tired of the three-way late-night fight with Carson and Dick Cavett," Griffin told New York's *Sunday Record* ("Merv Griffin: Now He's Bucking the Networks," March 12, 1972). "All America watched the three networks, and nobody was going anywhere. Viewers stayed with the show that had the big stars. They'd read the night's listings and figure out which of the three they'd want to watch."

Merv's exit from the Tiffany network was anything but harmonious. Even with all the mud-slinging in the press, one CBS bigwig confirmed that Griffin's tenure with the network wasn't entirely worthless. "I admit we made money from the show," said CBS programming exec Perry Lafferty to *TV Guide*. "But when Merv dropped to only about 20 percent of the total audience, some of our key stations began to defect."

CBS's replacement for *The Merv Griffin Show* would be a package of full-length movies—the very thing that had led to Griffin's late night stint in the first place.

With the Metromedia contract finalized, Griffin breathed a sigh of relief; his show would soon embark on yet another life in the syndication market.

Metromedia Producers Corporation (alternately known as MPC) was a company stemming back to the old DuMont Television network of the 1950s. TV buffs will recall that Jackie Gleason introduced *The Honeymooners* as a series of sketches on DuMont's *Cavalcade of Stars* in 1951. As a poor fourth among the prosperous networks, DuMont signed off in 1956. A year later, however, the company tied its fortunes to several radio stations in New York City, and subsequently changed its name to Metropolitan Broadcasting Corporation. After a series of corporate maneuvers and takeovers, Metropolitan would ultimately re-emerge as Metromedia. The company owned multiple television outlets, one of which was WNEW-TV (Channel 5), the station that had "saved" the Westinghouse Griffin show from an almost certain cancellation in 1966.

In December 1971, as Merv contracted to syndicate his series through Metromedia, the company was producing first-run programs as well as distributing "rerun" favorites like *Mayberry R.F.D.*, and *That Girl*.

Finally, on December 6, 1971, *The New York Times* confirmed that CBS would replace the Griffin show with a package of movies from MGM and other major studios. Three days later, the paper reported that Griffin's new Metromedia series would replace the departing *David Frost Show* on New York's Channel 5, WNEW-TV (Merv's former flagship) as of March 13, 1972. This was another ironic move, since Frost had replaced the Griffin show three years earlier on the Westinghouse network. It was also announced that Westinghouse might redistribute 260 episodes of the Group W *Merv Griffin Shows* to local stations. For reasons that were never made known, the plan to replay Merv's best moments from the 1960s never came to fruition.

At the time, several Metromedia-owned stations carried Westinghouse programming and vice versa. The publication reported that Channel 5's contract with Westinghouse (Frost's distributor) was contractually able to move the Frost series to another time slot, thereby making way for the much-anticipated return of Griffin.

While Griffin took delight in recalling how his departure from CBS netted him $250, 0000 in severance pay, he also bemoaned how the network erased every *Merv* tape in its archive to recoup that sum. In fairness to CBS, there is reason to believe that the network did give the departing host the option of salvaging—at his own expense—many of the 500 shows he had hosted between 1969 and 1972.

Don Kane recalls: "They would ask Merv what he wanted to save, and all he would ever save were the interviews with politicians. He thought those were important and, of course, they were. Whenever he'd ask *me* what should be saved, I'd say, 'Merv, save the one with Lily Pons. Save the one with Jean Arthur; no one's ever seen her on a talk show before.'

"There were some marvelous people on those CBS shows, because we'd go for all the legends—and Merv enjoyed them all. But he didn't save the people I thought were legendary, even though these people had never done any other talk shows."

Luckily, a handful of episodes from the CBS era did survive; several of them have been released on DVD. Sadly, nearly all of Griffin/CBS shows ultimately fell victim to the bulk tape eraser.

Kane estimates that the network erased about a 100 "good ones" that warranted preservation. "One day Merv came in the office with a long list," recalls Kane. "And he said, 'They want to know what should be erased and what should be kept.' I checked the ones that *I* thought should be retained. But he didn't keep them because he'd have to pay for the tape. The network was charging him money to save his own tapes and he didn't want to pay for that. Merv was kind of tight with his bucks."

Kane says that while his former boss respected Jack Paar's viewpoint as to what a talk show should be, he adhered to his own credo as to which guests were most important. "Paar would have people like Alexander King and Oscar Levant on. But Merv wouldn't go that route after he'd moved to Hollywood, even though he'd had people like Norman Mailer and Jimmy Breslin as regulars in New York. After the move, the show took on a different dynamic."

No one—not even Criswell—knew what the future held for *The Merv Griffin Show*. After a turbulent two and a half years, it was finally good-bye to the Big Eye.

The last installment of the CBS series was taped on February 11, 1972. Unlike his departure from NBC, Griffin's exit from CBS offered no sad songs or emotionally charged farewells. It was a remarkably low-key affair, with no show-stopping performances. On hand to wish Merv good luck were old friends such as Pamela Mason, Joe Flynn, and Richard Dawson. Two rising newcomers to TV were featured: actor Lloyd Haynes (*Room 222*), and young Marcia Wallace, soon to be famous as the wry receptionist on *The Bob Newhart Show*.

Merv wrapped up by offering a backstage glimpse of Television City. He introduced a few of the unsung stalwarts that put the show together, including the cue-card boy. Finally, he recalled some of the "highlights" of the past two-and-a-half years, such as Zsa Zsa Gabor and her diamonds in close proximity to ex-bank robber Willie Sutton, and the infamous Abbie Hoffman flag shirt debacle. No clips were shown. Merv wasn't about to waste time, money, and energy on a ship that had already sunk. The decks needed to be cleared for the start of another new chapter—one that would restore the program to its previously envied status.

14. METROMEDIA MERV

During the late afternoon hours of March 9, 1972, nearly a thousand people patiently stood in line outside the Hollywood Palace Theatre to witness the rebirth of *The Merv Griffin Show*. With only 400 seats available to the public, a multitude of irate fans could be seen scampering in all directions after the pages uttered two dreaded words: "We're filled!" Located at 1735 Vine Street, the Hollywood Palace was a stone's throw away from the famed intersection of Hollywood & Vine. "You can't get more Hollywood than *this*," quipped one lucky ticket holder, taking his seat in the audience.

Once again, Merv had leased a theatre with a long and diverse history as his professional "home." Designed in a striking Spanish motif, the building was established in 1927 as the Hollywood Playhouse, a popular venue for legitimate stage productions. During the Depression years, 1735 Vine became known as the WPA Federal Theatre (named after the Works Progress Administration), with several government-sponsored programs headquartered within. Majestically rechristened as the El Capitan in the forties, the theater would host thousands of standing-room-only performances. Lucille Ball's radio series *My Favorite Husband* originated from the venue, as did Ken Murray's famous variety/stage show, *Blackouts*.

In the fifties, the El Capitan stage would become a hot spot for television broadcasting. It was there, on September 23, 1952, that Richard Nixon delivered his famous "Checkers speech." Numerous "live" programs, most notably *The Colgate Comedy Hour* and Ralph Edwards' long running *This Is Your Life*, emanated from the El Capitan. In September 1963, the property became the domain of Jerry Lewis, who re-established it as the Jerry Lewis Theatre. ABC spent a fortune renovating the theatre, updating its aesthetical and technical features, for its weekly *Jerry Lewis Show*. After Lewis' series was canceled in December, the network re-established the landmark as the Hollywood Palace. Perhaps the best-remembered program to emerge from this famous site was *The Hollywood Palace*, the vaudeville-style extravaganza seen on ABC every Saturday night from 1964 to 1970.

The marquee at 1735 Vine, which trumpeted some of the greatest names in entertainment, now emblazoned the theatre's current occupant: *The Merv Griffin Show*.

Assisted by most of the people who had been with him at CBS, Merv was ready to raise the curtain on his first show for Metromedia Producers Corporation. For Merv, this wasn't merely a "comeback" after his failed attempt to dislodge Johnny Carson; it was also the dawn of the final chapter in his career as a talk-show host.

The Merv Griffin Show had been off the air for nearly a month. During the hiatus, the star and his staff labored mightily to ensure that the Metromedia premiere would be a momentous event. Merv was ready for it. He'd shed nearly 30 pounds, looking nearly as svelte as he did during his best *Play Your Hunch* days. Without having to deal with the unrelenting stress of network television, Merv was once again at the top of his form.

As the orchestra, still under the baton of Mort Lindsey, struck up the familiar theme music, Merv walked onto the stage wearing the broadest smile possible. To the home viewer, the switch from network to syndication was imperceptible. The only discernible difference was that Merv was now on a different channel.

"It's like being away and coming home again," said Merv, after the thunderous applause had subsided. He offered a brief history of the theatre, pointing out its various accoutrements, particularly the fashionable "love seats" in the first rows. Merv also called attention to the new set, which was as stylized as his wardrobe, now supplied by Botony 500. In fact, Merv said his old hound's-tooth sports jacket had inspired the new design, consisting of a series of jagge-edged blocks created by art director Henry C. Lickel.

Griffin had ordered several renovations to the theater. Gone for good was the traditional runway that had been a familiar fixture at the Hollywood Palace. "Times have changed," said Merv, when asked why that portion of the stage had been dismounted.

In an unusual departure, Merv thought it best *not* to announce the selection of guests. "I'm going to let all of them walk out here and surprise you," he enthused. "Because if you don't know who they are, then you don't have a television set."

Merv kidded that Bob Hope was not among the invitees. "He only appears at disasters," said Merv. "And we're not one *yet*."

Merv chatted briefly about the history of his new theatre, pointing out the spot where Jerry Lewis's motorized desk had been stationed. The device, used by Lewis to conduct interviews, was equipped so that the comedian could rise up "to heaven or purgatory," right in the middle of a conversation.

"This Hollywood Palace lends itself to doing something that dramatic," said Merv. "But I told my staff: this is a simple talk show. I do not want to do anything spectacular." As he spoke, the set behind him parted, revealing an elaborate mobile bandstand slowly moving forward.

Earlier in the day at rehearsal, one of its wheels had gone flat. "Did you ever see a band with a flat tire?" Merv laughed. "All my life, I've wanted a motorized bandstand." Now he had one, and he wasn't going to worry that another flat might mar his opening-night song, "La La La La La La," a rather unusual choice. Steve Lawrence, the first guest, offered the more conventional "Ain't No Sunshine, When She's Gone," which he had just recorded for the MGM label.

By the time Merv brought out his next guest, Dinah Shore, a slight disturbance could be heard in the balcony. "Move back!" a voice yelled. "Louder!" said another. Merv continued chatting with Shore as though nothing was wrong. As they continued, the grumbling became more vociferous. Obviously annoyed, Shore said, "I keep feeling like somebody's talking back to me."

"Just a minute," snapped Merv. "What's the matter?" he asked, looking up at the balcony. "You can't hear a thing I'm saying?" Shore asked incredulously. Soon, the only voices being heard were the ones emanating from the balcony. "Wait a minute," said Merv in frustration. "One spokesman at a time. You can't . . . *what?* You can't *see?*"

Apparently, the panel of chairs had been placed too close to the edge of the stage, making it difficult, if not impossible, for balcony patrons to catch any of the action. Equally problematic was the less-than-adequate sound system, which had begun to fail during Shore's discourse.

Merv asked if any stagehands were in the house. There were. "Let's push this whole thing back," he ordered, "then we'll go on with the show." The crowd roared its approval. "I knew we were going to have a balcony problem," Merv sighed. "I just *knew* it." Shore looked up at the balcony and said, apologetically, "You're not missing anything!" To which Merv replied, "Oh, yes, they are!"

"In my life, I've *never* had an opening night go right," Merv confessed. "On CBS, CBS thought. . . ." That's as far as he got. Shore interrupted him to finish the story she'd started when the yelling began. "Did you think my story was over?" she asked Steve Lawrence. "I wasn't even listening, Dinah," said Lawrence nonchalantly. The audience laughed politely. Then, when Merv said, "tomorrow night we'll do the show from the balcony," everyone cheered. Shore dedicated her song, "The Best Is Yet to Come," to the new series.

The next interruption was a pleasant one. "Telegram for Merv Griffin!" announced a plump visitor to the set. It was Dom DeLuise, bearing a lovely bunch of *bananas*—instead of coconuts! DeLuise had been one of the opening guests on Merv's Westinghouse series. Merv regarded him as a good luck charm. This time, though, the evening had brought anything but good luck.

Because of the numerous technical glitches, the show was running behind schedule. Nevertheless, Merv took the time to acknowledge his 12-year-old son Tony, wife Julann, and actor Ross Martin (*The Wild, Wild West*) sitting in the audience. There was barely enough time to accommodate Angie Dickinson, who spent most of her segment talking about her then-husband Burt Bacharach.

Even Merv's cuff links were giving him trouble. He fumbled with them nervously, as he began to introduce the big draw of the night. His expression turned somber. "What?" he said to his producer off camera. "He's *downstairs?*" The groans from the audience resurfaced. "Now they're going to really come get us!" "Stretching" is a television term for filling in time. That's exactly what the panel did as everyone awaited the arrival of "Mr. Television"—Milton Berle.

Milton Berle was television's first superstar. In 1948, when his *Texaco Star Theatre* aired on Tuesday nights, movie theatres closed

early, and folks who didn't own a TV sets found an excuse to visit their neighbors who did. "Uncle Miltie" had made numerous
appearances with Merv through the years, particularly on the CBS
entries taped at Television City.

Merv: "Hello, Milton!"

Berle: "Hello, *Irv!*"

Berle said he'd been watching the show backstage. "I haven't been
so thrilled since I won Totie Fields on *The Dating Game.*" Some of
Berle's wisecracks fell flat. "Hey, you died," he barked at his fellow
guests, "Now let *me* die."

"You were never funnier," he told Merv, commenting on the
opening monologue. "And that's a shame."

Berle aimed his venom at the "outcasts" in the balcony. "If you
knew anybody, you'd be sitting *here,*" he said, pointing to the more
desirable seats downstairs. That remark registered the biggest laugh
of the night. "Those folks on the *shelf* are right," snapped Berle. The
comedian recalled the time in which a balcony audience, in that
very theater, revolted because they couldn't see him on the stage.
"And they kept moving me back and back and back—until finally
I went off!"

Berle seemed to be taking over as host, critiquing Merv's jokes
and calling for the commercial breaks. His temerity came to a
screeching halt when the next guest, Dionne Warwick, accidentally
knocked a table onto his foot. "I'm suing Motown," barked Berle, as
he took Warwick's coat. "Milton," said Merv sternly, "can I run my
own show?" Berle shot back a look that communicated: "*Can* you?"

In one of the show's brightest moments, Warwick, Lawrence, and
Griffin did an impromptu rendition of Bacharach's "What Do You
Get When You Fall in Love?" while seated on the panel. After the
song, Warwick began speaking softly and the ire of the studio audience resurfaced. "Louder, louder!" they shouted.

The sound in the studio was loud enough for the nation's critics. "It's the Same Old Merv Griffin," observed Rex Polier in his
column for the Philadelphia *Evening Bulletin* (March 14, 1972).
Polier noted that Griffin's new show bore a remarkable resemblance
to the old one. Which old Griffin show? "Take your pick of either
his earlier syndicated one or the show he just recently bombed out

from CBS with," wrote Polier. Griffin's guests, in particular, failed to impress the critic. Polier felt that Dom DeLuise came off as simpering, while Milton Berle was too overpowering. His review didn't mention Shore, Lawrence, Dickinson, and Warwick, even in passing.

"It is a little puzzling what Griffin thinks he can accomplish with a new talk show that he couldn't in three years with CBS with a contract that gave him everything but the executive dining room," Polier concluded. "He doesn't appear to have any unplumbed depths."

TV Guide observed that Berle had insulted his host venomously. In reality, it was simply a case of Berle being Berle. Even if Uncle Miltie's zingers had been delivered maliciously, Merv would have handled the situation with his usual aplomb. Over the years, producer Bob Murphy would frequently attest that Merv wanted all his guests to outshine him. "He loved to listen and he didn't try to top you," said Murphy. One can view thousands of Merv's shows and not find him even remotely rattled by a seemingly hostile guest. On the rare occasions when someone may have made a snide remark, the audience almost always sided with the host.

The Metromedia opener had been an unrestrained show. Even with all its near calamities, Merv would liken the experience to a vacation in Hawaii compared to his last days at CBS. The new show embodied an energy that was lacking during those awful last episodes on the network.

What the critics didn't mention was that in several major markets (including New York and Los Angeles), the new syndicated Griffin show had performed remarkably well against its network competition.

To say that Griffin had stellar names on his guest list would have been like saying the Hollywood freeway had traffic. His first week showcased: Jean Stapleton (*All in the Family*), Jack Klugman (*The Odd Couple*), Totie Fields, author/sexologist Dr. David Reuben (*Everything You've Always Wanted to Know about Sex, But Were Afraid to Ask*), The Lennon Sisters, Jack Jones, Sergio Mendes, Donald O'Connor, Connie Stevens (*Hawaiian Eye*), Barbara Feldon (*Get Smart*), Ann Miller and Dusty Springfield. He wrapped up the week by offering the first theme show of the new series: a "Salute to Italians" with Frankie Avalon and Dom DeLuise. Curiously, the Italian edition happened to air on Friday, March 17, which, of course, was St. Patrick's Day!

"Even though Merv was a singer," says Don Kane, "the Metromedia execs would try to talk him out of singing as much as possible." From his earliest days as a talk-show host, Merv had always managed to belt out a tune in the first segment of the show, especially since his monologues had always been marked by brevity. "Johnny didn't sing. Neither did Dick Cavett. But Metromedia didn't see it that way," recalls Kane. "They felt that if he opened with a song, he would lose the home audience. And they didn't want that, of course. So they tried to talk him out of singing at the beginning of the show, though he could stick in a song at the end." Kane says that Metromedia wanted songs, but they didn't want them sung by Merv Griffin. "Merv was a good singer," says Kane. "But he wasn't Frank Sinatra. And he wasn't singing anything brand new or particularly brilliant at that point. He was singing the cover songs of other people."

Nevertheless, Kane believes the vocal talents of his former boss were underrated. "Of all the singers we had on the show," says the former talent coordinator, "Merv liked Dick Haymes the best." Kane claims that Merv actually envied Haymes. "I'll never forget the first time we got Dick to be on the show at the Hollywood Palace. Dick had been in England for a number of years and hadn't been doing too well. He came back to the United States and wanted to re-enter the market here. I asked Merv about putting him on the show and he said, "Sure." And I remember Dick rehearsing all around the theater, and Merv moving around—from the orchestra to the wings, then up to the balcony. Merv came to me and said, 'He's still got it.' Merv loved Haymes' singing voice, so we put him on a couple of times."

Early in the Metromedia era, Merv was surprised (or at least *pretended* to be surprised) by the appearance of a "walk on" guest. It was Johnny Carson. "I think that was one of those shows where our guest was supposed to bring on a protégé," recalls Don Kane. "And the gimmick was that Doc Severinsen brought Carson on!"

Gimmick or not, the sight of the two rival hosts, standing face-to-face, was a show within itself. The only other time the two men had been on television together was when Merv subbed for host Bud Collyer on an episode of *To Tell the Truth* with Carson as a panelist. Johnny's younger brother Dick joined the proceedings, making the show something of a family reunion. "They looked quite a bit alike," says Kane. "When Dan Smith left the show, it was very sudden and I was surprised. And I think Merv hired Dick because he was Johnny's brother. But even so, Dick happened to be an excellent director."

In May 1972, Johnny Carson relocated *The Tonight Show* to the NBC studios in Burbank, California—just a few miles away from the Hollywood Palace. The move didn't worry Griffin in the least. With Merv's show now airing mostly in prime time, as opposed to late night, Griffin and Carson were no longer in direct competition. Despite the fact that Hollywood offered a larger pool of celebrity guests, the two shows would still occasionally battle over certain stars.

It was also in the spring of 1972 that Douglas Fairbanks, Jr., a previous guest on Merv's Westinghouse show, was scheduled for an appearance at the Hollywood Palace. The veteran actor resided in New York and Florida, but would make frequent trips to the West Coast. Hours before he was slated to appear on the air with Griffin, Fairbanks received a call from someone at NBC. Apparently, *The Tonight Show* was in need of one more powerhouse guest, and Fairbanks was the prime choice to fill the bill. Having already accepted the invitation from Griffin, the debonair actor politely said no to Carson's people. "After that," said Fairbanks, "They never asked me again." Years later, a photograph of Fairbanks and Carson, taken at a black-tie event, would reveal that the men remained on friendly terms.

Booking the show had become significantly easier for the talent coordinators and producers. "I didn't think there was anything to the job," recalls Don Kane. "But you still had to deal with difficult people and difficult situations."

Some show-biz personalities, particularly actors who rely on scripted words, can sometimes come off as dull or repetitious in a forum in which they are expected to converse extemporaneously. "Part of the problem," says Kane, "is that a lot of them do not have any recollections or stories that can be told on TV," says Kane.

"They sit there and stare at the host while he tries to get something halfway amusing out of them."

Charlton Heston was an iconic actor and a prestigious name for the Griffin show. "The only time he came up with anything good on the air was when someone asked him about wearing a dress in *Ben-Hur*. With that, he lightened up a little bit. But some of the others never lightened up; they never had a good story or any recollection about somebody or something."

Fred Astaire also fit into this category, according to the talent coordinator. "To me, he was the greatest musical star we've ever had," recalls Kane. "But on the air he had nothing to say about anybody that he'd worked with. He was kind to his co-stars— Ginger Rogers, Eleanor Powell and Gene Kelly. But he told no stories. What about doing *Band Wagon*? What about Judy Garland? He remembered nothing about working with her in *Easter Parade*. I mean, if he did, he wasn't talking."

Griffin's staffers had to watch their Ps and Qs around certain stars. Kane recalls an incident in which one of Merv's writers, dispatched to Joan Crawford's hotel room for a pre-show interview, angered the actress by plopping his feet up on her coffee table. "She was so infuriated that she personally phoned Merv about it," Kane recalls. "And we had to use some heavy-duty smooth talk on her before she arrived at the studio."

By this time, the aging actress had grown "considerably hard-looking," recalls Kane. "But she still loved coming on. She'd be drinking Pepsi with vodka in it, and everyone knew she was drinking heavily. She certainly wasn't fooling anyone."

On one occasion, Crawford nearly didn't make it to the set. "She fell down right in the green room. Someone said, 'Are you ready, Miss Crawford? And she stood up and fell flat on her face. This happened at the Hollywood Palace."

Ever the trouper, Crawford got up, went out on the stage, and did the show.

Kane notes a significant distinction between Crawford and her professional rival, Bette Davis. "Unlike Bette Davis, who made relatively few career mistakes, Crawford had made a lot. The end of her career was bad; she should have skipped the last four or five pictures that she made. Davis remained tough as nails till the end, whereas Crawford had grown vulnerable in her last years."

Merv had always held a special place in his heart for Las Vegas, a town he relished as an around-the-clock playground, a Mecca of entertainment. Having performed there with the Freddy Martin Orchestra, and as a single, it was now a source of pride for him to be doing his show there on an "intermittent" basis.

"Merv actually began doing shows from Vegas while he was on CBS, when Walter Kempley was still producing," recalls Kane. "He had started doing them at Caesar's Palace, but would eventually move on to the Riviera Hotel."

Metromedia's ad campaign promised "dazzling showgirls in lavish costumes," along with Vegas headliners like Robert Goulet, Totie Fields, Johnny Mathis, Jimmy Dean, Jerry Vale, Carol Lawrence, George Kirby, and Phyllis Diller.

Kirby, a Griffin favorite, was touted in Merv's publicity releases thusly: "Comic George Kirby adds that when he first came to Las Vegas years ago, blacks were not allowed in the casinos. So tough guy Bugsy Siegel sent a crap table backstage and ran his own game with help from obliging black performers."

The glamour and glitz of Vegas inspired Merv to exploit his vocal abilities more zealously. In one memorable sequence, he offered a respectable rendition of *The Look of Love*, surrounded by a bevy of beauties from various shows along the Vegas strip. One showgirl was featured in the renowned Folies Bergere; another from the Casino de Paris; another from the Latin Fire; and yet another from the French Love Connection.

To usher in a week's worth of Vegas shows in October 1972, Merv made a spectacular entrance by riding Tana, the elephant. The same segment would focus on one of Merv's life-long preoccupations: money. One million dollars, in ten-thousand-dollar bills, was grandly displayed on the stage, amid heavy security. At the time, only 119 ten-thousand-dollar bills were in existence. "And wouldn't you know," proclaimed a Metromedia press release, "that a Las Vegas casino would own 100 of them. The 100 bills were "held aloft by Merv Griffin from the stage of the Circus Maximus at Caesar's Palace, the originations of all Merv Griffin Las Vegas shows."

Though the Vegas segments were enormously popular in prime time, they presented something of challenge with regard to booking. "You'd think being in Vegas, there would be a ton of available talent," says Kane. "But we often had to bring in talent a great deal of the time, because there weren't enough acts in town for us to use. Otherwise, we'd be having the same people on the show we'd used a month earlier."

One night in December 1972, Merv turned the Caesar's Palace stage over to legendary musical artist Isaac Hayes. Presented under the title "Isaac Hayes and The Stax Memphis Sound," this special one-hour edition featured many of the biggest artists on the famed Memphis-based soul music label.

Merv could be effortlessly generous when it came to singers and musicians he genuinely respected. If the big shots at Metromedia had no use for Merv's vocal chops, other producers and artists did. In the early 1970s, Merv belted out popular tunes on variety hours hosted by Della Reese, Tim Conway, and Sonny & Cher. His distinctive (and underappreciated) flair for sketch comedy also surfaced on these programs. A January 1973 episode of *The Sonny & Cher Comedy Hour* accorded Merv a punchline worthy of Don Rickles. It was scripted, of course, but a zinger nonetheless. In a parody of Richard Bach's *Jonathan Livingston Seagull*, Merv and Sonny Bono are a couple of seagulls, replete with elaborate feathers and paste-on beaks. "Jonathan" (Merv) discloses what he'd like most of all in the wake of his recent success. It was something he could share with every bird across the land: "a great big statute of Johnny Carson!"

As with Merv's previous series, each Metromedia installment would boast at least one or two major stars. Bette Davis, for instance, was the draw on Merv's 1973 salute to director William Wyler. The panel included stars that had worked in several of the director's best films: Davis (*Jezebel*; *The Little Foxes*); Walter Pidgeon (*Mrs. Miniver*; *Funny Girl*); and Olivia de Havilland (*The Heiress*). Wyler was one of those personalities who steadfastly avoided talk shows, but he graciously submitted to an interview in the program's final moments.

Davis had journeyed to Los Angeles from her Connecticut home, at Griffin's expense, solely for the purpose of paying tribute to her former director. "This must be very important to you, because you came all the way to Hollywood to do this show," said Merv, "and we are *not* famous in show business for paying a great deal of money!" Davis smiled. "No," she said, "we certainly didn't come here for the money!"

Walter Pidgeon was more straightforward about money, a subject Merv was always more than eager to discuss. The veteran actor hadn't been on the Griffin show in several years. His last appearance had been a tribute to the great director, Mervn LeRoy some three years earlier. "Why didn't you ever answer our calls?" asked Merv. "We've always treated you well." Pidgeon looked at his host beseechingly. "You don't really want to know, do you, Merv?"

"It's not the money, is it, Mr. Pidgeon?" The actor looked Merv right in the eye. "*You're damn right it is!*" said Pidgeon, puffing vigorously on the cigarette Merv had lit for him. The audience burst into laughter and applause. Merv's persistence in addressing the actor as "*Mister* Pidgeon" did not go unnoticed.

Pidgeon: "What's this mister stuff that you're giving me now?"

Merv: "Okay, *W.P.*"

Pidgeon: "You can always tell when a young fellow's been well brought-up; when he has respect for age, and this gentleman always has it."

Merv: "Do you know where it came from? Five years of working with Arthur Treacher. I learned respect *so* fast!"

Indeed, Griffin had always gone to great lengths to treat his guests with the utmost respect. "Occasionally, if we were dealing with a legendary star that the younger staff wouldn't know," says Don Kane, I'd do the pre-show interview myself."

Kane says he would do the pre-show interviews of stars like Davis and Pidgeon because the younger members on Griffin's staff knew very little about them. "The trouble was that Merv sometimes hired people as pre-show interviewers that were not qualified. They were either friends or show-biz hangers-on. Merv liked to surround himself with people that he was fond of. But they weren't always the most capable. "Luckily," says Kane, "Merv's head talent coordinator throughout the

'70s, Paul Solomon, was very capable. In fact, he was the *most* capable. He had been with the show in New York. Tony Garofalo had also been a talent coordinator very early on, but I remember him primarily as a writer. He was a talented guy, and he'd write about four or five gags for Merv to use at the opening of each show."

Kane says that many of the pre-show interviews were conducted in the afternoon, and the guest would show up that night. "There wasn't a whole lot time spent on research, so unless you knew the person's career, you weren't going to get a very good interview."

Several of Merv's recurrent themes did not require extensive delving or fact-finding. The "fashion show" is one entry that falls into this category. Merv would invite the wives of several top Hollywood stars to model the latest creations. One such segment, airing in 1973, included the spouses of Johnny Carson (Joanna Holland); Dick Martin (Dolly Read); Clint Eastwood (Maggie Johnson); Sammy Davis, Jr. (Altovise Gore); and Aaron Spelling (Candy Marer). Though all the women were glamorous and captivating, the most intriguing interview came from the third Mrs. Carson. Merv's easygoing banter with her, which included a few mild zingers about Johnny, came off as the undisputed highlight of the night. The fashion show theme was so well received that it would become an annual event, similar to the Photoplay Awards presentations. For the 1975 edition, Mrs. Johnny Carson would again be featured as the lead guest.

With many of Hollywood's legendary comedians still active in the early '70s, Merv and the staff wasted no time in booking as many of them as possible for various salutes and tributes.

"Burns, Benny, Berle—many of the great comedians enjoyed doing Merv's show, now that most of them weren't weighed down by a weekly series," says Kane. "There were very few comedians that I knew who had actually retired. Burns was still coming on the show when he was pushing ninety. And I think all of them simply liked the acclaim and being remembered."

Kane notes that by the early 1970s, most of America's veteran comedians had embraced the talk show circuit as a good avenue for appreciable exposure. "They weren't like the younger, up-and-coming comedians who *needed* to be on in order to advance their careers," says Kane. "But they would come on to plug a book, a movie, or a TV special." Kane notes how Bob Hope, NBC's biggest draw, always tapped into *The Tonight Show* before each and every special. "He took no chances," says Kane. "And he was smart to also do Merv's show within a day or two." Kane notes that Hope was good to the end. "He never became tottering or wobbly."

Since the comics were also on everybody else's talk show, it became necessary at times to dream up a fresh angle for a legend like Jack Benny, who'd been a favorite on all the major talk shows, including Merv's Westinghouse and CBS incarnations. Younger viewers knew Benny as the lovable cheapskate who stashed his fortune in an underground vault, and was perpetually 39-years-old. By the 1970s, however, few remembered that Benny had had a respectable career in movies. His screen career was launched with *The Hollywood Revue of 1929*, a vaudeville-like extravaganza in which Benny appeared as one of the masters of ceremonies. After he'd attained superstar status through radio, Benny became a comedy star in movies: *Broadway Melody of 1936*; *The Big Broadcast of 1937*; *Artists and Models* (1937); *Buck Benny Rides Again* (1940); *Charley's Aunt* (1941); and *George Washington Slept Here* (1942).

Benny thought his finest work in films had been achieved in Ernst Lubitsch's *To Be or Not to Be* (1942), a comedic farce about a troupe of actors putting on a play in Nazi-occupied Warsaw, eventually foiling the enemy. The film would mark the last screen appearance of Carole Lombard, who was killed in an airplane crash two months before the release date. Benny's biggest bomb, which he would poke fun at most irreverently, was Raoul Walsh's *The Horn Blows at Midnight* (1945). It's essentially a fantasy about an angel (Benny) assigned to blow "the last trumpet" to signal the end of the world. It also signaled the end of Benny's movie career; from then on, he would make only guest appearances on the big screen.

Benny's movies had been largely forgotten. Thus, Griffin's staffers decided that a fresh approach to the comedian's appearance on the show would be a salute to his screen work.

On April 27, 1973, Merv opened the show by walking on stage alongside Benny. Merv joked about Jack's peculiar way of walking. (Merv to Jack: "Bob Hope *copies* your walk!") The two of them noted that Jack's walk was oddly linked to the lyrics in his theme song, "Love in Bloom."

On the panel, the conversation focused on the topic for which Benny was there in the first place—his movies. At one point, Merv leaned toward Benny and asked, quite earnestly, "Do you remember your first laugh on a stage?" With that, Benny fired his best dead-pan expression at the host without uttering a word for nearly 30 seconds. The audience roared as Merv sat there, looking like a little boy who had been caught stealing cookies. Finally, Benny broke his silence. "That's the *silliest* question I've ever heard," he said indignantly. "I've been in show business 60 years and you're asking me if I can remember the first laugh. I can't remember the *last* laugh!"

This ad-lib would rank as one of Merv's favorite moments on television. In the years that followed Benny's death, from pancreatic cancer on December 26, 1974, Griffin would host several nostalgic tributes to the beloved comedian. The first of these aired in 1976, with a guest list that included singer Gisele MacKenzie, Benny's longtime producer Irving Fein, and Mel Blanc, a Benny stalwart who was also the vocal embodiment of all the legendary Warner Bros. cartoon characters. Three years later, Griffin assembled what would essentially be a Benny cast reunion comprised of Mel Blanc, actor/comedian Phil Harris, announcer Don Wilson, singer Dennis Day, and writer/producer Milt Josefsberg.

Lucille Ball was no stranger to the talk-show circuit, having made multiple appearances with Carson, Cavett, Mike Douglas, and others. Though Ball had made many prior appearances with Griffin, her October 1973 visit was particularly memorable because it was essentially a family affair. Sharing the spotlight were Ball's kids, Lucie Arnaz, Desi, Jr., and husband Gary Morton. Gale Gordon, who co-starred on *The Lucy Show* and *Here's Lucy*, also made a rare appearance.

A scene-stealer in many of Ball's escapades, Gordon was frequently on the receiving end of massive volumes of water. On more than one occasion, with his trousers wringing wet, Gordon looked like a man who'd had an accident. These slapstick scenes earned Gordon an endearing nickname: "Soggy Crotch." Apparently, such a moniker was deemed too suggestive for markets that played Merv's show in the daytime. Today, it seems unfathomable that such an innocuous utterance would need to be bleeped, but bleeped it was. This was another indication of how rigid television censorship was, even in the rapidly progressive '70s.

The president of the Academy of Television Arts and Sciences, Robert Lewine, was on hand to present Ball with a plaque commemorating her multiple Emmy nominations and wins. Lewine showed a video clip of Ball at the 1967 ceremonies, accepting her award as best female actress in a continuing series (for *The Lucy Show*).

Ball seemed genuinely touched by this presentation. She was also treated to a musical clip, which had not yet been "color corrected," from her forthcoming film, *Mame*.

The bonus would be an appearance by Bob Hope, who starred in four films with Ball: *Sorrowful Jones* (1949), *Fancy Pants* (1950), *The Facts of Life* (1960), and *Critic's Choice* (1963). Hope hadn't been announced at the beginning of the show; his appearance had been planned as a surprise. Nevertheless, those who stood on line outside the theater were keenly aware that "ski-nose" would be on the show that night.

"After the show with Lucy and Bob Hope, we covered the premiere of *Mame* (1974)," recalls Don Kane. "We did the preview at the Cinema Dome Theater in Hollywood, and Merv was outside interviewing Lucille Ball. And off to the side was this woman who had been standing there for a while. She had an attack of some sort and fell down. Medical attention was summoned immediately. Lucille looked over and saw what was happening, but never missed a beat," says Kane. "She went right on talking to Merv and didn't say a word about what was going on. She was so professional!"

Kane remembers Ball playing hard-to-get on one occasion, so unlike her affable, daffy sitcom persona. "You have to remember that she was an actress who did comedy, and was *not* a funny woman off-screen," recalls the former talent coordinator. "You had to really set her up to get a joke out of her. One time, RKO wanted to do a retrospective of their films and asked if we could help publicize it with film clips or something." As everyone familiar with Ball's career certainly knows, Ball had been a contract player at RKO from

1935 to 1942. It was at that studio during the filming of *Too Many Girls* (1940) that Ball met her first husband, the Cuban bandleader Desi Arnaz. After achieving iconic status with their groundbreaking sitcom *I Love Lucy* (1951–57), Ball and Arnaz purchased RKO and absorbed it into their burgeoning production company, Desilu.

"I thought for sure we could get Lucille to come on and we could show something from *Stage Door* (1937) and *The Big Street* (1942), which I thought were her two best movies for RKO." I called her and asked her to come on and help us promote the studio. She asked who would be on with her. I told her 'Douglas Fairbanks, Jr. would be on, and her response was, 'Wow!'"

Though Kane hadn't actually booked Fairbanks at that point, he knew that Ball had worked with the actor in the RKO "screwball comedies" *Joy of Living* (1938) and *Having Wonderful Time* (1938).

Ball told the talent coordinator that if Fairbanks would be on the show, she'd be there as well. "She thought Douglas Fairbanks, Jr. was hot stuff," says Kane. "And this was years after his career had wound down. But he was still Hollywood royalty and had remembered working with Lucille at RKO."

In a 1990 interview, Fairbanks recalled working with the famous redhead in those two films. "She was very talented, but I didn't think she had a flair for comedy," Fairbanks recalled. "Obviously, I was wrong."

Groucho Marx was another comedian of the first rank who made a steady stream of appearances on the variety/talk circuit. Groucho, master of the sardonic putdown, made several visits to the Griffin stage, the first of which had taken place on the Westinghouse series in April 1967.

"Merv wanted to do another evening with Groucho," notes Don Kane. "And even before Groucho said yes, we began putting the show together."

"The Salute to Groucho Marx," as the program would ultimately be titled, was slated for taping in mid-February 1974, and would air in early March. The time was ripe. At 83, Groucho was enjoying a remarkable revival, thanks to theatrical reissues of such imperishable Marx Brothers triumphs as *The Cocoanuts* (1929), *Monkey Business* (1931), *Horse Feathers* (1932), *Duck Soup* (1933), *A Night at the Opera* (1935), and *A Day at the Races* (1937). In the months to come, Groucho's classic quizzer, *You Bet Your Life* (which debuted on radio in 1947 and flourished on NBC-TV from 1950 to 1961), would win a new legion of fans through syndicated reruns. The vast majority of Marx devotees were high school and college students.

As plans for the tribute continued, Don Kane continued to "conspire" with Marx's manager/companion, Erin Fleming, to get the comedian on the show. Kane, along with the rest of the staff, brimmed with anticipation when he learned that Marx had finally said yes. There was one proviso: Fleming would *have* to sit on the panel alongside Groucho. Also on the bill would be actor Orson Bean, actress/singer Kaye Ballard, and Marvin Hamlisch. Ballard's connection was her recent role as Groucho's mother in the touring production of *Minnie's Boys*, a musical based on the vaudeville careers of the young Marx Brothers. Hamlisch had provided the piano accompaniment for Groucho's 1972 concert at Carnegie Hall.

Kane recalls: "Even though the audience was obviously thrilled to see Groucho in person, I went down the aisle and got everyone to stand up for him. Groucho appreciated that and got acclimated from it. He reveled in the applause and I think it was good for him at that point in his life. Comedians do not like to be forgotten; they enjoy being in the spotlight and it keeps them going in a special way."

The Griffin tribute would also support an effort to get *Animal Crackers* (1930), a long-unseen Marx Brothers feature, back in theatres. Sitting in the audience was 19-year-old Steve Stoliar, a student at UCLA. "I was there that night with my friend Daryl, who was co-chairman of the Committee for the Re-release of Animal Crackers," recalls Stoliar.

Filmed on a sound stage in Astoria, New York, *Animal Crackers* was the second film starring The Four Marx Brothers; it was also the one that introduced Groucho's immortal theme song, "Hooray for Captain Spaulding." "The copyright had expired on the film and it reverted back to the authors and composers of the play," explains Stoliar. "And when Universal acquired Paramount's pre-1949 film library, *Animal Crackers* was included, but the studio didn't have the legal right to reissue it."

Thus was launched the campaign to get *Animal Crackers* cracking again, and Merv was only too happy to offer publicity for the cause. At one point in the show, Fleming called attention to the young students. Says Stoliar: "I expected an Ed Sullivan moment where the host says, 'In our audience tonight, we have. . . .' and I would stand up to take a bow. It didn't turn out that way. But it was exciting for us to be in the audience of The Merv Griffin Show, and to have Erin throw the spotlight on us, but not literally, since the camera stayed on her and Groucho. Not long after that, Universal relented and brought the film out." In July 1974, Stoliar landed a job as a secretary/archivist to the legendary comic, and would work for him during the last three years of Groucho's life.

"Groucho was in a sobering mood that night because of the imminent death of two of his closest friends," remembers Stoliar. The two friends, composer/screenwriter Harry Ruby and screenwriter Nunnally Johnson, had had a long association with Marx. Ruby had written several songs that Groucho had sung through the years (including the unforgettable "Father's Day"), as well as co-writing scripts to several early Marx Brothers films. Johnson had kept up a correspondence with the comedian (as did a number of other luminaries, such as Dick Cavett) and his letters were ultimately included in Marx's 1967 book *The Groucho Letters*.

"Groucho mentioned that most of his friends were either dead or dying," says Stoliar. "And he added: 'If you want to see what smoking will get you, go visit my friend Nunnally Johnson, who has emphysema.'"

As a tribute to the ailing composer, Groucho and Fleming offered a duet of Ruby's song "Dr. Hackenbush" (a number deleted from *A Day at the Races*), with accompaniment by Hamlisch. "It took a bit of cajoling to get Groucho in the right mood for that," recalls Don Kane. "But Merv didn't mind, since he knew Groucho was not in great condition to chatter. He was satisfied with having him say a few things, and singing that old song. That was enough for him."

In May 1976, Groucho would make his last television appearance on Merv's "Salute to Ernie Kovacs." In his book *Making the Good Life Last*, Griffin recalled the ailing Marx in his final days: "A series of small strokes had dulled his razor-sharp intelligence, and the caustic wit that had skewered so many victims was now gone." Even though Groucho was able to summon up a few remembrances of Kovacs, Merv didn't want to burden him with superfluous questions or requests. Wisely, he focused on the other guests: Edie Adams (Kovacs's widow), Milton Berle, and Mickey Rooney. Groucho Marx died on August 19, 1977 at age 86.

Booking iconic stars such as Lucy and Groucho, whose careers are long and varied, required additional research and clearance for film clip usage. "We'd come in to work around 9:30 or 10:00 a.m.," says Kane, "and by the time the staff had gotten their assignments as to who they were going to interview that day, it would be noon. Then they'd have a discussion as to what these great stars were going to talk about during the show."

Kane confides that some of Merv's young staffers weren't even familiar with the legends. "They were 25-years-old," says Kane. "They didn't know or care who Mel Torme was, or Rosemary Clooney, or Margaret Whiting. These are the people I was interested in, and Merv was interested in them as well, so I could steer him into doing those kinds of shows."

Despite being connected with one of the nation's preeminent talk shows, Kane often found it difficult, if not impossible, to book certain guests. Getting Bette Davis to come on was easy "because she wanted to be there," says Kane. "Getting Kate Hepburn was hard."

There were certain stars that either flat out said no, or were too demanding. "I tried to get Marlene Dietrich," recalls Kane, "but she demanded $100,000, and there was no way Merv was going to pay that." The talent coordinator also had his sights set on William Powell and Myrna Loy, best remembered for their series of *Thin Man* movies for MGM, Charles Chaplin, Greta Garbo, "and a couple of others I wanted, but couldn't get."

Some of the show's guests had unusual requests. For example, Kane remembers actor Cliff Robertson as being one of the more gracious guests on the program. "But the thing I remember most about him is that he'd arrive early at the studio, take off his coat, jacket, and pants, and say, 'Could you get these laundered for me? He'd show up in dirty clothes and would want them cleaned and pressed so he could wear them on the show." Kane thought this was odd in view of the fact that the actor "was married to a millionairess!"

With the show now permanently based in Hollywood, there were enough available superstars for more custom-made "theme" shows throughout the '70s and beyond.

"Some of the theme shows just happened because of the people we could get at the time," says Kane. "Quite often, we could assemble a group of people that had a connection to one subject. I know a lot of Broadway-themed shows came about that way, as did shows featuring the great band singers; those are the ones I really pushed for. And Merv was always familiar with those performers, so there was never any problem and they were entertaining shows."

Kane says that during this period, the early-to-mid-1970s, it was often difficult for some legendary performers to get exposure on national television. Nobody wanted them, according to Kane. "So it was no trick to get them on the show. Jack Carter once told me, 'If you don't get on TV at least once a month, your career is dead.' And he'd said that in the seventies."

One guest in particular came as an enormous surprise to Griffin. "I got Donald O'Connor to come on," recalls Kane. "He had never been on Merv's show. And Merv had said, 'You'll never get him to come on.' And I said, 'Oh, I think I *can* get him. And I did. Merv was quite impressed. He was also very pleased when I got him Wayne Newton. But there were other people who, for unknown reasons, were never on the show and I never found out why."

Like many a good talent coordinator, Kane had a knack for coaxing reticent show- biz legends (like as Lily Pons) back into the spotlight. Of the many veteran actors Kane snagged for the show, Kane says Jean Arthur was his proudest accomplishment.

One of the most glamorous heroines in films of the 1930s and '40s, Jean Arthur is a faded name today. A native of Pittsburgh, New York, Arthur got her start as a model, then landed a contract with Fox Studios where she made her screen debut in *Cameo Kirby* (1923), which was followed by a succession of small roles in equally nondescript silent films, including several westerns. She appeared with Buster Keaton in *Seven Chances* (1925), but did not receive screen credit for her small role as a receptionist.

Because of her early roles in silent films, Kane had invited Arthur to appear on Merv's "Salute to the Silent Screen" in December of 1970. Though flattered at the invitation, the actress turned him down because she felt that her finest work had been achieved in the talkies. Indeed, by the mid-thirties, after considerable stage work and roles in numerous sound films, Arthur finally achieved star status in films like *The Whole Town's Talking* (1935) with Edward G. Robinson and *Public Hero No. 1* (1935) with Lionel Barrymore and Chester Morris.

Director Frank Capra further enhanced Arthur's reputation in three of his classics: *Mr. Deeds Goes to Town* (1936); *You Can't Take it With You* (1938); and *Mr. Smith Goes to Washington* (1939). From there, Arthur would go on to receive an Academy Award nomination for Best Actress for her role in the romantic comedy *The More the Merrier* (1943) opposite Joel McCrea. After achieving the pinnacle of success, she began turning down film offers. Even so, she would add two more hits to resume: Billy Wilder's *A Foreign Affair* (1949) with Marlene Dietrich, and George Steven's *Shane* (1953) with Alan Ladd, her last film.

Jean Arthur was not known to make public appearances. As far back as 1940, *Life* magazine dubbed her as a "reigning mystery woman" akin to Greta Garbo.

Kane recalls how he finally procured the notoriously reclusive actress for appearance with Griffin: "Jean Arthur did not want to go on television, but she did it only because she'd seen a couple of Disney movies with Helen Hayes playing little old ladies. And Jean thought she could possibly get one of these little old lady-type roles." Kane says he was stunned when he received a call from Arthur's agent. "He called one day and said, 'Do you know who Jean Arthur is?' And I just about dropped my pants, and said, 'Of course!' He said, 'Do you think Merv would be interested in having her on the show?' I told him, 'Yes, in a minute!' So I started calling her; she was teaching somewhere in the San Francisco area. I tried to talk her into coming on the show. She was interested, but very afraid. It took quite a while to convince her, and I told Merv about how frightened she was. I thought it would be a good idea to pair her with someone that she would be comfortable with. So we booked Frank Capra and Richard Arlen, along with Jean."

Acutely aware of Arthur's stage fright, Kane nervously awaited her arrival at the Hollywood Palace stage entrance.

Kane: "I remember standing by that door. But she didn't show up. Then, this little old lady came up to the door, and I heard her say, 'I'm looking for Mr. Kane.' I looked over and saw this frail little woman. Then I realized it was Jean Arthur, dressed in what looked like thrift store clothes, with a little bonnet. She looked *terrible*; no make-up, nothing. I held my breath, took her down to the make-up room and put her in the chair. They went to work on her, and after about a half hour, she began to look like Jean Arthur. While she was in the chair, I stood by to talk to her. Richard Arlen came in and said, 'Where's Jean? I've been looking for her.' And I pointed to the chair. Richard took a gulp, because he hadn't recognized her either. Then he made a fuss over her."

As a young man, Don Kane witnessed one of Arthur's most exhilarating stage triumphs in the Broadway musical *Peter Pan* (1950), which co-starred Boris Karloff.

"I brought my copy of the *Peter Pan* album and asked her if she would sign it," Kane recalls. "And she said, 'I never sign albums.' I said, 'Okay.'"

It was show time. "We were reluctant to put her on as the first guest," explains Kane, "because we thought she might freeze up. So we brought out Frank Capra to talk about her. And we told him, 'she's scared to death.' Capra, of course, knew her very well. His two favorite actresses were Jean Arthur and Barbara Stanwyck."

As expected, the director provided a good introduction, and a solid level of comfort, for the veteran actress, still suffering from stage fright. "She did the show," says Kane, "and she was quite pleased with it afterwards. In the wings, she turned to me and said, 'Where's that album?' I told her it was up in the office. 'Go get it,' she said. She signed it, and when she did, she said, 'You know, I was the *best* Peter Pan!' Now Mary Martin had played the part since, but Jean Arthur thought she was without a doubt the best." Jean Arthur died of heart failure in 1991, at the age of 90.

In the complex world of television talk shows, it is the talent coordinator who is burdened with the task of contacting agents and personal managers for the purpose of wringing an appearance out of one or more of their clients. Producers, too, will occasionally step in and make calls in this endeavor, especially if the talent sought is of legendary status. There are, of course, exceptions to the norm.

"I once saw Jack Lord [*Hawaii Five-O*] at a supermarket on Sunset Boulevard," remembers Kane. "It was about 9:00 p.m., and he was standing in front of me in the checkout line. I casually said hello to him. I made a bold move, told him that I worked for Merv Griffin, and said we'd really like to have him on the show. He was very cordial, and said, 'I'll have my agent get back to you.' And of course nobody ever got back to us."

Even stars with a more-than-casual acquaintanceship with Merv could prove difficult. Ethel Merman, for instance, had been a recurring guest through the years, having appeared on the first incarnation of the Griffin show. Merman and Merv would remain on good terms, even after the she bristled at having one of her appearances cut short. "Ethel was the first guest out," explains Kane. "She sang and did her interview. But we had a very long show that day, and Renata Scotto, a popular opera star at the time, happened to be on. Renata turned out to be quite good and was very lively, so Merv kept her on and dumped Merman's interview segment, which hadn't amounted to much." Kane would bear the brunt of Merman's wrath after the show aired. "You cut me out!" she yelled at the talent coordinator, who then pacified her with so much sweet talk that he had to go on a sugar-free diet.

Kane: "I told her, 'Ethel, you come on the show frequently. You had the first spot, you did your song, and got your plug in. We've never had those other guests on, and they'll never be on again. Don't be so upset.'"

On another occasion, Merman became overtly distressed when another performer dared to sing her signature song. The offending incident occurred when Griffin staged a salute to Irving Berlin. "We had Ethel and Howard Keel on that show," recalls Kane. "And they'd had a fight before the taping because I'd given Howard Keel her song. Ethel had about 8,000 songs by Berlin in her repertoire. Howard only had two songs, "The Girl that I Marry" and "There's No Business Like Show Business." And I had told Ethel that Howard was going to sing those two songs, and she would sing "Alexander's Ragtime Band," and "I Got Lost in His Arms," which she loved. She said, 'No, no, no!' "Show Business" is *my* song and *I'm* going to sing it!' I explained to her that if she did, there wouldn't be another number for Howard to sing. She argued with me profusely. Finally, I said, 'Look, Ethel, we've got to give him something else to sing.' She finally agreed. But when Howard was introduced to sing "There's No Business Like Show Business," Ethel made a point of saying, on the air, 'You know, he's singing *my* song!' She was that possessive of it." Merman's proudest moment on the show would come in 1982, when ASCAP president Hal David presented her with the Piper Award, an honor given to artists for their lifetime achievements in American music.

Just how difficult is it to land big name guest stars, even when you're booking for one of the premiere talk shows in the nation? "It can be difficult when you want certain people—and can't get them," says Kane. "On a show like Merv's, you'll get all the people that want to be on because they're on their way up. And there are others that want to be on because they're on their way down. But the people you really want are the ones that are hot at the moment. And they don't necessarily want to come on unless they have a specific reason to do so."

There is often difficulty in landing certain stars or acts—unless they are plugging a movie, play, book, or album. "Sooner or later," says Kane, "all of them will have something to sell or promote, and when that happens, you can get them booked at the drop of a hat."

That is, unless the star has a gripe with the host. Kane recalls the time Griffin had a falling out with a certain female singer who subsequently refused to appear on the show. "I got into a brouhaha over that one because she'd written a book and was turning up on every talk show in the world," says Kane. "Merv kept seeing her on all the other shows. 'Why don't we get her?' he asked. I explained that we had invited her, but couldn't get her to come on. 'Then I'll call myself,' he said. Merv made the call but couldn't reach her. So he came back to me again. "What's with her?" he asked. I finally had to tell him, 'Merv, it's because she doesn't like you.' After that, he never said another word about it."

Another pervasive problem in the talk-show business is booking restrictions. These might involve legal issues such as conflict of interest and undue competition, or simply a matter of bad chemistry. "I don't ever recall Merv telling me not to put somebody on, although I knew there were certain people in the business that he didn't like," says Kane. "We didn't bother with those folks because, in most cases, they just weren't important. But if they *were* important, they'd get on the show whether Merv was crazy about them or not."

Kane attests that his former boss excelled at what he did, and, as an interviewer, was second only to Johnny Carson in bringing out the best in people. "Merv was quick-witted and could handle any difficult person or situation. He didn't need prepared notes; half of the time, he didn't even use them. Merv also knew how to pick up cues from a guest. Joey Bishop, for instance, didn't. Mike Douglas was charming, but I don't think he was as good an interviewer as Merv."

Though Kane has admiration for Douglas' longevity on the talk-show scene, he equates his interviewing skills with Bishop's. "Mike's style was similar to Joey's. However, Joey could really come back at someone with a good wisecrack."

With greater artistic freedom at Metromedia, Griffin encouraged his staff to pursue new and edgy themes. One suggested theme involved the growing acceptance of the nudist lifestyle. Griffin's interest may have been sparked in 1965, when he and his wife attended a local stage presentation in which the players appeared in the buff. In his autobiography, Griffin recalled that after the shock of seeing everyone naked had worn off, it became apparent just how *bad* the actors were!

For a brief time, Griffin remained focused on doing a show about the inhibitions of people brave enough to shed their clothes. Don Kane recalls his boss contemplating the subject at several production meetings in the early '70s. "He always said he wanted to bring out these special guests in the nude to get everyone's reaction," remembers Kane. "Their privates wouldn't be shown on camera, of course, but the [studio] audience would definitely see them." Metromedia nixed the proposal just as quickly as CBS had done.

NBC was apparently more courageous than CBS and Metromedia. The network had no qualms when Tom Snyder tackled the subject of public nudity by taking his cameras to a California nudist camp. The provocative edition of Snyder's *Tomorrow* show, handled tastefully and intelligently, aired on November 19, 1973 following the Carson *Tonight Show*.

According to Kane, the nude theme prompted one of Merv's earliest disagreements with Metromedia. "The censorship people were always kind of uptight about what went out over the air," says Kane. "That was part of their job."

While Merv didn't have to grapple over censorship, he did experience a near calamity with the censor assigned to his show. Each network has its own standards and practices guidelines, enforced by the censor saddled with the disagreeable task of dealing with the program makers. The censors are a curious and mixed bunch. The range includes bright-eyed young folks on the way up, disgruntled old folks on the way down, and even sweet grandmotherly types. The big problem for Merv was that the watchdog Metromedia assigned to his show was anything but grandmotherly. "She was pretty nasty," recalls Don Kane. "This woman would come to the studio each night and help herself to a drink in the green room, then sit and watch the show to see if any objectionable material had to be edited out.

"One night we had Jack Paar as a guest, and she went after him— right in his dressing room. While I was talking to Jack before the show, she burst in and yelled, 'You're the one that got my son fired!' I could have slapped her silly. She really started in on him. I said, 'Ma'am, we're busy getting ready to do a show. Please leave.' But she wouldn't let up. Apparently, her son had worked on a project that Paar had been involved with years before in New York. Her son had been let go, and she blamed this on Jack Paar."

Usually, Kane would bring problems to the attention of the producer, Bob Murphy, or Merv's longtime stage manager, Ray Sneath. This situation, however, was atypical and very embarrassing; it involved an assault on the man to whom Merv owed his talk show career. As the confrontation grew more obstreperous, Kane felt compelled to go directly to his employer. "I said, 'Merv, you need to get security to throw this woman out. She's down there attacking Jack Paar.' This was before Paar was to go on and, of course, we wanted him to be in a good mood and funny."

At Griffin's frantic instruction, the woman was ushered out of the dressing room area. "After that," Kane recalls, "she was no longer allowed in any of the dressing rooms or even the green room. She would only be permitted to watch the show from the control room. And that took care of her."

15. MID '70s COMPLACENCY

Throughout the 1973–74 season, *The Merv Griffin Show* maintained consistently high ratings in first-run syndication. The program was airing in prime time on all the Metromedia-owned stations in major markets, including New York (WNEW-TV), Los Angeles (KTTV-TV), Chicago (WFLD-TV), and Washington (WTTG-TV). Some independent stations scheduled *Merv* comfortably in late-afternoon time slots, while others, like Philadelphia's WKBS-TV, a Kaiser Broadcasting station, aired the program at 8:30 p.m. Unlike Merv's previous talkathons, the Metromedia series was a winner from the get-go, demonstrating remarkable growth and prestige.

During the first quarter of 1972, shortly after the show's premiere, only 60 stations were carrying Griffin. By mid-summer, however, that number had swelled to 87, including 50 of the top 60 markets. By late 1973, the show was sold in over 100 markets across the United States and Canada, including 56 of the top 60 markets. To meet the needs of certain stations, a one-hour version of the 90-minute show was made available. As with the Westinghouse series, the one-hour version wasn't an abridgment; it was simply the first two-thirds of the program.

As he had done during his time at Westinghouse, Griffin produced several lavish specials that would be syndicated concurrently with the variety/talk entries. The first, and most memorable, was *Merv Griffin and the Christmas Kids*. Airing in December 1973, the one-hour show featured the top child actors of the day: Rodney Allen Rippy (known for his work in TV commercials and numerous movies); Ricky Segall (*The Partridge Family*); Eric Scott and Mary Elizabeth McDonough (*The Waltons*); Kim Richards (*Nanny and the Professor*); and the Mitchell Singing Boys.

Unlike most holiday specials that showcase kids, this one sidestepped the "cutesy" route. Merv didn't talk down to the kids. He sang with them, interacted with them intelligently, and allowed them to shine on their own. The visuals throughout the production were stunning. Thanks to art director Henry C. Lickel, the Griffin stage in Hollywood was transformed into a wintry village that could have done justice to Currier & Ives. The concept was credited to Merv Griffin, but Murray Schwartz, the William Morris agent who had worked his way up to president of Griffin's company, was credited as the show's executive producer. The *Christmas Kids* special was so well received that it begat a follow-up treat several months later—*Merv Griffin and the Easter Kids*.

In 1974, the trade paper ads boasted the impressive number of Emmy Awards the syndicated show had garnered. In the category of best variety/talk or public service show, the awards had gone to Bob Murphy as producer, Tony Garofalo, Merv, and Murphy walked away with statues for best writing. Dick Carson won for best direction.

One of the more unsettling subjects discussed on Merv's show in early 1974 was demonic possession, owing entirely to the recent success of *The Exorcist* (1973). The film, based on the best-selling novel by William Peter Blatty, garnered 10 Academy Award nominations, and would rank as one of the top-grossing releases of the decade. The guest lineup included Blatty (who also produced the movie), director William Friedkin, Father John Banahan, and three members of the cast: Ellen Burstyn, Max Von Sydow, and Linda Blair. The extensive publicity, fueled by record-breaking ticket sales, aroused considerable discussion in the mainstream press. "But when Merv Griffin has devoted an entire program to it," noted one observer, "it's officially a cultural phenomenon."

Many memorable shows of the mid-seventies focused on topical fads of the era, one of which was transcendental meditation. Griffin was instantly intrigued by the practice, referred to as "TM," and encouraged his staff and associates to embrace it. "Merv insisted we try that transcendental meditation stuff," says Kane. "He was in to it, but not very long. We even had classes at his house."

Don Kane recalls that there was at least one TM session at the house Griffin had been renting during the time his divorce was pending. "Merv was renting a place that director George Cukor once owned. The place had three or four other small houses connected to it and people like Spencer Tracy had used it for years. So we were going up there one night to do this TM thing, and as we pulled up to the street in front of the house, there was an elderly couple standing there, just staring at us. They were caught in the headlights like deer. And the woman turned out to be Norma Shearer. I almost died right there."

Kane recalls that the actress had "a clouded eye" that had been cleverly disguised by the studio lighting technicians. "She was with Marty Arrouge, her husband at the time, and she was just staring at us, looking slim and pretty, but with that clouded white eye." Kane thought he might be able to snag the actress for an ultra-rare appearance on the Griffin show. Unfortunately, nothing ever came of that chance encounter. "As it turned out," says Kane, "that was the only time any us associated with Merv ever saw Norma Shearer."

Griffin's fascination with TM culminated in a 1975 theme show devoted to the topic, with Maharishi Mahesh Yogi, founder of the World Wide Transcendental Meditation organization. Other guests on that special edition included Clint Eastwood, Mary Tyler Moore, Congressman Richard Nolan, and Dr. Bernard Glueck. One of the most visually stunning aspects of the taping was the set, which was decorated with enough flowers for at least 20 weddings.

After the Maharishi's appearance with Merv, there was a tremendous surge of interest in the TM movement. That interest, however, waned very quickly, and by the late seventies, the practice was just another passing fad of the decade.

Other important topics included self-improvement (with regard to either one's health or wealth), substance abuse, and rape—topics not generally addressed on a daytime variety talk show in the '70s. Such sensitive entries were interspersed with the highly-rated Las Vegas editions, which Merv was now presenting on a weekly basis. Each month, the program would tape a string of shows at Caesar's Palace for airing on Friday evenings. A Metromedia trade ad from the 1974–75 TV season says it all: "Friday Night is Now Vegasnite." The other four nights of week were "Mervnites." The ad boasts the Vegas entries as "a great new plus to the number one nationally syndicated talk-variety show."

One of Merv's out-of-studio expeditions resulted in an unmitigated disaster. It occurred at a time when Paramount Pictures was promoting its silly new comedy called *Won Ton Ton, the Dog Who Saved Hollywood* (1976). The studio asked Griffin if he'd be interested in covering the premiere.

Set in 1924, the film is a spoof obviously inspired by Rin Tin Tin, with dozens of cameos by show-biz veterans. "It was a terrible picture," recalls Kane. "But Merv agreed to cover the premiere, and the gimmick was that all the stars would bring along their dogs."

An elegant arrangement of trees and hedges adorned the front entrance to the theater where Merv greeted the stars as they arrived with their pets. "It was a very classy set," Kane recalls. "But the best thing about the whole chaotic affair was singer Robert Goulet. As he and Merv were talking, one of Goulet's two dogs took a dump right there on the carpet. Merv tried his best to cover up what had happened, but the two of them started laughing so hard that they scooted on to the next guest."

The next guest happened to be comedian Marty Allen. "He came up to Merv," Kane recalls, "looked at the pile of shit, and said, 'I see Robert Goulet has been here!' I thought that was the funniest line ever! We all screamed."

There would be more screams that night. Several of the dogs that followed apparently took a cue from Goulet's German Shepherd and "added to the mess that was already there," says Kane. Director Dick Carson carefully mastered the shots, making sure none of the "doo-doo" would be seen on camera.

A star-studded party was held after the movie. "They set up a throne-type chair with a red carpet leading up to it," says Kane. "And in the chair sat a big police dog. They tried to get as many stars as they could to pose next to the dog for pictures. Bob Godfried of Paramount was doing all this, bringing stars over to the throne. And Mae West came in."

A legendary sex symbol of the early-1930s, Mae West had made most of her best movies for Paramount, among them, *She Done Him Wong* (1932); *I'm No Angel* (1933); and *Belle of the Nineties* (1934).

"They brought Mae over to meet the dog and she was afraid of it. They told her, 'Mae, you can get closer; he won't bite you.' But she wouldn't get any closer. As you'd expect, she was dressed to the nines. Finally, she did put her hand out a little bit, like she was going to pet the dog. Then she started to leave. And they said, 'Mae, wait a minute! Adolph Zukor is here!'"

The Hungarian-born Zukor was the founder of Paramount Pictures, and largely responsible for Mae West's successful career at the studio. "So they wheeled Zukor in, who was 103 at the time," explains Kane, "and put Mae West on one side of the dog and Adolph Zukor on the other side. And he could only look down. He was in this chair, looking down at his crotch. He wasn't going to have anything to do with this dog. Mae didn't seem to care about him. I don't think she even remembered him. It was embarrassing."

Years later, Merv would invariably cite the premiere of *Won-Ton Ton, the Dog That Saved Hollywood* as the biggest disaster in the show's history.

It was also in 1976 that Merv would move his production unit into a facility at Sunset and Vine, in the heart of Hollywood, naming it the Celebrity Theatre. In addition to the new studio, the Griffin show added a young member to its staff, one who would flourish until the end of the series.

"I grew up in San Francisco and then moved to San Mateo," says Peter Barsocchini. "I started working for Merv in '76. When I was in college, there'd be these charity events at the tennis club where I worked. Tennis was big in the seventies, and [Clint] Eastwood and Merv would do these charity things. Merv was there one day and we started chatting about San Mateo. And then somebody who was with him said, 'You're the same guy who writes the music column for that newspaper....' blah, blah, blah. Then I got a call from one of Merv's producers, and the next thing was that I ended up going to L.A. for an interview because, as it happens with television shows, they wanted to reach a younger audience. They asked me, 'Can you get us music acts?' They had plenty of showbiz people and talent coordinators. So I really came in from that angle and started doing interviews of the music people. And because I had a background as a journalist, I did pre-interviews to prepare Merv and his guests for the show, which was something I was already used to doing.

"I started working for them when I was 24, and the thing is, I was already writing. But I wasn't really sure I wanted to go to Hollywood. It was actually my girlfriend at the time who said, 'Do it, because you'll regret it if you don't try.' So I gave it a try. And then it was fun. It was just a great job. Being a talent coordinator, you could get anybody on the phone, anywhere in the world. Talk shows were different then; it wasn't so much the celebrity attack culture. It wasn't the TMZ world that we live in now.

"Merv established his new studios as TAV [Trans American Video], at Sunset and Vine. At that time I had no idea of the storied history of that place, and how far back it went in television. It was a good setup for Merv, particularly because the post-production facilities were better; everything they needed from a technical standpoint was right there. That was part of Merv wanting to integrate the various facets of his businesses."

Griffin, who had always produced his shows in leased theatres or network-controlled studios, now owned every inch of the plush surroundings in which he would thrive. Even the video cameras that taped the show each night were the property of Merv Griffin Productions.

Barsocchini recalls: "That was when it was decided, we're outsourcing this, why don't we own it? Merv was smart in that regard. He wanted to own every aspect of the business he was in, and that contributed to his enormous wealth. Big changes turn on small things."

The move to TAV required changes in the set and presentation of the program itself. "Part of that was necessitated by the move from the Hollywood Palace down to TAV, which had a smaller stage," says Barsocchini. "You couldn't put a big orchestra behind the set and pull it forward; it wasn't deep enough. It was a matter of logistics. At TAV you'd have a semi-circle of guests and the band. And he had to cut down the size of the band because that became, basically, a cost item. Things were changing and so were the budgets for shows. Also legendary was the quality of the jazz musicians in his band: Herb Ellis on guitar, [trumpeter] Jack Sheldon, and Richie Kamuca, the tenor sax player. These guys were legends. But they cut the size of the band down because TAV was smaller; and to put them on one side of the stage would have been awkward. And besides, Merv liked change. He didn't like anything to stay the same for too long. He needed that constant refresh, and felt that it kept people on their toes."

Ask Barsoccchini about his favorite guests on the Griffin show and he'll start off with two words: Sophia Loren.

"She was one of my favorite guests," admits the former producer, "because she was genuine. There are a lot of stars where there's the public version and the private version. Sophia was *real*. She's Italian and, at the time, I spoke a little better Italian than I do now. When I went to meet her, she said, 'I'm so scared about being on TV and being asked so many questions!' And I told her, 'It's okay. Merv is easy and he's not going to embarrass you.' Again, it's not like today where somebody might stick a microphone in her face and ask something like, 'So, what about that affair you had while you were married to Carlo Ponti?' Merv wasn't going to go that route with her. She didn't want to do it, but she liked Merv, and she agreed to come on. I think it took Don Kane, moving heaven and earth and going over to the Beverly Hills Hotel where she was staying, to talk to her, and assure her that it's going to be okay and explain what Merv was going to ask. When she came to the show, she sat there backstage and said, 'Just hold my hand!' And it turned out great. She's such a sweet lady."

When the show wasn't focused on politics or entertainment, it explored world culture. From the late 1970s into the early '80s, the program ventured to several exciting locales around the globe, including France (for the Cannes Film Festival), Italy, Spain, and the Holy Land.

According to Barsocchini, the European jaunts were an enticement by which the most sought-after stars could be procured. "At the time, the lure was, 'You've got a trip to fabulous Italy, first class, all expenses paid,'" the produces recalls. "Sometimes we had to go to the star's spouse, because the star wasn't interested in going, but the spouse was. And you'd have to work that angle. And yes, it was always a little more complicated, because crews over there work differently. In Italy, when it was lunchtime, everything stopped. Merv could be in the middle of an interview and they say, 'We'll be back in an hour.' But those shows helped to keep Merv fresh."

Barsocchini recalls two shows Griffin originated from the Holy Land in 1976: "We were shooting in Jerusalem at the cave where they attribute the location of Jesus's manger. It's a holy site, so we had to get permission to do a song, a religious hymn for Christmas, there. We had set up some playback equipment for the recorded music, with strings for the song [to be lip-synched]. And we had to get it right on the first take because we were only given 20 minutes to do it. That's because pilgrims from all over the world get down on their hands and knees as they pass through there. At one point, we had to test the audio and were talking to somebody in the truck; he had to turn on the audio to test it. All of a sudden, down there in the cave with all these pilgrims, religious people, and priests praying on their knees, comes this ethereal string music. And I saw the looks on people's faces: 'Oh, my God, it's the second coming!' 'It's a miracle!' But, again, for Merv, this was the kind of thing that would keep him fresh. Doing a show like that back then wasn't as common as it would be now. Today you can do an interview with anyone on the planet on Skype! Back then, you had to go where the action was. So to go to Israel and come back with some tape meant more back then than it would today."

One exhilarating jaunt to Venice, Italy resulted in two days' worth of shows that provided ample time for Merv's two biggest passions: food and tennis. A planeload of stars including Mel Brooks, Carl Reiner, Gene Wilder, Gene Hackman, and others, joined Griffin at the famous Excelsior Hotel where much wine, pasta, and culture were consumed.

"We'd book the guests and bring them over on a plane," recalls Don Kane. "And then if there were certain stars in Europe, we'd pick them up as well, like Trevor Howard. Princess Grace was already in Cannes for a tournament. The hardest one was when we brought Jack Paar and Carl Reiner over for one of these things. And Carl Reiner worshipped Jack Paar; he thought he was the most marvelous thing that ever came down the alley. We got there, and it rained every day for six days, and the tournament in Cannes was rained out. So we had to fill in with other interviews. Supposedly, I was going to have Charlton Heston, who I knew was a big bore because I'd interviewed him before. So I traded him for Jack Paar. And I got all the good stuff, because Paar had a marvelous repertoire of stories and was very funny. And Carl Reiner was just about as good. We did shows every day, with Jack Paar and Carl Reiner, and other people now and then. And we wound up doing five shows with them, with no tennis at all. Then, on the last day we were supposed to be there, the sun came out. They started playing tennis at nine in the morning and kept going until five in the afternoon. And they took these tennis games and interspersed them into the other shows so there would be tennis in every show, every day. You never knew that it was all faked. But Jack Paar and Carl Reiner saved our lives in France.

"I also booked the show in Venice. I'd spent three hours with Trevor Howard and a writer, a reporter who knew everybody. He and Trevor were going to be interviewed in the square, in front of San Marco, in Venice and they went to a famous bar in Venice.

"They sent me over to keep track of Trevor Howard, because he was drinking. So I went over and joined them. They were drinking Bellinis—peach juice and champagne. Then they finally started eating something. We were there three hours. Trevor was getting high, the reporter guy *was* high, and I had had quite a bit. Finally, it was time to go. And when the check came, both of them excused themselves. One went to the phone and the other went to the toilet. And I got the bill for everybody, which was over a couple hundred dollars. I made Merv Griffin pay for it. But it was worth it, because Trevor Howard was just fascinating. I made a terrible mistake in that I said something to him that I wouldn't have said to anyone. I told him, 'The thing that I admire most about you is that you only accept good roles in good pictures. You never do any junk.' And subsequently, I found out that Trevor Howard had done an awful lot of junk over the years. We only saw his good films, because only the good ones came to the U.S. But years later, with cable TV, we saw all these bum movies he had made. But he was okay with it; he talked about his wife on the plane. They weren't getting on too well. He wasn't so great as an interview, but in person he was very interesting."

Has Don Kane ever considered penning his memoirs? "No," says the former talent coordinator, "because I couldn't write all the good stuff with some of the people still alive. I walked in the dressing room one time and saw Redd Foxx and Sammy Davis, Jr., both smoking joints, and they're higher than a kite, getting ready to go on with Merv. They said, 'Don't tell anybody.' I saw a lot of stuff you couldn't write in a book because you'd get sued or be called a liar. Actors are not necessarily very disciplined. I've never met an actor who didn't think the world was centered on him. They eventually put a protective web around themselves, and it's all about them. It's rare to find one that isn't; you'd have to find one that's no longer in the business. This was also true with Merv. It was all about Merv, all the time. It was all about Joey Bishop, all the time. Even stars that aren't important, it's all about them. Performers, I think, build that shell to protect themselves against anybody who doesn't like them or want them. It's definitely an ego business and they're all insecure way, way down."

In a business where egos are remarkably fragile, talent coordinators and producers of talk shows must walk a tenuous tightrope to keep their guests happy. While some of Merv's best moments in television resulted from bringing diverse personalities together, a few near-disasters occurred by attempting to mesh personalities from within the same profession. "Some personalities simply don't want to share the spotlight with anyone else," says Don Kane. "They feel that this is their moment and they want it all to themselves. You get into situations where a guest won't say those words, but that's the net effect of it."

What often seems like a logical combination of personalities at a production meeting doesn't always pan out that way on the air. Barsocchini recalls the time Walter Cronkite and Barbara Walters had been booked to appear on the same program.

"When Cronkite found out that we had also booked Barbara to come on, he came up with some bullshit excuse. 'Oh, I can't. I'll do it another day.' And that was too bad. I don't know if Barbara Walters will admit it, but it broke her heart. She was so excited about being on with Walter Cronkite. But a lot of the 'old boy' news guys didn't consider her a newsperson; they considered her a celebrity. And we look at Barbara Walters today as sort of an eminent person. But back then, the Harry Reasoners and the Dan Rathers had come up through the journalists' world and Barbara didn't. She was always just a television personality. Another important thing is, back then, the network news still mattered. The CBS Evening News *mattered*. The NBC Nightly News *mattered*. Today, there's probably nobody under the age of 50 who could tell you who the anchors are."

Yet a theme show, by its very nature, usually necessitates bringing together people from the same field of endeavor.

"That was the kind of thing we were always trying to do," says Peter Barsocchini. "The art of booking a talk show has always been: if you can get *this* person, you can get *that* person. It often becomes a juggling act with some dangerous cards to play. If you look at a lot of the comics, and the language they use to get somebody's attention, it all reflects on the pop culture. We don't see too many intellectual comics today; we're seeing more and more of the 'shock' comic coming out."

Was it easier for a rookie comic to land a spot on the show, as opposed to a fledgling actor? "Yes, if they were funny, it was easier," says Barsocchini. "Merv did not watch the soap operas. So if there were a young actor on one of the soaps, we'd say, 'Merv, you've got to put this guy on.' And he'd say, 'I don't know who that is.' But we'd book him anyway because we knew how hot those shows were. And then they'd come on. We booked the actors who played Luke and Laura on *General Hospital*; they were the biggest soap opera stars at the time. The audience would go crazy and Merv would invariably be surprised. He thought they'd only react that way for Sean Connery. And it was interesting, because the audience would react differently to movie stars than they would to television stars. Today, it's all sort of blended. But back then, when a big movie star would come, the audience would almost get quiet. That's because they were used to seeing them on a 60-foot screen, and it was almost disorienting to see them walk into the studio. Then, when we had a TV star on, like Bob Hope, people were so used to seeing him in their homes that they felt like they knew him. Today, because of social media, everybody's everywhere, and the nature of celebrity has changed."

Theme shows continued to dominate the Griffin show into the late seventies. In 1977, Merv devoted an entire program to "great achievements" with Los Angeles Lakers superstar Kareem Abdul-Jabbar, author Alex Haley, and actor Louis Gossett, Jr. Jabbar talked candidly about the pressures of being a star athlete. (Jabbar: "They don't pay you to play; they pay you to win.") Haley stole the show that evening, as he expounded on the 12 years he'd spent researching and writing his best known book, *Roots: The Saga of an American Family,* which sold 1.6 million copies and spawned a record-breaking ABC mini-series that garnered multiple Emmys, one of which went to Gossett for his role as Fiddler.

In 1978, Merv's viewers would witness one of the saddest fare-wells in show business history. Totie Fields, who attributed much of her success to the syndicated Griffin show, made her final television appearance with Merv shortly before her death.

For years, Fields had lived with Type II (or "adult onset") diabetes. "The disease brought on a heart attack that led to phlebitis in Totie's leg," explains Kane. "And that, in turn, led to her losing that leg. From then on, her health went downhill. Totie had come to L.A. from New York. The hospitals really couldn't do much for her. She wanted the public to be informed. And on the night that she did the show, she was perspiring profusely. You could see that she was very uncomfortable. But she got it together and tried to do some humor early for the show so it wouldn't be too heavy. And Merv explained why she had come along with her doctors from Cedars Sinai Hospital, all well-known specialists in Los Angeles. The idea was to set up some sort of clinic or program at Cedars to educate people about diabetes, heart attacks, and the other complications associated with the disease. She had asked to come on the show. Merv wouldn't have done a show like that ordinarily. Of course, he would have had her on anytime. But he wouldn't have had her on with her doctors. Totie died before the show aired, and Merv taped a new opening for the episode, rather than dumping it. He knew it had been important to Totie and thought it should air as a tribute to his good friend."

In the fall of 1978, Merv announced that his show would originate from Manhattan for six of the 48 weeks it would be in production.

"But poor, show-business-scorned New York City is reacting as if a blessing had been bestowed from on high," wrote Philadelphia TV critic Rex Polier. Griffin's main offices and production facilities would remain in Hollywood, his show's home base since 1970. "I've been amazed that nobody was doing a national talk show from the largest city in the world," Griffin told Polier, adding that the Manhattan episodes would be taped at the famous Ed Sullivan Theater. Ironically, most of Merv's guests on his first round of New York shows were residents of Los Angeles.

The first of the "new" Manhattan editions aired in late October 1978. It was at this time that the program sought out yet another political heavyweight. "We had Speaker of the House Tip O'Neill in New York at the Vivian Beaumont Theater," recalls Barsocchini. "And he gave the big bullshit politician interview. But we went out to dinner with him afterwards and that's when it got interesting. We went to a place that he knew—there were actually about 12 of them—and Tip O'Neill knew his way around a glass of scotch. And his glass was never empty. It kept getting refilled and refilled. And I'm looking at this guy, thinking how can somebody drink this much and *still* be so articulate? But he was a Boston-Irish politician, and the conversation was more genuine. I wish *that* was the interview we could have put on TV."

Though Barsocchini wasn't with the show when Richard Nixon had made his disastrous appearance in 1967, the producer would have a memorable encounter with him nonetheless. "We were in New York at the time and we were going do the interview [with Nixon] at The Ed Sullivan Theater. Nixon had a book coming out [*The Real War*], but he did not want to do the show with an audience. He wanted it to be just him and Merv."

Four years had passed since Nixon had resigned from the presidency. Nevertheless, "It was still too raw for him and he knew that with an audience, there might be booing," says Barsocchini.

"I happened to be in my office one night, I was the last one there, and the phone rang. I picked it up and a voice said, 'Hi, this is Dick Nixon.' And I was thinking, aw, who *is* this?' And it really *was* Dick Nixon. There was no secretary, or anybody. So I said, 'Do you mind if I call you back?' And he said, 'that's all right.' I did have a contact number, and I called and got an assistant. They put me right through to Nixon. He said, 'I just wanted to call myself, because I've got an issue with my phlebitis and I am not going to be able to do the show tomorrow. I didn't want Merv to think I'm getting cold feet.' He said he could hardly walk and it would too hard for him. I said, 'Mr. President, we can come to you or reschedule.' And whatever happened, happened. But we *almost* had him."

In October 1979, *The Merv Griffin Show* celebrated episode number 2,000 for the Metromedia network. Some 1,100 attendees competed for seats at the show's new home in the Big Apple: the Vivian Beaumont Theater at Lincoln Center. Governor Hugh Carey was on hand to help Merv mark the special occasion, which included appearances by Kris Kristofferson, comedian Robert Kline, and Ann Miller, then starring on Broadway in *Sugar Babies*.

The show was enjoying an incredibly smooth run in Manhattan. "I wish I could spend 48 weeks a year here," Griffin told *The New York Times* after the celebratory taping. When it was over, the star hosted a lavish by-invitation-only party held at the theater.

16. HIGHS AND LOWS IN THE '80s

At the dawn of the eighties, Merv Griffin was still a rock-solid success as a syndicated daytime talker. On July 1, 1980, the *New York Daily News* announced that the "Irish leprechaun" had just signed a new deal with his syndication company, Metromedia Producers Corporation. The headline said it all: "Make Merv the New $6 Million Man."

According to the article, Griffin's new contract would be worth somewhere between $6 million and $7 million per annum. The Griffin show would remain based in Hollywood, with periodic jaunts to New York, Las Vegas, and several European locales.

Merv was now being seen on 100 stations in the United States, and 15 stations in Canada. More important, the show was still enjoying prime-time exposure in 12 major American cities. Despite the strong ratings on New York's Channel 5, where the show still played at 8:30 p.m., some sobering rumors began to surface. The alarm was triggered when Griffin's outlet in San Francisco dropped the series, amid reports that the station in Chicago was about to do the same. A Metromedia spokesperson quickly quelled any backlash by pointing out that it's commonplace in television for a station to discontinue a show, only to have another station in the same market pick it up.

Interestingly, the same article reported that former CBS president Robert Wood, the exec who had delivered the cancellation notice to Merv in December 1971, had recently taken over as head of Metromedia.

Undaunted by any temporary setbacks, Merv remained focused on the program. He continued to play Las Vegas. "The ratings were stacked higher whenever Merv brought the show to Vegas," says Don Kane. "Merv felt that there was a special energy in that town that worked well for the show. And he aimed to keep those shows fresh with new and amazing acts."

Peter Barsocchini concurs: "Merv loved Las Vegas and enjoyed working there," says the producer. "He'd go out and play tennis, have dinner, and sometimes catch a show or just pop around town to see what was going on." Barsocchini recalls one Vegas jaunt during this period in which Merv believed he'd discovered a unique act. "He came back and said, 'I've found one of the most incredible acts. How could you guys have missed it?'" Merv looked at the young producer and talent coordinators and asked, "When was the last time you saw a duck start to dance?"

"A dancing duck?" Barsocchini recalls saying. "What's he talking about?"

"And Merv said, 'Well, I've booked this man and he'll be showing up at 11:00 for rehearsal.' And this swarming-looking guy showed up with a cage, some contraptions, and a couple of ducks. And it was literally the funniest thing when he came out to do his rehearsal and asked, 'Where's the electrical outlet?' We couldn't understand why he would need an electrical outlet. We had lights, and everything he needed. And he said, 'Yes, but I need an outlet to plug in the hot plate.' We asked him what the hot plate was for. And he said, 'What do you think makes the ducks dance?' And of course Merv went nuts and had somebody call the S.P.C.A., and the guy got busted." Needless to say, that incident cooled Merv's zest for booking acts for a while."

Were there any guests that Griffin wanted, either in Vegas or Hollywood, but couldn't get? The answer is yes, according to Barsocchini. "But it's a pretty small list," says the producer. "Merv had always wanted Cary Grant on the show. But Grant didn't want to do it. Barbra Streisand didn't want to do it, either." Occasionally, Merv would suggest people that he thought the audience would want to see. But if they were retired, they stayed retired."

Doris Day had played a pivotal role in Griffin's early career. The iconic actress/singer had made appearances on Merv's late-night CBS show in 1970, and his syndicated series in 1975.

"Merv wanted Doris Day on again, and I can remember asking her, 'Would you do the show?' And she said, 'I just don't do that anymore.' But he never expected to get any mysterious-types, like Howard Hughes. We'd sit around with Merv sometimes and just spitball as to who's the most impossible guest that everybody wants. And many of them remained impossible. And then again, sometimes, we would get someone like Sophia Loren. I think Merv's favorite ideas [for bookings] were people that were *super* movie stars. The old school, big time movie stars rather than professional celebrities. The icons of movies, those were his favorites. But a lot of them just didn't want to do it.

"He really wanted to sit down with Streisand and do a whole show with her. They had appeared together at The White Correspondents' Dinner [in 1963]. But when she became a *super*-superstar, she would only do certain things like the Barbara Walters interviews; she may have done *The Tonight Show*. But she didn't want to sing unless it was on her own special. I asked her myself because she was a close friend of someone I knew. And she said, 'Maybe, when I'm doing a movie, I'll do it.' But she just didn't want to do it."

Though *The Merv Griffin Show* was firmly entrenched in Los Angeles, with periodic visits to Las Vegas, Merv's dalliance with New York seemed to have intensified. In September 1980, he geared up for another week's worth of shows from the Vivian Beaumont Theater. "I'm the first to come back to New York on a regular basis," Griffin told Earl Wilson (*New York Post*, April 3, 1980). "I figure we'll all settle in Kansas."

He also told the columnist that the latitude of talk shows had changed: "It's different now. You can say anything as long as it sounds clinical and is not a dirty joke. We had a psychiatrist talking about women demanding multiple orgasms."

While on the East Coast, Merv embarked on a seven-city book-signing tour to promote his long awaited memoir, *Merv*. He came up with a clever gimmick to promote the book on his own show.

On September 24, 1980 the Griffin show began with Dick Cavett taking the stage at the Vivian Beaumont Theater. "I suppose you're wondering what happened to Merv," he said in a semi-serious tone. "I guess you didn't see today's papers. . . ." he joked, causing few people to sigh uneasily.

Authors had been coming on the Griffin show for years to plug their books. "And now," Cavett announced, "Merv has entered the august circle of authors, as you probably know." Cavett explained that Merv had tried to get on his own show, "but the producer felt that he just didn't have it." He then introduced a black-and-white clip of himself chatting with Merv on the Westinghouse show in 1965. When it was over, Merv walked onto the stage to thunderous applause. For the next hour, Merv Griffin would be a guest on his own show, with hosting chores turned over to the highly competent Dick Cavett.

Cavett was an ironic choice for this assignment, not so much because he was a former late-night rival, but because he'd been one of Merv's staff writers nearly two decades earlier. The two hosts reflected on Merv's childhood and early career, and the years leading up to the emergence of *The Merv Griffin Show*. They recalled working together on the old NBC series, and the back stage drama that nearly ruined the Montgomery Clift segment. Their reminiscences were interspersed with dozens of highlights ranging from newsmakers like Bobby Kennedy and Richard Nixon, to the memorable laugh-makers such as Richard Pryor, Jerry Lewis, Jack Benny, and others. There was also a series of clips showcasing Arthur Treacher's contribution to the earlier phase of the series. For the finale, Merv sat at the piano and offered an uplifting rendition of "As Time Goes By," accompanied by a succession of nostalgic photos on the screen.

Cavett praised *Merv*, the book, as "revealing," stating that it wasn't just another piece of "fluffy showbiziana." Nevertheless, some critics complained that the tome wasn't revealing enough, adding that the reader comes away not knowing if Merv, the private citizen, is a Republican or a Democrat.

If selling a book was a staple of the variety/talk show, by the early '80s it had become a *must* for both the best-selling or up-and-coming author. "Writers were happy to come on and promote their wares," says producer Barsocchini. "But today, with social media, there are a thousand ways people can promote their product. Back then, it was a huge coup for an author to get on *The Merv Griffin Show*, because an appearance could result in a best seller. It's the same thing with people in the movie business. For example, in 1985, you could go to the theater and see *Out of Africa*. Today, you couldn't sell *Out of Africa* to Universal in a billion years. They'd say, 'Who's going to go to that? We want *Fantastic Four.*' But back then, that was a major product; today, it would be an independent movie. Movies of the 1970s like *The Godfather, Apocalypse Now, The Conversation*—those were major-studio films that, today, wouldn't be made by a major studio. They'd be indies."

The variety/talk show has always proven to be a haven for the comedian, especially the struggling beginner. Throughout the late '70s, the Griffin show had three talent coordinators booking comics for Griffin. Don Kane says he exercised caution when it came to booking the comics. "I was careful not letting other people who weren't involved in that aspect book the show," he says, "so I booked it myself."

"Almost every night, I'd go to clubs like the Improv or the Comedy Store and look for a new comedian. We introduced a great many comics. We had a delay of a couple of weeks before the show aired. And quite often, Merv would be the first to have one of these new comics on, and then the comic's manager would get the word out. And then the word would get to Carson, who would then have the comic on before our show aired. And this made Merv look ridiculous. He'd be saying, 'And now, for the first time on television, please welcome so-and-so, when in fact, that same comic had been seen three days earlier on Carson.

"Merv would get upset because a lot of people wanted to credit Johnny Carson as their discoverer," says Kane. "A lot of comics, in particular, were supposedly discovered by Carson which simply was not true. I would book them from the Improv, or some other club, and they'd come in and tape our show, which wouldn't air for a couple of weeks. And in the meantime, their manager or agent would get them on *The Tonight Show*. I didn't appreciate that at all and called a few of them on it. But according to them, it was more important to be discovered by Johnny Carson. Johnny was still going big, and by the early '80s, Merv wasn't doing as well."

Case-in-point: Jerry Seinfeld. "We had Seinfeld first," says Kane. "I put him on before he'd done anything else, and the show aired on Thanksgiving Day of 1981." Kane remembers the incident with acute clarity, since Seinfeld's agent had invited him to a party at which Doc Severinsen (Carson's bandleader] was also in attendance.

"I went to the party and we all watched Seinfeld on Merv's show that night. And he had done very well. But the same stuff he'd done on Merv had been seen three or four nights earlier on the Carson show. That's because Jerry had taped Merv's show first, but it aired later."

Aside from scouring the clubs looking for new talent, Kane also tapped into the connections he'd made during his time with *The Joey Bishop Show*. "I even put Joey on with Merv a few times," recalls Kane. Bishop's most notable appearance on the Griffin show had been a 1976 "Salute to Philadelphia." The comedian shared the bill with fellow Philadelphians Jack Klugman, Lola Falana, David Brenner, and James Darren.

"Merv didn't treat Joey too well," notes Kane. Apparently, something of a rift had developed between the two stars. Bishop clung to the notion that Griffin Productions would produce a game show for him to star in. "The name of it was *That's Right, You're Wrong*," recalls Kane. "And I think that title had been around before, but Bishop wanted to emcee it. Merv fiddled with it, but he never got it off the ground." There may have been a problem with underwriting the pilot for the show. "Merv would never put his own money into anything like that; he always had other people use their money. He was smart about that," says Kane. "This was more than a decade after Joey's talk show had gone off the air."

In keeping with the tradition dating back to the Westinghouse era, Merv continued to interview many high-ranking government officials and dignitaries during the Metromedia period. These included Secretary of State Henry Kissinger and Prince Charles. Among the major coups in this vein: former Presidents Gerald R. Ford and Jimmy Carter.

The 39th President of the United States, Gerald R. Ford, was described by Merv as "one of the sweetest human beings" he had ever known. In a very relaxed, informal interview taped at a local TV station in Fresno, California, Ford offered a bittersweet account from his high-school days. As a part-time employee at a small hamburger stand, Ford noticed a man staring at him intently. "Are you Leslie King?" asked the man. "No," answered Ford. "Are you

Junior King?" the man asked. Again, Ford said, "No." Finally, he asked, "Are you Junior Ford or Gerald Ford?" Ford. of course, said yes. "And the man said 'I'm your father.' I'd never seen him before." Father and son had lunch together. "As he drove off," Ford recalled, "he said 'here's $25.00. Spend it the way you want to.' And, for all intents and purposes, I never saw him again."

Several months later, Ford appeared for a formal interview at the Celebrity Theater before a live audience. Well aware of the coolness that existed between Ford and his successor, Jimmy Carter, Merv asked, "Did Mr. Carter do damage to the country in those four years?" "I wouldn't put it *quite* that way," said Ford, politely. "Yes, you would!" retorted Merv, devilishly. "I think I heard you do it, as a matter of fact." The audience chuckled. Indeed, the years of Carter's presidency (1977–81) had witnessed high unemployment, long lines at gas stations (a result of the Arab oil embargo in 1979), double digit interest rates, and, finally, the seizure of the American Embassy in Tehran wherein 52 Americans would be held hostage for 444 days.

"I think he could have done a better job," Ford admitted. Ford said his biggest disparity with his successor was on "the economic side."

"When Jimmy Carter became president, we had reduced the inflation rate to 4.8 percent. It's today [1981] at 11 percent or 12 percent," he said without rancor.

Ford also criticized Carter's lack of rapport with foreign leaders, citing that many, though not all, of them never felt "warmth" toward his successor. "And if you don't establish a personal relationship with a foreign leader, it makes it much more difficult for the two to work together on a common problem."

On the subject of nuclear proliferation (a "fearsome thing" in Merv's words) the former president said: "There is the so-called nuclear club that includes Great Britain, France, the Soviet Union, ourselves, and the People's Republic. There are others who are suspected of having a nuclear weapon capability, such as India, Israel, and maybe one or two others. I say they're *suspected* of having it; we aren't sure they have it. That always presents a fear that some country who does have it will act irresponsibly in the use of it and, of course, that could set off a very serious conflagration that would have repetitive sequences that would not be good for the world as a whole."

On a lighter note, Ford debunked a myth of long standing about his early career.

"Ronald Reagan might not be the first actor in the White House," said Merv. "Weren't you a model in New York?" Ford smiled and said no. "That was a tale that got off on the wrong track. Let me tell you the story. When I was in law school, I invested in Harry Conover's model agency. He needed cash and I had $1,000. And I was a partner of his, not as a model, but as an investor. But it went from that investment to the idea that I was a model and [as] that, I never qualified." Ever the consummate businessman, Merv asked, "Did you double your investment at least?" Ford laughed. "We did well," he said cheerfully. The audience laughed, too.

The following year, 1982, Merv sat down with Ford's successor, Jimmy Carter. The interview began with Merv reminiscing about the president's mother, Miss Lillian, who, six years earlier, had danced with Andy Williams as he crooned "Moon River" on the Griffin stage at Caesar's Palace in Las Vegas.

Carter was a one-term president having lost his bid for re-election to Ronald Reagan. "Is that an awful feeling of rejection," asked Merv. "It must be terrible."

"Yes, it is," said Carter thoughtfully. "It's better not to be rejected in any circumstances, but to be rejected by people that you really love, as we loved and still love the people of this country was heartbreaking to us." In addition to losing his bid for re-election, Carter disclosed that he also lost the business he had cultivated, Carter's Warehouse. "When I left the White House," said Carter, "We had sold Carter's Warehouse to pay off our debts. And we came out very well on that."

Merv asked Carter if he had departed the White House a poor man. "No, I still had some land that has been in our family since the Indians left Georgia. It's not valuable land. We weren't destitute, but we didn't have much money."

"But a president doesn't get rich in office," Merv deduced. "No, I lost a lot of money in office," admitted Carter. "But it was a great experience and well worth it, of course." The conversation reverted back to election night, 1980.

Merv: "Is the first question one asks themselves after a defeat, 'What did I do wrong? Why did I lose?'"

Carter: "No, we could see it coming. For the last few hours, as you may remember, most people do, the exact first anniversary of the hostages being seized in Iran was Election Day. And the front cover of all the news magazines and the prime stories on television and so forth was the hostages when I was trying to get re-elected. And the feeling of impotence, the inability of a great nation to get 52 people back to freedom was very discouraging to me and to all the people in this country. And I was the personification of that. I was the president. Why doesn't the president get those hostages home? He must be impotent himself."

Carter recalled how his pollsters, during the last week of the campaign, had informed him that he was running "just about an even race" with Reagan. Then, when the Iranian parliament announced that it was considering releasing the hostages, and didn't, the result was a "despairing wave" across the nation.

On November 4, 1980, Jimmy Carter carried a mere six states, plus DC, and garnered 49 electoral votes. Ronald Reagan, the Republican challenger, carried 44 states and won 489 electoral votes, easily winning the election.

"I empathize with politicians," says Peter Barsocchini. "Every person they meet has a story for them; they want to shake their hand, they want a picture taken, and it becomes a pain in the ass. But the atmosphere backstage at the Griffin show was one where everybody was well trained not to annoy the guests, or ask, 'Would you sign a book for my grandmother?' or something. They knew to leave them alone. This was their quiet time before doing an interview on television. And we were well aware of that. I remember a specific incident where a page just wanted to shake [Carter's] hand, and he was not having anything to do with that. Reagan was gregarious, like Bill Clinton. I later saw Bill Clinton in private, and to watch him work a room is a work of art."

17. STILL TALKING, BUT IS ANYONE LISTENING?

By the early-1980s, *The Merv Griffin Show* had amassed an enviable collection of industry awards and scrapbook-worthy reviews. As the decade progressed, the pages in that scrapbook were beginning to look a bit yellowish. Times were changing. Daytime talk shows were changing. After a decade of complacency with Metromedia, the format that had once clicked was now beginning to seem passé. In keeping with the industry standard, the running time of the program would be trimmed to one hour. This was not particularly vexing, since Metromedia had, from the beginning, offered the program in a one-hour format to accommodate the needs of certain stations. Even Johnny Carson had scaled back *The Tonight Show* to one hour.

The new format was initiated shortly after Peter Barsocchini and Betty Bitterman had assumed the reins of production. "We had been doing 90-minute shows up to that time," says Barsocchini. "But that format wasn't going to work. Merv was still on Metromedia in New York and Los Angeles at 9:00 in the evening, and there was no way a ninety-minute talk show was going to survive at that time. And the business itself was starting to change, and so the show went to an hour."

The local stations had established a policy of selling more commercial time per hour, so a "60-minute" program, minus commercials, would now run about 43 minutes. This meant that the Griffin show would no longer be able to intersperse oddball guests or audience-participation games into the proceedings. The relaxed atmosphere of the sixties and seventies was quickly fading into the past. Worse yet, the easy-going style of Merv, Mike, and Dinah was being eclipsed by the more sensational, tabloid-style topics featured on shows like *Donahue*.

Having watched a million of these shows," says Barsocchini, "by today's standards, you watch the early ones and pace is glacial compared to what we're seeing now. It's very interesting to see how everything old is new again," says the producer. "You see somebody come in like Jimmy Fallon, who was not a great actor, not a great comedian, yet he could do it all pretty well. And that makes for a perfect host, which was sort of the formula that worked for Merv. And it still works."

When the show was trimmed to an hour in 1982, there were significant cutbacks in personnel, and certain jobs were combined as a cost saving measure. For instance, Don Kane had been promoted from talent coordinator to associate producer, but he still had the responsibility of booking guests for the program.

As it turned out, the new associate producer's time with the show was coming to an end. Kane says he never left the program. "The program left me," he confides. "Although I did quit once, when we went to Europe to do the show from Cannes." Kane had gotten into a rift with Merv's secretary when she appropriated his first-class seat on the chartered jet. Kane said he'd remain with the show, but only if Merv would fire the secretary.

"After Cannes, we went on vacation," says Kane. "I went to London, and sat next to Trevor Howard, who had been at the film festival in Cannes. We chatted all the way. When I returned to Los Angeles, I didn't hear from anybody, and I figured it was over. Then I got a call from Merv, and he said he wanted me to come in. "Did you get rid of her?' And he said, 'I can't. She knows too much about my day-to-day business. But I'll make a deal with you. I'll tell her she must *never* speak to you again, and to ignore you from now on.' Reluctantly, I said, 'All right,' and went back to work. Six months later, when they were going to another festival in Paris, they hired a girl as a special booker for that trip. I knew something was fishy when this girl started booking stuff for Paris. I said I'd do certain things and Barsocchini said, 'No, you don't have to.' I found out they were edging me out when someone at a club, a comedian, came up to me and said, 'I heard you're getting fired!' I told him that I hadn't heard any such thing, and he said, 'That's the word that's out.' I figured that's what hiring this girl was about. So I slowly started taking all my things out of the office, and nobody ever said anything to me. When the time came for them to go to Paris, I never received a ticket. So I just went home. They all went off to Paris, and I never heard from Merv or Bob Murphy. Nobody had ever said 'boo' to me. They just avoided the whole subject.

"When they came back from Europe, I sent them a letter saying that I was owed 11 years' severance pay, plus vacation pay. And for the next 14 weeks, I'd get a check as though I were getting paid. But nothing was ever said to me about leaving. 'You're fired,' 'get of here,' nothing like that at all. Then I was invited to be on someone else's show, talking about Merv, and booking stuff, with a comedian that had done the show. I went on and was very kind to Merv. I said nothing but positive things. And Merv had obviously seen it, because he kept asking people at the office, 'Did you hear what he said about me?' and so on. But I never heard from Merv again, although I ran into him a few times in Palm Springs."

Producer Bob Murphy had, by this time, been promoted to production executive. Recalls Barsocchini: "Once Bob moved up when I came in, he was still there, of course, if he was needed. He was basically overseeing the game shows and didn't really get involved in the talk show. If there was any budgetary issue, I might talk to him about it; to intercede with New York about the budget. But his day-to-day involvement with the talk show had stopped. And he couldn't wait because that's a burnout job, and he had moved on to greener pastures with the game shows. Those game shows had become the mother lode; they practically print money! According to Merv's deal, even after he'd sold the shows to Coca-Cola and Columbia, he still retained a piece of them after they hit a certain recoup point, which they did. Merv sold it, but still owned a piece, ad infinitum."

Not only was the show's running time cut, its title was likewise truncated. By early 1982 it had suddenly become *The Merv Show*. "They've taken the name *Griffin* out of the title," Merv quipped on the air. "I wonder if they're trying to tell me something."

Indeed, they were trying to tell him something. "That was the result of market research," says Barsocchini. "Merv had been doing his famous theme shows and had already devoted time to serious subjects. But this was the effect of Phil Donahue and some of the others. And for the type of entertainment that Merv Griffin, Mike

Douglas, and Dinah Shore had done, the marketplace was changing. And the demographics of the audience were changing and market research said there had to be more informational segments. I don't think Merv was thrilled about that because he was, essentially, an entertainer."

The new title may have been catchier, but it had no discernible effect on the ratings or marketability of the show, says Barsocchini. "Again, you get a pile of research that says, basically, everybody calls it *Merv* anyway. Does it really need to be called *The Merv Griffin Show*? So they shortened it to '*The Merv Show*' for a while.

"It's interesting because King World later leaned on Oprah at one point and told her she had to go more tabloid," remembers Peter Barsocchini. "She ran into that when it became the Maury Povich issue of 'let's have the cousins on who've had three children together.' She thought it over and refused, saying she'd sink or swim doing what she does. And it was the right choice for her."

One highly topical entry presented under the show's truncated title was the 10th anniversary celebration of *Ms.* magazine, seen on June 30, 1982. The lead guest was the magazine's co-founder and editor, Gloria Steinem. Though Steinem had name value as a respected voice in the feminist movement, Jane Fonda, Lee Grant, Loretta Switt, and Carole King complimented her appearance on the panel. Merv set forth the tone of the show. "If there's anyone who still believes women are the weaker sex—*get out*," he warned at the outset. He wasn't kidding. What followed was an hour that chronicled the substantial strides made by women since the inception of *Ms.* in 1972. "Now we have names for things," Steinem said poignantly. "Now we have words like battered women and sexual harassment." A decade earlier, such things were just called life, Steinem said. The emergence of new opportunities for women in the workplace, particularly in traditionally male-dominated fields, was also discussed. To further the point, actress/director Lee Grant commented that in recent years, one rarely saw an all-male crew on movie sets. The audience snickered; it looked as though Merv's crew was comprised entirely of men. Not so, protested Merv, taking justifiable pride in the fact that he'd placed women in high-level jobs over the years. "The producer of my show *used* to be a woman," he continued, as the snickering intensified. What Merv meant, of course, was that Betty Bitterman, one of his erstwhile producers, had been a valued member of his creative team before she accepted a more substantial assignment from Home Box Office.

The marketing research continued to flow in. Griffin gamely complied with certain recommendations by conducting several interviews news-anchor style, at a table, face to face with each guest. For a very brief time, he would also employ a co-host. These trendy modifications did not enhance the show's reputation or its popularity. By the fall of 1982, the old format was restored along with the show's original title. To no one's surprise, the discontinuation of the informational segments went largely unnoticed. What *was* noticeable, however, was the fact that Merv had also reverted back to the traditional desk-and-sofa format, the hallmark of the American talk show since the days of Jack Paar. The Griffin set was given a complete makeover, decorated with elegant furnishings, colorful paintings and fixtures. Despite its contemporary look, the new set reminded longtime viewers of the old one at Westinghouse.

The reduced emphasis on musical entertainment necessitated more changes. With the band now downsized, the artists began lip-synching. The show's theme music, "The Dream Theme," was also heard on a record.

"That's because Merv wanted a big orchestra version of the song, rather than have an eight-piece band playing it," Barsocchini explains. "He wanted that big, lush arrangement of it, with strings and everything. And with the music acts, as recording became more sophisticated, the artists felt that you couldn't replicate their sound in a TV studio. Certainly the rock and roll acts didn't want to do TV because it just didn't play on TV. Bruce Springstein didn't want to be coming through a three-inch speaker. Now he did on your car radio. But that wasn't the sound they wanted coming across on TV. They didn't want to come in and lip-synch. Some acts didn't care. But it was sort of in step with the changing of the times. Recording was more complex and, besides that, there just weren't a lot of singers that were so great that they could just walk in and sing."

During this period of experimentation, the Griffin show would devote entire editions to blockbuster movies. These programs not only celebrated the films, but also the camaraderie of the actors in them. On hand for a tribute to *Rocky III* (1982) were Sylvester Stallone, Burgess Meredith, Mr. T, Talia Shire, and Carl Weathers. Similarly, William Shatner, Leonard Nimoy, and DeForest Kelley appeared to promote the release of *Star Trek II: The Wrath of Khan* (1982), much to the utter delight of "Trekkies" everywhere.

Merv's *Rocky* and *Star Trek* salutes remain two of his best-remembered shows of the 1981-82 TV season. Hardcore Griffin fans, however, will often cite the November 1981 salute to Grammy winner Olivia Newton-John—then celebrating her tenth anniversary in show business—as their favorite episode. It was an energetic gathering of mega stars, with a fresh-faced John Travolta recalling his work with Newton-John in *Grease* (1978), Karen Carpenter, Richard Carpenter, and Rick Springfield. A happy mix of music and lighthearted chatter, the Newton-John tribute ranks as one of the best entries to emerge from Merv's transitory period.

Another observance during this phase was the old rawness of the sixties that would occasionally resurface with remarkable vigor. Such was the case in October 1982, when Dr. Edgar Berman was booked for an appearance at the Beaumont Theater. Berman had been on the show in Los Angeles, where, according to Merv, "he turned the place upside down." This came as a surprise to no one familiar with Berman's book, *The Compleat Chauvinist: A Survival Guide for the Bedeviled Male.* In the book, and in his personal appearances, Berman postulated that men should fight the good fight to prevent the downfall of their specie at the hands of militant feminists.

Berman was no crackpot. A highly accomplished surgeon, he was noted for two groundbreaking operations in the 1950s. The first procedure involved the implantation of an artificial esophagus into a human being; the second was a heart transplant performed on a dog. In the late fifties, Berman had served as president of an organization called Medico, which provided medical assistance to developing countries. During the sixties, he'd been the personal physician to Vice President Hubert Humphrey. It wasn't until 1970, in the wake of the feminist movement, that Berman gained national attention by asserting that women shouldn't hold leadership positions because of their "raging hormonal imbalances." Berman's eyebrow-raising statement cost him his post on the Democratic National Committee's subgroup, the Committee on National Priorities.

The primary evidence in Berman's argument was a set of studies indicating that females use the left side of the brain, whereas males use the right side. "First of all, I don't think women are inferior to men," he told Merv on the air. "But men *do* use the right side of their brain, which is the side of the brain that is the most creative, the most spatially related, mathematically, etcetera."

Berman got no farther. Seated next to him was actress Elizabeth Ashley, who uncorked a rambling discourse of disagreement. "That is factually, provably wrong," Ashley argued. "That's the problem with actresses," said Berman. "They're always trying to get in on the act." The audience snickered. "Well, you'll have to give her the right to in a minute," said Merv wryly.

"I don't want you to make a total fool of yourself in front of America," said Ashley, moving farther away from Berman on the couch. "My dear," snapped Berman, "I'm a scientist. You're an actress." Berman said "actress" as though it were a dirty word. Merv frowned.

Actress or not, Ashley vigorously defended her sex in an ensuing tussle of words. It was Berman's spot and he wasn't about to let up. "Now, it's not that the right side is superior to the left side," he continued. "It's just that the values that society places on it are greater." Berman then rattled off a myriad of great accomplishments in diverse fields, all of which, according to him, had been pioneered by the right side of the male brain.

"Well, then," Merv interrupted, "what does the left side provide, doctor?"

Berman said the left side offers greater verbalization and manual dexterity, marked by gentleness and peacefulness. And in contrast, the right side of the male brain is associated with more aggressive and "war-like" behavior, which explains why men prefer football instead of knitting. The audience chuckled.

Merv quizzed Berman: "Isn't this a time of enormously successful women in every field?" Merv and Ashley rattled off the names of several women who had achieved success in various professions. Unimpressed, Berman dismissed each of them as inferior to their male counterparts. At this juncture, director Dick Carson made sure Ashley remained in the picture; he captured her open-mouthed, how-dare-you expressions as Berman continued his argument: "I'm for equal opportunity and equal pay. But no amount of consciousness-raising, assertiveness training, or affirmative action is going to make a French poodle into a Doberman Pincher, or a Sophia Loren into a Nelson Bunker Hunt. It's just an impossibility. The glands say so."

Ashley, of course, matched Berman zap for zap. Merv smugly asked if there was a doctor in the house. *Another* doctor. There was—the resolutely astute psychologist, Dr. Joyce Brothers. She, too, was peddling a new book: *What Every Woman Should Know About Men.* "Let's get to the right side of the brain, which you don't use, Joyce," Merv snickered.

"First of all," said Brothers, "the new studies indicate it is true that for little boys, the right side of the brain develops earlier than in little girls. And for little girls, the left side of the brain develops earlier than in little boys. But the new studies also indicate that, in adulthood, women use *both* sides of the brain, and men tend to remain right-brained."

The audience roared. Brothers said that these biological differences shouldn't be construed as inequality. She pointed out that inequality is a political as well as an ethical concept. "Difference is a fact," she said.

"The only thing is," Berman smirked, "the right and left brain, if she knew, are in competition, not cohesion." This latest assertion led to a lengthy discussion about the preponderance of women in the workplace and in politics. And Brothers made her most cogent point by suggesting that the world might be better off with more sensitivity and understanding—qualities associated with the left side of the brain.

The two doctors continued balancing the same points over and over. After a much needed commercial break, a third party weighed in: the British stage and film actress Hermione Gingold. At 84, the "wise, witty, and *liberated*" Gingold could still reprise the outspoken candor she'd demonstrated on the old Paar show and Merv's earlier series.

"I adore men and a lot of men have adored me," Gingold admitted. "And I think we have to put up with them and do our best," she said in her accented monotone, curtailed by applause. Merv asked her if she'd always been the dominant one in her relationships. "Yes," she replied forcefully, "but I've been very careful not to display it." The audience applauded. "After all, it doesn't cost you anything, it makes him happy, so let him *think* he's the dominant one."

Merv asked Gingold about the role of intelligence in a relationship. The aged actress admitted that she'd known very clever men and very stupid men, and had had affairs with both sorts. "Was that this week?" said Merv, relieving some of the tension on the panel and scoring a huge laugh. "I think both sexes have a lot to be said for them," said Gingold. "And if only they'd shut up trying to find out which is better," she said, looking at Berman, who nodded in agreement.

Throughout the entire contentious discussion, which at times sounded like an over-modulated medical symposium, Merv did his best to remain impartial. He made sure both sides were afforded ample airtime, and demonstrated his skill as a moderator. He did, however, step in when Berman berated the talents of certain women in the arts, including Sara Caldwell, a respected opera conductor and impresario. And he reminded Brothers that a woman would not be above "pushing the button" in matters of war.

The entire episode seemed like a throwback to *The Merv Griffin Show* of old. If more of the later entries had embodied this level of engrossing commentary, the ratings might have ensured a longer life for the rapidly declining series.

With the ratings still sagging, a device to boost the show's popularity materialized through the publication of a book, penned by Merv and his producer, Peter Barsocchini, *From Where I Sit: Merv Griffin's Book of People*. Released in 1982, the volume is a compilation of Merv's impressions of "the world's most interesting personalities" who had appeared on his show up to that time. The roster includes Jack Benny; Orson Welles; Richard Burton; Gene Wilder; Henry, Jane and Peter Fonda; Joshua Logan; Jack Paar; Alfred Hitchcock; Francis Ford Coppola; Henry Kissinger; the Kennedys; and Barbara Walters. Though the book isn't merely showbiz fluff, much of it is anecdotal. The most interesting chapter, from a historic perspective, is Merv's recollection of the 1980 edition with conservative journalist William F. Buckley sparring with Judge John Sirica over sentencing issues in the Watergate trials. Despite an extensive tour to several major cities in the United States, the book did little to bolster the program's ratings.

Amid speculation within the industry that the Griffin show was slipping, several unflattering articles began to appear. On December 2, 1982, syndicated columnist Gary Deeb reported that a certain Metromedia exec was "sick and tired" seeing *Merv* in prime time on his company's stations in New York, Los Angeles, and Washington. Deeb also noted, quite accurately, that Griffin's contract with Metromedia stipulated that the show be broadcast in prime time. Despite this, Los Angeles's KTTV-TV, a Metromedia station, was shifting *Merv* from prime time to a late afternoon slot. This seemed to echo the CBS debacle of 13 years earlier. It was also disclosed that Griffin had threatened to sue Metromedia for making the switch.

"That really didn't have an effect on the production of the show," says Peter Barsocchini. "We were under pressure to turn out product. On these types of talk shows, you're just constantly consumed. For Metromedia, the whole nature of prime-time syndication was changing. And the audience that they were going after was not really the audience that would watch a talk show, one that would kick back and watch authors talk about their books. The pace of television was quickening. The very nature of the business was changing, and there was more coming into the market. They wanted to put it on in the afternoon, where it was in the rest of the country. Part of his contract with Metromedia stipulated that it would be on in prime time in New York and L.A., so there was a lot of saber rattling back and forth. Merv retained [attorney] Melvin Belli for a while in San Francisco to talk with Metromedia's lawyers about that issue. And, of course, everything becomes a negotiation. Later, when King World came into the picture, the writing was on the wall—try and do something in which you operate from strength, not from somebody who wants to change the business model."

As the 1980s progressed, it became painfully obvious just how rapidly the climate of daytime talk shows was changing. The daytime variety/talk format, once a surefire moneymaker, was now dying a slow death.

"That's the nature of television," says Barsocchini. "When you watch a show from the golden age of TV, you can see how much of it relates to the time in which it was produced. There are certain things that are *timeless*, that work forever. And then you have stuff from some of the greatest writers of shows like *Sgt. Bilko*. They remain classics. The same is true of *I Love Lucy*. But, again, the pace was different. Commercials were two minutes back then. Some of that had to do with technology, because up until the 1970s, not everyone had television sets with remote controls. People would put on a show and sit down, and they wouldn't want to get up from their chairs to change the channel.

"Someone who foresaw that in a bigger way was Michael Crichton. When he created *E.R.*, he had read studies about the attention span of someone who had a remote control. And he decided to change the story on the screen every minute and 22 seconds. So you'd have a minute and 22 seconds of George Clooney, then you'd cut to Noah Wyle. [Crichton] said, '*We'll* be the remote control for the viewer!'

"The attention span of the viewer has changed, and you need something more, so if they don't like *this* character, they might like *that* character. When networks develop shows today, you'll see more and more of them with deep casts. There's more character development today because people have more choices.

"Look at the pace of talk shows today, as opposed to when Merv was doing them. There was a slower pace when we were doing the Griffin show. We'd have the author's spot, the star's spot, the comic's spot. But the shows went on much longer. There was also a power shift back then. At the time, there were only a few shows. So it was a huge thing to get on *The Merv Griffin Show* or *The Tonight Show*; that's how you were going to sell yourself. And now there are a million venues, so the power shifted from the shows to the stars. It was a totally different time. You could say to somebody like Jane Fonda, 'We want to ask questions about your dad because everyone's interested.' And a publicist would say, 'Okay, okay.' But today, you'd get something like, 'She won't talk about this, and you cannot ask about that.' So it's a different ball game."

The game was far from over. There were still more powerhouse shows awaiting Merv's loyal viewers. One night in 1983, an unknown singer appearing in a New York nightclub utterly bedazzled Merv. In fact, Merv was so impressed by this young woman that he invited her to appear on the show the following night, at the Vivian Beaumont Theater. The singer, who had also worked as a model, turned out to be 21-year-old Whitney Houston.

Houston appeared on the show with Clive Davis, with whom she'd recently signed a contract for Arista Records. If Merv was taken aback by Houston's gifted voice, he was downright flabbergasted when he learned that his "discovery" was the daughter of Cissy Houston, who had appeared on his show, as did her aunt, Dionne Warwick.

"You won't forget her name," said Merv of Houston, who wowed the audience with her performance of "Home," from the musical *The Wiz*.

The year 1983 would hold several remarkable chapters of *The Merv Griffin Show*, including a rare segment with Prince Charles and Princess Diana, their first appearance on an American talk show. The coup of the year, and the one that would generate the most controversy, was Merv's hour-long visit with the 40th President of the United States.

Merv's friendship with Ronald and Nancy Reagan dated back to the time when Merv was a contract player at Warner Bros. In the early '70s, while Reagan was governor of California, he and his wife made several appearances (together and individually) on Merv's CBS and Metromedia shows.

Though Merv had interviewed several American presidents, he'd never done a one-on-one with a *sitting* president. In fact, no other variety/talk show host, up to that time, had invited a sitting president to appear on their show. Therefore, it was a triumph in September, when Griffin announced that he would bring his cameras to the living quarters of the White House for an exclusive chat with the Reagans.

"It was certainly because of his relationship with them that he got to do that interview," says Peter Barsocchini. "Michael Deaver, Reagan's deputy chief of staff, put us through our paces in terms of where to meet. We had to go back to the White House in advance, and meet with Deaver, to tell him what Merv was going to ask because he didn't want Reagan blind-sided. 'How come you're hiding around Iran Contra?' [laughs].

"I remember one of the things that *I* asked Reagan while I was talking to him, because he got to the interview early while Merv was still in makeup. And I'm sitting there waiting, and in walks the President of the United States! 'Hello, Mr. President, Merv will be right with you.' And Reagan was *exactly* as you thought he would be. That's just who he was, and he talked to us. I asked him 'What's the worst part of the job?' And he said the worst part was standing up in front of the press and sounding like an idiot, because you can't disclose what you know for reasons of national security or diplomacy. You can't tell what the *real* story is. As the president, you can't do that even if it makes you look foolish sometimes, and that makes it difficult. And every president says the same thing."

With trouble fermenting in the Middle East, Merv asked Reagan if the weariness following the Vietnam war "hampered" his ability to honor America's commitments around the world. Reagan said people referred to this as "the Vietnam syndrome."

The president admitted that the problem did indeed have an effect, particularly in his dealings with Congress. "First of all," said Reagan, "I'm not about to get us into another Vietnam. But we have to recognize that unlike the old days when you depended on coastal artillery batteries and knew that an enemy would have to come to your shores by ship and invade, in this world today your lines of defense are all around the world. You can't stand by and see the Middle East lost to the western world, or to our own country for that matter."

Reagan continued: "I've always felt that the real immorality of Vietnam was for our government to ask young men to go there, give their lives, for a cause that our government—that never decided we must win. Now I don't know how you ask someone to fight and die for a cause that isn't worth winning."

Merv solemnly brought up the subject of that near-fatal day, March 31, 1981. "After the assassination attempt on your life, Mr. President," said Merv, "did your personal priorities change?" Reagan pondered the question for a few seconds. "Well, no," he said softly. "I can't really say. I think I had them pretty well in line. But, Merv, I had to feel, after and as I learned later how close it was, I had to realize that any time I've got left, I owe to Him." The President looked upward.

On the subject of the nation's economic condition, the president commented that he was pleased ("very much so") with the recovery. During the 1980 presidential campaign, and in the early years of the Reagan administration, the term applied to Reagan's economic policies was "Reaganomics." Merv noted that the term was now rarely heard. "Yeah," the president beamed, "That's because it's working. We never called it Reaganomics. I never used the word. Our critics and opponents, who thought it was the wrong plan, they called it Reaganomics. And they called it that because they were insisting that it wasn't going to work. But now it's working and we have recovery coming, and I've noticed that no one calls it that anymore."

The second half of the interview focused on the First Lady, who shared a few lighthearted anecdotes, including one about the time her skirt accidentally dropped to the ground during a White House meeting.

In its review, *The New York Times* likened the Reagan interview to a baseball game ("Hitting Home Runs with Merv Griffin Pitching," September 28, 1983). The publication noted (not inaccurately) that as the "easy questions" were pitched, the president batted them out of the park.

The Griffin show had provided a Republican president with an hour's worth of airtime in which to expound on foreign policy, nuclear arms, the economic plan, and the burgeoning role of women in politics, without rebuttal from the Democrats.

Not surprisingly, the *Times* stated that the program might arouse envy among the opposing party, noting that president's interview was "Emmy Award-level mastery." Indeed, the eyes and ears of the opposing party were acutely tuned to every eloquent word Reagan uttered. "We make a practice of watching those appearances closely," said Bob Neuman, the spokesman for the Democratic National Committee, in the *Times* review. Neuman also told the publication that there was very little that the Democrats could do with regard to demanding equal time.

"This kind of TV exposure goes with the office," said David R. Gergen, the White House director of communications, noting appreciatively that few incumbents had "maximized it" as effectively as Reagan.

Several political pundits expected a backlash of criticism. "There really wasn't any negative feedback," says Barsocchini. "Most of the reviews would be something like, 'Merv tosses softball to Ronald Reagan. They were pissed, for one thing, that Reagan would give Merv Griffin an hour while he wanted to talk to The New York Times as little as possible. But what was Merv supposed to do? Was he supposed to go in there with [tough questions]? That was not the nature of his show nor was it the nature of that interview. And it really was Merv's belief that you could talk to somebody about their laundry and they would reveal themselves to the astute viewer as to who they are. With politicians in particular, if an interviewer asks hard-edged questions, the politician is so prepared for that and they'll give you a bullshit answer. On the other hand, if you ask something about their kid, they might say something revealing without even intending to. So if you really want to know who that person is, you're not going to get there by grilling someone like Bill Clinton about Monica Lewinsky. But if you talk to them about their mom or something where you can come at it obliquely, you're much more likely to get something revealing."

Like his predecessors who sat in the producer's chair, Peter Barsocchini had to deal with the Secret Service. "I remember one time we were having Nancy Reagan on when Ron was in The White House, and there was a detail of about 18 Secret Service agents. They were there the day before checking things out, and it's always a very complicated thing, moving anybody around from Washington."

18. SYNDICATION—THE GIFT THAT KEEPS ON GIVING

The television syndication industry received a major boost in 1971 when the Federal Communications Commission, under persuasive pressure from broadcasters, enacted the Prime Time Access Rule. The rule, which had been passed the previous year, decreed that the three networks, NBC, CBS and ABC, could no longer dominate the first hour of prime time. That meant that all programs scheduled in the 7:00 to 8 p.m. time block had to be filled by local stations.

Merv was dubious of the ruling when it was made known to him. In April of 1970, he briefly discussed the new law on his show with FCC commissioner Nicholas Johnson. "If I own a local station somewhere," Merv told Johnson, "and you said to me, you've got an hour at night and you can do what you want with it, I'm going to buy some old, cheap reruns, put them on, and sell them to local sponsors." Johnson explained to his somewhat startled host that that wouldn't be the case. Because the programs had to be "newly made," old, cheap reruns would be strictly prohibited, from seven to eight o'clock, on all stations affiliated with networks. The ruling went so far as to decree that the networks couldn't even broadcast the *news* during the first hour of prime time.

Ironically, it was Don McGannon, president of Group W Productions, who had effectively lobbied for this ruling. McGannon's position was understandable; his company was an industry leader in the production of first-run syndicated programs. McGannon argued that, for years, the three major networks had monopolized four hours of prime time viewing each evening, much to the detriment of independent producers and syndication companies. Since few local stations had the time or budget to produce their own shows, this change in the law would result in a bonanza for first-run syndication units such as Group W/Westinghouse.

Though Merv didn't realize it in 1970, the ruling would result in yet another golden nugget for his expanding production enterprises at the end of the decade and beyond.

In January 1979, Griffin Productions (later Merv Griffin Enterprises) premiered *Dance Fever*, a weekly half-hour musical variety series that cashed in on the then-current disco craze. Its format, which included young couples competing for cash prizes, fit perfectly into the early evening time slots requiring "newly made" shows. Though Merv took credit as creator and executive producer, he placed the writing chores in the capable hands of Tony Garofalo. With distribution through 20th Century-Fox Television, *Fever* would prove financially profitable throughout its eight year run in the syndicated market.

Griffin would later enter into association with King World Productions, one of the most successful syndication outfits in the history of television. Interestingly, King World's initial success wasn't attributable to a made-for-television property, but rather a series of theatrically released movie shorts. In the mid-1950s, King acquired the rights to *The Little Rascals*, which dated back to the 1920s and '30s. From the successful re-distribution of these vintage ten and 20-minute film comedies, King World built an empire.

In 1983, Griffin and King World successfully launched a syndicated reboot of *Wheel of Fortune,* hosted by former Los Angeles weatherman Pat Sajak. The following year, *Jeopardy!* would re-emerge, with Alex Trebek presiding as host. In most markets, the two programs aired back-to-back, from 7:00 to 8 p.m. It was also in 1983 that King World had acquired syndication rights to *The Merv Griffin Show*. Ironically, as the two venerable game shows soared on the rating charts, *The Merv Griffin Show* continued its steady decline.

"King World wanted those game shows," says Peter Barsocchini. "That's what they knew how to do. In order to get the whole package that they ultimately wanted, *The Merv Griffin Show* was bolted into the deal because, at that time, Metromedia was evolving into something else. And the Griffin show really didn't fit into what Metromedia was becoming. King World was the hottest syndicator in the business, because of *Wheel of Fortune*. So the business side of Merv sought to leverage their desire for the game shows so he could get more life out of the Griffin show. He played his business cards there because, again, the landscape was changing. The demographics were changing. The young women who were watching Phil Donahue in the eighties didn't grow up watching Merv Griffin in the sixties. Nor Dinah, or Mike Douglas, or John Davidson, Douglas's successor."

Ironically, it seemed as though every time an unfavorable report was published about bad ratings for the Griffin show, the Griffin *empire* prospered. In January 1984, Merv Griffin Productions had reportedly set a record, as evidenced by statements from the company's president, Murray Schwartz. According to Schwartz, the company was expected to have a record $20,000,000 in production during the coming year. He told *Variety* that the company expected to hit a gross of "around $70,000,000 for 1984–85," and would turn out "13 hours of programming weekly."

In October 1985, New York columnist Cindy Adams reported that Merv had again expanded his already substantial real estate holdings by acquiring the entire corner of Sunset Boulevard and Vine Street in the heart of Hollywood. His television facilities, including the TAV Celebrity Theater, also dominated the same four-acre spread.

In his third and final memoir, *Making the Good Life Last*, Griffin recalls being asked who, among his thousands of guests, was the most interesting. At first, he toys with the reader, giving every indication that his answer will be noncommittal. It's a ridiculous question, he asserts, since the pope and bin Laden could both qualify as "interesting." A few sentences later, he cites Orson Welles as the most interesting person who sat on his couch.

Welles was no stranger to the talk show circuit. By the mid 1970s, he had logged an impressive number of appearances on most of the major variety/talk and interview programs, including *The David Frost Show*, *The Dick Cavett Show*, and Carson's *Tonight Show*. Welles was among the many international figures Merv had chatted with on film, albeit briefly, during a 1965 European jaunt. The "boy genius" would sub-host for Merv in 1982, but his first full-fledged interview on the Griffin Show had taken place in 1976.

"When Welles did Merv's show that first time," recalls Barsocchini, "he didn't want to go down memory lane." That edict came as a big letdown not only to Griffin, but also his senior talent coordinator, Paul Solomon, who spent weeks unearthing old reviews and compiling multiple photographs and film clips. As it turned out, not one bit of this priceless material would be used. It didn't matter, because Welles was captivating enough to pull off the appearance without any nostalgic schmaltz. Additionally, the value of his name, in terms of publicity, would ensure future visits to the program.

In March 1979, as the Beverly Hills Chamber of Commerce bestowed the annual Will Rogers Memorial Award on Griffin, Welles was on hand for the tribute. The event, which took place at the Beverly Hilton Hotel, marked the first time the award had been given to a talk-show host.

"Welles, a frequent guest on the Griffin show but a rare one at testimonials," said *Variety*, "gave the rites a touch of class—and thoughtfulness and pertinence—not commonly encountered on the roast beef circuit." During the proceedings, Welles gave Griffin high marks for his ability to listen without endlessly trying to be funny ("a weakness in some of Merv's competition"), for being amused as well as amusing, and for being "intellectually concerned."

Much of the praise lavished on Merv that night could have easily been applied to Welles. Born in Kenosha, Wisconsin on May 6, 1915, George Orson Welles was a child prodigy destined for phenomenal success in theater, radio, and film—all by the time he was 25.

His stage triumphs included a production of Shakespeare's *Twelfth Night* (which won first prize in a competition at the Chicago World's Fair in 1933) and an all-black version of *Macbeth* in 1936. Then, in 1938, Welles's name would become a household word. On Halloween of that year, he adapted the H. G. Wells (no relation) classic *The War of the Worlds* for his "Mercury Theatre" radio program on CBS. Presented as an authentic-sounding news bulletin, the broadcast shocked tens of thousands of unwary listeners into believing that Martians were invading New Jersey!

In 1941, Welles would solidify his place in cinema history with the release of *Citizen Kane,* a production he co-wrote (with Herman J. Mankiewicz), produced, directed, and starred in. Hailed as a stylistic masterpiece, *Kane* aroused the ire of the powerful newspaper baron William Randolph Hearst, whose life story had obviously been the inspiration for Welles' largely unflattering portrait. Though praised as one of the most influential movies ever made, *Citizen Kane* was not a commercial success. The film garnered nine Oscar nominations but won only one award, for best screenplay. Many believed Hearst had campaigned vigorously to derail the film in any way possible, including having it panned, if not ignored, by the press. As a result, Welles lost much of his clout with RKO Radio Pictures, the studio that had financed and released the picture. Over time, the director's career would be ravaged by false rumors and ongoing political pressure.

None of Welles' subsequent movies, including *The Magnificent Ambersons* (1942), *Journey Into Fear* (1943), *The Stranger* (1946), and *The Lady from Shanghai* (1947), was considered "box office." Nevertheless, he would continue to make films in the United States and abroad, including the well-received *Othello* (1952). Even so, many in Hollywood believed that Welles's best years were behind him. He would prove them wrong by writing, producing, directing, and co-starring in *Touch of Evil* (1958), the *tour de force* that reestablished his genius. Many critics and film historians still regard the film as the last true *film noir* classic of the "golden era." Though Welles made movies during the 1960s and into the '70s, *Citizen Kane* is the title that immediately comes to mind whenever his name is mentioned. Modern filmmakers remain influenced by his directorial style, marked by keen focus on action as well as dialogue.

Long before he reached old age, Welles had been the survivor of battles with studio executives and media tycoons; a failed marriage to the preeminent sex goddess of the 1940s: Rita Hayworth; and a series of health problems stemming from his obesity.

"He was an interesting cat," says Peter Barsocchini of the veteran auteur.

Welles and Barsocchini dined together at Ma Maison in Los Angeles, where the topic of discussion was one for which they shared equal passion—food. "You could ask him anything on the subject and he'd have something interesting to say," says Barsocchini. "On this particular occasion, he was talking about the difference between eating and dining, and how *dining* was rapidly becoming a lost art."

High on Griffin's list of interview topics was Welles's marriage to Hayworth. The couple married in 1943, had one child (a daughter) and remained together until 1947. It was after their divorce that Welles directed and starred with Hayworth in *The Lady from Shanghai.* By the 1970s, Hayworth's heyday had long since ended. She had been stricken with a disease that most people had never heard about.

"It was very difficult for him to talk about Rita Hayworth because, at the time, not much was known about dementia and Alzheimer's," explains Barsocchini. "People didn't know that *that* was Rita Hayworth's affliction at the end of her life. So Orson didn't want to get into those areas of discussion. Of course, if we knew then what we know now, things would have turned out differently."

On October 9, 1985, Welles arrived at TAV studios, via the chauffeured limo that the show had provided, for his long-anticipated appearance with Merv. He was pale, haggard looking, and walking with a cane. "Orson Welles was obese, there was no question about it," Barsocchini says of the six feet-two inches tall, 300-pound filmmaker. "And he seemed to be perspiring with a kind of clammy thing going on. His breath seemed to be short and he just didn't look well. But he did the show and got through it."

Shortly before the cameras rolled, Welles told Merv that he felt "expansive" and would talk about anything. *Anything.*

Looking every one of his 70 years, Welles was now willing to take that dreaded stroll down memory lane. Sharing the panel with him would be his biographer, Barbara Leaming, whose book, *Orson Welles: A Biography,* had recently been published. The staff retrieved the mountain of research that had been tucked away since 1976.

On the air, Welles immediately commented on Merv's svelte appearance. "You've lost that 20 pounds that you lost last year!" he said wistfully.

Then it was time to get down to business. "I'm not essentially a happy person, but I have all kinds of joy," offered Welles.

Of Rita Hayworth, Welles recalled her as "one of the dearest, sweetest women that ever lived."

Merv mentioned Hayworth's disappointing appearance on his CBS show, before she had been diagnosed with Alzheimer's. Airing on July 12, 1971, "A Tribute to Rita Hayworth" didn't hold much in the way of an interview. The most probing question Merv got to ask was: "Did you find Orson Welles overwhelming?" The most revealing answer Hayworth gave was: "No, but I think he found *me* overwhelming!"

Griffin recalled that when he and Hayworth vocalized "Let's Take an Old-Fashioned Walk Together," several of his staffers thought the actress was drunk.

"I never believed that she was a drunkard," said Welles, "I didn't know about Alzheimer's disease, but I believed that something *like* that was wrong with her. When that began to happen, I wasn't seeing her, but I was hearing these stories and it was foreign to her nature. It was so unlike her."

Welles said that he had been with Hayworth longer than any of the other men in her life. Intrigued, Merv asked if Hayworth, whose real name was Rita Cansino, had ever exhibited a "Latin temper." Welles said that his former wife had never expressed anger towards *him*, but would "throw stuff around the house" whenever the name Harry Cohn was mentioned. Cohn, the tyrannical head of Columbia Pictures, had had a contentious relationship with Hayworth during her years under contract to that studio.

On May 14, 1987, Rita Hayworth died of Alzheimer's disease.

Welles also recalled another goddess of the golden era, Marlene Dietrich, with whom he'd once done a magic act. "She was the most loyal friend that anyone could ever ask for," said Welles. "Her professionalism was impeccable."

Had *Citizen Kane* been a boon or a detriment to Welles's career? "It was a great piece of luck," he said. "It was good because people liked it. "If they *hadn't* like it, it would have been bad." That was the extent of the great man's discourse about his best-remembered film.

Welles and Barbara Leaming left the TAV studios happy. Their segment together had gone well. Hours later, however, Welles would suffer a fatal heart attack at his home.

"Orson was one that we regarded as part of the family of the show," Barsocchini remembers. "And his death was a loss to many.

He really liked Merv, because he knew Merv wasn't going to go for the jugular and talk about the scandals of his life. Or ask questions like, 'Do you feel like a failure because your biggest success occurred when you were 25?' So he was comfortable with Merv. And the two of them could share references. They could discuss movies and things that a 19-year-old wouldn't know what Orson was talking about. But Merv, of course, *did*, and it was a good venue for Orson."

In retrospect, it can be argued that the great filmmaker's interview with Griffin was innocuous and unrevealing. Nevertheless, in August of 2013, the final appearance of Welles ranked number 46 on *TV Guide's* "60 Greatest Talk Show Moments." Two other Griffin shows also made the list: Captain Mitsuo Fuchida's 1965 interview ranked number 25, while Whitney Houston's debut came in at number 41.

Merv's staff began to pay closer attention to numbers and statistics. On October 24, 1985, the show began with its off-screen announcer, Carol Bilger, trumpeting the lineup of guests: Robert Wagner, John Standing, and eight-year-old Maia Brewton. The three actors were there solely to promote their new weekly series called *Lime Street*. Merv interviewed them separately. After a commercial break, Merv casually mentioned that he had a surprise for Wagner. "Before I let Bob go," said Merv, "I have an important announcement to make—important to me."

With the use of computers, it was now easier to keep track of the number of guests that had appeared on the program, dating all the way back to day one. "The staff has been keeping account for the last few months, right up until today," Merv smiled. "And it turns out that the exact 25,000th guest on *The Merv Griffin Show* just happens to be this popular star, Mr. Robert Wagner." As a special surprise, the staff also booked Shelley Berman—Merv's first guest on his October 1, 1962 debut. Berman, who hadn't been announced at the start of the program, added just the right touch of nostalgia to the panel. Merv asked him if he remembered anything about that first historic episode. "If I did," Berman joked, "I don't think I would have come back."

No film or video clips were available from that first show, and no one bothered to dig up any vintage still photographs for the occasion. Merv was never one to focus too much on the past; he felt it was better to relish magic moments connected to the present. Sipping champagne, the proud host and his special guests gathered at center stage, behind a row of multicolored cakes that spelled out 25,000. Everyone in the studio audience was treated to a sampling of the colorful sweets. After the taping, a private party was held for the staff and various personalities who had appeared regularly on the program through the years. The magnitude of 25,000 interviews seemed overwhelming, even to a seasoned talker like Merv Griffin. "It's a lot of lip movement," he said wryly. Generating publicity for the show had always been a top priority to Merv. His staff saw to it that photos of the celebration were widely circulated to newspapers and periodicals.

There was plenty of lip movement on an edition devoted to the cast of a recently launched, and soon-to-be adored, TV series called *The Golden Girls*. On November 5, 1985, Merv hosted Betty White (one of his favorite guests), Bea Arthur, Rue McClanahan, and Estelle Getty. Nowhere is Merv's devilishness more evident than in his interviews with the "girls." Rather than focusing on the new show, he decided to grill the women about their love lives.

"Do you enjoy the company of men your own age?" Merv asked Betty. "Do you prefer younger, older?" he continued, leaning in closer. Betty said that from a young age, she'd always preferred "mature men." With that, Merv planted a row of passionate kisses on her arm. The audience howled.

Merv found Bea Arthur to be a tougher cookie. "Tell the truth," he whispered to the white-haired actress, "have you been picked up recently?" "You mean by the network?" she answered, feigning innocence. Bea finally admitted that she'd been picked up recently, in Toronto. Then, after pondering the question, she gave Merv her famous "Maude" look of exasperation. "Are you bringing up an age thing, Merv? Because if you are, I'm going to *hit* you." She was kidding, of course, but her mildly outraged response resonated well with the audience. Always the consummate pro, Bea Arthur recognized the importance of making sparks fly for good talk-show camaraderie.

The "Golden Girls" segment would become one of Merv's most popular, and most requested, entries. The positive audience reaction to it may have inspired Merv's one-hour special, *Secrets Women Never Share* (1987), which was also well received.

Merv's final season on the air (1985–86) would have its share of ups and downs. One of the "downs" involved unfavorable coverage in the pages of *TV Guide*, a weekly favorite that had featured him on its cover several times in the past. Now the publication was raising a few eyebrows with an article titled "When He Starts Rubbing His Nose with His Knuckles, Watch Out!" (November 23, 1985). It characterized Merv as a tough, no-nonsense, and, at times, abusive boss.

"When *TV Guide* did that story about him, they talked to me," recalls Peter Barsocchini. "They asked, 'How do you define Merv Griffin?' And I told them that Merv's the kind of person that, if you lived in a town somewhere, and there was a nuclear holocaust, you'd want Merv Griffin in that town. Because when its time to rebuild, he's the guy who could figure out a way to get things going again.

"The truth is, like anyone of accomplishment, Merv could get pissed off at people and let them know it. If he felt you weren't carrying your weight, he'd get pissed off. He was writing the checks. Much of being a celebrity with the press is like Charlie Brown and Lucy and the football. They get burned sometimes. There's plenty of that. That's why today you see the big stories with nine layers of publicists between them [the celebrities] and the media. Some stars know how to handle it. George Clooney knows how to manage it; he knows the game. But some get burned a few times. Every celebrity has their story about a journalist who burned them. And you can get somebody pretty pissed off."

Griffin, of course, was more than mildly annoyed by the piece in *TV Guide*. "But that goes with the territory," concludes Peter Barsocchini. "If there was somebody who had rubbed him the wrong way, and he didn't like him or her, they'd get their five minutes to knock Merv down a peg."

In one of the more neutral portions of the article, Griffin offered a then-and-now assessment of topics relevant to the talk show landscape. "In the '60s, there were so many controversial issues," he said. "Now what is there? Nuclear war? I am against it. The contras in Nicaragua? Who cares?"

By the mid-1980s, Merv Griffin Enterprises, a company that employed some 800 people, was churning out 15 ½ hours of national TV programming per week. The shows that were masterminded by Griffin, *Jeopardy!*, *Wheel of Fortune*, and *Dance Fever*, were well established hits lined with gold. The same, however, could no longer be said of *The Merv Griffin Show*.

"What If They Gave a Talk Show and Nobody Listened?" asked the *New York Daily News* in its February 23, 1986 edition. The paper reported that WNEW-TV (Channel 5) had canceled the Griffin show, and would be airing the program that night for the last time.

The cancellation meant that Merv would no longer have an outlet in New York City. *The Merv Griffin Show* had been a solid fixture on Channel 5 for years, in the mid-to-late '60s, and from 1972 forward, after the demise of Merv's CBS series. Now Griffin had suffered another defeat, resulting in the loss of the nation's largest and most influential market.

The cancellation was sadly ironic. It was New York's Channel 5 that had rescued the show from possible cancellation when it was underperforming in 1966. Various media sources speculated that the latest crisis to hit the series was attributable to the impending $2 billion takeover of Metromedia by Rupert Murdoch. (Channel 5, as noted earlier, was a Metromedia-owned station.) Metromedia had sold its holdings, including its production subsidiaries, to Murdoch's 20th Century-Fox organization. Most or all of the stations in the group dropped Griffin in favor of movies in the Fox library.

A spokesperson for Channel 5 dispelled the "takeover" theory, claiming it was simply time for a change. Nevertheless, the ratings told the story succinctly. When the station aired *The Muppet Movie* (1979), in the Friday evening slot usually occupied by Griffin, the viewing audience doubled. The handwriting was on the wall.

The situation was disconcerting. Griffin had replaced movies on CBS in 1969. Two-and-a-half years later, CBS replaced Griffin with movies. More than a decade later, after perfecting a formula that had proven bankable, Griffin's biggest market was dumping him—for movies. This latest station defection coincided with a regrettable shift in audience tastes. Merv's intelligent, easygoing style, once praised by the critics, was now being described as "bland," "kissy-faced" and "obsequious." One reviewer went so far as to describe him as "boot-licking."

The most positive aspect of the *Daily News* piece came as no surprise to those familiar with Merv's business acumen. It concluded with a blurb regarding rumors that the Coca-Cola Company was about to acquire Griffin's production company for a then-astounding $250 million. "With that amount of money," said one observer, "one could buy a lot of coconuts." As a man with the Midas touch, Merv had worn many hats through the years, juggling his time between business meetings and the rigors of hosting the syndicated show, which he loved.

"We were well aware that the numbers for the show had been declining," recalls Peter Barsocchini. "You looked around and saw the style of talk shows, and knew that the format of the daytime variety talk show wasn't going to exist anymore. Oprah was on the ascent; Phil Donahue was on the ascent. We knew it was coming. You could see it in the demographics, the ratings, and where the ad dollars were going. It was very much like today, where things are changing even faster. In entertainment, distribution is destiny and those companies were looking for a different business model for the demographics that they wanted. And it was time. From 1983 to '86, you could see how television was changing. It was costing more money to produce *The Merv Griffin Show* than it did to produce Phil Donahue or Oprah Winfrey, so it became a numbers thing. The idea that someone would be sitting home watching the show had changed, too, because more people now had to go to work. In many families, both parents were out working and it was a different time."

Merv Griffin had saved the show from imminent cancellation before. Could Griffin, a man who was at his apex when he had a problem to solve, improvise yet another comeback? Could he keep the show alive?

The *New York Daily News* would answer those questions on March 31, 1986: "There's New Life for Merv Griffin." Apparently, there was enough of an uproar from Griffin loyalists to prompt WOR-TV,

Channel 9, to salvage the ailing program. Though Channel 9 was headquartered in Secaucus, New Jersey, the station served the New York metropolitan area. The volume of complaint letters protesting Merv's departure from the airwaves was reminiscent of the NBC cancellation in 1963.

As a result, *The Merv Griffin Show* was slated to join the Channel 9 lineup as of April 21, 1986. Some creative juggling was in order. To make room for Griffin, the station had to shift two of its most popular game shows, *Tic Tac Dough* and *The Joker's Wild*, into later time slots.

Through all this maneuvering, Griffin had reached a parting of the ways with his distributor, King World Productions, Inc., and its barter division Camelot Entertainment Sales. During its headstrong years in syndication, through Metromedia Producers Corporation, the Griffin show had been seen on roughly 130 stations. By 1986, however, that number had dipped below 50. Consequently, King World dropped *The Merv Griffin Show*, but retained distribution rights to *Jeopardy!* and *Wheel*. The closing credits of the *Merv Griffin Shows* produced in 1986, would bear the corporate logo of its new, and final, distributor—Merv Griffin Enterprises.

Throughout the spring of 1986, the press focused largely on the Griffin/Coca-Cola deal. By this time, Merv Griffin Enterprises held among its assets: Trans America Video ("TAV"), the facility at which the Griffin show was produced; a string of radio stations; a close-circuit TV company for racetracks; and Vine Street Publishing, a corporate entity set up for the purpose of handling the music rights to songs Griffin had composed for his various productions. One of these, "Think" (the snappy little tune played on *Jeopardy!* as contestants write their answers) earned tens of millions over the years. Understandably, Merv liked to keep those hefty royalties "in the family."

There is a time-honored axiom in show business that it's better to leave the audience wanting more. After showcasing more than 25,000 guests, over a period of 23 years, it seemed that it might be time for Merv to hang up his microphone.

Barsocchini recalls several chats he'd had with his boss on the subject. "On several occasions," says the former producer, "Merv had always said, 'If I get up in the morning and I'm not dying to do the show, that's when I'll stop doing it.'"

Merv was no longer dying to do it. The big question was: Could Merv Griffin, the eager beaver who couldn't wait to get to the studio each day, settle into retirement—at least from the show? "Yes," says Barsocchini. "I would say he was done with doing his talk show by that time. He had other interests. But he was a little nervous about what comes next because he was so used to doing that [show] every day. Merv knew, at a business level, that that format was done."

In August 1986, Griffin's company released a press statement confirming that the final installment of *The Merv Griffin Show* would be taped at the end of that month. The Griffin finale would be seen on the 40 stations that were still carrying it. By contrast, Merv's other proud achievements, *Jeopardy!* and *Wheel of Fortune,* continued to be widely heralded as the most successful shows in first-run syndication.

On September 5, 1986, the last edition of the *The Merv Griffin Show* was aired with a minimum of publicity and a maximum of videotaped highlights. It was the 3,780th installment of the series since Merv had joined Metromedia in 1972. There was no studio audience. Merv sat alone in the middle of the theatre, with dozens of reporters in the aisles snapping copious photographs of him. "It was a somber day for him," recalls Barsocchini. "And it was understandable because he had been doing that show, basically, since 1962, in various formats. And that was a long, long run."

Like Steve Allen had done on his Westinghouse finale, Merv would play to an empty house, introducing choice video clips between reminiscences. An air of nostalgia permeated the studio as Merv presented some of show's funniest moments: Richard Pryor and Jerry Lewis spitting water on the host, and each other; Jack E. Leonard getting pelted with pillows by an irate Totie Fields (he had insulted her weight); a nervous Don Rickles trying to stay on the good side of Mr. T.; and the famous clip in which Jack Benny's deadpan stare put an instantly-humbled Griffin in his place.

The host retreated to his glass-top desk on the stage. "Well, this is the last time for me in this familiar setting," offered Merv, cueing up clips of the controversial newsmakers of the seventies: Gloria Steinem, Gore Vidal, and Spiro Agnew among them. Then, from the control room, he introduced what he considered to be the "privileged interviews" with the political heavyweights: Richard Nixon, Bobby Kennedy, Gerald Ford, Jimmy Carter, and Ronald Reagan.

There was a special montage dedicated to Arthur Treacher. The highlights included Merv and Treacher gleefully indulging in some "dramatic" readings (with comedic twists, of course) and a wonderful segment in which the veteran actor joined Hermione Gingold in a light performance of "I'm Glad We're Not Young Anymore."

During the final third of the program, Merv paid tribute to Dick Carson: "The best director I could ever steal from his brother." Then he acknowledged his assistant director, Kevin McCarthy who, according to Merv, probably had the best collection of outtakes of stars saying and doing things they shouldn't have. "And if after today, you sell them," Merv jokingly told McCarthy, "I get 50 percent!"

As the show went to its final commercial break, Mort Lindsey played "There Will Never Be Another You," a perfect choice for the last song he would play on the air. Merv spent his final moments of the hour at the bandstand, acknowledging Mort, who had been with him since 1965.

Finally, he said: "For the first time now, I can tell you we *won't* be right back after this message." Then he looked into the lens and said: "*Th-th-that's all folks!*" echoing Porky Pig's famous closing line. The credits crawled up the screen one last time, and *The Merv Griffin Show* became part of television history. After the taping, the star retreated to the privacy of his office where he sat alone in a contemplative mood. His fans wouldn't have to wait very long to see him back on the tube. Merv would soon be chatting on another venerable talk show—the one hosted by the man who had been his professional rival for the past two decades.

19. LIFE AFTER THE MERV GRIFFIN SHOW

Merv Griffin hadn't been on *The Tonight Show* since his last stint as guest host in 1962. On September 5, 1986, Merv returned to the program—as a guest. "You win," he said to Johnny Carson, several hours after the final edition of *The Merv Griffin Show* had been broadcast. The bemused Carson did not hear (or pretended not to hear) what Merv had said. "I say, you *win*," Merv repeated, in the most facetious way possible. Now that the two gray-haired hosts didn't have to compete for guests or ratings, they could attempt to outshine each other in the laugh department.

Carson got the ball rolling by calling attention to Merv's recent weight gain. Merv made jokes about Carson's perceived laziness. Carson noted that certain aspects of his career paralleled Merv's, particularly with regard to their on-air longevity. With that, devilish Merv deduced that they would be equal in years—*if* Carson's vacation time were factored into the equation! The audience howled, and the duel of ad-libs continued.

The King of Late Night was between marriages at the time. He would marry his fourth and final wife, Alexis Maas, in 1987. Merv's constant companion at the time was Eva Gabor. Though Carson had always been notoriously reticent to discuss anyone's marital status, he hit Merv with: "When are you and Eva getting married?" Unfazed, Merv shot back: "When are you and Alexis getting married?" Carson changed the subject.

The nostalgic clip of Merv asking Jack Benny if he remembered his first laugh was shown. The 30-second vignette was the catalyst for the two hosts to share memories of the late comedian and other greats that appeared on their respective shows. The atmosphere was a far cry from 1962, when Carson's producer had Merv's name needlessly bleeped from the soundtrack.

Merv's business acumen was duly noted. He acknowledged the recent sale of Merv Griffin Enterprises to Coca-Cola. The soft drink giant was diversifying into multiple entertainment ventures and had recently acquired Columbia Pictures, as well as TV producer Norman Lear's Embassy Pictures. The usually calm and collected Griffin had been in a pensive mood as he awaited that enormous bundle of cash to be wired into his account. As a result of this lucrative deal, Griffin would be included on the *Forbes 400* list as one of the wealthiest people in show business.

Griffin would make another appearance with Carson in 1989, and a final one in 1990. Assessing these *Tonight Show* appearances today, one wonders if Merv harbored a trace of resentment that he didn't inherit the program back in 1962. "It played out as it should have played out," says Peter Barsocchini. "Johnny had that edge that worked so well in late night. And, in the end, everybody won."

There could never be any dispute that Merv was the winner in the financial arena. Though Merv no longer owned *Jeopardy!* and *Wheel of Fortune*, his name would continue to appear in the closing credits of both shows as creator (even though he frequently credited his ex-wife, Julann, with the creation of *Jeopardy!*). He also continued to profit handsomely from the musical themes he'd composed for both shows. He took great delight in noting that "Think Music," the brief musical interlude used on *Jeopardy!*, had earned millions in royalties by the mid-1980s.

"He retained a position as creator and executive producer of both shows," notes Kevin Sasaki. "And he continued to generate royalties from the use of the music he had written for them. It was funny, because you'd always hear those themes, especially the one from *Jeopardy!* We were at Trader Vic's one night and someone was humming it. Merv looked at me, laughed, and patted his wallet!"

On the last edition of *The Merv Griffin Show*, Merv announced the development of a new variety program, *The Cocoanut Ballroom*, a nostalgic throwback to the big-band era. The proposed series would also serve as a showcase for a singing group called the Merv-Tones. A pilot episode was produced, but it never sold. It didn't matter. Merv had enough on his plate with highly lucrative enterprises that included hotel ownership, racehorses, radio stations, vineyards, and extensive real estate holdings. He would occasionally squeeze in a network project, such as *Secrets Women Never Share*

(1987) and several *Merv Griffin's New Year's Eve Specials,* the first of which appeared in 1990.

In 1988, Merv became interested in gaming and sought to invest in Resorts International, the company that owned Resorts Hotel and Casino in Atlantic City, and Paradise Island in the Bahamas. At the time, Donald Trump held the controlling percentage of stock. The press took great delight in reporting all the details of the takeover process that ensued between the retired talk-show host and the billionaire real estate developer. "Merv did what he had to do and he just loved the great press reviews he got," says Sasaki.

"He's the Man of the Moment," blared the front-page headline of the *Philadelphia Inquirer* on November 17, 1988. The paper reported that some 500 enthusiastic admirers showed up to greet Griffin, the proud new owner of Resorts Hotel and Casino. It took a team of police officers to clear a path for Merv and Eva Gabor to "squeeze" their way into the hotel. This was a major moment for a former boy singer who once crooned at the nearby Steel Pier with the Freddy Martin Orchestra. Thirty-nine years later, he was photographed holding the keys to one of the most venerable landmarks on the boardwalk.

"The Resorts deal not only encompassed Resorts International in Atlantic City, but also Paradise Island," says Sasaki. "That was part of the deal. That's how Merv got involved in the Bahamas. And he was going to have fun with that as well. We created an annual event down there called The Star Sports Spectacular. We'd bring down sports stars and movie stars to play tennis and golf for a weekend. And the place got a lot of press. All the TV shows would go there. We'd fly in *Entertainment Tonight* and they would cover the weekend. Merv had a ball with that. The properties included a casino/hotel; a more exclusive, upscale property called the Ocean Club; and another with a big tower that was part of Paradise Island Resort. Merv also had a private home there. And of course, he had a place in Beverly Hills and a home in Carmel Valley. When he really got into the millions, he built a huge ranch in La Quinta, located a little east of Palm Springs. He liked that area because it was less developed. If you look at what he created there, you'd see no reason to ever want to leave. It included a racetrack, and it was

near a private airstrip only a few minutes away from his house, and
he could fly in and out on his private jet. When you traveled with
Merv, you flew on his jet!

"He got involved locally as he felt it was important; he supported
the La Quinta Arts Foundation, which was a big deal for him. He
served as chairman of their board, or president. He'd host parties
and be present at their annual arts festival. He'd bring his band
and perform that night, under a tent. Jack Sheldon came out and
performed with him. Mort and Judy Lindsey would also be part of
that crowd. Merv had his little group that would keep close to him."

Venues such as the Cocoanut Ballroom and Griff's Restaurant
were popular components of the Beverly Hilton Hotel, which
Griffin had purchased in late 1987.

"He would have lunch by the pool almost every day," says Sasaki.
"I think he loved being in the hotel. And of course, the Beverly
Hilton was sort of a main *Californiaesque* hotel with a beautiful
pool. Sitting out there, especially when the weather was good, was
just a wonderful place to be. Merv would have everyone there, producers, friends like Nancy Reagan, they would all come and meet
him at the pool."

Griffin and Nancy Reagan shared the same birthday, July 6. "On
their birthday, she would join him there, and they would have a
little birthday lunch. It was nice for him because people got to
gawk a little."

Sasaki remembers how his boss appreciated simple things. "I
gave him a money clip one year," Sasaki recalls. "Now with Merv,
there was absolutely nothing he needed—*ever*. But on the inscrip-
tion, I put, 'Merv Griffin, or M.G., our nation's innkeeper.' He
thought that was just wonderful. And that's how I saw him. He
was the greatest hotelier you could have, because of his hands-on
nature and his love for people. One of his most famous lines was,
'I actually go and put the chocolates on people's pillows.' I think
he genuinely loved speaking to people. And people would always
come up to his table whenever they'd see him. For being who he
was, he made himself fairly visible at the hotel. He would talk to
people, and he usually enjoyed those conversations unless, of course,
he had something that was pressing. He took the time to chat with

people and he loved that interaction, which made him a great hotel owner. And people respond to that type of interaction.

"I think one of the things that made him successful was his curiosity about *everything*. If he was interested in a certain business, or an issue, he had the wherewithal to investigate and possibly get himself involved. It was always interesting to attend a meeting with him because you never knew what he was going to throw out on the table. And that wasn't the Merv who had done a five-times-a-week talk show. I think in doing that talk show, what made him a wonderful host was his curiosity about people and talking to them about everything.

"Merv had a very youthful outlook on everything, and you never felt like you were with an ancient person. That's what had made him successful; he tried to keep up on everything. He was a big news junkie. He loved to have the news on all the time to keep up on things. As an entrepreneur, he had to promote his businesses. He was always promoting his hotel. I remember booking him on the Jay Leno *Tonight Show* because there was a big event at the Beverly Hilton that he needed to talk about. Jay, of course, was excited to have *Merv Griffin* on his show. They got to chatting and laughing because Merv loved to banter. And he didn't even get a chance to promote what he had gone on there for! By the time the interview was over, Merv hadn't said a word about it. Commercial break and it was 'Thank you, Merv, for being here!' When Merv left, he said, 'God, I didn't even promote the event.' He was kicking himself. But he had gotten caught up in a funny repartee, which was entertaining, but didn't serve the original purpose. But that was Merv. He didn't have it in him to go there just to promote something. Through the years, Merv did everybody's show and they loved him. He was really a well-liked man, so he traveled through circles very easily."

Though he no longer hosted a daily talk show, Griffin continued to nurture new talent. Kevin Sasaki remembers Griffin's best "discovery" of the 1990s. "Merv came to me one day and said, 'You're going to meet a young fellow, and he is energy personified.' I worked on the campaign that would introduce the world to Ryan Seacrest," Sasaki recalls. "Merv had developed a game show for young people called *Click*. He told me, 'You're going to do a number on this guy because he is going to be a big star.' And I said, 'Okay!'

"We went to the studio where they were taping *Click*, and out runs this skinny blond guy named Ryan. Merv said, 'The two of you need to know each other because Kevin is going to promote you.' And so we started where one would start, by doing little things. We got him photographed for Old Navy, and put a promotion together for that; and we got him some interviews."

Click would remain popular in syndication from September 1997 to September 1999. Despite its relatively short run, "it got Ryan to the next step up, and the rest is history," says Sasaki. "I remember one thing he said to Ryan: 'It's fine to be a host on television, but the trick and the key is to *own* it. Own your own productions.' And that was a great piece of advice to impart."

In 1995, Merv Griffin was diagnosed with prostate cancer. "There was a part of him that didn't want to address certain things," says Kevin Sasaki. "And I think that when he first discovered that he had something, he really didn't want to do anything. And if I recall correctly, he got on his yacht and went on a cruise. In some ways, he just wanted to get away and not address the problem, not think about it, and just have some time to himself."

In a December 1995 appearance on CNN's *Larry King Live*, Griffin spoke openly about his condition. Prior to that, he had not disclosed his condition to the press.

Sasaki: "He had given an interview to the *National Enquirer* because, as he said, 'I don't want them to come out with a story that I'm dying. What I'd rather do is actually speak to them, so that not if, but *when* the story comes out, it will actually be true.' And that was very smart on his part. And he was fine for a long time. He used to joke about the radiation, and the 'zapping.' It was a minimal sort of thing and he was able to carry on. It didn't put him out. And after that, you didn't hear anything more about it."

In 1998, Merv was honored with a Golden Palm star on the Walk of Stars, the Palm Springs equivalent of the Walk of Fame on Hollywood Boulevard. After the ceremony, Merv posed for pictures and spoke to reporters. A man in the crowd walked up to Merv and tapped the back of his shoulder. It was Don Kane. "I always knew you'd wind up in cement," Kane told his former boss.

Merv smiled and greeted Kane warmly, as though it only been a short time since they'd last seen each other. "We talked as if nothing had ever happened, and everything was just fine between us," Kane recalls. "My being released or fired was never brought up. I was never actually fired. They had simply moved on and left me behind."

Merv the entertainer had pretty much given way to Merv the mogul, a journey he chronicled in the aforementioned memoir, *Merv: Making the Good Life Last* (with David Bender; Simon & Schuster, 2003). In addition to numerous Emmys, Merv was the recipient of the Television Academy's Life Achievement Award in 2005. He was also inducted into the Hall of Fame of the Academy of Television Arts and Sciences.

In 2007, Merv experienced a recurrence of his prostate cancer. A doctor told him the disease had spread. Even in the face of serious health concerns, Griffin's zeal for business and ability to improvise never abandoned him. The "retired" host had never really retired; he continued to manage his multi-million-dollar empire and develop new game show projects. When work was over, he'd be on his yacht ("Griff") or flying his plane.

By summer 2007, it had become obvious that Merv was not a well man, according to Sasaki. Merv was admitted to Cedars Sinai Medical Center in Los Angeles. "At that point, the symptoms were pretty bad. They had checked him in, so it wasn't just something that he could get fixed and go home," says Sasaki.

Merv Griffin died on August 12, 2007 at age 82. Tony Griffin and Governor Arnold Schwarzenegger delivered eulogies at Merv's funeral, which was by invitation-only. For years, Merv joked about what his epitaph would be. His gravestone reads: "I will not be right back after this message."

20. THE LEGACY OF THE MERV GRIFFIN SHOW

The Merv Griffin Show would remain entrenched in American pop culture long after it had vanished from the airwaves. The 1997 episode of *Seinfeld*, aptly titled "The Merv Griffin Show," remains among the most popular episodes of that sitcom. In the 2006 film *Running with Scissors*, a film set in the 1970s, Annette Bening's character has delusions of becoming a celebrated author and landing a guest shot on *The Merv Griffin Show*.

Over the years, much has been said about the television industry not preserving its rich heritage of filmed and taped archives. A scant amount of footage is extant from Merv's NBC series; a considerable number of the 1,061 shows he did for Westinghouse are missing; and only a handful of entries from the CBS period have survived.

Installments from the Metromedia and King World years have been preserved. Peter Barsocchini recalls the near-loss of studio tapes spanning the later years of the show. "When I came in as producer in late '79, early 1980, I would read these things they were sending me that asked which shows we wanted to keep, I said, 'Why are we erasing *any* of these? You don't know who's going to become the next superstar.' But those decisions were driven by the cost of videotape back then, and the digital world has changed all that. It's a shame, but that doesn't mean all the Merv Griffin shows were something for the Smithsonian. But you never quite know what you have until you get to the fullness of history. There's Tom's Cruise's first interview. A singer's first song; a comedian's last appearance. Whatever it is, it becomes significant."

In 2014, *The Merv Griffin Show* resurfaced in a 12-disc DVD set produced by Reelin' In the Years Productions, and released by MPI Home Video. In 2016, reruns of the program began airing on the cable station GetTV. (Ironically, reruns of Carson's *Tonight Show* were resurrected on Antenna TV that same year.)

"Merv was so diverse," concludes Kevin Sasaki. "He imparted a lot of things, including *Jeopardy!* and *Wheel of Fortune*, that will continue to remain. He's one of those people we call pioneers, an innovator who initiated things that are still followed today. He maintained that ability all through his business years, which made his enterprises as successful as they were. He put his entire being into anything that he got involved with. That's what got him up every morning. You don't find too many people like that these days."

Julann Griffin once had a discussion with her former husband about how history might treat him. "He said to me, 'When I die, no one is going to remember me.' He gave me the impression that, in his mind, he hadn't done anything worthwhile." One of the things Julann reminded him about was that, for quite some time, people of color had been depicted on television in stereotypical roles and shown rioting and looting on the nightly news. "Merv started to hire black comedians, people like Richard Pryor and Dick Gregory, because he thought they were talented. But what happened was that, when audiences saw blacks in a different light, they opened up their hearts, and that helped change the world. He tried hard to be a good guy in this world."

How do we sum up Merv, the talk-show legend, as opposed to Merv, the media mogul, in the 21st century? Merv was the consummate showman and a broadcaster of good conscience, one who didn't acquiesce to network executives, corporate blacklists or public opinions.

Steve Allen introduced topical, and often serious, subjects at midnight and brought his cameras outside the studio. Jack Paar did likewise. Merv, however, was the first to tackle these things in the afternoon, on a major network, at a time when television was still in its adolescence. While Merv provided plenty of breezy hours with the "Richie" Pryors, the Henny Youngmans, and the Gabors, he also gave us rare insight into controversial figures like Westbrook Pegler, Bertrand Russell, and Timothy Leary. Though the other hosts interviewed the great political leaders and newsmakers, it was Merv who always seemed to listen, absorb, and react more clearly with an unwavering alacrity.

More than 25,000 personalities glistened on *The Merv Griffin Show* over a period of 23 years. The shows represent a time in which people on talk shows actually *talked* — and listened to each other. An appreciable number of the tapes have been painstakingly preserved for future generations and, thanks to the digital age, can be relished over and over. The Merv Griffin archive of shows remains one of the most compelling time capsules of America's cultural and social history from the mid-1960s to the mid-1980s. More than anything else, it is that repository of distinguished programming that will likely be the lasting triumph of Merv Griffin.

TV SERIES HOSTED BY MERV GRIFFIN

Song Snapshots for a Summer Holiday, **a.k.a.** *Song Snapshots*
   (CBS), 1954

Look Up and Live (CBS) 13 weeks, 1955

The Morning Show (CBS) 6 months, 1956

Going Places (ABC) 6 months, 1957

Play Your Hunch (CBS) 12/59 – 7/62
(ABC) 1959, (NBC) 12/9/59 – 10/62

Saturday Prom (NBC) 1960-61

The Merv Griffin Show (NBC) 10/1/62 – 3/29/63

Talent Scouts (CBS) 1963

Word for Word (NBC) 1963-64

The Merv Griffin Show (Westinghouse Broadcasting Company)
   5/65 – 6/69

The Merv Griffin Show (CBS) 8/69 – 2/72

The Merv Griffin Show (Metromedia Producers Corporation)
   3/72 – 10/83; King World 10/83 – 9/86

The Coconut Ballroom (Syndicated) 1986

EMMY AWARDS WON BY
THE MERV GRIFFIN SHOW

1974: Bob Murphy, producer, for Outstanding Talk, Service, or Variety Series.

Tony Garofalo, Bob Murphy, Merv Griffin, for Best Writing for a Talk, Service, or Variety Program.

1975: Dick Carson, director, for Outstanding Individual Director for a Daytime Variety Program.

1977: Bob Murphy, producer, Outstanding Talk, Service or Variety Series.

1981: Peter Barsocchini, producer, Outstanding Talk, Service or Variety Series.

1982: Merv Griffin, host, Outstanding Variety Series.

1983: Peter Barsocchini, producer, Outstanding Variety Series.

Dick Carson, director, Outstanding Individual Direction for a Variety Series.

1984: Bob Murphy, executive producer, Peter Barsocchini, producer, Outstanding Variety series;

Merv Griffin, host, Outstanding Variety Series.

1985: Dick Carson, director, for Outstanding Direction in a Talk, Service Show.

ONGOING TV SERIES PRODUCED/ PACKAGED BY MERV GRIFFIN:

1963: *Word for Word*

1964: *Jeopardy!*

1965: *Let's Play Post Office*

1967: *Reach for the Stars*

One in a Million

1970: *Joe Garagiola's Memory Game*

1975: *Wheel of Fortune*

1979: *Dance Fever*

1990: *Monopoly*

1991: *Ruckus*

1992: *Click*

1997: *Merv Griffin's Crosswords*

MOVIE APPEARANCES BY MERV GRIFFIN

I Confess – Warner Bros. (1953) – voice only

Cattle Town – Warner Bros. (1952), Dennis Morgan, Philip Carey

By the Light of the Silvery Moon – Warner Bros. (1953), Doris Day, Gordon MacRae

So This is Love – Warner Bros. (1953), Kathryn Grayson

The Beast from 20,000 Fathoms – Warner Bros. (1953), voice only

The Charge at Feather River – Warner Bros. (1953), voice only

Three Sailors and a Girl – Warner Bros (1953), Jane Powell, Gordon MacRae

The Boy from Oklahoma – Warner Bros. (1954), Will Rogers, Jr.

Phantom of the Rue Morgue – Warner Bros. (1954), Karl Malden

Hello, Down There – Paramount (1969), Tony Randall, Janet Leigh, Jim Backus, Roddy McDowall, Charlotte Rae, Richard Dreyfuss

Two-Minute Warning – Universal (1976), Charlton Heston

One Trick Pony – Warner Bros. (1980), Paul Simon

Slapstick (of Another Kind) – The S. Paul Company/Serendipity Entertainment Releasing Company and International Film Marketing (1982), Jerry Lewis

The Man With Two Brains – Warner Bros. (1983), Steve Martin

Alice in Wonderland – Irwin Allen Productions, CBS-TV (1985), All star cast

Murder at the Cannes Film Festival – Exclamation Productions/ Merv Griffin Entertainment/Shavick Entertainment (2000), French Stewart, Karina Lombard, Bo Derek

BIBLIOGRAPHY

BOOKS:

Franklin, Joe, *Joe Franklin's Encyclopedia of Comedians*; New York: Bell Publishing Company, 1979.

Cavett, Dick and Christopher Porterfield, *Cavett*, New York and London: Harcourt Brace Jovanovich, 1974.

Galanoy, Terry, *Tonight!*, New York: Doubleday & Company, Inc., 1972.

Gregory, Dick, *The Shadow that Scares Me*, New York: Doubleday, 1968.

Griffin, Merv, with Peter Barsocchini, *Merv*; New York: Simon and Schuster, 1980.

Griffin, Merv, with Peter Barsocchini, *From Where I Sit; Merv Griffin's Book of People*, New York: Arbor House, 1982.

Griffin, Merv, with David Bender, *Merv: Making the Good Life Last*, New York: Simon & Schuster, 2003.

Keylin, Arleen and Suri Fleischer, *Hollywood Album*, New York: Arno Press, 1979.

Paar, Jack, *My Saber Is Bent*, New York: Trident Press, 1961.

Rosenbaum, Jonathan, *Discovering Orson Welles*, Berkeley and Los Angeles, California: University of California Press, 2007.

Shanks, Bob, *The Cool Fire*, New York: W. W. Norton & Company, 1976.

Shulman, Arthur, and Roger Youman, *How Sweet It Was*, New York: Bonanza Books, 1966.

Vance, Jeffrey, *Chaplin: Genius of the Cinema*, New York: Harry N. Abrams, 2003.

ARTICLES:

"Treacher Suggests Autograph Fee," Lee Mortimer (The Movies), *New York Mirror*, January 1942.

"Belittles Song Craze Effect," Dan Richman, *New York Morning Telegram*, March 25, 1955.

"All the Charm Is Still There," *New York Journal-American*, John McClain, May 19, 1955.

Leahy, Jack, *New York Sunday News*, February 28, 1960.

"This Is Merv Griffin, Who Does Not Keep a Wolf at Home," *TV Guide*, August 20, 1960, pp. 17-18.

"Six City Caper," Peter Levinson, *TV-Radio Mirror*, January 1962.

"Merv Griffin Show," (review), *Variety*, October 3, 1962.

"Johnny Carson Show," (review). *Variety*, October 3, 1962.

"Old Merv Griffin Has a Farm, Ee Aye, Ee Aye, Oh," Edith Efron, *TV Guide*, October 3, 1962, pp. 6-9.

"Merv Griffin Has Ambitious Plans for Daytime TV Show," Doc Quigg, *New York Morning Telegraph*, October 9, 1962.

"Merv Griffin Turns 'Tonight' Into Day," Elinor Klein, *New York Herald- Tribune*, November 18, 1962.

For the Record, Henry Harding, (column), *TV Guide*, February 9, 1963, p. A-5.

"Merv Griffin: Star by Day," Virginia Kelly, *Look,* February 12, 1963, pp. 73-77.

"Merv Griffin to Rejoin N.B.C.," *New York Times*, June 12, 1963.

"Griffin an Untalented Host on CBS's Talent Scouts," Kay Gardella, *New York Daily News*, July 4, 1963.

"Merv Griffin's Legiter," *Variety*, June 17, 1964.

"A Dazzling Performance," Jules W. Rabin, *The Long Island News and Owl*, November 13, 1964.

"Griffin to Get Talk Show," *New York Times*, February 23, 1965.

"Griffin's Ready to Go with Nighttime Show," Kay Gardella, *New York Sunday News,* May 9, 1965.

Griffin review, *New York Herald-Tribune*, May 11, 1965.

"Griffin a Strong Entry in Late Night TV Race," Kay Gardella, *New York Daily News*, May 11, 1965.

"Merv Griffin Show," (review), *Variety*, May 12, 1965.

"Merv Griffin Relies on Actors for Talk," Jack Gould, *New York Times*, May 13, 1965.

"James Bond Sings," *New York Times*, May 24, 1965.

"3rd All-News Station Planned," *New York Times*, June 19, 1965.

Russell's Reviews, *New York Herald-Tribune*, June 23, 1965.

"Satire on Merv Griffin Show," *New York Times*, June 28, 1965.

"Merv Griffin – A Truly Busy Star," Ben Gross, *New York Sunday News*, July 3, 1965.

"Merv Griffin: Man of 1,000 Faces," Dorothy Ferenbaugh, *New York Times*, July 18, 1965.

"Merv Griffin's 'No,'" *New York Herald-Tribune*, October 22, 1965.

"Griffin-Carson Talent Feud," Matt Messina (News Around the Dials), *New York Daily News*, January 27, 1966.

"Carlin Charges 'Merv Griffin Show' is Interfering with Comic's Career," *Variety*, June 15, 1966.

"George Carlin, Merv Griffin Settle Tiff Sans Arbitration," *Variety*, June 24, 1966.

"He's Merv Griffin – Period," Robert Higgins, *TV Guide*, November 11, 1966.

"Carson Defeats Bishop and Paar in Ratings Race," *New York Times*, April 26, 1967.

"Griffin Poses Chief Threat to Carson Show," John Horn (A Look at TV), *Philadelphia Inquirer*, May 3, 1967.

"Griffin Shifting into Prime Time," Robert E. Dallos, *New York Times*, May 17, 1967.

"TV's Merv Griffin, They Talk, He Listens," Betty Rollin, *Look*, April 16, 1968, pp. 98-102.

"Arthur Treacher: Call it Mastery," Jerry Tallmer, *New York Post*, June 29, 1968.

"Merv Griffin Show Will Move to C.B.S. in 1969," Robert E. Dallos, *New York Times*, August 6, 1968.

"Griffin to Be Contender in Carson, Bishop Slot," *Newsday* (N.Y.), August 6, 1968.

"When Merv Griffin Shifts to CBS-TV…" *Variety*, August 28, 1968.

"They Say…" *Philadelphia Evening Bulletin*, October 6, 1968.

"'Start in the Sun, Merv,' Said the Voice," Nora E. Taylor, *Christian Science Monitor* (Boston), October 25, 1968.

"Treacher's Fish 'N Chips," *Variety*, March 26, 1969.

"Move Over Jackie Gleason…" George Maksian, *New York Daily News*, July 27, 1969.

"…And Griffin Makes Three," Neil Hickey, *TV Guide*, August 16, 1969, pp. 16-19.

"CBS-TV's Guests Cop Out as Griffin Pulls a Flop-Out," Kay Gardella, *New York Daily News*, August 19, 1969.

"Talk, Talk, Talk," (Television/Programming), *Time*, August 29, 1969, p. 52.

"Johnny Carson Shows Early Speed in Late-Night Race," Richard K. Doan, *TV Guide*, August 30, 1969, p. A-1.

"Battle of the Talk Shows," *Newsweek*, September 1, 1969, pp. 42-47.

"N.Y. Numbers Derby Make Merv Nostalgic for Good Ol' Syndie Days," *Variety*, December 17, 1969.

"C.B.S. Keeps Pleas for Peace Off Air," *New York Times*, December 31, 1969.

"A Reluctant Merv Griffin Studies Move to Hollywood," Clarence Peterson, *The Chicago Tribune*, January 18, 1970.

"Merv Would Be Happy, Afternoons in Philly," Rex Polier, *Philadelphia Evening Bulletin,* January 21, 1970.

"Griffin Back at Old 4:30 Start, in 3 Markets in CBS Reversal," *Variety,* January 21, 1970.

"Merv Griffin, a Solo Owner, May Go Public," *Variety,* January 28, 1970.

"At Home with Mrs. Merv Griffin," Rita Delfiner, *New York Post,* February 14, 1970.

"Arthur Treacher – 76 and All That," Ira Peck, *New York Times,* July 19, 1970.

"Griffin Show Will Miss Treacher's Performance," Ben Gross, *New York Daily News,* July 24, 1970.

"Merv Griffin to Stay in East – But Will Keep Suitcase Packed," Richard K. Doan, *TV Guide,* July 25, 1970, p. A-1.

"Griffin Show Moving to Coast," *New York Times,* August 2, 1970.

"Griffin Paging Illson-Chambers," *Variety,* August 5, 1970.

"Merv on New Course," Tom Macklin, *Evening News,* (Newark, NJ), August 11, 1970.

"60 Disrupt Taping of Griffin Show," *New York Times,* August 28, 1970.

"TV: Big Bands Swing on Nostalgic Griffin Show," Jack Gould, *New York Times,* January 21, 1971.

"Sullivan, Griffin May Be Nearing End of the Road," Richard K. Doan, *TV Guide,* January 30, 1971, p. A-1.

"Merv Griffin Asks Out, Beats CBS to the Punch," George Maksian, *New York Daily News,* September 4, 1971.

"Merv Loses Bid to Wipe Face Off Those Yo-Yos," New York Post, September 24, 1971.

"Films Will Replace Griffin on Feb. 14," Jack Gould, *New York Times,* December 6, 1971.

"Jeeves of the Movies," Earl Wilson, *New York Post,* February 5, 1972.

"It's the Same Old Merv Griffin on Channel 48," Rex Polier, *Philadelphia Evening Bulletin,* March 14, 1972.

"When a Network Makes a Disastrous Mistake," Bill Davidson, *TV Guide,* July 8, 1972, pp. 20-25.

"Griffin Lineup Now at 87," *Variety,* July 19, 1972.

"My Life in Talk Shows," Walter Kempley, *True,* February 1974, pp. 30-31; 60-61; 104.

"Arthur Treacher Dies on L.I. at 81," *New York Daily News,* December 15, 1975.

"Welcome Back to N.Y., Merv," Rex Polier, *Philadelphia Evening Bulletin,* October 18, 1978.

"Producer: The Pressure is Terrible!" Eugenia Sheppard, *New York Post*, November 27, 1978.

"Talkshow as Art Form in TV: Welles," *Variety*, March 21, 1979.

"Carey Joins Merv Griffin to Observe Anniversary," *New York Times*, October 27, 1979.

"Merv Comes Home," Earl Wilson, *New York Post*, April 3, 1980.

"Make Merv the New $6 Million Man," George Maksian, *New York Daily News*, July 1, 1980.

"Will Talk Show Host Be Silenced?," Gary Deeb, (Syndicated), *Philadelphia Daily News*, December 2, 1982.

"Hitting Home Runs with Merv Griffin Pitching," Francis X. Clines, *New York Times*, September 28, 1983.

"MGP Sets Mark," *Variety*, January 25, 1984.

"Prospector Merv," Cindy Adams, *New York Post*, October 18, 1985.

"When He Starts Rubbing His Nose with His Knuckles, Watch Out," Mary Murphy, *TV Guide*, November 23, 1985, pp. 51-58.

"What If They Gave a Talk Show and Nobody Listened?," Brian Moss, *New York Daily News*, February 23, 1986.

"There's New Life for Merv Griffin," George Maksian, *New York Daily News*, March 31, 1986.

"'That's All,' Says Merv," *New York Daily News*, August 22, 1986.

"He's the Man of the Moment," David Johnston, *Philadelphia Inquirer*, November 17, 1988.

ADDITIONAL SOURCES:

Merv Griffin Presents…Mort Lindsey, (LP), notes by Merv Griffin, Dot Records, 1966.

That Regis Philbin Show, (TV program), Group W/Westinghouse Broadcasting Co., syndicated, 1965.

A Tinkling Piano in the Next Apartment, (LP), Arthur Treacher, MGM Records, 1965.

The Tonight Show Starring Johnny Carson, (TV program), Carson/NBC, 9/5/86.

AUTHOR'S INTERVIEWS:

Allen, Jayne Meadows – February 22, 2009

Ballard, Kaye - June 11, 2014

Barsocchini, Peter – February 20, 2015

Fairbanks, Douglas, Jr. – April 24, 1991

Fisher, Albert – October 15, 2009; February 8, 2013

Garofalo, Tony – March 14, 2013

Griffin, Julann – September 16, 2015

Kane, Don – June 12, 2014; July 11, 2014; November 7, 2014

Larson, Jack – October 6, 2013

Rock, Monti, III – December 14, 2015

Saphire, Rick – March 20, 2015

Sasaki, Kevin – May 21, 2015

Shanks, Bob – March 26, 2007; August 20, 2007; February 20, 2013; March 20, 2015

Sinclair, Rob – March 15, 2015

Stoliar, Steve – February 7, 2016

INDEX

Made in the USA
Columbia, SC
20 November 2019